ALI AND LISTON

ALI AND LISTON

The Boy Who Would Be King
and the Ugly Bear

BOB MEE

A Herman Graf Book
Skyhorse Publishing

Skyhorse Publishing books may be purchased in bulk at special discounts for sales promotion, corporate gifts, fund-raising, or educational purposes. Special editions can also be created to specifications. For details, contact the Special Sales Department, Skyhorse Publishing, 307 West 36th Street, 11th Floor, New York, NY 10018 or info@skyhorsepublishing.com.

Skyhorse® and Skyhorse Publishing® are registered trademarks of Skyhorse Publishing, Inc.®, a Delaware corporation.

Visit our website at www.skyhorsepublishing.com.

10 9 8 7 6 5 4 3 2 1

Library of Congress Cataloging-in-Publication Data is available on file.
ISBN: 978-1-61608-369-4

Printed in the United States of America.

CONTENTS

INTRODUCTION

In Louisville, Kentucky, in July 2004, to cover what turned out to be Mike Tyson's unexpected defeat by the London heavyweight Danny Williams, I sought out Muhammad Ali's childhood home. As Sky colleague and friend Dave Culmer and I drew up opposite the white-boarded house, by complete coincidence BBC men Mike Costello and Steve Bunce were there, interviewing Ali's brother, Rahaman. When they had finished, I had a chat with Rahaman, sitting on a step under a tree. In the summer sun, he dropped his voice a little for just the briefest of moments and recalled how he and Ali used to sit there as boys, dreaming their dreams of all they might do with their lives. There was no need to fill in the pause that followed. Finally, he said: 'Don't feel sorry for Muhammad. Because Muhammad don't feel sorry for himself.'

Tyson was to box Williams in the Freedom Hall, where long, long ago Ali had made his professional debut against Tunney Hunsaker, a part-time fighter and full-time policeman from Fayetteville, West Virginia. Tyson had also gone to see Ali's old house. A police officer had given him a lift. In that week, Tyson seemed to know his time in the business that had made and broken him was almost up. He also knew that in years to come nobody would be making small but splendid pilgrimages to the house where he had been raised. Nobody would be opening, as they were shortly to do in Ali's honour in Louisville, a museum in his name.

There aren't any museums in Sonny Liston's name in St Francis County, Arkansas, either.

There are those who have seen a little bit of Liston in Tyson: the darkness, the apparent ability to self-destruct, the tendency to embrace chaos at every turn. There was, however, no similarity in the way they expressed themselves in interview. Tyson laid out either himself or the side of himself he chose to be on that particular day to be picked over by anyone who was paid to be there. To understand how manipulative Tyson was you had to become experienced at listening to him. It is fairly safe to believe that listening to Liston was an altogether different experience. If Sonny gave writers more than a sentence or two, it took on the significance of the Gettysburg Address.

When I began this book, I looked back at my Louisville notes for one of Tyson's confessional monologues in front of writers. His words carried an intimacy that led some to claim he had spoken to them and them alone. Perhaps that is why, in spite of all that he did, Tyson in general received a pretty sympathetic press. Liston got little or no understanding. Neither did he ask for any.

In Louisville, Tyson said:

> The pressure of fighting, it drives you crazy. Some guys do crazy things. It's all very well calling a fighter a nut, but you don't know the pressure of getting bashed upside the head in front of, say, 100,000 people . . . Sometimes when you are successful you get a lot of money, but it restricts you from being you. I'm pretty cool now. I'm rounded . . . but if somebody gives me a whole garbage can of money, I might start being a psycho. I have mistreated a lot of people. I was a monster not too long ago . . .

At the end of 2006, I was in Little Rock, Arkansas. Again, on a day when work was slow Dave Culmer and I took a trip out into the cotton fields. We went up the interstate towards Memphis, pulled off at a place called Palestine and turned north into the cotton fields and swamps. There isn't anything or anybody to tell you where Sonny Liston was born and raised. One or two might guess, but that's all it would be. We drove up dirt tracks where Liston might have walked, past creeks where he might have swum. We were in the right area of St Francis County, near Johnson, where the piece of land called the Sand Slough was. Liston was born there in a fragile wood-board shack. His mother, Helen, once said she put cardboard on the walls to keep out the wind. That home, from three-quarters of a century ago, would have been long gone.

As we eased the hire car over the rutted tracks, the satellite navigation system stopped working. Out of the car, with the bare land stretching to the horizon on one side and a swamp full of dead trees on the other, it was eerily quiet. I took a few strands of cotton left behind after the harvest (and have them still in the drawer of the desk at which I write). For a fleeting minute or so, I could feel what it might have been like to grow up here, to know this and only this, to live in a time where the past was remote and confused. And without the past, what could the future have meant? The Listons, Helen and her husband Tobe, who was the son of a slave, bent their backs over these cotton fields for a meagre living until some time in the mid-1940s when Helen walked out for a dream of prosperity and a back that ached less. Sonny went too and, as far as anybody knows, never came back.

Dave and I, enriched by whatever it was that we learned, pulled out along the dirt roads, back to a place the sat-nav recognised, on to tarmac and the twenty-first century, ate at a friendly place called Catfish Island, left it at that.

Liston's resting place is easy to find: it's in Paradise Memorial Gardens, Las Vegas, under the flight path of planes landing at McCarran International Airport. You'll see his metal plaque on the ground near the place where they bury babies and children. The plaque says: 'Charles "Sonny" Liston 1932–70' and below, starkly, 'A Man'.

From the moment I read the newspaper and magazine cuttings handed down to me by the journalist and television commentator, Reg Gutteridge, I wanted to use them to explore the story of Ali's two controversial world heavyweight championship fights with Liston in 1964 and 1965. The first ended with Liston, supposedly one of the toughest men ever to walk this planet, sitting in his corner complaining of a sore shoulder, and the second was a muddled first-round knockout that had people yelling 'Fix, Fix, Fix!' in the arena.

It was a volatile, unpredictable time in a country troubled almost to breaking point. Ali, when he was still Cassius Marcellus Clay Jr, challenged Liston for the title only three months after the assassination of President John F. Kennedy. The man arrested for killing him, Lee Harvey Oswald, had been killed even before extensive interviews could be carried out. Oswald's murderer, Jack Ruby, claimed he acted alone on a furious impulse. Very few believed him.

Slavery had been abolished a hundred years before, but African Americans were still in psychological chains, battling for the right to be educated, to walk the streets without worrying which white person they might bump into, which seat on a bus they might flop into, or into which eating house they might walk and ask to be served.

To be black in America in the early to mid-1960s was to be a part of an underclass, separated from the rights granted to all Americans by their own constitution. The peaceful, honourable Civil Rights movement was, in the north at least, the acceptable face of the quest for change, but, as always in times of social strife, there was reaction and counter-reaction. Protest and resistance take many forms, and there were those who preached violence and even segregation. One such organisation was the Nation of Islam, and it was to this group that the young Cassius Clay would turn. Suddenly, after winning the heavyweight title, he was no longer the brash, funny, irritating boy with God-given speed in his feet and fists but a misguided champion of a shadowy, subversive cult that seemed to counter racism with racism. On top of that, Ali, as he became, proclaimed his opposition to the Vietnam War, which was perceived at that time by most Americans as a just war against a genuine Communist threat. He rejected what the majority, black as well as white, felt was the responsibility of every fit American male of suitable age: he refused to do his duty and was, well, just so ungrateful.

The flipside of Ali was Liston, who had no apparent political or religious beliefs, no apparent interest in the well-being of anybody outside his own household, and who had Mob connections. Some said Liston was manoeuvred by the criminal underworld from the moment he stepped into a professional ring, not long after he was released from a Missouri prison, until the day he died in mysterious circumstances in that Mob paradise, Las Vegas.

The cuttings collected by Reg Gutteridge when he was working on the fights between Ali and Liston paint a dramatic picture of a world now consigned to the past. I felt it would be an exciting adventure to use them to recreate what it was like to be there at that time. Too many histories rely on memory, on interviews carried out long after the event, and while some of these can provide material of value too often they are unreliable. I acknowledge that sometimes it takes a while for truths to emerge but against that memories are so often altered to suit an agenda or are inaccurate. That is why I felt Reg's mass of contemporary material was so relevant. He knew about this project before he died and was happy for it to happen.

I am English and this story will be published, at first, in Britain. Therefore, I would ask any American readers for a degree of tolerance. Some of the knowledge you have learned from the cradle is not taken as read by a British audience.

It has been an amazing journey of discovery. I knew Liston's tendency to be virtually monosyllabic with the media allowed them to build a myth of the brooding, menacing ogre, but I found, yes, a sad man but one with a strange sense of humour, if not haunted then certainly made suspicious by a world that gave with one hand and snatched away with both, a man who sought redemption and acceptance by winning the heavyweight championship of the world but who found only disappointment, rejection and constant reminders of the moral debt it was felt he owed his country. In the end, I found a disillusioned man who became what it seemed the world wanted him to be. Reg always said beneath the surface Liston had a vulnerable heart. I believe him.

I have explored the heritage and childhoods of both men in an attempt to provide detail, and I hope this helps the understanding of what made both men who they were. Neither man's childhood and adolescence were particularly significant to writers at the time, of course, and inevitably details of those early years have had to be pieced together and reassessed from earlier historical accounts.

I take in Liston's championship wins over Floyd Patterson and then the fights with Ali – including the one that never happened and which has so often been ignored, when Ali was struck down by a hernia that some suspected might have been the result of his being poisoned. I listened to the first fight live on radio in the middle of the night at the kitchen table of our home in Leicestershire when I was ten years old. My father woke me, and we tiptoed downstairs. He put his finger to his lips and whispered: 'Don't tell your mother.' I remember wanting Liston to win and not knowing why. The rematch, of course, was the bizarre night in the small town of Lewiston, Maine, which for a modern equivalent might be the same as a Lennox Lewis–Mike Tyson fight descending on Whitby or Southwold.

I feel that by investigating the combined stories of Liston and Ali through the newspapers and magazines of the time, and film footage, I have discovered a little more about what it was like to be there at this tumultuous time in history. I was a child when these events happened, and I knew about Martin Luther King, Malcolm X, the race riots and the war in Vietnam but I had not appreciated the details of the African American struggle, the day-to-day reality of what it must have been like to have been born black in this most complex of societies.

Shortly after completing the first draft, after considering what Ali meant for my generation, yes as a boxer, but also as a symbol of resistance, of the right of the young or the disenfranchised to challenge the perceptions of the moral majority, on 20 January 2009 I was driving on an English motorway, listening to the radio. Barack Obama took the oath as the first black president of the United States of America, an event that would have been unthinkable in the 1960s when black people had to steel themselves to find the courage to take up a place at a certain school or university, let alone sit in government. I pulled into a service station to listen as the speech began with the words 'I stand here today humbled by the task before us, grateful for the trust you have bestowed, mindful of the sacrifices borne by our ancestors . . .'

Obama was talking for all America to all America, but to African Americans his words obviously carried extraordinary significance. I didn't know then that among the crowd sat the 67-year-old Muhammad Ali, once so vocal, so full of loud, opinionated, resistant youth and now dimmed by the onset of Parkinson's and wrapped up in a black overcoat, scarf and hat, with a blue rug over his knees to keep out the cold. We don't know what Ali thought as he sat there, but it was good, and poignant, that he lived to see it.

I hope you enjoy this story as much as I have investigating and writing it.

1

MAYBE THEY THINK I'M SO OLD BECAUSE I NEVER WAS REALLY YOUNG

Charles 'Sonny' Liston's grandfather, Alexander, was a slave on the sprawling farm of a white landowner, Martin Liston, between Poplar Creek and Huntsville, Mississippi, not far from Winona on what is now Interstate 55. African slaves lost their names, and, out of convenience if nothing else, once freedom came it became normal practice to identify themselves by using the name of their former owners. And so Alexander, who called himself Alex, became Alex Liston.

The lot of the slave was romanticised by 'white' literary fiction, and in many of the movies of the first half of the twentieth century the sun shone, the Negro slaves sang as they toiled in the fields of benevolent masters and mistresses. The men were strong, the women plump. The truth is that African people were systematically stripped of their dignity for generation after generation until the vast majority no longer knew who they were or where their grandparents and great-grandparents had lived. Even when slaves tried to build new family lives they did so often only to have them torn apart when children, husbands or wives were sold on. A Quaker from Virginia once described the misery: 'Husbands and wives are frequently separated and sold into distant parts. Children are taken from their parents without regard to the ties of nature, and the most endearing bonds of affection are broken for ever.'

When freedom eventually came, there were those who restlessly travelled the country searching for loved ones. In the 1870s and 1880s, newspapers for black readers carried a steady stream of notices taken out by people anxious for knowledge of the whereabouts of wives, brothers or sisters, parents or children. What were people to do if their families were in pieces? The temptation must have been to drift, but this would have been balanced by worry that if the missing loved ones came back there must be somebody still there to welcome them.

Slavery left its survivors with psychological as well as physical scars and with damage that would be passed on through their children and children's children. For generations, their role had been to serve and to work. Education, if any benevolent owner bothered to give them any, was minimal. Therefore, in the world that the freed slaves were cast into, there were very few lucrative careers open to them. Their inclination would have been to act as they knew best, to work the land or, if they drifted to towns and cities, to work for others, often for menial wages with no rights to speak of. And for white people, the idea that blacks could contribute to the whole by taking responsible posts would have been alien. They freed the slaves, but they expected them to carry on their role as third-class citizens, and the easiest way for people to enjoy their freedom rather than discover troubles and difficulties through it was to conform. Black people remained poor, uneducated, uncertain where they had come from or where they might go.

Although upon receiving his freedom Alex Liston could have travelled, he chose to stay close to home. With his wife, Fannie, and their first four children, Ned, Rachel, Joseph and Frank, he set up on land near that belonging to Robert Liston, son of the man who had owned him. Perhaps he or Fannie had family who might come back, or perhaps they just felt safer and more comfortable closer to what they knew and where pretty much everybody knew everybody else. Local churches were focal points for these spread-out but relatively insular communities. Martin Liston was one of the founders of Bethel Methodist Church on the Bethel Road which links highways 407 and 413, and there was a baptist church used by black folk at Pinkney Grove, and another, called Shiloh, not far east of Poplar Creek.

According to the 1910 census, Tobin Liston, Sonny's father, was born in January 1870. Another family in the area were the Winfreys, ancestors of the television host, Oprah (though she has said the roots were purely biological, she had no other connection with them). One of the Winfrey daughters, Cornelia, known as Cora, married Tobin Liston in 1889. He was 19, she was 16. Their first child, Ernest, was born in Kilmichael, Mississippi, in November 1889. More than 40 years would separate Ernest, known as Ernie, from Charles, known as Sonny, but they were half-brothers.

Over the next twenty years they had a total of thirteen children, seven of whom were still surviving by 1910, when they were still in Mississippi. At some point in the next five years or so, either the marriage ended or Cora died, and Tobe took up with a young girl, Helen Baskin, who was nearly thirty years younger than him. It was Helen Baskin, who became Helen Liston, who was Sonny's mother.

Helen was born in February 1898 to Martha Baskin, who married Joe McKelpin the following year. He might or might not have been Helen's father, but in 1900 they were living in Poplar Creek, near the Listons, listed under the name Kelpa. They had another newborn daughter, Ida. Like Alex and Fannie Liston, they were illiterate farming folk, renting or sharecropping.

When Helen was 17, she gave birth to a child named Ezra Baskin Ward, on 6 August 1915. His father was Colonel Ward, son of a sharecropper named Jerry Ward. Colonel was not a military rank but his given name. In the 1910 census, Colonel was newly married to a 17 year old named Mattie. Perhaps he was still married when he became the father of Helen's son, or perhaps not. Perhaps he might have wanted to settle down with Helen but could not, or maybe he was just another married man with a wandering eye. Ezra, known as E.B. Ward, was under the impression that Colonel died not too long afterwards and that he was 'poisoned by a lady'.

Tobe and Helen went looking for a fresh start, moving across the state line into Arkansas with those of Tobe's children who still needed looking after or who wanted to go. Helen left the infant E.B. behind in the care of her mother, Martha. They found a place to call home in the area of open land north west of Forrest City in St Francis County and settled down to sharecrop, paying rent in the form of three-quarters of what they grew to the landowner, a black farmer named Pat Heron. Helen said Tobe loved it, and she knew he would never leave.

Almost half a century later, Sonny Liston would tell the Kefauver Committee, during its investigation into Mob involvement in boxing, that his father had 25 children. He didn't know exactly how they were divided up between his mother and Tobe's first wife, Cora, but he tried to remember those he had known in an interview with *Sports Illustrated*, published on 17 July 1961.

> My mother had either 12 or 13 children. No, I'm sure it was 13. E.B. Ward, he's the oldest, a boy child almost 40 years old now [in fact, he was 45]. It's been a good while since I seen him. Next comes J.T. I always call him Shorty. And he's close behind E.B. After J.T., there's Leo and then my sisters Clarety [Clara T.], Annie and Alcora, Curtice [Curtis], me and Wesley. Annie and me was closest, and I see a lot of her. She always kids me because I was bigger than her, yet she would rock me to sleep. Curtice and J.T. get together with me sometimes, and I saw Wesley, the baby, in '58 or '59, but the others have wandered off someplace.

Leo Liston was said to have been shot dead in Michigan; Annie and Curtis moved to Gary, Indiana; Annie married a man named Wallace. Curtis and Alcora, who was supposedly as quiet as Sonny, both died in 1982 in their early 50s. Helen Liston told Sonny's first biographer, A.S. 'Doc' Young:

> All my children grew fast. They were healthy children. I made them go to bed early. They didn't have any television to watch until twelve o'clock at night. My children ate their food, washed their feet and went to bed after it got dark.

The best we can do in identifying Tobe's legion of children is by looking at the census returns. Surprisingly, given what we are told by Helen in Young's book about Tobe's attitude to education – that he considered if a child was old enough to sit at the table and eat, then it was old enough to work in the field – he always declared he could read and write.

Cora stated in the 1910 census that six of her thirteen children had died, which leaves Ernest (b. November 1889), Bessie (January 1891), Latt (October 1894), William (October 1895), Jane, who becomes James in another census! (December 1897), a daughter whose name is too faintly written to be legible (1901) and Cleora (1905). Then in the 1920 census we also find Ada (1910) and Willie May (1913), which makes a total of 15 for Cora.

The 1930 census shows that Helen, after E.B in 1915, had Clara T. (1919), Glitt, aka Clytee (1920), J.T. (16 August 1921), Leo (1923), Annie (1924), Alcora (November 1927), Curtis (15 October 1929), which just leaves Charles and Wesley to come after 1930.

From the moment he rose to the top of the heavyweight division at the turn of the 1960s, Sonny Liston's background and age was a subject for sometimes wild conjecture. Some said he might have been born as far back as the early 1920s and for years he added to the mystery, claiming at various times to have been born in Little Rock or Pine Bluff, Arkansas, and even Memphis, Tennessee. When a date of birth was needed for him to enter the 1953 Golden Gloves tournament, 8 May 1932 was settled on. Very few believed him. Not many believed his mother, Helen, either when she said, in talking to Doc Young, that she thought it was 18 January 1932.

Part of the problem was that Sonny did not know himself. Why would he? Out in the place he was raised in the Sand Slough, in the wide open farming lands of Arkansas, men and women lived by seasons, by the times of the year when jobs needed doing to grow their crops of cotton, corn, sweet potatoes and whatever else they could. As year piled upon year, it is easy to understand that, with nothing written down, exact dates could become hazy and unimportant.

Father Alois Stevens, who encouraged Sonny's boxing while he was in jail in St Louis, said:

> We tried to get his birth certificate for the Golden Gloves, but it was impossible. Sonny was born in Arkansas country, and I'm afraid in those days officials weren't particular if they recorded the birth of a Negro child or not.

When it emerged, by his own admission during his time as heavyweight champion, that he had daughters of 17 and 13, the theory that he was much older than he said gathered in strength. These daughters, however, remain shadowy figures who lived with him and his wife Geraldine for a time and then appeared to drift into obscurity. And, of course, Sonny looked as if he aged ten years in half an hour when he lost his world title to Cassius Clay in Miami in 1964. His age became something of a joke.

This would remain a detail of minor significance were it not for the effect the speculation and scepticism had on Liston. Jack McKinney, who wrote for the *Philadelphia Daily News*, said:

> When guys would write that he was 32 going on 50 it had more of an impact than anybody realised. Sonny didn't know who he was. He was looking for an identity, and he thought that being champion would give him one. Sonny was so sensitive on the issue of his age because he did not really know how old he was.

While it is probable that he did not know the exact truth, he knew what he was saying was not that far out. It can only have aggravated his sense of isolation to have nobody believe him. Once, Liston, pondering the scepticism, said: 'Maybe they think I'm so old because I never was really young.'

The impression that he did not seem to be able to tell the truth about his age widened the already substantial social gap between Liston and the writers. Here was a man who, by the time they knew him, had already been jailed for a series of dumb, thuggish street crimes and again for attacking a police officer; a man whose ring career appeared to be controlled by the odious mobster Frankie Carbo; a man who had supposedly worked as a strike-breaker for the Mob in their St Louis factories; and who could barely be bothered to react when asked the simplest of questions, like when and where he was born.

In the eye of the moral majority, which tended to be condescending when dealing with people who were uneducated, poor and black, Liston had little or nothing to recommend him. He was a bum from a bad background and could barely write his name. That was all they needed to know. Given his ability with his fists, it was only a small step for the newsmen of the world to create an ogre out of a mixed-up, largely dysfunctional, ostracised man.

The story that Sonny was brutalised by a violent, merciless father has all too easily been accepted. 'The only thing my old man ever gave me,' Liston was quoted as saying more than once, 'was a beating.' He gave the impression that he was whipped by his father whenever the old man's mood took him. Tobe, of course, was not around to deny the allegations. He had died in hospital in Forrest City, Arkansas, on 22 November 1947, when he was 77 years old.

It is possible that when Sonny was young, Tobe whipped him hard enough to leave physical and psychological scars. By Helen's testimony to Doc Young, the young Charles was not the fastest of workers in the field. If Tobe, in trying to teach his children to farm the land and help the family grow enough to survive, lost his temper with any or all of them and went too far in punishing them, there would have been nobody around to remonstrate. By the time he was eight years old, Helen said Charles was working full time in the fields. He had not had enough time to learn to read and write.

If the systematic whippings happened, it is likely this was when Charles was very young, for by the time he was 11 or 12 Tobe would have been in his early 70s. Helen also told Doc Young that she herself was 5 ft 1 in., and that Tobe was 5 ft 5 in. She thought Sonny might have got his heavyweight build from an uncle, who was large. And so while little old Tobe might have retained an intimidating psychological authority over his big adolescent son, it is hard to imagine him handing out much in the way of corporal punishment. Helen came to her late husband's defence: 'He didn't whip them as much as people say he did. But he hollered at them a lot. The biggest thing he did was whoop and holler. He whooped and hollered so much nobody paid any attention to him.'

What is beyond dispute is that Sonny had no time for his father. I have discovered no kindly or forgiving reference by the son about the father. He resented the way he was treated, and it is easy to see how a boy, who would naturally want to be loved and approved of, could be hurt and damaged by what he perceived as rejection. The fact that Sonny harboured these feelings at all suggests he was not the insensitive brute people have chosen to believe him to be.

His uneasy relationship with his father perhaps made it inevitable that sooner rather than later, Sonny, or Charles as he was then, would leave the sandy patch of land alongside the slow, swampy waters of eastern Arkansas where Tobe and Helen Liston raised their children for the best part of 30 years. Inevitably, as word spread of better-paid jobs available in the industrial cities, people began to migrate towards them. And at some time in the mid-1940s, Charles Liston's sister Alcora took off north to St Louis. E.B.Ward told Liston's biographer, Nick Tosches, that Charles then went to live with E.B. and his family for about a year. They were sharecropping on a farm in Parkin, Arkansas. E.B. said Helen and another of her sons, Curtis, arrived and stayed for one harvest, then went on to St Louis, where by then Alcora had become Mrs Alcora Jones. It was not a complicated journey. Trains had been running between Parkin and St Louis since the 1850s.

In other words, it seemed that Sonny, perhaps because he was no longer able to get on with his father, was sent to live with his half-brother, or else took it upon himself to go and nobody stopped him. Only later did he go looking for his mother in St Louis. Given those circumstances, it is uncertain whether or not he went to St Louis out of convenience, because maybe he had outstayed his welcome with E.B., or simply felt like moving on, or because of some deeper adolescent need to remain closer to his mother for a while longer.

Public-record research shows that by 1946 Helen was living in Forrest City, first at 220 North Beach Street and then at 114 Union Street. Maybe she did not really know where she was going, except away from the farm and Tobe. By the following year she was in St Louis, working in a shoe factory. She did not appear to experience any guilt at going:

> There wasn't too much of a problem about the children getting taken care of. I didn't have but one little fellow that needed to be taken care of. He was six years old. The rest of them could make a day [day's work].

This suggests that the baby of the family, Wesley, was born around 1940, when Tobe was 70 and Helen 42. The 1940 census, which is likely to be released for public scrutiny from at the earliest 2012, should tell us more about when Sonny Liston was actually born, but my suspicion is that 1932 was not an unreasonable estimate.

And so the Liston family broke apart. Tobe remained on the farm with Sonny's brother, J.T., and both J.T. and Wesley stayed in the area after their father's death. Wesley eventually farmed nearby in Cherry Valley.

Sonny Liston's roots, even if he did not know or understand them, are of relevance when we come to consider what type of man he was. The effects of slavery only two generations back, his parents' move to Arkansas, the apparent failure or refusal of his father to show love, the decision of his mother to move away, and his choice to follow her to St Louis, all combine to give the sense of an emotional instability, and he might well have had a subconscious yearning to find security.

Perhaps he looked for it in the company of the hard men who drifted through the contemporary construction jobs he found in St Louis; perhaps he looked for it when he stood up to gang leaders in jail; and once free again, perhaps he sought it through what he thought would be an honest living in professional boxing. In the end, he did find a level of security through the loyalty and persistent support of his wife, Geraldine, and it seems entirely understandable that he found consolation and a kind of freedom in the company of children.

This was no ordinary man.

2

THIS IS THE ATOMIC AGE, PEACHES

Cassius Marcellus Clay and his younger brother Rudolph Valentino Clay were also descendants of slaves but, unlike Sonny Liston, they had white slaveowner's blood on their mother's side – rapist's blood, as Cassius would call it when he and Rudolph converted to Islam in 1964. Through their father's line, however, they were linked to the remarkable emancipationist, also named Cassius Marcellus Clay, who lived on the estate known as White Hall in Madison County, Kentucky. In contrast to abolitionists, emancipationists aimed to remove slavery by gradual, legal means. Abolitionists just wanted shot of it in any way possible. Cassius Clay owned slaves but was also said to have been one of the first to set them free. Two of his slaves, named Jonathan and Sallie, who took the name Clay, were the great-grandparents of the man who would become the heavyweight champion of the world.

As far as we can tell, the family, far from resenting the connection, were pleased to take his name. Cassius Clay Sr, the champion's father, declared to Jack Olsen, who wrote a fine series for *Sports Illustrated* and a biography: 'Yes, indeed, the original Cassius Marcellus Clay battled against slavery at all times. We're proud of him.'

The emancipationist Cassius Clay had set up an anti-slavery newspaper in Louisville and endured the horror of his son being killed by an angry mob. He withstood attempts on his own life. Two of his daughters were persistent champions of women's rights, and in 1855 he provided land and symbolic support for Berea College, which was specifically designed for the purpose of providing both white and black students with a chance to be educated. Its motto is still 'God Has Made Of One Blood All Peoples Of The Earth'.

In an astonishingly rich and varied life, Cassius Clay fought and survived being captured in the Mexican War of the 1840s, was Abraham Lincoln's ambassador to Moscow and was involved in the negotiations to bring Alaska into the United States of America. In his 80s, he was accused of abducting a 15-year-old white girl. When a posse of seven men rode up to his home, he fired a cannon at them. It transpired that he had married the girl with her family's consent. The marriage, however, did not last. Still, he was not done with excitement. At the age of ninety-three, he killed two burglars, shooting one and knifing the other. He died in his bed of old age.

We have no evidence of it, but the possibility is that slaves at his home had a better time of it with this maverick, forward-thinking man than most did, and once free, while unable to climb far up the social scale, they might have had more vision of what was possible and a more heightened sense of purpose and adventure. They had seen first hand how big things could be achieved.

According to census returns in Virginia, Jonathan Clay was born around 1824, while his wife Sallie was much younger, born around 1847, which fits with the presence of an unnamed three-year-old black slave on the Clay property in the 1850 census. Jonathan and Sallie's seventh child was Herman Clay, who would become the grandfather of the champion. Herman, born in 1876, worked as a labourer on the railroad and late in life was a chauffeur. One of his daughters, Coretta Clay, recalled to Jack Olsen that when the family moved house in Louisville when she was young, they set to and restored what had become a run-down building. Coretta said:

> There's some people that say coloured people are plain old lazy, they don't want anything. You put new houses for 'em on this street and in no time it's just gonna be all slummed up again because they don't care. Well, you should have seen this house when we moved into it in the 1940s. No trees, no paint, yard had nothing in it, no grass, not anything. The brick was just black with dirt, the mortar was old and rotten, and Cassius's granddaddy was living then, and he taught us, and we put on overalls after we finished work every day, and we would scrape out all the old mortar, and we got some tools and we tuck-pointed the whole place. About seven of us at home then, and we did the whole place in about six weeks. And then we plastered and papered the inside.

As Coretta spoke, Olsen said her mother, Herman's widow, Edith, by then 75 years old, was sweeping the house with a broom. This was a family that had pride in its image and part of that image was its tradition and history. While in Arkansas, Helen Liston was putting cardboard on her shack to keep out the wind, the Clays had a brick house. And while Helen and Tobe parted, even though the relationship between Cassius Clay Sr and his wife Odessa was far from an easy one, they stuck it out.

The champion's father was born in Louisville on 11 November 1912. There was another brother, Everett, who was a clever enough mathematician to attend Indiana University but whose wild streak left him a dead man, possibly by his own hand, by the time he was 30. One sister, Mary, was educated – a schoolteacher who when Jack Olsen went to see her was sitting by a stack of books on geometric function theory and topology. She was also drinking bourbon from a half-pint bottle wrapped in paper.

Cassius Sr was an egocentric, frustrated artist turned sign-writer. He was proud, erratic and colourful. He liked to entertain, especially in the years when journalists were in town to talk to him about his son, and in order to provide value he sometimes found it convenient to concoct stories that suited whatever he felt should be his image that particular day. He had a habit of turning conversations around to the subject of his achievements, real or imagined, such as when he declared himself to be a great breeder of poultry. There is no evidence to suggest he was anything of the kind.

He had a tendency to roam, and when the drink had hold of him he could rage. And sometimes his rage would be aimed at the good, gentle woman he married. Three times Odessa Grady Clay had to call the police to ask for protection from his temper. By 1966, Cassius Sr had an arrest sheet that included reckless driving, assault and battery, and disorderly conduct. He once treated Olsen and other writers to a ride around town in his battered Cadillac convertible with Odessa in the back. He wore a red hat, red sports jacket, leather boots and a black and white checked overcoat, and he serenaded the gathering with 'A Lovely Way to Spend an Evening'.

> The car was cold and a rasping noise came from under the hood while the broken speedometer needle spun wildly. The heater was out of order, the cigarette lighter was defunct, and the horn honked whenever Senior made a turn.

From the back seat, Odessa told him not to cut up cars on the road, to which he replied: 'You gotta cut 'em off, this is the Atomic Age, Peaches. Judgement Day round the bend. You back in another age.'

Angelo Dundee, who would train Cassius to the heavyweight championship of the world, said at one point he wondered where on earth the boy learned his antics from: 'And then I ran into his father. And I knew. His father looked like a young jitterbug himself, ageless, in the same shape as a young man and just as sharp.'

Odessa Lee Grady Clay kept a photograph of her father, John Lewis Grady, on a sideboard in her home. Although officially listed in the census as black, he had fair skin, blue or grey eyes, and his hair was long. His First World War draft registration card in 1917 gave his race as Ethiopian. John Lewis Grady was a coalminer, one of more than seven hundred workers at the St Bernard Mining Company in Earlington, in Hopkins County, Kentucky. In 1920, John and his wife Birdie, formerly Birdie Morehead, lived in the area of Earlington identified in the census only as south and west of the railroad. Their eldest child, also John L., was four, and Odessa was two. By 1930, they were in Louisville, John still a labourer with a coal company, while Birdie worked as a hotel maid. John L. was fourteen, Odessa thirteen and little sister Arletha nine. Odessa told biographer Thomas Hauser that her parents separated when she was a child, but at least at the times of the census returns of 1920 and 1930 they were together in one household with the children. Odessa said she saw little of her father, and, as her mother struggled to raise them, she often lived with an aunt. When she was 16, so around 1933, she met 21-year-old Cassius Marcellus Clay.

There are claims and counter-claims over Odessa's heritage, one being that her grandfather, Abe Grady, was from County Clare in Ireland. However, the US census suggests he was born in Kentucky. Another family history source suggests Abe was the son of a white American farmer and slaveowner James Grady, who had at one point graduated from medical school in Virginia. This same source says Abe Grady's mother was a black slave on the farm. Certainly, Odessa's mother, Birdie Morehead, was descended from a female slave, known only as Dinah, who was owned by Birdie's grandfather, Armistead S. Morehead in Logan County, Kentucky. Dinah, it is believed, was only 14 when she gave birth to Birdie's father, Thomas. Armistead, who got her pregnant, was 30. It was this incident in the family history more than any other that gave the by-then Muhammad Ali ammunition to declare the white blood in his veins to be that of rapists.

The first of the Moreheads on the records at the moment is a Captain Charles Morehead, who was born in 1739, but the family of his wife, Mary, has been traced back to emigrants with the family name of Norman from Somerset, England, half a century before that. Odessa was to say that her fairer skin, her mixed blood, was one reason the members of the Nation of Islam had no time for her. Long before that, however, just after half past six in the evening of 17 January 1942 at Louisville General Hospital, she and Cassius Marcellus Clay Sr welcomed their first son into the world.

3

I FIGURED I HAD TO PAY
FOR WHAT I DID

By 1947, Helen Liston was living in a room at 1017 O'Fallon Street, just off North 10th St in downtown St Louis, and earning money in a boot and shoe factory. Charles had joined her, making the 200-mile journey north by train.

> I figured the city would be like the country. And all I had to do was ask somebody where my mother lived and they'd tell me she lived down the road a piece. But when I got to the city there were too doggone many people there, and I just wandered around a lot.

At one point, he said he asked a wino on the street where Mrs Liston lived, and by some freak chance he happened to know. Another time, he said the police picked him up and, after consulting their records, delivered him to her address.

Helen is supposed to have said she answered the door to find him standing there. She asked why he had come – probably not the welcome he had dreamt of – and he said he was tired of life in the Arkansas fields. Liston himself said when he knocked on the door his brother Curtis opened it. Another time, Helen said she found him after the police had picked him up.

An unlikely story was perpetuated that he tried school in St Louis but left because he felt ridiculed. The tale ran that he was too slow and uneducated to learn alongside youngsters of his own age so had to squeeze his bulk into chairs in a class of small children. He was humiliated and did not go back. He repeated this to the Kefauver Committee in the 1961 investigation into Mob influence on boxing. Given the fact that he was already fourteen or fifteen by the time he arrived in St Louis, and had not had any apparent education since he was eight or nine, it seems unlikely that he saw any point in attending a school. It is possible that the story refers not to his time in St Louis but to when he was back in Arkansas.

Helen said at one time she got him into night school, but she had to go with him or he would go somewhere else. She says she also got him jobs in a poultry house and on an ice wagon. If the jobs happened, they didn't last long. He did say he worked with a construction gang – and this seems to have been a crucial element in his development from a country lad into a delinquent teenager old before his time.

> Those guys treated me like a man. They thought I was one because I could work as hard and as long as they could, and I could do more than hold my own in a fight. It was a tough bunch. Many of them had been in jail and others were headed there. But they were the only friends I had, and they influenced what I did and thought.

By this time, Helen had left him again, returning briefly to Arkansas and then to live in Gary, Indiana.

Whatever he was doing by day, by night he was hanging around the streets of St Louis. He said he was once given a gun but was too naive to know what to do with it. When he fired it into the sky and saw a flame burst from it, he threw it onto the ground.

He talked of how his life of crime took root:

> We broke into this restaurant about two in the morning and got away. But after we had gone ten blocks we decided to stop and get some barbecue – and then the police came along and barbecued us. I got out on probation. I was 16 then, weighed over 200 lb.

In the 1960s, Liston also talked to journalist Lionel Crane of the *Sunday Mirror*, who had been assigned to ghost Sonny's life story. Liston was uncooperative for days, then gradually opened up. Remembering St Louis, he said: 'Nobody don't want a bum. Down there is a lonely place. There ain't nobody going to leap down and say, "Hey, fellow, do you want a hand?" Not for me there wasn't, anyways.'

Helen Liston was asked, around the time Sonny won the championship, whether or not any of her other children had been in trouble with the law: 'No, it hurts me when I think about the trouble Sonny's been in. I think he fell in with the wrong people.'

His crimes were serious in that they were violent, yet as miscreants go he was some way short of Al Capone. He and two associates mugged one man for $6 plus $1.50 in loose change. Another robbery yielded $9; an assault on a man just one block from his home in O'Fallon Street pulled in a substantial haul of

$45, but a fourth attack harvested a nickel. And all the time Charles wore the same shirt – yellow with black checks.

Then in January 1950, perhaps around the time he turned 18, he and some other ne'er-do-wells used a gun when raiding cash registers at a night café and a filling station. On the charge sheet, his age was put down as 22, which is what he might or might not have told them, which later fuelled the suspicion about when he was born. He was also described as a labourer, which ties in with the construction job. The court sentenced him to five years in Missouri State Penitentiary at Jefferson City. His time behind bars began on the first day of June 1950. He was one of 3,000 prisoners, about a third of them black. 'I didn't mind prison,' Liston said. 'I figured I had to pay for what I did. No use crying.'

Liston said he carried clothes to the dry cleaner, ran messages, did jobs he was asked to do; a warder named W.P. Steinhauser said he lugged boxes of vegetables to the kitchens. Father Alois Stevens, a St Louis priest who worked at the prison, said: 'It was considered a break if a man was given a job. The state paid the prisoner five cents a day or ten cents if he worked in a shop.'

In the exercise yard, where white gangs ruled, he stood his ground. There was a story that in five minutes he left three white gang leaders unconscious on the concrete floor of an enclosed room known as the hole. After another violent brawl, it was said that the prison chaplain, Father Edward Schlattmann, offered him the chance to try boxing. As with much of Liston's youth, the exact truth is hard to pin down. There was apparently nothing on his official prison record that showed he was problematic to staff, beyond being told off for playing craps and for shouting when in a queue for something. Steinhauser told Doc Young: 'We had no trouble with him at all. He was all right.'

Schlattmann's successor as chaplain and athletics director was Father Stevens, then in his mid-30s. It is Father Stevens who is generally credited with encouraging Liston into boxing on a serious basis. He organised a boxing team and said Liston was pushed forward by other prisoners to do it seriously: 'He was very shy and uncommunicative, but he was very good. We staged boxing shows every Monday, and Sonny fought in every one of them.' He said later: 'Sonny was just a big, ignorant, pretty nice kid. He wasn't smart-alecky, but he got in little scrapes. I tried to teach him the alphabet, but it was hard to impress on him the importance of it.'

'The can was no party,' Sonny said. 'But after I started fighting, I had it pretty good. I could train, and I had special privileges.'

Andrew Lyles, who said he shared a cell with Liston for a year, described him as shy. Another inmate, Joe Gonzalez, claimed he was the first person to call him Sonny.

Young asked what Father Stevens felt about Liston's level of intelligence.

> He's no fool. He's not dumb by any means. He's just not had any formal education. But he's pretty shrewd. He has a great sense of humour. He learned to write his name and a few other little things in Jeff City. But he could count money. He learned that a long time ago.

After two years, in June 1952, Liston was moved to the minimum-security 'prison farm', ten miles outside Jefferson. By then he had improved dramatically as a boxer.

As the date of Liston's parole neared, Stevens called Robert L. Burnes, a journalist with the *St Louis Globe-Democrat*. Burnes recalled the conversation:

'I have a fighter down at the penitentiary,' said Stevens. 'How do I get him started in the fight game?'

Burnes offered a joke. 'Well, it would help, I suppose, to spring the fighter first . . .'

Stevens remained serious. 'Don't worry about that part of it. I've talked to the parole board. The members are interested in helping the boy if we can start him in something worthwhile. What I want you to tell me is how I can get him a fight with Rocky Marciano.'

Burnes explained patiently: 'In the first place, Father, even if this boy of yours is any good, it would take him years to qualify for a match like that. In the second place, this is an old, old story. We are always hearing about some kid who is the toughest guy in the neighbourhood. But put him in the ring with a boxer of any experience and the tough guy will never lay a glove on the professional.'

Stevens was adamant Liston was different. 'Help him get the chance. This is a poor Negro boy from Arkansas – broken home, big family, can't read or write. This is the only hope he has of becoming a decent member of society.'

Burnes contacted a former pro light-heavyweight, Monroe Harrison, and Harrison agreed to go to the jailhouse. He had no easy means of getting there, so he invited Frank Mitchell, who had a car. Mitchell managed some local fighters, the best of whom was a featherweight, Charlie Riley, who had recently fought Willie Pep for the world title. (Mitchell had been installed as publisher of the *St Louis Argus*, a weekly newspaper for black readers, by his mother, Nannie Turner, who was its business manager. His father, Willie Mitchell, had founded it. Turner told *Sports Illustrated* in 1961: 'I made Frank publisher. That's the best job there is. I wouldn't make him editor. He doesn't like to sit around and write.')

The St Louis police did not appreciate Mitchell's better side. By 1961 he had been arrested 26 times. Mostly he was picked up for illegal gambling, though none of those charges stuck. The best the police could get him for was a few speeding violations.

The fact that one of his boxers had fought for a world championship might be an indication that he knew people who had influence, especially as before he boxed Pep in St Louis in January 1950 'Chillin' Charlie Riley' had won only five of his last twelve fights. Pep knocked him out in five rounds. Mitchell was known to associate with John Vitale, who was the head of what was euphemistically known as the St Louis Crime Family between 1935 and 1954, when he 'retired'.

Harrison and Mitchell went up to the prison for a sparring session, taking along another trainer, Tony Anderson, who was a leading light in the St Louis amateur programme, and a local, preliminary-level professional heavyweight, Thurman Wilson. Liston and Wilson did two or four rounds, depending on the source, after which Wilson had taken enough. 'Better get me out of this ring,' he is supposed to have said. 'He's going to kill me.'

Burnes remembered Harrison bursting into his newspaper office.

> He's on the roly-poly side and seldom moves at anything faster than a leisurely amble, but he was hurrying that time.
> 'Mr Bob,' he said, 'you found me a live one this time . . . that boy Sonny's got the prettiest left jab I've ever seen.'

On 30 October 1952, Liston was paroled into the care of Father Stevens, Harrison and Mitchell. Stevens would supervise, Harrison would train, Mitchell would manage. (Father Stevens later denied his involvement, declaring he stayed 'out of things'.)

Parole board member John Fels told Liston:

> I'm not sure we're doing the right thing, but I am impressed by the fact that so many people have offered to help you. Don't let them down, boy. If you do, the first minute you get into trouble I'll see that you come back here.

Harrison, who was not above dreaming up stories to present his jailbird heavyweight in a better light, remembered buying him a chicken dinner. Liston sat staring at it.

'Why don't you eat it?' said Harrison.

Liston looked at him and said: 'I don't know how.'

Harrison would play checkers with him and talk boxing.

Burnes felt Liston was frightened when he was in St Louis straight after his time in jail. He spent a lot of time listening to the radio in the room Mitchell found for him at the YMCA in Pine Street. Lying on his bed going nowhere was what he was used to doing at night. Mitchell also organised him a job in a steel plant, but it doesn't seem to have lasted long.

Johnny Tocco, who ran a gym Liston used on the corner of Cass Avenue and what is now North 14th St, said:

> He was a loner. He wouldn't talk to nobody. He wouldn't go with nobody. He always came into the gym by himself. He always left by himself.
>
> The police knew he'd been in prison, and he'd be walking along, and they'd always stop him and search him. So he went through alleys all the time. He always went around things. I can still see him, either coming out of an alley or walking into one.

Liston's official amateur status was to last just 11 months, yet in that time he proved himself a natural fighter. His official date of birth came when he entered the Golden Gloves tournament in 1953. He couldn't enter unless he had one, so somebody came up with 8 May 1932. Harrison began to put around sanitised versions of Sonny's story, including the 'school humiliation' episode. Nobody really knew what to believe – when he was in the ring or out of it.

His first win was in the St Louis Golden Gloves, and he went on to compete in Chicago, where he pulled an astonishing upset over the previous year's Olympic champion, Ed Sanders. That put him in the national finals in March 1953 and only five months after walking out of the penitentiary gates he won that by defeating the respected Julius Griffin of New York. Griffin dropped Sonny in round one, but this raw novice from St Louis got up, steamed back and won the decision.

When he tried his luck in the 1953 AAU event, he lost in the quarter-finals to a 17 year old from Philadelphia, Jimmy McCarter, whom he would later employ as a sparring partner. In the Kiel Auditorium in St Louis in June 1953, Liston boxed against a touring team from Western Europe. He was matched with Hermann Schreibauer, who had won a bronze medal in the European Championships a few weeks earlier. In front of 7,500 fans, Liston overpowered the man from Munich in two minutes sixteen seconds of round one.

Tony Anderson, the head coach of the St Louis Golden Gloves team, said Liston was the strongest fighter he had ever seen:

And I've seen them for more than 30 years. Although he has only had about six months of training, we've never had a heavyweight in Golden Gloves who was so good.

The boy is still crude, and he's no Joe Louis – yet – but he's much faster on his feet and has more speed than Louis had at his age. In fact, he's one of the fastest big men I've ever seen.

That's what most folks don't realise. They see how strong he is, but he's still awkward and he doesn't look fast.

After describing him as shy and quiet, Anderson added: 'He likes to train, likes to box and likes to keep in condition. He works as a furnace feeder in a steel foundry because shovelling coal all day keeps him fit.'

Monroe Harrison said: 'He's an ideal boy to handle.'

By the beginning of September 1953, following a lengthy meeting involving Stevens, Harrison, Mitchell, Anderson, Burnes, Liston and John Fels of the parole board, professional boxing had a new heavyweight. A contract was drawn up: Liston would get 50 per cent of his purses, Mitchell and Harrison the other 50, all expenses coming from their half. All Sonny said during the discussions was: 'Whatever you tell me to do, I'll do.'

4

THAT'S WHY YOU CAN'T BE RICH

When Cassius Marcellus Clay Jr arrived in this world on 17 January 1942, the family lived at 1121 West Oak Street in Louisville, Kentucky. His brother, Rudolph, followed on 18 July 1943. Rudolph's second name was originally Arnett, but some time later their father changed his mind and replaced Arnett with Valentino. When the boys were still small, the family moved into the home they would remember, at 3302 Grand Avenue, a white-boarded house of four rooms.

Cassius and Rudolph went to school and played games in front of their home, which was lawned, with a tree overhanging the steps where they sat talking about what they would do with their lives, dreaming their dreams. Cassius would tell his mother that one day he would buy her everything she wanted.

Louisville in the 1940s was as segregated as anywhere else, though not especially dangerous. Cassius Sr told a story that is hard to countenance now of when he and Odessa were downtown at the time Cassius Jr was a small child. The little boy wanted a drink of water, but when they asked at a 10c store, the shop girl refused, saying she would lose her job if she served them.

Cassius Sr was angry, bitter and resentful towards white people, an attitude that, while understandable, was a contributory factor in his sons' eventual seeking-out of the Nation of Islam. Jack Olsen felt this strongly when putting together his 1967 biography of Ali, recounting incidents the father had related to him. 'When I was a boy,' said Cassius Sr, 'seemed like every darned day you'd read in the paper . . . a lynching, a burning of a Negro . . . Now wouldn't that turn you against the white man?'

He spoke of an incident in Louisville at the turn of the 50s when a black man of about 21 was accused of raping a white girl and killed, even though the girl said they were having a consensual relationship. He explained to his sons when they were small boys that white people got the opportunities, that they ruled everything.

Odessa Clay said Cassius began asking about basic race issues when he was only three years old, which shocked her. Because of her fairer skin, he asked her if she was black or white.

Mary Carter, Cassius Sr's sister, did not share her brother's extreme views, though she knew well enough the injustices and horrors that existed. She also understood the frustration that influenced the way he thought: 'It's according to how you look at things. Sometimes people want to blame their shortcomings on somebody else.'

Cassius Sr had ability as an artist but had no chance of earning a living through art. Instead he painted signs in Louisville, wherever the jobs came in. He painted KING KARL'S THREE ROOMS OF NEW FURNITURE on Market Street. He painted A.B. HARRIS, M.D., DELIVERIES & FEMALE DISORDERS on Dumesnil Street. JOYCE'S BARBER SHOP was his, too. And PACIFIC PLYWOOD PRODUCTS CO., 1299 12 ST. With his sign-writing and Odessa's work as a maid and cook, they got by.

Once, according to *Time* magazine, young Cassius demanded of his father: 'Why can't I be rich?'

His father touched his hand and said: 'Look there. That's why you can't be rich . . .'

The sprawling city on the banks of the Kentucky River was home, but not a single one of its black-skinned citizens could mix socially with the wealthy white folk who enjoyed the spectacle and excitement of the Kentucky Derby at Churchill Downs or the sophistication and class of the Seelbach Hotel on Fourth Street.

That said, it was not the Deep South. While black youngsters might be verbally abused, Louisville was generally peaceful enough. Rudolph Clay, by then Rahaman Ali, told Thomas Hauser: 'If we were in the wrong place, white boys would come up in a car and say, "Hey, nigger, what are you doing here?" I never got into any fights. No one attacked me.' But then he never fell in love with a white girl and knew how he had to behave in order to minimise the chance of anything happening to him.

The murder of Emmett Till affected the young Cassius deeply. It was in August 1955 that 14-year-old Till from Chicago was visiting relatives in Money, Mississippi, which is about 50 miles west of where Sonny Liston's parents were born and raised.

It was a moment of crazy over-familiarity with a young white woman, Carolyn Bryant, that cost him his life and made America take temporary stock of itself. The details of what he did were never made clear with any consistency. Certainly, he offended and worried Mrs Bryant. Some said he touched her hand when he paid for some gum in the store she ran with her husband, Roy, who was out of town at the time. Others said he attempted to touch her waist or that he called out 'Bye, baby' as he left and might even have wolf-whistled when she left the store to get a gun from a car outside. What is plain is that the Chicago boy was showing off to his new teenaged Southern friends and had forgotten the warnings he had been given by his mother, Mamie, about how to behave in the South.

Money was a small, suspicious community where white women did not generally sleep in a house without a white man present. It was also a poor town. Most of the customers at the Bryant store were black sharecroppers.

Three nights later Emmett was awoken in the house of his great-uncle, Moses 'Preacher' Wright, driven out of town, smashed to a pulp and thrown into the Tallahatchie River, weighed down by a 70 lb fan from a cotton gin around his neck. When his body was discovered, he was identified by a ring that belonged to his father.

Roy Bryant and his half-brother, John William (J.W.) Milam were arrested, charged and tried in a trial that drew surprising interest around the country. In the summing-up by the defence, a lawyer told the all-white jury that their ancestors would turn in their graves if the verdict was guilty. He said, 'I'm sure every last Anglo-Saxon one of you has the courage to free these men.' They did, after deliberating for 67 minutes, including a drink break.

The following year, protected by the double-jeopardy procedure whereby once acquitted, they could not be retried for the same crime, Bryant and Milam admitted they killed Till, when a journalist, William Bradford Hule, paid them $7,000 for their story. Milam said:

> I'm no bully, I never hurt a nigger in my life. I like niggers – in their place. I know how to work 'em . . . As long as I live and can do anything about it, niggers are gonna stay in their place. Niggers ain't gonna vote where I live. If they did, they'd control the Government.
>
> They ain't gonna go to school with my kids. And when a nigger gets close to mentioning sex with a white woman, he's tired o' livin' . . . My folks fought for this country, and we got some rights.

Milam said it was when Emmett Till talked back to him that he made up his mind to kill him, to make an example of him.

In an interview with Devery S. Anderson on a website dedicated to Emmett, Mamie Till said the attention her son's murder received surprised her:

> It really did, because what happened to a black person in the United States

was 'ho-hum'. Whole families disappeared and nobody raised an eyebrow. The black people were afraid to talk about it because they knew that if they opened their big mouths, they would disappear as well.

She felt that by attending the trial she was risking her life, but she felt compelled to honour her son, that it was her moral business to be there. As she listened to the evidence, she knew Milam and Bryant were guilty, but the hostility of the white crowds made her realise they would not be convicted. She and the black people who were with her left town in two cars when the jury retired. They heard the verdict on the radio and could hear the cheering and uproar in the background of the broadcast. 'We knew that had we been there, we could have been lynched,' she said.

Emmett's body was laid in an open coffin in Chicago for five days so that people could walk by and see for themselves what had been done to him.

I mean, to hear they hung people on a tree, that they cut their fingers off and passed them out for souvenirs, to hear that, to read it, is one thing. But to actually see it with your eyes, that is a different thing. And 600,000 people, which is a conservative estimate, walked by and looked at Emmett. People from all over the world came . . .

Cassius Clay was 13, a year younger than Emmett Till, when Emmett was murdered. He said the case made a deep impression on him. It is possible it made a deep impression on 23-year-old Sonny Liston, too, as he worked at making a name for himself as a professional boxer in the dark, smoky clubs of St Louis, but if it did he never said. Then again, perhaps nobody ever asked.

In December 1955, when Cassius was just short of 14 years old, an African American woman, Rosa Parks, boarded a bus in her home city of Montgomery, Mississippi, and sat in the first row of seats reserved for black people at the back, behind the seats for whites. The driver, James F. Blake, had a history of enforcing the unwritten rule that when the white seats were full, the 'front' of the bus stretched as far as the driver wished it to stretch in order for white people to sit. Black people, even if they were already sitting down, had to stand.

Rosa Parks said Blake had ordered her off a city bus years before when, after dropping her purse, she momentarily sat in a 'white' seat to pick it up. Even though she had paid, he drove off, leaving her to walk five miles home in the rain. This time she refused when Blake told her and three other black people to stand to allow whites to sit. She was arrested.

It was not the first act of defiance that year in Montgomery. Earlier, 15-year-old Claudette Colvin had refused to give up her seat to a white hobo. She had been handcuffed and forcibly removed by the police. However, she was pregnant and unmarried, and the National Association for the Advancement of Colored People decided that they could not use the incident for political benefit.

Rosa Parks was a respectable married woman in her middle years, active in the NAACP, and her protest was used to set off a rapidly organised reaction. Some even accused her of pre-planning the incident, but she explained:

> I had plenty to do without having to end up in jail. But . . . we had endured that for too long. The more we gave in, the more we complied with that kind of treatment, the more oppressive it became.

Edgar Nixon, president of the NAACP, and an Alabama College professor, Jo Ann Robinson, stayed up all night producing 35,000 handbills that declared a boycott of the city's buses on the day of Rosa's trial.

> We are . . . asking every Negro to stay off the buses Monday . . . You can afford to stay out of school for one day. If you work, take a cab, or walk. But please, children and grown-ups, don't ride the bus at all on Monday.

Rosa Parks was fined $10 with $4 court costs.

Dr Martin Luther King, pastor of Dexter Avenue Baptist Church, led the organising committee, which took on the name of the Montgomery Improvement Association. As many of Montgomery's 50,000 black residents travelled around the city by bus, even a one-day boycott had a significant effect. Encouraged by its success, they extended the action and many of the city's buses remained idle for more than a year as black people shared car lifts or just walked, no matter how far, to get to work.

On 30 January 1956, Dr King's home was bombed, and in March he and a hundred other African American residents of Montgomery were arrested on an astonishing charge of carrying out an illegal boycott: in other words, for choosing not to travel by bus and asking others to do the same. Dr King was fined $500. However, the stand held, and on 13 November 1956 the US Supreme Court ruled that segregation on buses was unconstitutional.

The Civil Rights movement would change the way a nation thought, but it would take time and a great deal of sacrifice. With rallies, meetings and marches across the South, it was a momentous time to be young and black. Cassius Clay, although already politicised to a minor degree by his father, took part in only one demonstration in his teenaged years. That was when a teacher at his school organised a protest outside a restaurant where black folk could not eat. A white woman emptied a bucket of cold water over him from an eighth-floor window. He didn't get involved again.

At the age of 12, in October 1954, Cassius had taken up boxing on the invitation of a police officer, Joseph Elsby Martin. The boy's new red-and-white Schwinn bicycle had been stolen while he was at a fair at the Columbia Auditorium, and he wanted to know what Officer Martin, who was in his boxing gym in the basement of the building, was going to do about it. Martin didn't find the bike but found the world a fighter. In 1961, by which time he was no longer associated with his most famous pupil, he told *Sports Illustrated*:

> In the past 20 years, I guess I've taught 10,000 boys to box, or at least tried to teach them. Cassius Clay, when he first began coming around here, looked no better or worse than the majority. About a year later, though, you could see that the little smart aleck – I mean he's always been sassy – had a lot of potential. He stood out because, I guess, he had more determination than most boys, and he had the speed to get him someplace.

He won his amateur debut over three 3-minute rounds on a split decision over another novice named Ronnie O'Keefe, and before his first year with the gloves on was out he had boxed on a local television show called *Champions Of Tomorrow*. When Cassius Sr saw his son box, he exclaimed: 'Oh, he's a real Joe Louis!'

Martin, who was 38 when he first met Clay, was a good coach. He had guided his own son, Joe Jr, to a National Golden Gloves title. Cassius would train in Martin's gym and in Chickasaw Park, the main park in Louisville where blacks were allowed to relax. At 15, he had his first headline in the local *Courier-Journal* after he stopped a lad named Donnie Hall in the fourth round. A black trainer, Fred Stoner, also worked day to day with young black boxers at the Grace Community Centre. Cassius hung out there sometimes. Stoner's input has been undervalued, but at the time Cassius boxed Archie Moore in 1962, Cassius would say: 'I was taught by Fred Stoner, a poor, coloured man who had nothing going for him.'

Jimmy Ellis, his boyhood friend and later sparring partner, who would himself become World Boxing Association champion, said Cassius was always ready to call someone out, to get under their skin. And always, always, he worked incredibly hard. 'He'd box and box,' said Ellis.

He'd box three or four rounds with one guy. Then he'd sit down. Then another guy would come into the gym and he'd go three or four rounds with him. Then he'd come out and hit the heavy bag. And then he'd go three or four rounds with another guy.

Martin said Clay's habit of winding up opponents was there from very early on and was not developed as a publicity stunt or to sell tickets. He just saw it as a way to gain psychological supremacy before a fight began – and, perhaps even more relevant, of drumming up his own courage. Usually, it was kept within reasonable limits, but occasionally it would spill over into the unacceptable.

At the Olympic trials in San Francisco, Martin had to sit him down and tell him to stop because it was alienating people. He went so far as to threaten to withdraw him from the competition. Another time, when Cassius was boxing in Chicago in an inter-city Golden Gloves match, Martin was not with the team. He had a phone call from the managers, who could not control Clay's tongue. Apparently, he had been insulting the heavyweights. (He was a light-heavy.) Martin had to talk to him on the phone and cool things down. 'He was always a loudmouth, liked to talk, but of course I kept him curbed. When I thought he was talking too much, I made him shut up.' It was at that amateur event in Chicago that, according to his aunt, he was first influenced by the Nation of Islam, which had its headquarters in the city. He was 16 years old.

Cassius attended, first, Virginia Avenue Elementary School, then DuValle Junior High and from September 1957 Central High School (which was for black students only). He was in trouble only once, when he threw a snowball and it hit a teacher. Hauled before the disciplinary board, he informed them he was very sorry and then added that one day he was going to be the heavyweight champion of the world.

Whereas the teenaged Sonny Liston was drifting aimlessly on the St Louis streets, at the same age Cassius Clay knew exactly what he wanted and, being his father's son, was prepared to tell anybody who would listen all about it.

One time Cassius raced the school bus for 20 blocks on Chestnut Street past astonished folk trying to get to work. He would break out into a shadow-boxing routine in the hall or in front of the mirrors of the restrooms. Surprisingly, an English teacher, Thelma Lauderdale, said that in her class at least Cassius was shy, quiet and meditative, though he often drew pictures instead of writing things down. However, perhaps most tellingly, there was an argument over an unfinished English paper. Mrs Lauderdale, a Methodist, refused to accept it because he wanted to write it on the subject of the Nation of Islam. The stand-off was settled by the head teacher, Attwood Wilson. Cassius was allowed to give his paper orally – and to talk about life as an amateur boxer and where the sport had taken him. Wilson said: 'One day our greatest claim to fame is going to be that we knew Cassius Clay or taught him . . .'

In four years of senior high school, the requirement was that a student gain a minimum of sixteen unit passes. To get a unit pass, you needed at least 70 per cent. Cassius got sixteen unit passes, seven of them with exactly 70 per cent. A character assessment ruled him 'above average' in health, 'average' in scholastic zeal, honesty, effort, social attitude, initiative and intellectual ability, and 'fair' in emotional control and leadership. By the age of 15, he was working part time for 60 cents an hour in the library of Nazareth College, carrying books around, waxing tables, doing whatever was asked of him.

In the early '90s, *Sports Illustrated* writer William Nack found a girlfriend, Mildred Davis, who appears to have been close to Cassius during his last year at school. He kept her guessing. He had a habit of sipping water from a bottle laced with garlic, supposedly to keep his blood pressure down. He would reek of it. He refused to eat pork, apparently because he believed it raised the blood pressure. Similarly, he wouldn't drink soda because of the sugar and acid in it. He carried his money folded in a small purse like an old lady. In Mildred's house, he was always polite, almost to the point of being old-fashioned. Once, he said he would run her home from an evening show at school. As he didn't have a car, she wasn't sure how that would happen. She soon found out. For 13 blocks, she had to walk in her high heels as he ran and jogged backwards and forwards alongside her. And once, perhaps in some kind of forerunner of his requirements later with his first wife Sonji Roi, he told her that when they were married she would have to wear her skirts longer in order to look like a lady.

Already there was evidence enough that, even if he were not yet confident enough to speak about it, the teachings of the Nation of Islam were interesting him. He wanted to avoid pork, perhaps because of blood pressure and perhaps because Islam forbids it. He wanted Mildred to dress more soberly. He wanted to write his school essay about the movement. However, for the time being at least, any interest in religion was submerged beneath the typical aspirations of a teenager who believed the whole world was spread out before him. Davis said one evening they sat on the porch of her house and he told her:

Pretty soon, we're gonna get married, and we're gonna get a real big house with a swimming pool. All the kids in the neighbourhood are gonna come over. We gonna have a lot of kids. And they'll swim in the pool.

The general estimate of the Louisville folk who knew these things was that Clay only had two street fights in his life, neither of them of his making. One was when a grown man decided to take him down a peg and nailed him with a surprise shot as Clay was jogging around a corner. Cassius hammered the man until he screamed: 'Get him off me, get him off me . . .' The other was when two youths goaded him into retaliating and he knocked one down with a single punch. The incident left him near to tears. 'I never did bother nobody,' he said. 'Didn't want to get hurt.'

Joe Martin remembered that when they were away on boxing trips, Cassius would read the Bible before going to bed. 'He didn't chase women, and I never heard him say a curse word in my life,' Martin said.

This was when Odessa was still taking both of her boys to the Baptist church. Years on, Muhammad Ali would say: 'I've changed my religion and some of my beliefs since then, but her God is still God. I just call him by a different name.'

If a professional fighter came to town, Cassius made it his business to go along to see what was happening, maybe to introduce himself. In 1957, he picked the brains of top-level trainer Angelo Dundee for three hours when Dundee was in Louisville with Willie Pastrano, later the light-heavyweight champion of the world. Dundee remembered him even then as a serious student of boxing. In 1959, when Dundee and Pastrano returned, Clay pestered them into letting him spar. Dundee didn't like it but let him have a round. Pastrano could do nothing with him and knew it. 'The kid kicked the hell out of me!' he said.

When he graduated from Central High School on 11 June 1960, he was ranked 376th in a year of 391 students, but it didn't matter. Over a span of 6 years from the age of 12 until he was 18 Clay won, according to some sources, 134 of 141 amateur contests, according to others, 176 of 181, culminating in his selection as the USA's light-heavyweight representative for the Rome Olympics. He deserved it, too: in 1959 and in 1960 he won the National AAU light-heavyweight championship, he was the National Golden Gloves light-heavyweight champion, then added the heavyweight crown. He also won the light-heavyweight competition in the Olympic trials in San Francisco, after the plane from Louisville had passed through a storm that terrified him. He threw away his return ticket and, after borrowing money from a referee, caught the train home.

He had wanted to turn professional before the Olympic trials, but Martin persuaded him to wait. It was the police officer who sat him down after he returned on the train from San Francisco and told him he needed to deal with his fear and get himself on the plane to Rome. Of course, he knew Martin was right. And, of course, he went.

Sugar Ray Robinson said, in his autobiography by Dave Anderson of the *New York Times*, that before the Olympics, Cassius asked him to be his manager. Sugar Ray, who had never met him before, told him it was impossible because he was still boxing and wouldn't have time to do both. Robinson said Clay had waited for three hours in the hope of bumping into him. As a result, the great man kept an eye on his career, and from time to time acted as an unofficial adviser.

They called it the greatest sporting festival to grace the Italian capital since the fall of the Roman Empire. More than 5,000 competitors from around the world, the largest number for any Olympics up to that point, descended on Rome. It was the Olympics when Abebe Bikila, the barefoot runner from Ethiopia, changed the face of marathon running, when the great Australian, Herb Elliott, broke the world 1500m record, when the formidable Tamara Press won the women's shot, and her sister Irina the sprint hurdles. It was the Olympics of Dawn Fraser and Anita Lonsbrough, of Wilma Rudolph . . . and of Cassius Marcellus Clay Jr.

In his opening bout on 30 August 1960, he beat a Belgian named Yvon Becaus in the second round. Becaus was a perfect first opponent, not really much of a test. (Later he had a brief, unsuccessful professional career.) Then he outscored Gennady Shatkov of the Soviet Union, a unanimous decision that made it clear he could win the gold. Shatkov had been Olympic middleweight champion in 1956 and twice a European champion, and now at 28 had moved up to the light-heavyweight division.

In an interview published on www.eastsideboxing.com in 2005, Shatkov said he was asked to move up to light-heavyweight for the good of the team by the Soviet trainers, who wanted to put another boxer in at middleweight. He said he felt, as team captain, he could not refuse. 'I had to drink water right up to the weigh-in,' he said, 'just so that I could get in over 75kg.' He said because Clay was taller and bigger than he was, he couldn't beat him at long range, his normal game, and so was forced to try something different. For two rounds, he felt he held his own, but in the third Clay stretched clear. Shatkov went on to become a professor in the Department of Theory and History of State and Law at Leningrad University and later entered the university management. 'You know if you were to tell me after my defeat to Ali that he is a future legend and superstar, I wouldn't have likely believed you,' he said.

In the semi-finals, Cassius repeated a previous victory over the American-based Australian Tony Madigan who, at 30, was in his third Olympic Games. This was Madigan's first medal. During a stay in Britain, Madigan had also won the 1954 ABA middleweight title. He could fight, but while some of his supporters felt he was unlucky in both of his meetings with Clay he admitted he lost them.

In the final, Cassius wrapped up the gold with another decision, this time over Zbigniew Pietrzykowski, a 26-year-old southpaw from Poland. Once again, Clay the man-child was fighting a seasoned veteran. The Pole had won a bronze in the Melbourne Olympics as a light-middleweight, when he lost in the semi-finals to the great Hungarian Laszlo Papp. He would win bronze again in Tokyo in 1964, plus five medals in European championships. Pietrzykowski's wrong-way-round stance, his experience and cunning made things difficult for two rounds, but by the third, the young man had him worked out. Clay peppered him with raking punches, bloodied his nose and claimed the gold with another 5–0 unanimous verdict.

Cassius used the Olympics as a platform to launch himself as a celebrity athlete as well as a fine boxer. When he wasn't competing, he went around introducing himself to other sportsmen, exchanging lapel pins and handshakes and talking to them about their achievements as well as his own. However, his room-mate, the light-middleweight Wilbert 'Skeeter' McClure, said behind the noise was a young man who was extremely serious about his sport. He trained ferociously hard. And in front of girls, he was tongue-tied and almost sheepish.

In Rome, one of Clay's media interviews brought the oft-repeated exchange with a journalist from the Soviet Union, who asked him how he felt that he could win a gold medal for his country and still not be able to eat in some restaurants in his home town. His reply was magnificent in its patriotic innocence:

> Russian, we got qualified men working on that problem. We got the biggest and the prettiest cars. We get all the food we can eat. America is the greatest country in the world and as far as places I can't eat goes, I got lots of places I can eat. More places I can than I can't. I ain't fighting off alligators and living in a mud hut.
>
> Russian, there's good and bad in every country, and if there weren't good and bad, we wouldn't be talking about Judgement Day.

When he won the gold medal, he didn't take it off for two days, even sleeping on his back with it laid on his chest.

On the way home, he and Joe Martin stopped off in New York. A businessman sponsor from Louisville, Billy Reynolds, installed them in a suite in the Waldorf Astoria (next to the one used by the Duke and Duchess of Windsor) and gave him money to buy presents for his family. Cassius spent $450 on watches for his father, mother and brother.

When they were back home, he talked modestly of meeting world heavyweight champion Floyd Patterson, who himself had won Olympic gold at middleweight in Helsinki in 1952.

> Floyd came by to see me. We had a little talk. It was a friendly talk, but if possible I would like to fight him one of these days. I didn't look at him right and he didn't look at me right, but we were friendly.

Back home in Louisville, he drove down Walnut Street in a pink Cadillac with the great sprinter Wilma Rudolph alongside him. He was 18; she was 20. Wilma had won the 100m and 200m gold medals in Rome, and another in the 4 x 100m relay. Cassius had met her in the Olympic village, and she was visiting him from her home in Clarksville, Tennessee.

Rudolph's victory parade in Clarksville had been the first integrated public event ever held in the town. Rome had been her second Olympics after Melbourne in 1956. One of a family of twenty children, she had overcome polio to become the best female sprinter the world had ever seen.

As they drove through Louisville, he began calling out to the crowds that he was Cassius Clay and he was the greatest – and then he introduced Wilma as well. 'She is the greatest!' he cried out.

Wilma told him to sit down, sank back into her seat and waited for the show to stop, but he wouldn't let up until she had stood up and taken a bow. Thirty years on, she said: 'I saw him at the very beginning. It was bedlam. I always told him, "You should be on stage."'

Cassius and his brother had been raised as Baptists by their mother, and by Rome the seeds of their conversion to Islam had been sown. However, for the time being, spiritual concerns were less important than the desire for material gain. He told journalist Huston Horn:

> Last Sunday, some cats I know said, 'Cassius, Cassius, come on now and let's go to church, otherwise you won't get to Heaven.'
>
> 'Hold on a minute,' I said to them, 'and let me tell you something else. When I've got me a $100,000 house, another quarter million stuck in the bank and the world title latched on to my name, then I'll be in Heaven.
>
> 'Walking around making $25 a week, with four children crying at home 'cause they're hungry, that's my idea of Hell.'

The question of which direction his career would take following the Rome triumph took a while to solve. For two years, he had been courted by Billy Reynolds, who ran Reynolds Metal Company and who had shelled out for his stopover in New York. Reynolds' offer was a ten-year contract, with Martin remaining as an adviser, but word reached him that the family had problems about that. Martin believed Cassius was, at that time, still afraid of his father:

> We were all at Wilson Wyatt's office in Louisville to sign a contract for me to manage Cassius and train him. One of the lawyers took me aside and said, 'I hate to tell you this, but old man Clay will not sign any contract with your name on it.'
>
> I said, 'Why? What's he got against me?' and the lawyer said, 'Either it's because he thinks you've done something for his son that he couldn't do, or because you're a police officer.' Later I read that the old man didn't like cops in general and me in particular.

According to *Time* magazine, they ignored offers to manage him from Cus D'Amato, Archie Moore and Pete Rademacher.

When an alternative came from a syndicate of eleven wealthy Kentucky businessmen, this was immediately more attractive – especially as it came with a $10,000 signing fee, a minimum guaranteed salary of $4,000 for two years, plus training expenses, rising to $6,000 for four years and 50 per cent of the purses, however they were earned. (For example, they split equally his $500 fee for appearing in the movie *Requiem For A Heavyweight*.) And the syndicate had no problem with leaving Martin out of the deal.

And so, Officer Joe Martin stayed on his policeman's wages of $408 a month when the young man he had nurtured and trained for six years turned professional. At times in the ensuing years Martin seemed hurt, disappointed, that his contribution to the moulding of Cassius Clay into an Olympic champion was dumbed down. 'Let's just say he fell off the Christmas tree, a gift-wrapped champion,' he said once.

The syndicate retained the option to renew the contract up to October 1966, when they had the right to make Clay another offer. Fifteen per cent of his purse money went into a pension fund that could not be touched until he was thirty-five or had retired from boxing. Some more was invested in US Government bonds.

The 'head' of the syndicate, which called itself The Louisville Sponsoring Group, was Bill Faversham Jr, who had made a fortune as vice-president of the Brown-Forman distillery in Louisville. This was responsible for, among other brand names, Jack Daniel's. Faversham's father, William Sr, had been a professional actor from London who had made his name on the Broadway stage. After being forced to drop his Harvard studies because of a family financial shortfall, William Jr also spent six months acting in Broadway shows. While there, he kept in shape in the New York gym belonging to the old champion Philadelphia Jack O'Brien. He settled in Louisville after the war and joined Brown-Forman.

He also persuaded the Brown half of Brown-Forman, W.L. Lyons Brown, to join the syndicate. Linked to W.L. was another investor, William Sol Cutchins, who was president of the Brown-Williamson Tobacco Company. Cutchins was a Princeton graduate, and his grandfather had been a 15-year-old private on the Confederate side in the Civil War.

James Ross Todd, 26, was installed by his father, a Kentucky Republican politician and lawyer, because, as he put it: 'Daddy had enough on his mind without getting involved in prizefighting.' Todd was treasurer.

Vertner Degarmo Smith Jr was James Ross Todd's godfather. Chairman of a liquor distribution business, he had once employed Odessa Clay as a cook. He had done a stint as vice-chairman of the Kentucky State Racing Commission. After becoming involved in Clay's career, he told Huston Horn of *Sports Illustrated* in 1963 that he had recently read a good book about boxing. Unfortunately, he could not recall its title.

Robert Worth Bingham, thirty, was the son of the owner of Louisville's two newspapers, the *Louisville Times* and the *Courier-Journal*. He had taken to buying *Ring* magazine every month. With Bingham on board, Cassius was more likely to get a better publicity ride.

Then they had 29-year-old George Washington Norton IV, known as Possum. Said to be distantly descended from Washington's wife, Martha, his father owned the local NBC radio and TV franchise. Young Possum's previous business dalliances were some way short of the big league: neither of his two racehorses ever got to run a race, and the professional football team, the Louisville Raiders, into which he put $1,000, went bust.

Unlike Possum, Patrick Calhoun Jr, a retired boat builder, was a horse-racing expert. By his own admission, however, he knew nothing of boxing.

Elbert Gary Sutcliffe was a retired farmer with a 300-acre estate running alongside the Ohio river. He said he didn't know Cassius Clay but had shaken hands with him. He got involved because the project was recommended to him, and the boxer's credibility was confirmed by a friend named Either One Richardson. (Apparently, said Huston Horn for *Sports Illustrated* in his 1963 article, that was his real name. His parents couldn't decide, so asked his grandmother which of two names she preferred – and she told them 'Either One.') Said Elbert Sutcliffe: 'Either One knows Cassius and he says he's a good boy. That's good enough for me.'

Archibald McGhee Foster was an advertising executive. One of his previous enterprises was a sponsorship deal with ABC's *Wednesday Night Fights* series. He was the link with Angelo Dundee. Foster said: 'Dundee is the best trainer and free-wheeling psychologist in boxing, and he's so clean he's practically antiseptic.'

And finally, J.D. Stetson Coleman chaired a drug company in Georgia, an oil business in Oklahoma, a bus firm in Florida. His wife owned a candy company in Illinois. 'We think we can keep him out of the financial trouble Joe Louis got into, which almost made me sick to see,' said Coleman.

> In Cassius we saw a good local boy with a clean background from start to finish. With the proper help and encouragement, he could bring credit to himself and his home town.
>
> There are plenty of wolves who would leap at the chance to get their paws on Cassius, to exploit him and then to drop him. We think we can bring him along slowly, get him good fights and make him the champion he wants to be.

For six weeks, Cassius was sent off to learn under Archie Moore, the world light-heavyweight champion, and Dick Sadler in San Diego. It didn't work out. Clay said he got homesick; Moore, who had wanted to manage as well as train him, said he was just a restless youngster who couldn't settle. Moore also wanted him to take a part in training-camp chores, as he believed it would make the boy understand the need for discipline. Cassius, who saw himself as a boxer first, last and always, felt he needed no lessons in dedication and did not want to scrub floors or wash dishes. He challenged Archie to a spar. Archie said he did not spar with amateurs. They were never going to get along.

After returning to Louisville, a deal was struck with Angelo Dundee for $125 a week, and Cassius was packed off to Miami, where Angelo ran the Fifth Street Gym, which was owned by his elder brother, Chris, who had been promoting fights for a quarter of a century.

Angelo took an initial dislike to Clay's boasting and tendency to compare himself favourably to boxing's all-time greats. After all, he had barely begun in the business Dundee knew so completely. Gradually, though, they became accustomed to each other. Cassius listened and learned. Dundee adapted his style from what was needed to be a successful amateur over the 'sprint' distance of three rounds to what he would require to box hardened professionals for fifteen. He increased his power, put more snap into his jab.

While Clay was confident in his boxing ability and his charismatic personality earned him acquaintances readily enough, he admitted he struggled to cope with the changes in his life. He was living in a tough part of town in an apartment the syndicate rented for him. Dundee asked if he was all right in that neighbourhood and Cassius said he was, but he might have not wanted to seem ungrateful. He told Huston Horn:

> The hardest part of the training is the loneliness. I just sit here like a little animal in a box at night. I can't go out in the street and mix with the folks out there because they wouldn't be out there if they was up to any good.

Nevertheless, as lonely as he was, he could see the wider picture and kept a grip on his ambition and vision:

> All this temptation and me trying to train to be a boxer . . . But it takes a mind to do right. It's like I told myself when I was little. I said: 'Cassius, you going to win the Olympics some day, and then you're going to buy yourself a Cadillac, and then you're going to be the world champ.'
>
> Now I got the gold medal, and I got the car. I'd be plain silly to give in to temptation now when I'm just about to reach out and get the world title.

5

I AM NOT A SOCIAL FRIEND OF MR CARBO'S, MR CHAIRMAN

The boxing world into which Sonny Liston was launched, with his small-time management team of Monroe Harrison and Frank Mitchell, was way beyond his comprehension. For Liston, fighting was a way to earn some honest money, and that was probably the sum of it when he stepped into the ring at St Louis Arena on 2 September 1953 for a 33-second win over a light-heavyweight named Don Smith. He had a two-year contract with Harrison and Mitchell, renewable for two years, and when he wasn't fighting or working, they agreed to pay him $35 a week. Good money. Honest money.

Liston wouldn't have recognised the corrupt influences that would, in the not-too-distant future, take over his career – and the likelihood is that, even had he known, he wouldn't have thought about it very much. Mitchell, who knew the dark side of life well enough, admitted they were out of their depth. 'We were babes in the woods,' he said.

Johnny Tocco, who ran the Ringside gym in Las Vegas after moving there from St Louis in the 1950s, felt it was just a matter of ordinary fact that Liston was 'moved' by the Mob from the very start. It was the world of *The Untouchables* come to life. One of Mitchell's associates, John Vitale, ran the St Louis Crime Family from 1935 until 1954. By 1961, his rap sheet totalled fifty-eight arrests – and just three convictions.

At the end of his year-long probe into the way boxing was run by the US senate sub-committee led by Estes Kefauver in 1961, Kefauver went on record as stating that Liston's career had, as of December 1960, been controlled undercover by Philadelphia hoodlum Frank 'Blinky' Palermo; the notorious, one-time Murder Inc. villain Frankie Carbo, otherwise known as Mr Gray; and John Vitale. Their frontman as official manager from 1958 was Joseph 'Pep' Barone. Carbo, stated Kefauver, had even received payments from Liston's fight purses while serving time in jail for illegal management of fighters and undercover matchmaking.

Back in the 1930s, it was widely accepted that figures like the giant Italian Primo Carnera were promoted, managed and regally ripped off by professional criminals. The middleweight champion Jake La Motta cynically summed up the 'connected' boxer's dependencies and allegiances as 'win one, throw one'. Carnera was metamorphosed from a glorified circus act into a contender courtesy of a string of bent fights. Some will always suspect that even Carnera's world heavyweight title win over defending champion Jack Sharkey in 1933 was Mob-influenced. Sharkey, as he would have done, denied it passionately, but his manager and even his wife had doubts.

Leon See, who managed the early part of Carnera's career, claimed in his book *Le Mystère Carnera*, that thirty of the Italian's fights between 1928 and 1931 were fixed, including two against the popular American contender Young Stribling. A syndicate which included the gangsters Owney 'the Killer' Madden – who also controlled Max Baer and was said to have a hand in the rise of heavyweight champion James J. Braddock – Frenchie DeMange and 'Broadway' Bill Duffy, bought See off. After a career that saw Carnera hold the world heavyweight title for two years and have more than a hundred professional fights in supposedly the most lucrative weight division of all, Primo, who was by no means extravagant, returned to Italy in 1939 with $7,000 to his name.

With the decline of Joe Louis's long-time promoter, one-time ticket scalper Mike Jacobs, the International Boxing Club (IBC) assumed control of boxing. Jacobs, who had taken over as the promotional power in New York after the death of Tex Rickard in 1929, suffered a stroke in 1946 and eventually sold his company, the 20th Century Sporting Club, to Madison Square Garden in 1949. The Garden was run by the IBC which, it eventually emerged, was heavily influenced by Frankie Carbo. The IBC purported to be a force for good in a notoriously disorganised sport. Those who cared about the subject at all wanted to believe it was for real. Its frontman was an apparently legitimate businessman, James Dougan Norris, who originally through his father, also called James, had part-ownership of major arenas in Chicago, Detroit, St Louis, Omaha and Indianapolis, and the stake in the Garden. His family owned a grain company, he was a director in a sugar company and of a furniture mart in Chicago, and owned a horse-breeding enterprise in Kentucky.

It has been the perception that the heavyweight championship fell prey to the IBC because of Jacobs' decline, but rumours persisted throughout his ten-year 'dictatorship' that he himself had too close a business relationship with Frankie Carbo. Joe Louis defended his title against opponents selected by Jacobs. How much say in that did Carbo have? We'll never know. The FBI were certainly interested in the relationship and in April 1947 Adolph Alexander, a Deputy

District Attorney in Los Angeles, told them Carbo's reputation was that of the 'king fight-fixer' in the country.

In his book *James Norris and the Decline of Boxing*, Barney Nagler wrote that while Jacobs supposedly ran boxing, Carbo held court in the dining room of the Forrest Hotel on 49th Street, just a short walk from the Garden. 'He was surrounded at all times by a circle of stooges who rendered unto him the things that were theirs,' wrote Nagler. 'While newspaper columnists and reporters made continual references to Carbo's role in boxing, state and city boxing commissions throughout the country reacted as if he were a folk myth, existing only in the addled brains of journalists.'

Nagler described Carbo as Norris's Rasputin:

> When the Empire tumbled he would be revealed in the naked light of truth as its arch manipulator. His influence ran deep from the very moment the IBC was organised, though it was hidden from view by the imposing figure of Norris.

An FBI report of June 1946 by agent August J. Micek read:

> About 15 years ago, he [Carbo] became connected with the boxing game, first backing Babe Risko through Vito Genovese . . . Has since controlled Sammy Angott, Johnny Greco, Chalky Wright and Marty Servo, and is also interested in Freddie Steele, Popeye Wood, Tony Janiro and Tami Mauriello. Carbo said to control entire boxing game in New York City, even controlling Mike Jacobs, the promoter. He cannot be a manager of record because of criminal background but uses front men as name managers. Said to manipulate odds by causing fixed results in fights and to cash in heavily on fixed fights.

Paolo Giovanni, translated to Paul John, Carbo was born to Sicilian immigrant parents in New York in 1904. He was sent to a New York reformatory for juvenile delinquents when only 11, and at 20 he killed a cab driver who had refused to be a part of a protection racket in the Bronx. After going on the run, Carbo was caught and sentenced, astonishingly on a plea bargain for manslaughter, to between two and four years in Sing-Sing State prison in Ossining, New York. He was behind bars for 20 months. He was there in 1930 at the time of the census, described as a 25-year-old married man who was being put to work labouring for a road company – hard labour in other words.

Upon his release, and after more 'service' as a hired gun, he was charged in 1931 with the murder of a mobster from Philadelphia, Mickey Duffy, in an

Atlantic City hotel room. The charges didn't stick. Working for Louis 'Lepke' Buchalter, Carbo was arrested in Madison Square Garden in 1936 for the murders of two hoods from a rival enterprise, Max Greenberg and Max Hassel, three years earlier at an Atlantic City hotel. He was released when witnesses refused to testify.

On Thanksgiving Day 1939, along with Lepke, Bugsy Siegel, Harry Segal and Emanuel Weiss, Carbo was indicted for the murder of underworld informer Harry Greenberg, also known as Harry Schachter, in his car when it was parked in a residential street in Los Angeles. Abe 'Kid Twist' Reles, another Mob murderer, was 'singing' to the police about a variety of underworld crimes to save his own skin and was supposedly prepared to give evidence against Carbo in court. He didn't get the chance. He fell to his death from a window at the Half Moon Hotel on Coney Island in 1941. His room had been under police guard. The official verdict was suicide. Allie 'Tick Tock' Tannenbaum did talk in court, saying Carbo fired five bullets into Schachter and that Siegel drove the getaway car. Even so, the jury could not decide on a verdict.

Carbo was then said to have organised the killing of Siegel in 1947. Siegel had overseen the building of the Flamingo Hotel in Las Vegas with an estimated $6 million of Mob money but had skimmed large sums off the top. He was given a deadline to repay what he owed, failed to meet it and was taken out and shot dead at the home of an actress and socialite.

Carbo was involved in boxing from around 1933 when he had a piece of the world middleweight champion Ed 'Babe' Risko, whose official manager was Gabe Genovese, a Syracuse barber and a cousin of crime boss Vito Genovese. Gabe Genovese bought himself a piece of welter and middleweight champion Carmen Basilio when Basilio's original managers, Johnny DeJohn and Joe Netro, were trying to get him a fight for the world welterweight title. Basilio had already been robbed of a decision against the Mob-controlled Kid Gavilan in 1953, and DeJohn and Netro knew the score. They contacted Genovese, who said he could help them in return for a cut of Basilio's purses. In 1961, it was revealed that Carbo, unknown to Basilio, and via Genovese, had taken up to $80,000 from him.

Carbo and his associate Blinky Palermo allegedly promised Bronx middleweight Jake La Motta a shot at the title on condition he threw a fight with 'Blackjack' Billy Fox at Madison Square Garden in November 1947. La Motta lost in the fourth round and admitted throwing the fight before the Kefauver Committee in June 1960. Two years later he said how difficult it had been because Fox couldn't punch hard enough to hurt him and could not take a shot himself. In round four, La Motta lay on the ropes and covered up until the referee stopped the fight, with the crowd booing him. Carbo allegedly made $35,000 betting on the outcome. Fox fought for the world light-heavyweight title in his next fight and went down in one against the champion, Gus Lesnevich.

Blinky Palermo was also well known to police. He was fined $500 in Philadelphia in 1928 for attacking a man using knuckle-dusters. In 1934, he was jailed for 60 days for running an illegal lottery. He was arrested for threatening to kill a man in 1933 and for a hit-and-run killing in 1935, but the charges had gone away.

In June 1949, La Motta won the world middleweight title when Marcel Cerdan, the popular Frenchman who was the lover of singer Edith Piaf, retired with a shoulder injury in a fight that launched the International Boxing Club and provided them with a profit. Plans for an equally lucrative return ended tragically when Cerdan's plane to the United States crashed in the Azores, killing everyone on board.

A week after the first La Motta–Cerdan fight, Ezzard Charles fought Jersey Joe Walcott for the heavyweight championship at Comiskey Park, Chicago, and the IBC made another bundle. James Norris was the front man, Truman Gibson, a graduate of the University of Chicago, its officially salaried lawyer. Carbo's shadowy presence was never far away. To keep him sweet, Norris also employed Carbo's wife, Viola Masters, on an inflated salary in one of his companies, the Neville Advertising Agency.

Another fight known to have been fixed was the world welterweight championship in August 1951 between Kid Gavilan and Billy Graham at Madison Square Garden. Graham had refused an offer from Carbo and so was not allowed to win. The referee and one judge scored level on points but cast a deciding vote for Gavilan, while the third, Artie Schwartz, voted for Gavilan anyway. The crowd stormed to ringside in angry, riotous scenes, but decisions were never altered. The late Jim Brady reported that Schwartz said on his deathbed to Graham's manager, Irving Cohen, that he had been ordered to vote for Gavilan. 'I had to do it,' he was quoted as saying. 'It's bothered me all these years. The boys ordered me.'

Al Weill, who managed the legendary heavyweight champion Rocky Marciano, was appointed matchmaker of Madison Square Garden, and was said to have given Carbo a piece of Rocky to ensure he was able to find the right matches for him. Weill, it was said, had become involved with Carbo as far back as 1934 when he had a featherweight champion, Joey Archibald. When Weill was sacked from the Garden job, Billy Brown, whose real name was Dominic Mordini, took over. It was said his first port of call was Frankie Carbo. When Carbo was referred to in conversations, it became the habit not to refer to him by name but by a series of pseudonyms, the most famous of which was 'Mr Gray'. This was because it had become known the FBI had a nasty habit of tapping phones at the Garden and even in stores and streets nearby. Barney Nagler wrote that Mordini, aka Brown, had a piece of Connecticut heavyweight Nathan Mann along with Marty Krompier, who was a member of the Dutch Schultz gang. Mann, whose real name was Natale Menchetti, challenged Joe Louis for the heavyweight title on a Mike Jacobs promotion at the Garden in 1938.

Teddy Brenner, who made the matches at the Garden after the IBC folded and new owners had moved in, insisted both Weill and Brown had to deal with Carbo because Norris walked and talked with the hoodlums:

> Carbo had his fingers on the throat of boxing and could squeeze the air out of it any time he wanted to make a move. When Weill was Marciano's manager, he was controlled by Carbo. So was Felix Bocchicchio, who managed Jersey Joe Walcott.

When a manager named Mike 'Bananas' Sokoloff refused to deal with Palermo or Carbo, his world-rated fighter Percy Bassett lost controversially on points to Teddy 'Red Top' Davis and was, it seemed legitimately, excluded from the championship picture.

There were no such problems for Jimmy Carter, for whom Carbo engineered a lightweight title shot against Ike Williams, who was managed by Palermo from 1946 until the end of his career in 1955. Carter had won and then lost against Bassett in his two fights before taking on Williams in May 1951.

Williams was an outspoken character. He had attempted to get a Fighters' Guild started and had once been fined $500 for supposedly casting doubt on the honesty of the officials of the Pennsylvania Boxing Commission. He said he was offered money several times by Palermo to throw fights. In an interview with boxing writer Peter Heller in 1971, Williams said he had signed for Palermo because, even though he was NBA lightweight champion, he was being frozen out. Once he signed for Palermo, he found all of a sudden he could get fights. In August 1947, he unified the lightweight title by knocking out Bob Montgomery in the sixth round in Philadelphia.

Williams was specific about how and when he was ripped off:

> Two fights I had. I received thirty-three thousand four hundred fighting Beau Jack in Philadelphia. I never saw a penny of that. And thirty-three thousand five hundred, Jesse Flores in New York. I never saw a penny of that . . . I fought those two fights for nothing, and paid taxes on them.

Williams said he wanted the purse monies left with the New York commission so that he could use them to pay taxes in 1949, but behind his back Palermo collected them. When he challenged Palermo, he got nowhere. 'He started crying about he's broke, and he's going to get his brains blown out if he didn't pay some people, he said he needed my purses to pay off some old debts.'

Jimmy Carter, who beat Williams in the fourteenth round to become champion of the world, was managed by Willie Friedland, another frontman for Carbo. Friedland was also called Willie Ketchum. Carter lost and regained the world lightweight title three times between 1951 and 1955. Friedland's role was exposed under oath by another fight manager, Hymie 'The Mink' Wallman, during the Kefauver hearings. Wallman also said that Carbo was paid $5,000 for approving a world lightweight championship bout between Joe Brown and Orlando Zulueta in Denver in July 1957, and he gave sworn testimony that he also provided Carbo with information about which referees and judges would be willing to favour his fighters.

As early as 1952, the US Department of Justice was showing serious interest in the IBC as a monopoly. One attempt by Ray Arcel, the great trainer who worked with fighters from Benny Leonard to Roberto Durán, to promote televised boxing on Saturday nights acts as an illustration of how things were.

The IBC already staged TV bouts on Monday, Wednesday and Friday, and Arcel and his partners found their main events for Saturdays repeatedly fell apart until, miraculously, following a ridiculously large over-payment for advertising in the Managers' Guild magazine, things suddenly ran smoothly. Carbo was by then heavily influencing the Managers' Guild to control their members' negotiations with the IBC. Arcel's Saturday-night fight enterprise was cut short in September 1953 when he was hit over the head with a piece of lead piping and put into hospital. No one was charged.

The IBC also promoted Rocky Marciano, the world heavyweight champion from 1952–6 – as it had promoted his predecessors, Ezzard Charles and Jersey Joe Walcott (whose manager, Felix Bocchicchio, had a criminal past and a supposed business affiliation with Carbo). It was said at one time that Marciano's final fight, against Archie Moore, was a fix – that Moore, far from being denied a knockout when he floored the champion heavily early in the fight, was in on the action. That he stood off when Marciano was hurt and eventually rolled over in round nine. Nothing can ever be proved and why would Moore wait to round nine to go into the tank? However, the quoted sources of the allegation were Truman Gibson and Doc Kearns, who had managed Jack Dempsey and after the war managed Joey Maxim, the light-heavyweight champion from 1949 to 1951.

If it were true, it backfired on Norris. Marciano retired and Moore lost again for the vacant title to 21-year-old Floyd Patterson, whose single-minded, eccentric Italian-American manager, Cus D'Amato, refused to have anything more to do with the IBC and James Norris.

In 1955, the New York State Athletic Commission called Norris before them on a hearing into the alleged freezing-out by the Managers' Guild of a welterweight named Vince Martinez. During the hearing, which led to the closing down of the guild, he was asked about his connection with Carbo. He admitted he had known him for 20 years but insisted he was not professionally associated with him. 'I am not a social friend of Mr Carbo's, Mr Chairman,' he said. 'I know Mr Carbo. I talk to him. I have a cup of coffee with him occasionally.' Norris made the improbable declaration that he did not discuss fights or fighters with Carbo. Later that year, Norris was appointed president of Madison Square Garden.

The New York hearing, which closed in December 1955 after sworn testimonies which transcribed to 1,000 pages, dealt closely with Carbo. It was wide ranging, calling itself an Inquiry into Alleged Irregularities in the Conduct of Boxing in New York. The commission found there had been a flagrant breach of the law in that licensed managers admitted they had associated and consorted with a known criminal. The official decision included the following sentence: 'It is significant and worthy of comment that these very managers who admitted intimate friendship with Carbo kept no records of their finances, no bank accounts and did business strictly on a cash basis.'

The heat increased.

In September 1957, Norris had a heart attack shortly before a middleweight title fight between Carmen Basilio and Ray Robinson. During his recovery, he received visits from Carbo and a floral bouquet from Albert Anastasia, a New York Cosa Nostra boss who ran Murder Inc. after making his name as a hit man for Lucky Luciano. Anastasia was murdered the following month, killed by two gunmen in a barber's shop at the Park Sheraton Hotel on Seventh Avenue and 57th Street. In April 1958, Norris resigned because of ill health and Truman Gibson took over.

In June 1958, Palermo was picked up by St Louis police while in town for a world welterweight title fight between Virgil Akins and the once-avoided Vince Martinez and interrogated about his involvement in gambling and drug rackets. He admitted nothing and was released. However, when the hoodlum squad, as *Sports Illustrated* called them, went through Blinky's briefcase they found evidence of his connection to Liston in the shape of a hotel bill for Sonny in Chicago and food totalling $300 at Palermo's restaurant in Philadelphia.

When questioned about that, Liston said: 'When I went to Philadelphia they just told me to eat anything I wanted and sign my name.' He was living in an apartment building next to the restaurant.

Years later, in the *New York Herald Tribune* (in May 1965 before Liston fought Muhammad Ali in Lewiston, Maine), Jimmy Breslin recalled a story in which Palermo didn't like the way Liston had spoken to him, ripped a fire axe from a wall case and went after him. Breslin did not substantiate his source – and didn't provide the result of the altercation either.

In the summer of 1958, a grand jury in New York indicted Carbo, in his absence while said to be holidaying in Mexico, for conspiracy, undercover management of boxers and matchmaking without a legal licence in contests arranged and promoted by the IBC. And the heat was on for just about everyone else. A doctor recommended that Norris should not be brought before a court because the stress on his heart might kill him. Gabe Genovese, however, was indicted, arrested, tried and described as 'an evil and degrading influence on professional boxing for over two decades'. Genovese, it was claimed in court, was Carbo's bagman. He was sentenced to two years in jail, was released after little more than a year in Rikers Island and died not too long after that.

In January 1959, the Supreme Court broke up the IBC, declaring that it had conspired to control world championship boxing in the whole of the United States and was in contravention of the Sherman Anti-Trust Act. Norris was also ordered to sell his interests in Madison Square Garden, which he did within a month. On 31 May 1959, Carbo was arrested at a house in western New Jersey, not far from Philadelphia. Police officers said he was relieved when he discovered it was lawmen who had come for him and not rival gangsters.

On 25 August 1959, the Governor of California, Edmund Brown, declared that boxing smelled to high heaven. A few weeks later, a federal jury in California indicted Carbo, Palermo, Gibson and two others, Joe Sica and Louis Dragna, on a variety of charges ranging from racketeering to extortion and conspiracy. Gibson, the lawyer and self-styled respectable face of boxing, was led from his home in handcuffs. The charges centred on the interference in the management of Californian welterweight Don Jordan by way of threats made to and pressure put on his legal representatives, Jack Leonard and Donald Nesseth.

Leonard and Nesseth had declined an invitation to allow Carbo and his people to help themselves to a piece of Jordan. According to the court, as reported by *Ring* magazine in 1959, Carbo warned them to remember what happened to Ray Arcel and said: 'Nobody ever has done this to us. Somebody is going to get hurt. You'll never know what hit you.' Carbo also faced the old charges brought in New York, and government investigators were also interested in a little matter of $750,000 in unpaid taxes.

Three days into his New York trial, which came first, Carbo changed his plea to guilty on three of the seven charges against him. When he appeared for sentencing on 30 November 1959, prosecuting attorney Alfred J. Scotti read out an 18-page condemnation of the defendant. 'I believe it is fair to say that the name of Frank Carbo today symbolises the degeneration of professional boxing into a racket. This man is beyond redemption. He is completely impervious to public opinion.'

Before passing sentence, Judge John Mullen told Carbo: 'You had terrific, improper and illegal influence in the fight game. You enriched yourself to a degree I can't contemplate.' Carbo probably took that as a compliment. He got two years on Rikers Island. 'Thank you, Judge,' he said, as he was taken down.

In Washington DC, the subcommittee led by Senator Estes Kefauver began its deliberations on the state of boxing. During the hearing, Norris agreed to testify, admitted he was embarrassed by the fact that he knew Carbo and agreed that he had also been friends with a gentleman named Sam 'Golfbag' Hunt from Chicago. Hunt, by then deceased, was called Golfbag because he was known to carry a machine gun in a golfbag. He also had a grim sense of humour: when he fired, he sometimes shouted: 'Fore!'

The beleaguered Norris said he felt Hunt was a man who wanted in his heart to be a decent citizen. 'If he would want fight tickets, I would leave him fight tickets,' he said. 'If he wanted hockey tickets, I would leave him hockey tickets . . . To me he was not the type of individual that he has been portrayed.' Then he also agreed he owned a racehorse named Mr Gray.

Gibson acknowledged that the IBC had indeed paid Viola Masters, who was Mrs Carbo, $45,000 over three years. He said they had decided it was better to live with Carbo to 'maintain a free flow of fighters without interference'. Jack Bonomi, special counsel for the sub-committee, pressed Gibson further and asked why it was decided to pay Mrs Carbo instead of being up front about it and paying Carbo himself. Gibson admitted it was because 'it looked . . . better on our record'.

Carbo was taken out of his jail cell in December 1960 to testify to the committee. He answered 25 questions by taking the Fifth Amendment, repeating each time: 'I respectfully decline to answer the question on the ground that I cannot be compelled to be a witness against myself.' Similarly, Blinky Palermo, Frank Mitchell and John Vitale also took the Fifth Amendment when questioned on all subjects, including their involvement in the management of Sonny Liston. Lieutenant Joseph Kuda of the St Louis Police Department testified that police investigations revealed Liston was owned by Carbo (52 per cent), Palermo and Vitale (12 per cent each) and two others whose identities were still unknown (12 per cent each). When this possibility was put to Liston himself, he said he didn't know. 'You know your boss but you don't know who he's with. You know he pays you, that's all. But you don't know who he gets his money from.'

When Carbo stood in the Californian court with his co-defendants Gibson, Palermo, Dragna and Sica on the charges of racketeering and extortion relating to interference in the managerial contract of world welterweight champion Don Jordan, he alone refused to testify. All five were found guilty on 30 May 1961. Eleven days later, the judge who had heard the case, Ernest Tolin, died. Requests for retrials were refused. On 2 December 1961, after all the evidence had been reviewed by a replacement judge, George Boldt, the sentences were handed down.

Truman Gibson, the lawyer who had been the only one allowed bail, was given a five-year suspended sentence and fined $10,000. The others were jailed, as follows: Carbo twenty-five years, Sica twenty years, Palermo fifteen years and Dragna five years. All but Dragna also received $10,000 fines. Pending appeal, Palermo, Sica and Dragna were bailed. Carbo was sent to Alcatraz.

The court of appeals in San Francisco took until 13 February 1963 to complete the case. Dragna was freed, his conviction overturned. Sica got off on one of the three charges against him, but his sentence remained. The convictions of Carbo, Palermo and Gibson stood. When Alcatraz closed, Carbo was moved to McNeil Island off the coast of Washington State. He was eventually released from jail on compassionate grounds when he was dying and passed away at St Francis Hospital, Miami, in 1976. Palermo, whose sentence began in June 1964, was incarcerated at Leavenworth, Kansas, and was paroled in 1971. Incredibly, he was allowed to operate on the fringes of the fight game. He lived until he was 91, passing away in 1996 in a Philadelphia hospital.

It was into this world that Charles 'Sonny' Liston, raised in the cotton fields of Arkansas and turned into the dumbest of thugs by the St Louis streets, then reborn as a prizefighter in a state penitentiary, was thrown when he decided boxing would be his living from September 1953.

He was out of his depth from beginning to end.

6

WHERE YOU GOING? I DON'T KNOW

Sonny Liston's first three professional fights in 1953 – a one-round stoppage of Don Smith and points defeats of Ponce DeLeon and Ben Thomas – merited little or no interest outside St Louis. The fourth, a sixth-round stoppage of New Orleans heavyweight Martin Lee, was a supporting bout on a small show by a new promoter, Sammy Crowe, at the Masonic Temple at 4500 Olive Street. It drew 645 paying customers. Liston knocked Lee down twice with right hands in the sixth round and the fight was stopped. It got a mention in *Ring* magazine thanks to the local correspondent, known as Bus Burke, who boldly gave his address as a barber's shop in De Soto, Missouri.

Liston won his first seven fights, in St Louis and Detroit, before he lost a split decision over eight rounds against a slippery light-heavyweight named Marty – real name Marion – Marshall. Marshall was a father of nine who had a full-time job in the Acme Quality Paint Company factory. Sonny finished the fight with his jaw broken. Afterwards, he visited Marshall in his dressing-room. Marshall remembered he was 'holding his jaw funny' but didn't talk about it.

'You fight good,' he told Marshall. 'I'd like to get you again.'

Marshall, who needed the paydays, said: 'Any time.'

The *Detroit Free Press* said Marshall's switch-hitting, jerky style and speed confused Liston:

> As the fight wore on, Liston became more and more disturbed by his inability to catch up with the ever-moving Marshall, and the Detroiter took the play from him through the final three rounds to clinch his triumph. Liston suffered a possible fractured jaw in the fourth round.

Marshall said Liston was very raw then, and he could anticipate what he was trying to do. His long jab was easy to slip, and Marshall won by 'faking and moving'. Marshall said he didn't know Liston's jaw was broken, simply because the big man's expression never altered. 'He don't grunt, groan, flinch or blink. He don't do nothing. He just keeps coming on. He's discouraging that way.'

Frank Mitchell had been too busy to travel from St Louis to Detroit, then Liston returned with his jaw wired. Sonny didn't like losing, didn't like getting hurt, and he was mightily unimpressed when Mitchell handed him a dentist's bill for $20. Unable to work, Liston became a financial burden to Mitchell and Harrison, who had agreed to pay him $35 a week under the terms of his two-year agreement. Harrison, with a large family to feed, could not pay his half of Liston's wages. Mitchell said he bought out Harrison's side of Liston's contract for $600 and sold it on to a drugstore owner from St Louis, Eddie Yawitz. Harrison said this was not the case – that he sold his piece of Liston to Yawitz, not to Mitchell. He said he did so because his wife was in hospital suffering from meningitis. 'What with the hospital bills and the loss of her income, I couldn't keep up my end,' he said, stating that she went into hospital on 13 January 1955, and he sold his half-share of Liston to Yawitz for $600 in Yawitz's drugstore. Harrison declared the same thing in an affidavit to the US Senate Anti-Trust committee led by Estes Kefauver on 26 October 1960.

It's certainly true that Harrison was never a wealthy man. In the early 1960s, he was still working as a caretaker in Carr Lane branch school in St Louis. When Harrison died, his old friend Robert Burnes related another story, that one of the Mob boys actually tapped Harrison on the shoulder as Liston was in the ring, looking good, and informed him he was no longer needed, that Sonny was their fighter now. Maybe it happened, maybe not.

Eddie Yawitz worked with Bernard Glickman in the management of the St Louis welterweight Virgil Akins, and it was widely understood then that they were at the very least associated with, and at worst operated on behalf of, Frankie Carbo and Blinky Palermo. In other words, even if the tap on the shoulder never happened, Harrison sold his piece of Liston to the Mob.

Liston won a rematch with Marshall in six rounds but was given a count in round four. Marshall, who had taken the fight at three days' notice, believed it was a genuine knockdown; the Liston camp said he got his feet in a tangle and fell over. Well, they would, wouldn't they.

Next Sonny stopped a Pennsylvanian coalminer, Emil Brtko, in five rounds in Pittsburgh and followed that with inside-the-distance wins over Calvin Butler, Johnny Gray and Larry Watson. Then in March 1956 he outpointed Marty Marshall over ten one-sided rounds in their third fight, when Marshall was again a late substitute. In the ring, things were going very well, but the St Louis Police Department were beginning to take a closer interest.

They had no problem with Harrison, but he had gone, and they considered Mitchell an unwholesome influence. Mitchell's mother, the newspaper owner Nannie Turner, was his great defender. 'Frank took this poor boy out of the pen and made something of him,' she said. Mitchell was, of course, offended that he was not trusted as an honest citizen by the police. 'They've raked me over the coals, sent me through the wringer, given me the devil,' he said. 'I'm supposed to be a front man with the hoodlums.' Mitchell also said he met John Vitale innocently on the golf course when a starting marshall paired his twosome with Vitale's to make a four.

Mitchell believed Liston was easy meat for the police. 'Sonny has the mind of a 12-year-old child. He has no finesse, tact, whatsoever. He doesn't realise that he has to keep his name out of the paper. He's kind of mean, too. He hates policemen, they hate him.' The only time Liston shook hands on the street with a police officer, it was to play a childlike practical joke. He had a buzzer in the palm of his fist.

At first, Vitale sorted out a gym for Liston and installed a stove to heat it. He would sometimes peel off a $20 and give it to his new fighter. Eventually, Vitale gave Sonny and another Mitchell prospect $65-a-week jobs in one of his factories which made that old 'Mob staple', concrete. Vitale also had a vending-machine franchise.

Liston said his job for Vitale was the best he ever had:

> We'd get there in the morning and work for about an hour or so, and then John would show up and tell us we oughta do some roadwork. So we'd run for a while, then we'd come back and John would drive us to the gymnasium.

Liston, according to some, also acted as a paid thug for Vitale. He was a strike-breaker, who, when ordered to do so, would 'dissuade' anyone who looked like making problems. He was picked up repeatedly by the St Louis police, held overnight and then released. He didn't appear to understand that to be an athlete meant living the life. He improved because he worked at it in the gym and enjoyed knocking people out. Once out of the gym, he had no consistent direction.

'We wanted to break up Liston's association with hoodlums,' said a police captain, John Doherty. 'Every time we could jump Liston up, we did. We wouldn't tolerate beating any citizens up, robbing them, which he was known for.' Doherty said he talked to Liston himself on the streets around 20 times. Always the conversation was roughly the same:

'Where you come from?'

'I don't know.'

'Where you going?'

'I don't know.'

Doherty's orders to his men were to arrest all known gangsters on sight. 'If they don't belong in St Louis and if you haven't got anything on them, run them out of town.'

One of his targets was a 'heavy' – literally as he weighed around 385 lb – from outside St Louis, Barney Baker. Twice, when police flagged down Baker in his car, Liston was with him. (Baker, incidentally, was later linked to Jack Ruby, who killed Lee Harvey Oswald, who killed President John F. Kennedy.)

Doherty said he tried to make Liston understand that he couldn't make an honest living by associating with hoodlums, but it was no use: 'He's dumb, he's got a vicious temper, he's ill-advised . . .'

Another St Louis cop, Frank Burns, said when he was arrested, there would always be a pause as Liston gauged whether or not it was wise to go quietly or fight it out. 'He doesn't react, just stands there.'

Once Liston thought about fighting, but a detective, Bob Green, pulled his gun on him. 'You better unroll those fists, my man.' Liston did. Green admitted he was just stopping Liston because he wanted to know where he was going. Liston said mostly he was held overnight, perhaps two. It was just the way it was.

Robert Burnes said he was told by the Missouri State Athletic Commissioner, Charley Pian, that Captain Doherty did not like the company Sonny was keeping. By this time, Liston had also been arrested for speeding, failing to answer a summons and twice on suspicion of theft. The last two charges were dropped.

During the Kefauver Committee hearings in 1961, St Louis police officer Joseph Moose said reports suggested Liston's main job with Vitale was to 'keep the Negro labourers in line'.

Liston also said he had spent time working for one of Vitale's business acquaintants, Raymond Sarkis. His job for Sarkis was driving the businessman's car, a white Cadillac, and helping in the house. 'All I tried to do is work and make an honest living,' he said.

Years later, though, the Las Vegas referee Davey Pearl, who ran a 24-hour bar and who knew Liston well, said in the late 1960s Sonny had admitted to him a part of his job was to keep the workers under control.

At one point, a police officer wanted to take Liston to an interview room and give him a hiding but was overruled by Doherty. The conjecture was that this was a tough detective sergeant named James Reddick, who had fought in the Golden Gloves. Reddick said in 1961 that Liston was a bad man, end of story. 'He hangs out with a bunch of dogs. I'd like to show him how bad he is. If he ever crossed me, I'd baptise his ass.'

On the positive side, Sonny also met, while they were working in one of the factories, the one woman who would provide what stability there ever was in his life, Geraldine Chambers. At the time she was around thirty years old, Sonny six or seven years younger. She had a daughter, Arletha, who was born in 1944, when Geraldine was nineteen. There was another daughter, Eleanor, born around 1951. Sonny and Geraldine lived together in a house in St Louis Avenue, backing on to North Taylor Avenue.

On the night of 5 May 1956, Liston was arrested after a violent altercation with a police officer, Patrolman Thomas Mellow. Liston and Geraldine were sitting at home with her sister, Ada, and a cab driver, Willie Patterson, who had left his cab running outside. Mellow says he called out to Patterson to move his vehicle or risk a parking ticket. Liston interfered, words were exchanged – Sonny claimed Mellow insulted Geraldine – and things over-heated. Officer Mellow ended with a broken knee and a gash over his left eye that needed seven stitches. Liston also confiscated his .38 police-issue handgun, put it in a bag and had Patterson drive him to his sister Alcora's house, where he left it in a drawer.

Mellow was found where he lay, at the back of 2818 North Taylor Avenue. He was treated in hospital, released and then re-admitted. Liston and Patterson were arrested separately later that evening and eventually, on 28 January 1957, Sonny pleaded guilty to assaulting Mellow. He was handed what seems on the face of it a lenient sentence by Judge David J. Murphy: nine months in the St Louis city workhouse. He served seven. Patterson got 30 days.

In between the assault on Mellow and his incarceration, Liston was arrested four times – twice for suspected theft, once each for speeding and failing to answer a summons. Frank Mitchell said the police told Liston they were looking for an excuse to blow his brains out, that one day his body would be in the river.

When he was released from jail, attempts were made to persuade the Missouri Athletic Commission to deny him his professional boxing licence. A police officer was quoted as saying: 'Every time he fights, half the hoodlums in the country turn up in St Louis.' However, the Commission felt Liston should be given a chance and did reinstate him following a meeting with police representatives and an attorney.

Charley Pian, for the Athletic Commission, said the police insisted on putting plain-clothes men in the audience if and when Liston fought, just to see who was taking an interest. It was hardly surprising, given the circumstances, that Sonny found it near-impossible to get fights in St Louis. Mitchell, therefore, signed a deal with Chicago promoter Irv Schoenwald, a three-year contract in which Liston would get 50 per cent, Mitchell and Schoenwald would get 50, out of which they would pay the expenses.

By then Sonny and Geraldine had married, on 3 September 1957, according to biographer Nick Tosches, and had moved to 4439 Farlin Avenue.

In January 1958, twenty-two months after his last bout against Marty Marshall, Liston stepped into a ring against Billy Hunter of Detroit down the bill at Chicago Stadium. Liston, who had a 17 lb weight advantage, won in two rounds. Six weeks later, also in Chicago, he knocked out Ben Wise from Oakland, California, in four, significantly on a show sponsored by the International Boxing Club, which was about to part company with James Norris. Interestingly, in the other eight-round joint main event on this show, future WBA heavyweight champion Ernie Terrell won in one round.

Also interesting was the fact that Schoenwald's interests ended after that fight, after one month of the three-year deal. Later, Robert Burnes reported a hearsay conversation between the promoter and the attorney who had drawn up the contract, on 5 February 1958. When the lawyer asked if he still had his piece of Liston, Schoenwald said: 'Some of the boys in the fight mob came up to me one night and said they were taking Sonny east.' The lawyer, knowing the contract was legally valid, said they could easily take the matter to court. 'I'd rather sleep nights,' was the reply. It was a similar story to the one Monroe Harrison had apparently told Burnes.

As usual, Mitchell saw it slightly differently, offering the implausible explanation that only five weeks into the new contract it was obvious that they weren't going to get anywhere in Chicago, and so they decided to change direction: 'At one of those Chicago fights, I saw Blinky Palermo. He asked me the same question I had been asking myself. Why waste Liston when he was ready for the big time?'

Liston moved to Philadelphia after another altercation with a police officer in St Louis. The story ran that the policeman whacked Liston over the head with his nightstick and in return, a while later, the cop found himself head-down in a trashcan. So perhaps the Mob wanted their increasingly valuable but notoriously erratic heavyweight hope where they could see him. According to Martin Kane in *Sports Illustrated*, John Vitale lent him $200 to finance the move.

Sonny and Geraldine moved into a red-brick building, Hamilton Court Apartments at 101 South 39th Street. In Philadelphia, Sonny was officially guided by Joseph 'Pep' Barone, who had worked for Blinky Palermo in the gloriously euphemistic role of 'detail supervisor'. Barone denied Palermo was involved, said his only agreement was that if Liston reached the top then Frank Mitchell would be looked after. He agreed that in the past he and Palermo had done each other favours. 'I've known Blinky for a good many years,' he said. Barone had been involved with the fight game before but had never officially managed a fighter. There is no evidence that Sonny signed anything, but nobody was going to argue.

Back in St Louis to box in April 1958, with 46-year-old former heavyweight Willie Reddish replacing Jimmy Wilson as trainer, Liston beat Bert Whitehurst on points over ten rounds and then won his first televised bout, a third-round stoppage of Julio Mederos in Chicago. Mederos, a Cuban who had once beaten contender Roland La Starza, retired after losing to Liston, even though he was only 25 years old.

The hiring of Reddish was a good professional move. Reddish had boxed out of north Philadelphia. He lost decisions to Jersey Joe Walcott in 1936 and John Henry Lewis in 1937. Walcott would go on to become heavyweight champion while Lewis, when Reddish fought him, was the reigning light-heavyweight champion. Willie also beat two men who fought Joe Louis for the championship, Gus Dorazio and Abe Simon. He knew how to fight.

Liston's victory over Mederos prompted a gloriously inept piece entitled 'Heavyweight Hopefuls' by Lew Eskin in *Ring* magazine in August 1958. Sonny's lone trek in pursuit of his mother to St Louis, and his subsequent street-life and jail sentence, were sanitised into: 'Sonny moved with his family to St Louis while a teenager and soon got his start in amateur boxing.' The next jail term he served for assaulting a police officer was negotiated with equal expertise. 'Sonny saw no action in 1957 but he was not discouraged. He stayed in the gym and kept in top condition.'

In its October 1958 edition, *Ring* included a photo of Liston's 56-second demolition of Wayne Bethea and included him at number 9 in their heavyweight rankings. *Boxing Illustrated* wrote that Liston might well be the shot-in-the-arm that the division needed. Truman Gibson, for the IBC, offered Floyd Patterson $250,000 to defend against Liston, who had won 19 of his 20 professional fights. Patterson's manager, Cus D'Amato, who didn't deal with the IBC and knew very well what might happen if Liston were let anywhere near his man, knocked it back.

Next Liston fought Frankie Daniels, a 185 lb Californian who had just lost a ten-round decision to another heavyweight dangerman, Cleveland 'Big Cat' Williams. Liston demolished Daniels in one round. Then he had to go ten rounds for the second time with Bert Whitehurst in St Louis. He finished the year by stopping Ernie Cab in eight rounds in Miami.

Years later, Whitehurst, by then a science teacher who was planning a Master's degree in biology at the City College of New York, recalled the first time they fought. Initially, he was unable to get past Sonny's long jab. 'Every time Liston stuck out his left in the first round, it was as if he held a stick in his hand and the stick was telling me to stand back.' Whitehurst said his trainer, Charlie Brown, told him to slip the jab, step inside and work his own left. By doing that, he not only found a way to survive, he was able to work the body and tie Liston up. Over the second half, Liston re-established himself on the outside, but the body punching from Whitehurst had taken something out of him.

Tom Phillips, of the *Daily Herald*, quoted Whitehurst some time later, as saying: 'When he hits you with the left, it stuns you and knocks you across the ring, but he comes after you with the right so slowly that your head has had time to clear and you snarl him up.'

In their second fight, Whitehurst said his manager, George Gainford, who had guided Sugar Ray Robinson's career, told him to box on the outside. Crazy tactics, but he ran for six rounds. 'I took a good beating,' said Whitehurst:

> By then he was too tired to run, so I moved inside and again survived the ten. It was like being in the eye of a hurricane. On the outside it was hell, but in close it was calm and I was safe. If I had listened to Charlie Brown, I might have beaten Liston . . . but that's an old story. Liston's an excellent fighter, a mean fighter. But if I could get another shot at him, I'd quit teaching, give up studying, go into training and fight him, winner take all. And believe me I wouldn't do that unless I was convinced I could beat him.

Old fighters always talk a good fight.

It was in 1959 that Liston became a live contender. In February, he overpowered Mike DeJohn at Miami Beach. Rocky Marciano, at ringside, was impressed. Liston was shaken a couple of times in round three but kept punching and won in the sixth. 'Liston is not too far away,' said Marciano, whose endorsement was obviously something to be valued. 'His jab is the best I've seen since Joe Louis. He gets real force into his jabs, like Joe used to do.'

The beaten Mike DeJohn didn't join the fan club. 'He can't fight,' he said. The logic, therefore, was that DeJohn couldn't fight even more than Sonny couldn't fight. No one put that to him.

Liston talked to *Ring* magazine, told them he was born in Pine Bluff, Arkansas, and claimed to be 25 years old, which would have made 1933 his birth year. 'The *Ring* Record Book makes me 27 next May. I don't know where they got that.'

As approximate as he was about his childhood, he was candid about his misspent youth and first spell in jail – had no complaints: 'It was a stupid, crazy thing, a bad thing we did. We got what was coming to us.' He didn't own up to the assault on police officer Mellow. *Ring* again referred to a 'long lay-off'.

Interestingly, he said he had little or no money, and the deal for the DeJohn fight earned him next to nothing. Liston was apparently paid the TV money plus 50 per cent of the gate but also had to guarantee DeJohn $20,000. As Chris Dundee's promotion was a flop, after DeJohn had been paid Liston was led to believe there was nothing left.

Dundee, elder brother of Angelo, who would eventually train Muhammad Ali, began the job of turning Sonny into an ogre, citing his unusually large fists as evidence. 'Take a look at those hands,' said Dundee. 'I have the gloves made extra large for Liston.'

On another Dundee promotion at Miami Beach in April 1959, Liston stopped Cleveland Williams in three rounds. He admitted he took it too casually in the first round, was caught and shaken up. Williams couldn't seem to miss him with jabs and rattled him with right hands. Liston saw the crisis through, then overpowered Williams, knocking him down twice in round three. It was one of the 'big performances' of his career.

> I really found out about myself. If I had one weak spot anywhere, my chin, my heart, my body, I would have found it out with the whuppin' he put on me in that first round.
>
> I was never hurt real bad, no matter how it looked. I knew what was going on. Even when I sat down at the end of the round, I thought to myself, 'This cat's got to put it on me like that for nine more rounds to beat me, and I don't think he can do it.'

Willie Reddish told him to close the range, deny Williams room. He did that, outfought him on the inside and turned it all around.

Two months later, Floyd Patterson was knocked down seven times in three rounds and relieved of the heavyweight crown by the slow but heavy-handed Swede Ingemar Johansson. Of course, there was a rematch clause, which effectively froze out every other heavyweight in the top ten.

In August 1959, Liston offered more proof that he was ready for a title shot when he knocked out the veteran Cuban Nino Valdes in the third round in Chicago. He enjoyed that because when he was an amateur back in 1953, Valdes, who was then a seasoned professional, had embarrassed him in a sparring session.

'I got a contender and can't get nowhere with him,' said Pep Barone, as the Patterson–Johansson rematch was delayed by legal problems. Liston completed the year by stopping Willi Besmanoff in seven in Cleveland.

Interestingly, Frank Mitchell, who continued to hover around the scene, said Liston was very nervous before two fights on the way up – against Johnny Summerlin in 1954 and Valdes in 1959. 'Because he's big and strong, you don't realise unless you talk to him that he can be scared like anybody else.'

Across in Britain, where Henry Cooper was hoping for a world title shot, George Whiting of the *London Evening Standard* wrote in the February 1960 edition of *World Sports* magazine that Liston was too good for his own good. Angelo Dundee, who trained contender Willie Pastrano, and who would take up with the young Cassius Clay shortly, felt the same way. He said: 'Liston is the president of the Don't Wanna Know club. Nobody wants any part of that guy. He could kill you.' For his part, Pastrano said: 'I wouldn't walk into the same town, let alone the same ring, as that guy.' Trainer Teddy Bentham said: 'I wouldn't bet on a grizzly bear against Liston.'

In February 1960, Liston wore down Howard King for an eighth-round stoppage and the following month trounced Cleveland Williams again, this time inside two rounds. 'I had his ticket number goin' in,' said Liston.

Roy Harris, from the small Texan town of Cut 'N Shoot, had hung around for twelve rounds in a world title bid against Patterson, but Liston wrecked him inside one. Harris told me when he was a guest at the Lennox Lewis–Vitali Klitschko championship fight in Los Angeles in the summer of 2003 that his problem was that Liston was in range when you didn't expect him to be. Liston knocked him down three times. Of course, ever the proud old pro, Harris told me he could have gone on.

Twelve months after Johansson defeated Patterson, they fought again at the Polo Grounds. This time an undertrained Johansson was knocked out in the fifth round. Patterson had become the first man in history to regain the world heavyweight championship. A third match between them was inevitable. It was unfair, but everybody else would have to wait.

In July 1960, Liston blasted out the talented but erratic Zora Folley in three rounds. Folley counter-punched him successfully for the first round, then was knocked down on his face by a right hand in the second. Usually, when a fighter goes down like that, he doesn't get up, or at least not with any sense of what is going on. Folley not only got up, he fought back until he was floored again by a right hand almost on the bell. It took less than half a minute of round three, including the count, for Liston to finish it off.

'What happened?' said a confused Folley.

'I knocked you out,' said Liston.

They embraced.

'Oh, now I remember,' said Folley. 'And they told me not to worry about your right hand.'

Folley said later: 'My plan was to box him. I didn't. I thought I could knock him out.'

Folley still believed he should have won, that he threw it away by his own stupidity. He said he thought Patterson would be too quick for Liston but later changed his mind. 'It'll do me no favours saying it, but Liston would knock Patterson over with the first punch he landed.'

Liston liked Folley, thought him a man for taking him on head to head, toe to toe. 'He's honest and smart,' he said, 'and a gentleman besides being a darned good fighter. He's the kind of guy I'd be pleased to call a friend.'

Years on, when he got his long-overdue shot at the title against a peak Muhammad Ali, Folley was also treated with immense respect by the young champion. Folley, who had a wife and nine children, died of head injuries in a motel swimming pool in Tucson, Arizona, in 1972 at the age of 40. It was ruled an accidental death. He has a park in his home town of Chandler, Arizona, named in his honour.

Even with the Patterson–Johansson saga incomplete, Cus D'Amato was thinking beyond it. He wanted to avoid Liston and instead have Patterson take on Henry Cooper, perhaps in London. He travelled over to discuss the possibility with the British promoter, Harry Levene.

Liston got on with his job. In Seattle in September 1960, he took on Eddie Machen, who like Folley had been avoided by Patterson, or rather D'Amato. Machen, a cunning defensive boxer, gave Liston a frustrating night, backing off and going the full 12 rounds to lose on points. As he retreated, he would taunt Liston from time to time. 'Come on, Big Punch . . . Come on, show me that big, terrible punch.'

Liston swung away crudely, increasingly cross, increasingly frustrated. He couldn't set himself, because Machen kept moving, side to side, in and out, as well as away.

Machen acknowledged the power in Liston's left hand, said: 'The guy is all animal. Yes, he can fight.'

Liston thought Machen could fight, too, but said he had no interest in winning, just in lasting the distance. Machen, he said, was cute, knew his job, had clever moves and strong legs. Liston was annoyed at the criticism he got. 'All I tried to do was make the fight, and all he tried to do was live. They said I looked like a bum . . . I never heard nobody say Machen looked like a bum. Only me.'

Machen said he fought so defensively because he had damaged his right shoulder sparring with Willi Besmanoff. 'I needed the money,' he said.

'I was embarrassed to get into the ring with this unrated duck,' complained Clay. 'Truly, it embarrasses me to keep fighting these bums. I am ready for Eddie Machen and Ingemar Johansson and Sonny Liston and Floyd Patterson.'

Besmanoff was one of the few to pull the rug out from under him. 'Nobody,' said the beaten man softly and seriously, 'has a right to call another fighter a bum.'

Whatever Cassius said to attract publicity and attention, the confidence behind him was high. There was no need for 'tomato can' victims, never-could-have-beens woefully short on ability and ambition. Clay's opponents were good enough to give his career perspective.

Cassius had just turned 20 when he made his New York debut against Lucien 'Sonny' Banks from Detroit on a small show at Madison Square Garden in February 1962. The young man was still exuberant, not afraid to take a risk or two in order to land his long raking punches. In the first round, too soon, he went after Banks, left himself wide open and was nailed flush by a perfect left hook. He crashed backwards for the first knockdown of his career but got up, took the fight to Banks, floored him in the second and stopped him early in round four.

Going into that fight, Banks had won ten of twelve, nine of them by knockout or stoppage. He could punch. Crucially, however, he was inexperienced: he had not had even a single amateur contest. Clay got away with it. (Banks' story ended tragically. Three days after losing on a ninth-round knockout to Leotis Martin in Philadelphia in May 1965, he died of brain injuries. He was only 24.)

Understandably, Clay's team dropped him back a level after the surprise knockdown against Banks, but they brought him back only eighteen days later for a routine fourth-round stoppage of Don Warner in Miami Beach. Warner, from Philadelphia, was a fair puncher at his level but couldn't hold one. He had won only two of his previous eight fights.

In April 1962, Clay took four rounds again to beat the erratic George Logan from Boise, Idaho, in his first bout in Los Angeles. Back in New York, Billy Daniels lasted into the seventh, and in Los Angeles the ill-fated Alejandro Lavorante who, like Sonny Banks, was to die after a fight, was knocked out in five. That fight drew 12,000 fans.

Jack Dempsey saw how good Cassius was for a business that had been shaken by years of Mob involvement, by scandal and tragedy. 'I don't care if this kid can't fight a lick,' said the old champion. 'I'm for him. Things are live again.'

The Lavorante win took the 20-year-old Clay to his biggest engagement so far, against the man who had been briefly employed as his trainer, the former world light-heavyweight champion, 'The Old Mongoose' Archie Moore, in Los

Angeles, in November 1962. Cassius treated the public to one of his more excruciating rhymes, as he told the world that Ancient Archie would fall in four:

> Archie's been living off the fat of the land.
>   I'm here to give him his pension plan.
>   When you come to the fight, don't block the aisle and don't block the door
>   You will all go home after round four.

The Cuban fighters in the Fifth Street Gym had a name for the noisy young man who at least must have livened up the daily drudge of training. They called him 'Nino con boca grande' – or 'the boy with the big mouth'. Luis Sarria, who was to become his conditioner, had operated alongside Dundee as a trainer there since leaving Cuba when Fidel Castro took over. Sarria, who spoke little English, is an often unnoticed piece of the Clay jigsaw. He worked away quietly on his physical condition while others were making more noise. Sarria, in his early 50s when Cassius came along, brought welterweight champion Luis Rodriguez to Dundee after they decided together not to return to their home country. Sarria had been a pro fighter himself in the 1930s and around 1948 trained the Cuban amateur team.

Clay demolished Archie Moore, as he said he would, in round four. The image of him standing, long arms raised, as Moore lay on the canvas, was carried across the world.

The new year, 1963, began with Clay taking on former footballer Charley Powell in Pittsburgh. Powell had made his name by effectively ending the world-title aspirations of the Cuban Nino Valdes. Powell was big and strong but not overly talented. Clay taunted him at the weigh-in: 'You wait and see, you'll go in three,' he yelled and held up three fingers.

Powell didn't move, just said: 'Get your hand out of my face.'

Clay ranted on about how, if he lost, he would leave the country and eventually attempted to get right under Powell's skin with a cutting insult: 'B-I-G don't spell man.'

Powell laughed at him. 'I can't take no more,' he said. 'I'm getting out of here. He's too cocky. I didn't know he was that cocky . . .'

Powell's refusal to be fazed apparently bothered Clay, but whatever the outcome of the weigh-in banter, the result of the fight was what mattered. Powell, as Clay had said he would be, was knocked out in round three.

A year or so on, Powell said:

When he first hit me, I thought to myself, 'I can take two of those to get in one of my own.' But in a little while I found out I was getting dizzier and dizzier every time he hit me, and he hurt. Clay throws punches so easily you don't realise how much they shook you until it's too late.

Another former heavyweight champ, Jack Sharkey, was impressed. 'Clay has such good movement,' he said, 'that he can make you do exactly what he wants.' Former middleweight champion Paul Pender said Cassius was the first heavyweight he had seen who could take one punch but would be gone before the second one came.

For an interview in Louisville with Alan Hoby for the *Sunday Express*, Clay sat in a 'coloured café' on 12th and Chester Street he had frequented since he was a schoolboy. The young heavyweight ate two bowls of hot Mexican chilli and told the British writer: 'Eating, that's my only weakness. I'm always hungry.'

He told Hoby one day he would have an entourage of 20 or so people around him, with chefs, valets, secretaries and a manicurist as well as his sparring partners, parents and brother. They would travel everywhere in a double-decker bus. 'Yes, sir, I'll always be surrounded by people when I'm the champ.'

On the way out to his home at 7307 Verona Way, Louisville, he said to Hoby:

You think I'm romancing, don't you? Well, I'm not. I don't just talk, you know. I can box, too. I'm ambitious. I train as hard as I talk.

I want luxury. I want to be world famous. Most of all I want that heavyweight title.

The way I see it, I don't make money unless I draw people. And the only way I can draw people in this game is if I talk loud and long.

Hoby also saw Bill Faversham, then returned to say goodbye to Clay, who was doing more publicity work at Churchill Downs, home of the Kentucky Derby. 'Goodbye, goodbye,' he cried out from a distance and asked Hoby to send the articles he would write to him in the post: 'Just address the envelope Cassius Clay, USA . . .'

Around the same time he told *Time* magazine:

I'm gonna drive down Walnut Street in a 'Caddy' on Derby Day and all the people will point and say, 'There goes Cassius Clay.' Pretty girls will be there, and I'll smell the flowers and feel the nice warm night air. Oh, I'm cool then, man. I'm cool. The girls are looking at me, and I'm looking away. I'm wanting to know them worse than they want to know me – only they don't know it.

And, of course, the doggerel kept on flowing.

> This is the story about a man
> > With iron fists and a beautiful tan.
> > He talks a lot and boasts indeed
> > Of a powerful punch and blinding speed . . .

Angelo Dundee and the syndicate that bankrolled Cassius knew it was almost time. Just a couple of fights more and they would know he was ready for the big one: the heavyweight championship of the world.

8

IT'S NICE TO BE NICE

Sonny Liston was called before the Kefauver hearing – officially the subcommittee for Antitrust and Monopoly of the US Senate Judicial Committee in Washington DC – on 13 December 1960.

This was six weeks after Cassius Clay had made his professional debut. Liston was ranked number 1 challenger to Floyd Patterson and acknowledged as the most dangerous heavyweight in the world. In his last two fights, Sonny had beaten Zora Folley and Eddie Machen. He was living with Geraldine in Philadelphia.

The record of the conversation he had with Senator Estes Kefauver suggests he was doing, respectfully, what he always did with figures of authority who were friendly and polite in their manner towards him. He said what he thought they wanted to hear and revealed as little of himself as he could.

Kefauver: How much education did you get?

Liston: I didn't get any.

Kefauver: You didn't get any?

Liston: No, sir.

Kefauver: You didn't go to school at all?

Liston: No, sir.

Kefauver: You didn't have much opportunity, I guess.

Liston: Too many kids.

Kefauver: How many kids were there?

Liston: Well, my father had 25.

Kefauver: Twenty-five children?

Liston: Altogether.

Kefauver: Twenty-five children altogether.

At this point, Senator Everett Dirksen interrupted: 'I was going to say your father is a champion in his own right!'

Kefauver: Did you have to work to help support the other 24 children?

Liston: That's right.

Kefauver: What did you do?

Liston: Pick cotton.

Kefauver: You had a pretty tough time.

Liston: Yes, sir, I did.

Kefauver: You are 27 now. When did you leave Little Rock?

Liston: I left Little Rock when I was 13.

Kefauver: Where did you go?

Liston: St Louis.

Kefauver: Did your father move up there?

Liston: No, sir.

Kefauver: You did what?

Liston: I went back to the same thing.

Kefauver: Do you want to tell us about that? You are being very forthright. I say you are being very frank.

Liston: Then, after I got there, then I started to go to church. Father Stevenson, he started helping me, and then I got into a couple of fights up there.

Kefauver: Who did you say?

Liston: Father Stevenson.

Kefauver: When you were incarcerated over there?

Liston: Right.

Kefauver: He was a great help to you, Father Stevenson?

Liston: He was the one who got me started.

Kefauver: Got you what?

Liston: He was the one who started me in fighting. There was a boxing team in there. He said, 'You like fighting, so why don't you get into the boxing team?' I told him all right. And I started in fighting, and then I beat all the guys there, and he said, 'I'll see what I can do.'

Liston, of course, had not been born in Little Rock – his mother said as far as she knew he had never been there – and for some reason he always called Father Stevens by the name Stevenson.

John Bonomi, the senate committee attorney, interrupted the conversation to ask: 'Do you recall that you were arrested in St Louis, Missouri, August 12 of 1959, and questioned by some police officers concerning your relations with Mr Sarkis?'

Liston: I couldn't recall the date. I was arrested sometimes there. I don't carry a pencil around to see how many times I was picked up.

Bonomi: Do you recall on that date, August 12 of 1959, that . . .

Kefauver: On or about that date . . .

Bonomi: On or about that date, you stated to the St Louis police officers that John Vitale was the person who introduced you to Raymond Sarkis?

Liston: No, I don't. The way it was there – I mean I may have said anything because they just kept grabbing me, picking me up.

Kefauver: Is that your wife's handwriting?

Liston: I couldn't say.

Dirksen: Do you read at all?

Liston: No, sir, I don't.

Dirksen: Nothing whatsoever? Well, you can make out figures. I thought I saw your name signed here allegedly by you. Do you sign your name?

Liston: Yes, sir.

Dirksen: Do you sign your address? Can you sign your address?

Liston: No, sir.

Dirksen: Your house number? Who does that for you?

Liston: Well, I can write 5785.

Dirksen: Can you write the name of the street that you live on?

Liston: No, sir.

Dirksen: For instance here is a signature that says 'Charles Liston, 39 Chestnut'. Would you be able to write 'Chestnut'?

Liston: No, sir.

Dirksen: You wouldn't. But you can write your name?

Liston: Yes, sir.

Dirksen: And the number. Suppose your share of a purse, of a fight purse, was $25,000, and they handed you a cheque for it. Could you tell whether they were giving you a cheque for $25,000?

Liston: Well, not exactly.

Dirksen: You would have to depend on somebody else?

Liston: Yes, sir.

Dirksen: If there was a cheque for $25,000.

Liston: Right.

After being informed that the evidence suggested Frank Carbo and Blinky Palermo owned him, Liston said he didn't know about that: 'Pep Barone handles me.'

'Do you think that people like that [Carbo and Palermo] ought to remain in the sport of boxing?' asked Kefauver.

'I wouldn't pass judgement on no one. I haven't been perfect myself.'

When Joseph 'Pep' Barone had the opportunity to speak before the Kefauver Commission, he could not appear. He was in hospital, said to be suffering from deep depression and anxiety.

Liston knew what was happening. 'I got to get me a manager that's not hot . . .' he said, drily. 'Like Estes Kefauver . . .'

Kefauver made it plain that if Liston were to be allowed to box for the title, the sport ran the risk of Carbo and Palermo controlling the heavyweight championship of the world. Barone was expendable.

Rocky Marciano wanted to buy in, so did Joe Louis, even the Olympian Pete Rademacher, who had lost to Floyd Patterson in his pro debut, expressed his interest. None of them succeeded.

On 10 May 1961, Liston's interests went to George Katz, another Philadelphia businessman, who ran a picture-framing company and had previously managed a world-class welterweight named Gil Turner and several others, including Frank Cappuccino, who would go on to become a world-class referee. Katz was full of self-confidence and tended to waver between outlandish exaggeration and bland generalisation. Perhaps his finest line was: 'In all my years in boxing, I have never heard Frankie Carbo's name mentioned.' He claimed not to need any boxing income. 'I could retire tomorrow and just tour the world, only I don't fly, get seasick and can't swim . . . the first time Liston came to me, I turned him down. This is a headache, I said to myself. I don't know why I came back to managing fighters.'

Katz was proud of his defiant stance against officialdom – he admitted to having been fined by the state commissions of New York and Pennsylvania because he had stood up against them in the name of fair play. 'I called some of their officials bums,' he explained.

Katz said he turned Liston down initially because he was offered only 10 per cent, then changed his mind because he realised he would be inheriting a fighter whose career he did not have to spend money building up. Liston was already at the top, just waiting for a shot at the big one. 'Ten per cent of Liston could be $200,000 in two years,' he said, declaring himself honest and free of background obligations. 'No ifs, no buts, no nothings,' he said, adding, 'My only vice is smoking.' He also liked to say: 'It's nice to be nice.'

Senator Kefauver was expected to endorse Liston's career once Katz was appointed, but he hesitated. Washington sources told Lester Bromberg of the *New York World Telegram* that Kefauver was 'resisting pressure to sit in judgement on Liston's management'.

Bromberg quoted his source as saying:

> As matters stand, there are two courses which he could pursue – to extend the investigative stage of the boxing hearings to look into the Barone deal and the Katz contract, or to discourage Patterson or anybody else from counting on him to certify Liston.

The second option was quicker and less trouble but of course less 'official'.

A further complication for Kefauver was that the Pennsylvania Boxing Commission had no problems with Katz and no apparent record of any incidents of his claimed defiance. Alfred M. Klein, the Pennsylvania commissioner once said to have been a close ally of Kefauver, said investigations into Katz revealed he was clean, and therefore they decided to approve the business relationship and give Liston his licence to box. Klein said: 'They have testified under oath they alone are parties to the contract and there are no contrary contentions other than that of a conjectural nature.'

In spite of the assertion of his new manager that Sonny had lived a clean and beautiful life since moving from St Louis to Philadelphia, he couldn't keep away from trouble. He wasn't training. Lester Bromberg suggested he did go to Champs Gym once but stayed only a short time and then walked out.

John Gold went to visit Liston at his home in Philadelphia for a feature published in the *London Evening News and Star*. Sonny was late, Geraldine served him tea and showed him around the house, which was the first they had bought

– 5785 Dunlap Street in the Overbrook district, the west side of the city. Gold described it as being furnished in the 'French provincial' style, whatever that meant, and said it had green and gold furniture, pink walls, royal blue carpets, pink, yellow and purple cushions, and 'a great many china and plaster figurines, including a bust of Aphrodite, and five TV sets'.

'I furnished the house,' said Geraldine. 'But Charles is easy to please. He has very good taste. He buys all my clothes. He also bought the Aphrodite – and that thing over there.' 'That thing' was a large Buddha.

Liston arrived with a man who explained he was a bodyguard. As Gold asked his questions, Liston watched television. The only subject that seemed to rouse him was that of Cus D'Amato, Patterson's manager. Liston became animated, said he had visited D'Amato at his house and asked him personally if he would get his title shot, and said D'Amato had put a hand to his chest as if he were about to have a heart attack. 'I haven't been able to find him since,' said Liston. 'He's always on the move. He better be.'

Gold didn't get very far at all. Mostly Liston just grunted and went on watching television.

In a photo in a *Sports Illustrated* spread on 17 July 1961, Liston lay sprawled across Geraldine's lap, looking sad, a little haunted. She is looking down at him, as if worrying about an unknown future. By allowing such an intimate photo to be taken, Liston was making it plain that he wanted to be included in the human party, not excluded from it. It might also have been a move by Katz to smooth over some unwelcome publicity from more brushes with the law.

According to the fine article by Gilbert Rogin and Morton Sharnik which accompanied it, the photo was taken shortly after the newly licensed Liston's arrest for the alleged harassment of a 29-year-old woman, Mrs Delores Ellis, in Philadelphia's Fairmount Park in June 1961. Only a month or so earlier than that, he had been picked up by the police for loitering on a street corner.

Liston had plainly frightened Mrs Ellis when she was driving her car through the park. He had drawn alongside her in his Ford, flashed a spotlight at her and ordered her to pull over. The incident was interrupted by an armed park guard, John Warburton, who gave chase when Liston drove away at speeds of up to 80 miles per hour. When he was eventually pulled over, Liston was wearing boxing trunks. It was 3 a.m.

George Katz explained patiently that his fighter was going out to do his roadwork. Liston and another man who was with him in the car faced charges of impersonating an officer of the law, disorderly conduct and conspiracy, extinguishing the car lights to avoid identification and resisting arrest. They were allowed bail of $300. During the court hearing, Katz sat in the row behind Sonny. At one point, Liston leaned over and said to him: 'If I get time, you're entitled to 10 per cent of it!'

On 1 July 1961, the charges were dismissed by magistrate E. David Keiser, but it was suggested Liston and his friend apologise to Mrs Ellis. We assume they did. Katz tried to explain: 'Liston has a lot of good qualities. It's his bad qualities that are not so good . . .'

The Pennsylvania Commission, feeling let down after approving Liston's contract with George Katz and in their eyes in doing so giving him a break, suspended his licence on 14 July 1961 for that old chestnut 'conduct detrimental to boxing'.

His original co-manager, Monroe Harrison, was interviewed for the *Sports Illustrated* piece. He was working as a caretaker at Carr Lane branch school in St Louis and was photographed with his brush and pan, with smiling kids in the background:

> Sonny's the type of person that needs understanding. He's vicious all the way. Youth, all his youth. He needs someone to help him control his emotion. He must be kept busy until all that youth and strength leaves him, like it leaves all of us . . .
>
> I understood Sonny's language, befriended him. I fathered him around. He needs training. He needs love. The right people have to take an interest in the boy and treat him like a member of the family.

In the autumn of 1961, the Pennsylvania Commission decided to lift their suspension on Liston's licence. This was no doubt in response to a plan to screen both Liston–Albert Westphal from Philadelphia on 4 December and Floyd Patterson's world championship defence against Tom McNeeley in Toronto the same night, back-to-back, in theatres around the country. In boxing, money talks louder than moral outrage.

Alfred Klein, head of the Pennsylvania Commission, issued a message to Liston by way of a public statement:

> You now stand at the crossroads. Never again will you get such an opportunity to prove that you are a good man. What you do after this will determine the course of your life.
>
> I believe you will be a success. However, it is all up to you. Nobody else can do the job that needs to be done. Sonny Liston, you are on your own from this point on.

Klein also said:

> It has never been the purpose of the Commission to destroy the career of Liston or any other athlete. The unique circumstances of the programme projected for December 4th present to Liston an opportunity that if now denied to him could well accomplish irreparable damage to him both as a championship contender and as a man.

In the *New York Herald Tribune*, Red Smith wrote that this was the only appropriate action: Liston had served his time in Missouri and faced no criminal charges in Pennsylvania. *Boxing Illustrated* said when they had published pieces supporting Liston's case they had received a larger-than-usual postbag and it was 5–1 anti-Liston.

Then at the beginning of February 1962, Katz was suddenly replaced as Liston's manager by Jack Nilon, who owned a lucrative popcorn and peanut concession business. The contract was said to have cost the 41-year-old, slightly built father of six from Chester just outside Philadelphia $125,000. He said he knew nothing of the way boxing worked. 'Like some guys buy racehorses, I bought a fighter,' he said.

In another interview with British writer Alan Hubbard for *World Sports*, Nilon said:

> Let me make this clear. Sonny came to me. I did not go to him. Sure, I like the idea of managing the next world champion. Who wouldn't? But as for Palermo and those other guys they talk about, why what the hell, I don't even know them. And I don't want to. Sonny's my boy now. I like the guy. He's a big kid, a big, overgrown kid. Hasn't he been persecuted enough?

9

DON'T DUMP YOUR TRASH ON US

Sonny Liston disposed of Albert Westphal, a right hand dropping the quick but too small German on his face in the first round. Floyd Patterson survived a knockdown, again, but floored the horribly overmatched Tom McNeeley repeatedly for a fourth-round win. At long last, the stage was set for Patterson–Liston to materialise.

Not everyone went along with the party line that Liston was a ring monster. In *The Observer*, John Hanlon suspected Liston's ability was being inflated out of all proportion:

> He is pictured as a fearsome, all-powerful, mighty menace hovering over the division. It is an intriguing fancy being built, I suggest, by many who have never even seen Liston strike a blow . . . The truth is that Liston, so far, simply does not have the credentials to justify his name as a first-class ogre of the ring.

Hanlon felt Sonny was strong but ponderous and predictable. He pointed to the win over Eddie Machen being disputed and that Zora Folley was a notoriously erratic performer. The rest of the opponents, according to Hanlon, were second-rate.

Technically, Monroe Harrison also felt Liston was far from perfect:

> He has a push jab with a lot of power, but I'd have shortened the jab. He misses with his right, because his jab is so powerful it knocks the man back, so he isn't there when he throws the right. If they give him the title fight within a year and a half, I favour Liston. Otherwise, it's Patterson. Liston'll be too big, too old later on.

Harrison never earned much money out of boxing, but he knew his stuff.

Jack McKinney, the Philadelphia sportswriter who knew Liston best, did too. He felt Liston's ring style reflected his personality: 'Liston is not stupid, but his insights are impeded by his neuroses. Emotionally, he is a child. Stubborn, obdurate and completely lacking in flexibility. And this is the way he fights.'

Steve Snider in *The Jersey Journal* of 20 April 1962 suggested the arguments over Liston's suitability as a challenger were 'a bit silly'. He cited the historical precedent of Jack Johnson, who was shunned because of his colour until it was impossible to ignore him any longer, and who was considered socially unacceptable through his six-and-a-half-year reign. The dwindling army of boxing fans, wrote Snider, didn't care about this stuff, they just wanted to see if Sonny really was the best heavyweight in the world.

Hal Hennesey, arguing Liston's corner in *Boxing Illustrated*, pointed out that by its very nature the fight game didn't attract 'Little Lord Fauntleroys to wear boxing gloves and Oliver Twist to manage them'.

One of the more bizarre interviews Liston gave around this time was with, of all publications, *The Police Gazette*. He was virtually pleading for his title fight. 'What do I have to do to get it?' he told writer Pete Evans. 'Patterson says it's the Mob that keeps him from fighting me. But there ain't no Mob. I'm the only mob he's worried about.'

Liston was upset that his misdemeanours in Philadelphia the previous year – when he was picked up for loitering and then charged with the harassment of Delores Ellis, not to mention impersonating a law enforcement officer – had poisoned opinion against him once again.

> All that publicity didn't do me any good. But it wasn't as bad as the newspapers said it was. People are easily led against you and it's harder to get them to go along with you. I was brought up in a tough neighbourhood with tough guys. They were my friends. Their ways were the only ones I knew. I'm trying to change, but it ain't easy.

OK, it might have been one of his practical jokes, but did trying to change really include following a woman in her car in the middle of the night, making her think he was a police officer and pulling her over? It is easy to see why he was misunderstood.

On 16 March 1962, the month the *Police Gazette* interview was published, Liston's pleas were answered. He and Patterson signed contracts for a heavyweight championship contest. 'I'll knock him out,' said Sonny.

Patterson had met President John F. Kennedy at the White House in January 1962. A story was put about by Patterson in later years that Kennedy had asked him not to defend against Liston, but he had decided he must. The President had taken off his tiepin and given it to him as a souvenir of his stay. Outside, wearing a sheepskin coat, his breath billowing out as steam in the cold, Floyd seemed relaxed and content as he spoke with the press, but later he said he was so nervous he couldn't recall what had been said. President Kennedy, he said, had tapped him on the shoulder during the general reception and told him to stay behind when everyone else left. 'I still don't know what he asked me,' he said. 'I just kept saying yes, yes, yes, yes!'

When the contracts were signed, Patterson was asked if he minded the fact that he was already considered an outsider in the betting. He said that the odds had been wrong in the second Johansson fight, and he hoped there was a slight possibility they would be again. Liston, who signed his name deliberately and slowly, agreed he had said he would box Patterson for nothing and was smiling as he said: 'Well, I admit I said I wouldn't mind fighting him in the gym when there was nobody there to watch, but . . .' The sentence didn't need to be completed. Everybody laughed.

Even though the heavyweight division had the fight it needed to lend the championship some credibility, resistance to Liston the man remained high. On 27 April 1962, the New York State Athletic Commission announced it had refused a boxing licence to Sonny Liston.

The group that had negotiated the promotional contract, Championship Sports Inc., had wanted to put the fight on in Yankee Stadium or at the Polo Grounds. The three worthies who comprised the New York commission – Melvin Krulewitch, James A. Farley Jr and Raymond Lee – said 'no'. Liston was paying Barone the $75,000 for his contract in part-payments from each of his fights, beginning with $18,000 from the Westphal mismatch. In the considered opinion of Krulewitch, Farley and Lee, this might well be going not to Barone but to Blinky Palermo, who was still out pending an appeal against his sentence. They failed to see why they should approve the funding of his legal defence by allowing Liston to box under their jurisdiction.

Patterson's legal team didn't like the idea of moving the fight away from New York and thought there might be a loophole that would enable them to get out of it, but when the boxers had signed the contracts both sides had left the site and date vacant, to be agreed later by Championship Sports.

Patterson himself, already in light training at Highland Mills, in New York State, was surprised by the commission decision. 'I'm disappointed in the way he has been treated,' he said.

What's he done? He has already served his time. What if they did that to me? You know how many times I went to the police station when I was nine years old? About a dozen. I used to steal from fruit stores and what not, but they have forgotten all about that. I feel sorry for him. People keep pointing to Liston and saying, 'There goes the ex-con, the criminal.'

Patterson also acknowledged that it was his decision alone to take on Liston, against the advice of Cus D'Amato and the wishes of the Kefauver Committee – and also the National Association for the Advancement of Colored People, which viewed Liston as a negative advertisement for the cause.

'One night in bed I made up my mind,' Patterson said:

> I knew if I'd want to sleep comfortably I'd have to take on Liston . . . Some people said 'What if you lose and he wins? Then the coloured people will suffer.' But maybe if Liston wins, he'll live up to the title. He may make people look up to him.

On another occasion Patterson said Liston had fought his way to number one and he himself had no right to pass judgement on his character. Patterson gave Liston a fairer hearing than most.

The New York decision to reject the fight met with something less than universal approval among members of the press, especially as it was given by way of a statement, with none of the three-man commission available to answer questions. Columnist Joe Williams labelled it a 'hit and run' statement, declaring merrily: 'The spectacle of boxing commissioners lined up on the side of the angels, hymn books reverently clasped, heads uplifted in non-partisan spirituals, is so extraordinary, one stares in disbelief, reason becomes unhinged.'

They had no obligation to do so but California and Massachusetts felt they should follow New York's lead, which ruled out, in particular, Los Angeles and Boston as venues for the fight. Californian commissioner Douglas Haydon said: 'I don't feel Liston has sufficiently rehabilitated himself. Nor has he made too much effort toward eliminating the people with whom he has been associated.'

The Illinois Commission had no such qualms. 'If they want to bring the fight to Chicago, they can rest assured that Sonny Liston will be given the right,' said Illinois Athletic Commission chairman Joseph Triner.

Liston's attorney, Mort Witkin, declared the New York action 'unfair, unjust and un-American'. Witkin was reportedly, and if true no doubt by complete coincidence, also the attorney for Blinky Palermo.

The New York Commission would have none of it. In ruling against Liston, they were not insensitive to his past but said they had remained unconvinced that he was free of his associations with Vitale, Palermo, Mitchell and, by implication, Carbo. 'We cannot ignore the possibility that these long-time associations continue to this day,' said the official verdict statement. 'The wrong people do not disengage easily.' And so, the deal was done for the fight to be held at Chicago Stadium on 25 September 1962. The *Chicago Tribune* ran an editorial attacking the decision. 'Don't Dump Your Trash On Us' was the headline.

Irving Schoenwald, the Illinois promoter and insurance man who had once agreed a deal with Frank Mitchell to co-manage Liston before Sonny was moved to Philadelphia, was hired to do the on-the-ground work as the licensed name on the official lists.

Jack Nilon was by now trying to straighten out the financial end of Liston's career. At that time Nilon took one-third of Liston's gross earnings, while 10 per cent still went to his former manager, George Katz, and 10 per cent to head trainer, Willie Reddish. Nilon said he knew of no clandestine stakeholders and was planning to form a company, stock of which would go to Liston and to two of Nilon's brothers. True to his word, Nilon established Inter-Continental Promotions, with Liston as president and Nilon, with brothers Jim and Bob, in charge. Liston owned 47.5 per cent of the stock, the Nilons jointly owned another 47.5 per cent, and a law firm, Kassab, Cherry and Curran had the other 5 per cent. Pennsylvania's laws concerning conflicts of interest prohibited Jack, as Liston's manager, from holding promotional rights.

First Katz and then Nilon had been brought into Liston's career to put a respectable face to it, but Jimmy Cannon provided some weight for the New York Commission concerns when he wrote in the 20 September 1962 edition of the *New York Journal-American* that Carbo still had ties with Sonny's backroom team. Nilon told Cannon that he was introduced to Liston, not by any mobster, nor even a businessman, but by Father Edward Murphy, a Jesuit priest from Denver who was Liston's friend. Nilon also claimed never to have met Carbo or Blinky Palermo. However, two prominent members of the Liston team, Joe Polino and Archie Pirolli, were said by Cannon to have links to Carbo. Polino was the cut man, Pirolli ran the training camp.

Polino had worked with Joey Giardello when he was on the way up. Giardello would win the world middleweight title in December 1963 and always protested complete innocence against being involved with the Mob on the grounds that it took him more than 123 fights to become champion. However, he lost his licence in New York in 1957 because of the associations of his co-managers, Carmen Graziano and Tony Ferrente. The latter was found by Senator Kefauver to be close to Carbo and Palermo. Ferrente had, it was said, been a party to Carbo's whereabouts when 'on the lam' before Frankie was caught and thrown into Alcatraz.

Pirolli had worked for Palermo in Philadelphia. He had been by Ike Williams' side in a non-title fight with Johnny Bratton in Philadelphia in January 1949. While Williams was 'guided' by Palermo, Bratton was managed by Hymie 'The Mink' Wallman, another of Carbo's flunkeys, though he had an above-board business as a furrier. (Wallman would eventually lose his licence in New York for bribing a judge.) In other words, it was a Mob-owned fight. Sometimes too much can be made of connections, of course. Because somebody knows someone and sometimes works with them does not necessarily mean they are involved with them in anything more than a minor professional sense. Polino's trade was to train fighters and to treat cuts. Pirolli worked corners, organised training routines, and in Liston's case, the training camp. It does not make them villains.
Nilon told Cannon:

> I'm totally ignorant of the fight business. I needed a cut man . . . a trainer.
> I got Joe, who used to work with Joey Giardello. Then I couldn't go to the
> Pines Hotel, where Sonny was training in Upstate New York. I asked Joe,
> 'Do you know anyone who knows the fight business who can take care of
> a camp?' Joe recommended Archie.

Part of Pirolli's job was to act as controller of the press – he organised who would be favoured and who would not. Cannon described him as 'crabbed and vindictive'. If, in the absence of Sonny, writers were looking for a little background, some morsel of information they might turn into a story to provide a reason for their day, Pirolli could be belligerent. If he didn't like a question, asked not necessarily of him, he had a tendency to cut the writer dead with a curt: 'What are you, a cop or something?'

When Liston, as he frequently did, refused even the briefest of meetings with the press, it caused upset and stress. Men had jobs to do, deadlines to meet. 'Who the hell does he think he is?' said one rejected man from a national daily.

One of his colleagues replied: 'He thinks he's Sonny Liston, the next heavyweight champion of the world. And I'm afraid he's right.'

10

A BLUES SONG JUST FOR FIGHTERS

Boxing draws most attention when it can provide a situation where sports fans can identify two distinct sides of the drama. When Sonny Liston finally challenged Floyd Patterson for the heavyweight championship of the world in Comiskey Park, Chicago, on 25 September 1962, laid out before the public was the classic hero–villain scenario. In one corner was the champion, the sensitive, gentle kid from a deprived background who had once been the youngest heavyweight champion of all time, the all-time good guy, polite, respectable Floyd Patterson. And in the other corner, whether he liked it or not, was not the man Sonny Liston but the monster, the ogre, the brute with the giant fists and the Mob connections, the jailbird who was a symbol of all the lawless ills of America.

Who Sonny actually was didn't matter a jot. Any subtleties in his personality, any fears and doubts, sensitivities, the investigation of which might have spoiled the story, were ignored. Johnny Tocco, who knew Liston the man as well as the fighter and who trained him for the last fight of his career against Chuck Wepner, said much of the bad-guy image was a media creation. 'They made him a monster,' he said.

Two days before the fight, British writer Sam Leitch, who admitted he had seen Liston box only three rounds – a knockout win over Howard King the previous year – described Sonny in the *Sunday Pictorial* as 'that scowling slab of boxing zombie'. Leitch labelled the fight 'Saint v. Sinner'. 'He has no ring frillery. He scorns plans with the unschooled contempt of a man who grunts mostly in monosyllables.' And more. 'Sonny is the biggest, toughest, sharpest, most venomous, vindictive man in any sport today.'

That said, Leitch also included, well down the story, a brief testimony from Geraldine Liston, who had, after all, seen him for more than ten minutes. Geraldine said: 'He has paid for what he did when he didn't know better. Now he knows better.'

Peter Wilson, the *Daily Mirror* boxing writer whose work carried the legend 'The Man They Couldn't Gag', recognised Liston's ability but joined in the plot.

'He looks like a fugitive from a horror film.' Wilson was to use the same line in one of his pieces before Liston defended the title against Cassius Clay in Miami in February 1964. 'The man is like something that has strayed out of a horror movie. Sonny Liston – the Human Hammer.'

Liston certainly understood what was happening. 'A boxing match is like a cowboy movie,' he had said to *Sports Illustrated* back in July 1961:

> There's got to be good guys, and there's got to be bad guys. That's what the people pay for . . . Everybody thinks I should be mean and tough, but I'm not. Fighting ain't fun. In the ring I look tough because I'm trying to get the scare on the other guy. And the way some of these suckers fight, I guess they are scared.

The situation disappointed Floyd Patterson. 'The champion does not want to be typed as the hero who must slay the monster,' he told the *New York Times* in April 1962.

In the *New York Times* magazine Jack Murphy wrote: 'To Geraldine Liston, the champion is a nice, thoughtful man named Charles. To my notion, he's the meanest animal in the jungle.'

Liston was persuaded to allow Wendell Smith to ghost a first-person column for the *Chicago's American* in the build-up to the Patterson fight. The result was excruciatingly bad. Liston was credited with saying: 'In the beginning I want to emphasise that I have no intention of copping a plea in this presentation concerning the problems and troubles I have encountered during my life.'

Perhaps Smith was under pressure to produce and Liston was being uncooperative, but under a headline 'Sonny's Story of Childhood Squalor', Liston, who was not prone to complaining about his upbringing beyond a few moans about beatings from his elderly father, apparently said: 'We grew up like heathens. We hardly had enough food to keep from starving, no shoes, only a few clothes, and nobody to help us escape from the horrible life we lived.'

The short series of articles went on in the same stilted tone that bore no resemblance to the way Liston spoke and only an occasional resemblance to the way he seemed to think. However, the sentiment (if not the actual words) expressed at the end of the final piece was perhaps the most genuine part of the entire exercise: 'If I win, I won't throw my weight around, nor be an arrogant person. People do not like that kind of a champion and I want people to like me.'

With those words Smith had summed up Liston. However socially inept Sonny was at times, however inappropriate his behaviour could be, at this time of his life, before he challenged Patterson for the title, he wanted to be liked. He wanted to be one of the good guys.

The fight contract was a strange one. Liston was offered only 12½ per cent, instead of the customary 20 per cent. Of that, should he win, he would be paid $50,000 the day following the fight, the remainder to be held in trust until the rematch was signed. He didn't like the contract. In an attempt at doggerel so bad that not even Cassius Clay would have gone there, Liston told writers: 'I'm the poorest and I need the moorest . . .' Then, as if he couldn't think of another rhyme or had forgotten the one he had been fed, he said: 'Anyway, more than the 12½ per cent.'

Liston did not like long training camps but this fight was different. This was the big one that would define the rest of his career and bring with it wealth he could not have imagined for himself back in the cotton fields of Arkansas. He knuckled down to 12 weeks of work at The Pines, a resort at South Fallsburg, New York, after which he would move to Aurora Downs, a disused racetrack 38 miles from downtown Chicago.

As fight time neared, the fight would need all the publicity it could get, and with newsmen coming in from all over the world, they needed some access to the fighters in order to generate enough copy. Pirolli could organise media days at Aurora Downs, when Liston would be required to put up with the intrusion. At The Pines, things were far more private. One of the few visitors there was Liston's journalist friend from Philadelphia, Jack McKinney, who understood him as well as any, and whose writing is in such contrast to those of his fellow-tradesmen that at times he seems cast in the role of Liston's apologist. McKinney was sent to do pieces for the *Philadelphia Daily News* and *Sports Illustrated* and found Liston bored and irritable: 'I don't like this business of training six months or even three months for one fight. I can get my body right in three weeks, four at the most. I'll never start this early again.'

Some would later criticise Liston for bullying smaller sparring partners, but Patterson was smaller and quicker than he was. It made sense to fight smaller, lighter men. And there were still big guys whose job was to give Liston more of a physical test. Jimmy McCarter, who had beaten Liston way back in the 1953 National American Athletic Union championships, was one of them. He had played football in the US college system and had won the AAU title in 1956, then tried his luck as a pro fighter. It hadn't worked out. He had lost in three rounds to Alex Miteff, whom Cassius Clay trounced in six.

McCarter felt Liston wanted to put him down because of his college education. It is possible they didn't like each other, but more likely is that McCarter was resentful of the fact that he beat Sonny as an amateur and was now employed as a sparring partner. It's possible also that he just didn't understand or enjoy Liston's sense of fun. With his dislike of being cooped up in a training camp, it is unlikely that Liston would have chosen McCarter if he didn't want him around. He could have picked any one of a number of big, ordinary heavyweights around the circuit. The likelihood is that Liston remembered him from the old days, knew his career was coming to nothing, and felt like giving him some work.

Jack McKinney made detailed reference to Liston's hard work in training, but McCarter's view was the opposite. 'Sonny likes to talk about training,' he said, 'but he's lazy. He doesn't like to do roadwork and he does not like to be hit in the gut.'

McCarter felt Liston, famously uneducated, sneered at him for his university background. 'If someone had a question, Sonny would say, "Ask college boy, he knows all the answers."' McCarter didn't get the practical jokes, either. That said, we might have sympathy for him on the morning he awoke to the sound of a gun being cocked perilously close to his head. Sonny squeezed the trigger and fired a blank.

'I guess I annoyed him,' said McCarter. 'He was murdering all the sparring partners in camp except me. This he didn't like.' The one man he was grateful to in the camp was Willie Reddish, who took the time to work with him too until, according to McCarter, Sonny put a stop to it. 'I learned more than I had in my entire career,' he said. Reddish might have wanted to teach him in order to bring more out of Liston by having McCarter stay on the inside, test him physically and work the body.

McKinney, who was in the camp for eight days, said McCarter had got Liston wrong and pointed to one conversation he witnessed which suggested that far from disliking McCarter, Sonny actually cared about him. Liston asked why a man with an education would box. McCarter said it was the chance of making big money quick. Liston told him there was no point in doing that if you got your head scrambled before you got a chance to spend it. Many boxers choose to ignore the risk of brain damage. They know about it and leave it in the background as a vague possibility they hope and trust won't arise. Liston was not like that, which may have some relevance in his reluctance to take punishment later.

See, the different parts of the brain set in little cups like this [putting his fists against each other, the knuckles knitting together]. When you get a terrible shot – pop! – the brain flops out of them cups and you're knocked out. Then the brain settles back in the cups and you come to. But after this happens enough times, or sometimes even once if the shot's hard enough, the brain don't settle back right in them cups, and that's when you start needing other people to help you get around.

What is courage and what is common sense? When the madness of youth leaves a fighter is it fair to call him a quitter if he wants to avoid getting maimed or worse? On 21 September 1962, four days before Liston fought Patterson, the 25-year-old Argentine heavyweight Alejandro Lavorante was knocked out in Los Angeles by John Riggins, a veteran from Spokane, Washington. In his previous fight Lavorante had been knocked out by Cassius Clay, and in the one before that, he had been carried from the ring on a stretcher after losing in the tenth round against Archie Moore. After losing to Riggins, Lavorante was unconscious for two hours and was taken to the California Lutheran Hospital, where he was operated on to relieve pressure on his brain. The morning bulletin described him as 'very grim'. There was some hope when his arm appeared to respond to touch; however, the pressure on his brain built up again and he needed a second operation. He lingered on for 18 months and died on 1 April 1964.

Despite such stories, the 'college boy' McCarter could not leave boxing alone. He had three attempts at comebacks but didn't win another fight. He retired for good in 1973.

McKinney said Liston was in charge of his own camp. Nilon, Pirolli, Reddish and Polino all carried out his bidding. Liston enjoyed labelling the rest of the backroom team, some of whom had hard-to-define roles, Bums Incorporated. Bill Morefield, a Philadelphia restaurateur, was the camp cook. Raymond Munson woke Sonny for the morning run and usually accompanied him. Teddy King took photographs and made sure the equipment was in order. Reddish told McKinney: 'Sonny knows what he's doing. Some fighters have to be driven, but he's not one of them.' There was one morning that Liston announced: 'No workout. I smell rain.' He would have learned how to 'smell' the country weather way back in the days in Arkansas. An hour later, it was raining.

According to McKinney, far from being lazy, Liston got up at 4.45 a.m. to do a four-mile run along the track bed of an abandoned railway, vaulting the odd wire fence along the way. Later on, he took to running on the resort's hilly golf course.

Liston, who confided in McKinney to an unusual degree, admitted sometimes he felt unable to get out of bed when the alarm bell sounded, but when that happened he asked himself why he had to answer it. He knew the answer. 'Because there's another bell ringing about now just a hundred miles from here and Patterson's hearing that one.'

He would tell himself:

That's the way it has to be from here on in. I'll hear my bell and he'll hear his bell and we'll both get up and do just about the same thing and keep doing it until it finally comes up the night we both hear the same bell and we're inside the ropes together with the whole rest of the world looking on from the outside.

McKinney said during their walks together in camp, Liston would recite dialogue from television comedy acts like Redd Foxx and Pigmeat Markham, complete with sound effects. He added in the falsetto, the creaking doors. The writer would watch Liston lose his temper with a member of his team then be contrite a few moments later and want to make up. If he took money off a sparring partner at cards, he would sometimes give it back, knowing the man couldn't afford to lose but was playing the game to please him.

It was to McKinney that Liston uttered his immortal line: 'Some day they'll write a blues song just for fighters. It'll be for a slow guitar, soft trumpet and a bell.'

With the hard work done, Liston and his people moved to Aurora Downs, which had formerly been used to hold harness races and stock car meetings. By then the wooden grandstand was rotting and weeds had spread everywhere. There were two abandoned wrecks of stock cars rusting at the gates. Sonny prepared himself for becoming more public, as he was required to do. He trained indoors if it was raining, outside if the weather was good. He invited boys from a local reform school to watch him train, then let them sit in on the press conference. 'If I win this fight, you'll be able to see there is good and bad in everybody,' he said. 'The way things stand now, everybody thinks there is only bad in me.' As always he decided whom he would, and whom he would not, talk to. Harold Conrad, the head of public relations for the promotion, met Liston in the grounds at Aurora Downs. As a matter of habit he moved towards a handshake, only to be ignored. 'Aren't you speaking to me?' he said.

'I don't have to talk to you,' said Liston.

One young dreamer hitched a lift from Chicago to spar with the champion. The boy, whose name was Milton Mendly, arrived with a suitcase and a kit bag. To try him out, Reddish put him in with one of the sparring partners, then had to intervene because poor Mendly was so inept he was in danger of suffering serious damage. Jack Nilon was about to give him his bus fare home when Liston, who had been watching, said: 'That kid didn't come here for no handout. Let's give him a job.' Milton Mendly became, not a sparring partner, but the 'first assistant to the camp cook'.

Liston occasionally staged elaborate pranks to wind up onlookers and amuse himself. One favourite was to pretend to lose his temper with cut man Polino and appear to hit him in the face. Polino, who had actually caught the blow in his palm, which he held alongside his head, then spat out his 'teeth' – in fact, several white beans. He would stagger backwards, somehow grab hold of a golf club or a baseball bat and lunge at Liston, who would suddenly produce a gun and shoot him (with blanks). Visitors were taken in for long enough to be horrified . . . only to realise they had been had.

Jack McKinney was confused when people around the resort kept calling him 'Bobo'. Eventually he worked out what was happening. Liston had spread the word that he was Carl 'Bobo' Olson, the former world middleweight champion.

Liston's mood darkened at Aurora Downs. He had been in camp a long time by then. The fight itself was nearing, a time when fighters can become tetchy, and he did not enjoy the increase in demands on his time. While he liked talking to McKinney, he didn't enjoy having to give press conferences. One example of his changing mood was the way he treated the police officers who were working on the entrance to the camp. Given his general mistrust of anyone in authority, let alone those wearing a police uniform, it was not too far short of astonishing that at The Pines, McKinney saw him go out and chat with the police officer on the gate, explaining: 'The poor guy could go nuts standing there by himself all the time.' Yet at Aurora Downs, an officer with the same job told George Whiting of the *London Evening Standard* he couldn't wait for his job to end. 'One dollar seventy-five cents an hour for a seventy-hour week for the last five weeks and the mean son-of-a-bitch won't even speak,' he said.

The contrasts continued. As much as he disliked dealing with the media, he went out of his way to talk to *Chicago Tribune* writer David Condon, who was 35 minutes late for an 11.30 a.m. meeting at Aurora Downs and, upon arrival, nearly crashed into Liston's dark blue Cadillac. Liston told Condon and his photographer they would have to wait, as by then it was time for his sleep. Having slept, after at first mistakenly believing they had left to return to Chicago, he made himself available immediately. He told Condon his favourite musician was Ray Charles, that his toughest fight was with Cleveland Williams, that he was sorry his old amateur opponent, Ed Sanders, who had won gold at the 1952 Olympics, had died. Condon tried to probe Liston about any charity work he might have done but drew a blank. 'Favours aren't special, you do 'em from the way you feel in your heart and you don't tell about 'em. You do a friend a favour, you don't brag. You don't tell.'

He asked what Liston might tell fans who disliked him. Sonny tapped his fingers on the table and thought about it, then said slowly: 'I would like to say to the people that it's wrong to judge a man, to judge him by what they read because sometimes the biggest part is not true. These people should not judge a man until they know him personally themselves.' Developing that theme a little later, he said: 'Say, know what I want to tell people? Don't be jealous of the other man. He does better than you, OK, don't be jealous. More power to him.'

As for hobbies, he said he liked TV, music and baseball – 'I like the Dodgers.' When asked what the best thing was that had happened to him, he said: 'Meeting my wife.'

At one point, he agreed to do a joint interview with Ingemar Johansson, who had flown in from Sweden especially for the fight. Someone asked Johansson for a comment on the subpoena he had received concerning the small matter of $1 million in taxes allegedly owed to the US government. Johansson, when approached by someone he mistook for a fight fan, had put out his hand, expecting a greeting and a handshake, and instead found himself accepting legal papers.

Liston listened to this with great interest, as if suddenly finding an affinity with the Swede. 'That'll teach you to shake hands with strangers,' he said, with a broad grin. Then when another reporter asked a follow-up question, Liston gleefully advised: 'Don't tell him nothing. You'll just make it worse.'

Liston treated most press conferences with the same bored stare, as if the entire process was an irrelevance. Once he complained: 'You fellers look at the sun, then you ask me if the sun is shining . . .'

Budd Schulberg noted for *Playboy* that Liston often ignored the question altogether, substituting for words 'a stare that puts Karloff's and Lugosi's in the Bobbsey Twins' class'. He added: 'And when Liston did talk, his voice sounded muffled and distant, from some hole deep inside him, almost as if issuing up out of a tomb.'

Leonard Shecter, in the *New York Post*, said during workouts Liston would scan the visiting pressmen to check for those he did not like. 'He has a list of them . . . who he believes have been especially unfriendly. If there are many of them present, the post-training press conference goes badly.'

Shecter, as McKinney had at The Pines, felt Liston was in complete control of his camp, that Jack Nilon, who seemed to him to spend a lot of time running around with a clipboard, was no more than a 'head flunky'. 'Call me his adviser,' said Nilon, who added:

Put yourself in my place. This guy comes to you talking about a lot of money. This is a business with me. Anyway, I've done a lot. When we started out, we didn't have a licence to fight. Now we got a shot at the title. That's a pretty good three months' work.

Gerald Kersh did a background piece on the fight for *Playboy* and quoted Harold Conrad's response when he told him he was going to talk to Nilon.

'Now what the hell for?' said Conrad.

'Just to see.'

'There's nothing to see. Jack Nilon simply doesn't exist. Nobody can make anything of that character. He tried to publicise himself once. It couldn't be done.'

Jack R. Griffin of the *Chicago Sun-Times* covered a conference at Aurora Downs in the early part of the week of the fight, by which time Joe Louis had arrived and was spending time with and around Liston. Sonny complained that writers were concentrating too much on how good Patterson was:

All time I read how fast this Patterson is, how fast he is, how fast he is. What reason papers got to say he so fast? Who he ever get out fast? What you guys trying to do? You want to know about fast? You look over there at Joe Louis. Now that was speed. He didn't waste no time with nobody.

When somebody pressed the issue of Patterson's quick hands, Liston said: 'What he do, this guy, catch a bullet with his hands, or something?'

When another writer asked if Louis being at his camp helped him, Liston didn't seem to understand. 'I didn't box with him,' he said, appearing surprised. The writer tried again, explaining he meant was Louis an inspiration to him. It appeared the idea had not occurred to Sonny. 'It ain't gonna make us win, is it,' he said.

The questioning appeared to be going nowhere. Did he feel lucky to be given his title shot? 'Man, we lucky to be living . . . the way they shooting things at the moon, and all that.'

In the end, he got a question he could deal with. How long, wondered one hack, would the fight go. 'If it's a cold night, not very long,' said Sonny.

Liston built on his hunger, his excitement, and gradually his resentment towards Patterson turned into what he admitted was more cold hatred than anger. He needed it to drive himself on. It fuelled his adrenalin, made him, as the fight neared, difficult to be around. Patterson, he told writers, was prejudiced against his own kind because he hadn't given a black fighter a chance at the title since Tommy 'Hurricane' Jackson in July 1957. The last seven world-title fights had involved Patterson against white opponents. During that time, of course, it was Cus D'Amato who had selected Patterson's opponents, not Floyd.

Even in the sparring workouts before the media, and even though all the hard work was done, Liston didn't see the point in taking it easy on his hired hands. As one sparring partner put it: 'When he hits, he hits every cop who ever beat him.' Liston's working philosophy was plain. 'Fighting ain't fun,' he said. He had learned that back in 1954 when he laughed at a wisecrack the jerky, unorthodox Marty Marshall made, then had his jaw broken when Marshall cracked him with a right hand.

> It's like war. Either I'm gonna hurt him or he's gonna hurt me. That's why I don't smile in the ring. Why should I? If I could do something else, I would. I don't like earning my living getting hurt.

Lester Bromberg telephoned Marshall at work at a Detroit paint firm to see what he made of the fight. Marshall, who had retired from the ring three years before, said:

> I can't see Patterson beating him, especially since Sonny's got a good left hook now. I don't like Patterson's peek-a-boo defence and his jumping around. He doesn't hit heavy enough. If he tries to fight Liston, it could be over fast. If he tries to make a grabbing, holding, pecking fight like Eddie Machen, he'll still get knocked out. I say it will be seven, eight rounds at most.

11

HE MUST HAVE DIED LAST NIGHT

Floyd Patterson's autobiography, written by Milton Gross, had been released earlier in the year. Gross revealed later that at the end of the interviews he carried out, Patterson had said to him: 'When this gets printed I think I'll take a copy of it to a psychiatrist and maybe he'll be able to explain me to me.'

Patterson was born the son of a railroad worker near Waco, North Carolina, on 4 January 1935. His parents moved to the Bedford-Stuyvesant section of Brooklyn when he was a year old and moved around from apartment to apartment. His father, Thomas, worked in physical jobs all his life, and Floyd remembered him coming home so exhausted he fell asleep on his bed fully clothed without eating. His mother took what jobs she could in between raising her six children. Floyd was a troubled child, who had nightmares, fell into strange trances and walked in his sleep. His clothes were handed down from his father and were so ill-fitting he was laughed at in the street and, especially, in school. He took to staying out at night, stealing food and milk to eat, and put up a psychological wall between him and everyone else in the world. He refused to learn, and as he fell behind in class, stayed away, hiding in cellars, in movie-houses when he could find enough money to pay to go in, in subways and wherever nobody would trouble him. Eventually, for a combination of truancy and petty crime, he was sent, at the age of ten, to Wiltwyck School for Boys in upstate New York. It was there his life changed, though psychologically a great deal of damage had already been done. He remained shy, introverted, uncertain, even though teachers, psychoanalysts and psychologists worked with him and helped straighten his life out. He found he loved to immerse himself in nature and, from a white boy named Galento, he learned something of the ways of the countryside. He learned to read and write, and after running from gangs and being upset by racist taunts from time to time in Brooklyn, he found a world where racial and religious equality was a code. 'For the first time in my life, perhaps the only time in my life, it seemed colour didn't make any difference,' he said in his autobiography.

Among the sports he tried at Wiltwyck was boxing. He left there at 12 and went to a 'School of Opportunity', the Cyprus W. Field School at 113 East 4th St, New York City. After the day's study, he would go ten blocks uptown to the Gramercy Park Gym, where Cus D'Amato trained would-be fighters. When he moved on to the Alexander Hamilton Vocational High School to study metalwork, a teacher asked him what he would like to be. 'A professional boxer,' he said.

At first, he was not as naturally talented as one of his elder brothers, Frank, who went on to have a short professional career, but he learned fast and was only 17 years old when he won the Olympic middleweight title in the 1952 Games in Helsinki.

He turned professional when he returned to New York, making his debut in New York City in September 1952. Apart from a points defeat by the former world light-heavyweight champion Joey Maxim in an eight-round contest in Brooklyn in June 1954, everything went well. And in November 1956, following the retirement of Rocky Marciano, Floyd won the vacant world heavyweight title by knocking out 39-year-old Archie Moore, the reigning light-heavyweight champion who had also been Marciano's final opponent, in five rounds in Chicago. With that he became the youngest world champion in heavyweight history at 21.

Despite his success, Patterson remained difficult to know. By his own admission, he found it hard to look people in the eye and would rather stare at the ground when he was talking. He learned to overcome it, but to the outside world in his own way he was just as complex, just as difficult to fathom as Sonny Liston.

British writer Reg Gutteridge was among those who went to see Patterson in the final days of preparation at Marycrest Farm near Elgin, Illinois, where the owner, a Mrs Widman, worked for under-privileged children. The champion, who had been a 'lost child' once himself, didn't feel like working out and apologised. 'Patterson appeared in a boilermaker blue shirt and emerald-green baseball hat perched at a Popeye angle,' wrote Gutteridge in the *London Evening News and Star*. Patterson said he had already sparred 175 rounds, first in his camp at Highland Mills, New York, and then when he had first arrived at Marycrest, and now wanted to save his strength.

His headquarters were basic – a white clapboard cottage that Gutteridge said looked more like a shed, and a chapel containing a piano, organ and prayer books. The ring he was using was outdoors, on a hillside where donkeys grazed. The public were allowed to watch him train for a fee, the proceeds going to Mrs Widman's charity, but someone had stolen the collection box. It was said the champion had replaced the money – about $3,000.

The only worried man in the camp seemed to be the head trainer Dan Florio, who felt Patterson was just too calm. 'I gotta make him mad,' said Florio, a veteran who had worked in the old days with world champs like Tony Canzoneri, Joe Louis and Jersey Joe Walcott.

Patterson's Mr Reasonable mood was no act. When it was suggested to him that he might need to feel a bit more vicious, he said: 'It's a word I hate because I won fights without being vicious,' then added, as if almost reluctantly, 'But right now I've got some dislikes for Sonny . . . Talk is cheap. Liston's confidence is already on the surface. Mine is within.'

Florio's team included Ray Patterson, Floyd's younger brother. Cus D'Amato also appeared at times but was kept at arm's length. He was retained as official manager, paid his 33 per cent, but no longer had control over what Floyd said or did. One writer later described Cus as like an admiral in the Swiss navy. D'Amato did, though, entertain reporters by running a film called *The Floyd Patterson Story*, which set out to prove D'Amato's point that he had created the best heavyweight of all time.

Patterson said: 'Even if I beat Liston, the writers still won't recognise me as a great champion.'

He also told Gross: 'If you dig deeply enough beneath Sonny's hate, you'll find a layer of fear and underneath that there would be compassion, just as there is in everybody else.'

It was public relations man Irwin Rose's job to send out quotes supposedly from Patterson to small-town newspapers. This worked well until Floyd read one of them and publicly disowned his 'words'. This obviously caused a deal of embarrassment.

Most people liked Patterson or at *least* empathised with his struggle to succeed in spite of his psychological fragility. One of the few who wasn't convinced by Patterson the man was acidic New York columnist Joe Williams. In the week of the fight, he cited the champion's attempt to be *kind* and fair to Liston as evidence that he was a patronising fake. 'I've attended only *two* Patterson press conferences,' wrote Williams, 'and I walked out in the middle *of the* second one. Much of what he said seemed nonsense to me. Some of it, I felt, was pompous and insincere.'

Perhaps it was Williams, perhaps someone else, who was the subject of a Milton Gross anecdote. A writer, who had been consistently critical of Patterson, claimed he had been barred from the champion's training camp. Patterson sent word to him that this was untrue and offered to send a chauffeured limousine to bring him out to Elgin if he found it too difficult to get there himself. He added a condition – 'You must keep writing the same way you've always written about me. Don't change.'

George Whiting, for the *London Evening Standard*, said the only time Patterson expressed any criticism of or resentment towards Liston was when the subject of money came up. Liston's dislike of the 12½ per cent deal irritated the champion. 'For a guy who said he'd fight me for nothing it seems a nice payday,' said Floyd, who told reporters he was investing his money in the promotional company behind the fight, which should provide him with a lump sum from the contest itself and annual increments plus interest for the next 17 years. If it sounded like a tax loophole plan, that's exactly what it was, and it would have ramifications sooner rather than later.

The British newspapers were divided on who would win. Reg Gutteridge for the *Evening News and Star*, the *Daily Express*, the *Daily Mirror* and the *Daily Mail*, all went for Liston before the eighth, the *London Evening Standard*, the *Daily Sketch*, the *Daily Telegraph* and the *Daily Herald*, all went for Patterson, either on points or by late stoppage.

In his preview, Joe Williams was scathing of the quality of both protagonists. Labelling it 'The Battle of the Bums', Williams wrote:

> Liston is the unknown quantity. We know about all there is to know about Patterson. Quick hands, fast combinations, game, china chin. He's been on the floor so often he's developed a canvas back. Up to now he's always got up . . .

Williams, in spite of his sneering style, had a steady eye when it came to boxing. He felt Patterson was fortunate in the third fight with Ingemar Johansson in 1961 because if the Swede had been a good finisher it would have all been over early on when Floyd was knocked down.

The founder and editor of *Ring* magazine, Nat Fleischer, picked Patterson. The bulletin board in the press room had a space for predictions. By 20 September, five days from fight time, Patterson was ahead 15–12.

Cassius Clay said Liston would knock out Patterson within five rounds. Red Smith went for Liston but reminded his readers:

> This is the column that called all three fights between Rocky Graziano and Tony Zale wrong. That isn't easy to do. Practically anybody can be wrong two times out of three. It requires a special talent to go the whole distance . . .

Smith pointed out that the literary mob had turned out in force: Norman Mailer, James Baldwin, Ben Hecht, Budd Schulberg and Joe Liebling, and enjoyed a little dig at their pretentious ways: 'They're going to psychoanalyse Liston and explore Patterson's subconscious. They'll discuss motivations and compulsions and subliminations and character transfers.'

Smith said, contrary to sentimental opinion, a Liston win would be good for boxing:

> We will then have a heavyweight champion who is not a mixed-up, sensitive, confused muddle of complexes. We will merely have a great big ugly rough heavyweight prizefighter for champion. It will make life a lot simpler for all of us.

Al Buck, another *New York Post* correspondent, reported that Joe Louis was impressed by Liston's training session, in which he did light sparring with middleweight Allen Thomas and a long-retired heavyweight, Dan Bucceroni. 'I don't see how he can lose,' said Louis. 'Patterson has to have a plan. He can't make a mistake.'

In a ghosted piece for the *New York Journal–American*, presumably syndicated in other Hearst newspapers, Louis said he liked Liston's winning attitude. 'Unless he's fooled me, he's absolutely confident,' said Louis, who said in some ways Liston reminded him of Rocky Marciano, though he added that Liston had a cockiness that Marciano never had. Marciano, he said, continued to learn even when he was champion.

Louis felt Bob Satterfield, the erratic Chicago heavyweight, was a harder one-punch hitter than Liston, but Sonny threw his punches fast and hard enough. Joe felt the challenger did not have 'lightning reactions':

> He responds when he is going in one style – usually moving in. The off-beat stuff irritates him. Another thing I have noticed is that he cannot punch down well. That's because he never has learned – or won't learn – how to do it.

Perhaps the tactical brains behind Patterson noted what Louis had said and perhaps that was the thinking behind Floyd's instructions to stay low, jab, keep the hands high. Perhaps they were trying to make Liston punch down and therefore to render him less effective.

Perhaps.

As always, the public relations men did the best spin they could. Sometimes they could do it with the merest hint of proportion, enough to make newsmen understand that, all right, it was probably a lie but it might have a grain of truth to it – what is known as a 'sensible lie'. Sometimes, however, the lies were so outlandish they were funny.

Ben Bentley, Harold Conrad's sidekick, greeted Chicago writer Leo Fischer, who had been out of town covering a football game, with a hearty:

> Welcome home! How lucky can you get! Here you are back in town with an opportunity to write something about the greatest heavyweight championship fight held in Chicago since – well, since 1956, anyway.

Fischer pointed out 1956 was the last time there had been a heavyweight championship fight in Chicago, when Patterson beat Moore for the vacant title.

Bentley replied:

> Certainly, but has there been any worthy of your fair city since then? No, sir! Only the best is good enough for Chicago, and now we got it. The eyes of the world are on us. You are back in the fight universe. Doesn't it make you feel wonderful?

Their one-way conversation was interrupted by half a dozen phone calls, after which Bentley took up where he left off, with apparent sincerity:

> Those were friends of mine I haven't heard from in years. It almost brings tears to my eyes to be associated with an event that makes people want to renew old times and recall old memories.
>
> It's only incidental that they want tickets . . . No boxing match on record has drawn so many literati, so many top magazine writers and so many foreign correspondents. We already got authors of half a dozen bestsellers here looking for different angles. We got cartoonists of all sizes and shapes. We got famous columnists . . .

If that was 99 per cent comedy, Bentley was a tad more accurate when it came to analysing the way the sports world was moving:

> A live gate may soon be a thing of the past. Theatre-television, pay-TV and the closed circuit are coming in the future – not only for boxing but many other sports.
>
> I can see the day in boxing when you'll talk about gates not in the thousands but in the millions. This one is setting the pattern, with a box-

office take close to four million dollars from people who won't be within a hundred miles of Comiskey Park.

The *Daily Express* not only sent writers but also cartoonist Roy Ulyett, who told Wendell Smith, for *Chicago's American*, that Patterson was underrated and would prove his greatness by defeating Liston. 'I don't think Floyd is scared of this chap at all,' he said.

Gerald Kersh, a London freelance who declared himself unemployable because he refused to take orders, went for Liston by the sixth.

Nils Magnuson, sports editor of the *Aftonbladet* in Stockholm, did not bother to analyse it, explaining that he liked Patterson the man:

> I am pulling for Floyd and so is everyone else in Sweden. He made a wonderful impression when he was over there in 1960 on a visit. Forty thousand people turned out just to see him go through a routine exhibition of bag punching and rope skipping.

Joe Louis and Jim Braddock posed for a publicity shot in Comiskey Park 24 hours before the fight. Louis had knocked out Braddock in the eighth round there on 22 June 1937 to win the championship. Twenty-five years had passed since then. Louis, once so fabulously wealthy, owed the government around $1.5 million in back taxes and had no way of paying it.

Braddock said a lot had been made of Liston's jab, but if he couldn't hit Patterson with it, what then? 'If Floyd keeps sort of moving to Sonny's right all the time, Liston won't be able to land that left, and he might get a little panicky and start to press.'

Braddock thought back to his own title victory over Max Baer, when he was 10–1 in a two-fighter fight and still won a clear decision. 'I didn't let him land, and I think this fight, like mine, could go 15 rounds and, if it does, Floyd has got to outbox him.'

Ingemar Johansson felt Patterson's best chance was not to run but to use his speed in attack, to close Liston up, to hit him first. Patterson should not try to jab with him but should use his left hook and his combinations.

These days a big fight isn't a big fight without a row about the selection of gloves. In 1962, this was a rare thing, but another chance for some column inches in the newspapers in an attempt to move more tickets. In spite of the best efforts of the publicity team, the stadium was a long way from sold out.

The row first erupted eight days before the fight when Dan Florio complained to the Illinois Commission about the gloves Liston wanted to wear. Patterson wanted both boxers to use Everlast gloves padded with horsehair; Liston preferred Sammy Frager gloves which were foam-filled. Florio said he felt the Frager gloves did not provide enough padding across the knuckles. When Jack Nilon tried to say something, Florio shouted. 'You keep quiet. I don't know who you are, but I am Dan Florio, trainer of the champion.' D'Amato joined in; Nilon still wanted his say; Joe Polino, Liston's cut man, picked up one of the Everlast gloves and Florio snatched it back. It was all very silly, and the dispute rambled on for a while and then petered out. Afterwards, Florio was so steamed up, he grabbed the tie of writer George Whiting, from the *London Evening Standard* and said:

> You tell England there ain't gonna be no fight if they pull anything with the gloves. You understand? No fight. I don't care if it's one million dollars or ten million dollars. No fight. I seen guys in hospital and I seen other guys get killed with gloves like that.

The argument was reconvened on the day of the fight when it was the Commission's duty to run through the rules and sort out any administrative details that still needed to be completed. Nilon began protesting again about the Everlast gloves, but Liston cut through the big talk by trying on the gloves on display until he found a pair that fitted. They happened to be Everlast. He told Nilon: 'We'll be here all day. I'm going to use just one pair of gloves. Who's going to fight, you or me?'

The night before, Patterson had been driven to Chicago by his chauffeur, Ernest Fowler. Floyd's brother Ray was with him, so too were co-trainers Florio and Buster Watson. They settled in at the Oxford House Hotel. Floyd's mother, Annabelle, arrived with a friend. His wife Sandra was still undecided as to whether or not she could face it. His father stayed at home to look after Floyd's youngest brothers and sisters. It was decided that, as frosty as the relationship had become, D'Amato could be in the corner. Florio was the chief second, with Buster Watson and Florio's brother Nick also there.

Liston left it until the morning to travel up from Aurora Downs but arrived in plenty of time for the medical at 10.30 a.m., which was followed by the selection of the gloves, last run-through of the rules and the weigh-in.

D'Amato gave writers a last assessment for the evening editions – the fight would not start until 9.30 p.m. He predicted a Patterson win. As usual, not everything he said made complete sense, but he had such an air of authority about him that it sounded as if it did. He had the ability to command an audience's respect – even when that audience was a motley band of hard-bitten newsmen:

I believe Floyd's assets are of more value to him than whatever Liston has. I believe that Sonny is a predictable fighter . . . Floyd will not be intimidated. I wish I was as sure of going to heaven as I am that Patterson will not be intimidated.

When asked if he would think that way were he not connected to the champion, D'Amato replied:

Absolutely. I look at boxing coldly, without any emotion engendered by financial aspects or partisanship . . . Boxing is war. If you can deploy your own forces skilfully and at the proper time, you can defeat a superior force even if it's firmly entrenched in position.

Liston played to the gathering fans by trying on a giant white signed glove that might have weighed as much as 10 lb and was about three feet long. Somebody called out to ask if Patterson was his toughest fight.

'How do I know?' said Liston with a smile. 'I haven't fought him yet.' He added, 'He's a nice fighter.'

Joe Triner, the 68-year-old head of the Illinois Commission, ran through the rules that were routine enough for the time. Anyone knocked out of the ring could have a count of twenty instead of ten, and judges did not have to deduct a point from a boxer even if the referee, who would also score the fight, notified them specifically of a rule infraction. 'They don't have to take a point away just because he does.' Triner also said the names of the referee and two judges would not be made public until shortly before the fight. Nevertheless, the word had gone around that the refereeing job would go to Frank Sikora, a 63-year-old beer salesman who had done a good job in Patterson's defence against Brian London in Indianapolis in 1959.

At the weigh-in, in the Tally Ho Room on the ninth floor of the Chicago-Sheraton Hotel, the fighters offered their final quotes for newsmen.

Liston: 'Patterson is a pretty good fighter, but he's easy to knock down. I'm gonna knock him down and keep him down.'

Patterson: 'I am champion, and I mean to stay that way. Liston did all the talking, but he will discover that I may do little talking, but I do a lot of effective fighting. The battle is never going to be won on conversation.'

The fighters wore white towelling gowns. Liston arrived nearly half an hour late but still four minutes before Patterson. When a camera bulb exploded and made people jump, Liston burst out laughing. On the scales, Liston weighed 214 lb, Patterson 189 lb. When Sonny stared at him, Patterson refused to look back. 'See you tonight,' said the challenger. Patterson did not answer, turned and, strangely, asked where his security man was.

When the ceremony was done, Joe Louis signed autographs for about 15 minutes. Not many wanted the signatures of other champs like Jim Braddock, Barney Ross and Johnny Coulon. Cassius Clay posed for a photo with middleweight Henry Hank. Ross, according to Red Smith, went around asking what he could do for people.

Patterson said he would answer three questions. Nobody had anything much to ask him. Eventually they came up with what round he thought he would knock out Liston, what he thought of Liston and what he felt about conceding 25 lb. Patterson said he was prepared for 15 rounds, thought Liston was very good and very strong and that the weight difference did not matter. D'Amato, almost as if searching for a role for himself, questioned Joe Triner about what would happen in the event of a foul. Triner patiently explained the low-blow rule, that the protector was considered good enough to prevent a low blow incapacitating a man, and therefore if he went down and stayed down he would be counted out. When D'Amato questioned him further, Triner said the Commission and the referee would interpret other circumstances as they happened. D'Amato claimed it was all too vague, and Triner dismissed him: 'Just act very calm, Cus, you've done that plenty of times before.'

D'Amato tried to convince writers that Liston used a hypnotist to render himself immune to pain. If anyone needed a sign that D'Amato, who had never wanted the fight, was worried, in spite of his bold predictions, here it was.

Liston returned to his hotel suite several floors above where the weigh-in had been held and played cards with the bodyguards whose job it was to guard him until fight time, John 'Moose' Grayson and James Kelly. Also with him were his training team, wife Geraldine and her mother, Eva. In mid-afternoon, Sonny ate a 2 lb rare steak, his last meal before he entered the ring. At 7.45 p.m. he left the Chicago-Sheraton for the 15-minute journey to Comiskey Park. Geraldine stayed behind, pottering about the suite in a blue bathrobe, her hair in rollers. 'If he wins,' she told Georgie Anne Geyer of the *Chicago Daily News*, 'we'll feel it's God's will. If he loses, we'll feel it's God's will. No, I'm not nervous.' Geyer gave Geraldine's age as 30 (instead of 37) and declared her pretty and soft-spoken. Geraldine watched television and talked to her mother, then put on the outfit she had chosen for the post-fight celebration or commiseration: a gold-knit jacket and dress, and a mink stole. There were diamonds, too. 'I'm praying he'll win. Mostly, I'm just glad this tension will be over.'

When Frank Graham of the *New York Journal-American* returned from the weigh-in to a late breakfast with his wife and daughter at their hotel, he lamented the fact that in his preview of the fight he had picked Patterson. 'I just saw a dead man walking to the scales,' he said. 'He was all right when I saw him at Elgin. He must have died last night. He couldn't even look at Liston.' When asked about this later, Patterson said it meant nothing. 'I never look at any of my opponents in the face. It's no sign of being afraid. I just find it difficult to look them in the face.'

For the final editions before the fight took place, the *New York Post* canvassed leading figures in the African American population in the city as to who they wanted to win. The reasons differed, but the pick was the same: Patterson. A judge and civil rights activist Hubert Delany said: 'Patterson's not only an alumnus of Wiltwyck, on whose board I serve, he's a real gentleman and a credit to his profession. Can I say that of his opponent?' Baseball legend Jackie Robinson said: 'He has contributed so much to our way of life . . . Liston has no sense of responsibility of what the championship should mean . . . Floyd will still be champion, win, lose or draw.' Earl Brown, a planning and redevelopment commissioner, said he knew no sports figure that he admired more than Patterson. 'I know him,' he said. 'I don't know Liston.' And Percy Sutton, Manhattan representative for the National Association for the Advancement of Colored People, said: 'Hell, let's stop kidding, I'm for Patterson because he represents us better than Liston ever could or would.'

And, as always, there were the cynics, the knockers, those who find it so desperately hard to give anyone credit for anything. Teddy Brenner, matchmaker at Madison Square Garden, said one of those sceptics declared to him: 'Liston is a bum. The bum's got no defence against a hook. He gets sore at you if you miss him.'

'Who you picking?' said Brenner in an attempt at dry humour.

'Liston,' said the man. 'The other bum can't fight.'

Chicago's American revealed it had polled 50 writers in the press room and Patterson came out on top 28–22. Given that there were 648 accredited members of the media, that might not have been particularly representative, but among those who picked the defending champion were Frank Butler from the *News of the World* (points decision), Floyd's friend and ghost-writer, Milton Gross (ko 8), Dan Daniel of the *New York World Telegram* and *Ring* magazine (ko 10), Bill Liston of the *Boston Traveler* (ko 9) and Gay Talese from the *New York Times* (ko 9). Nat Fleischer, editor of the *Ring*, had already said he thought Patterson would win, as did Steve Fagan of the *Daily Sketch* and Donald Saunders of the *Daily Telegraph*. George Whiting of the *London Evening Standard* predicted Patterson would win in the later rounds 'against the weight of evidence and at the risk of next-day jibes'. Those for Liston included the former fighter from

Finland, Elis Ask (ko 10), London writers Peter Wilson (ko 8) Jack Wood (ko 7) Sam Leitch (ko 5) Harry Carpenter (ko 5), Desmond Hackett (ko 5) and Alan Hoby (ko 6). American writers Al Buck, Red Smith, Barney Nagler and Eddie Miller all said Liston and varied their predictions between rounds six and eight.

Barney Ross, the old three-weight champion, said he picked Liston to win inside five, but added the rider that if he failed to win early, then it was possible Patterson would take over. 'He must get Patterson out of there in a hurry, and I believe he will. Liston is a hungry man and a violent man . . . just too big and strong. He can hurt you with any punch that lands.' Ross felt, contrary to popular opinion, Patterson was not any faster than Liston. 'His hands are fast, but he isn't exceptionally fast on his feet,' he said. The old champion, who had held the lightweight, light-welter and welterweight titles in the 1930s, said he felt Floyd's pride would not allow him to run, that he would go to Liston and would be knocked out.

Rocky Marciano arrived late, said he preferred not to pick a winner, but offered his take on how he would have beaten both of them. He said he would have swarmed all over Patterson and driven him into the corners, while he would get inside Liston and work his body, then switch to the head to knock him out. 'The big problem,' he said, 'would be escaping that terrific left jab he shoots at you.' Marciano was asked if, six years on from his retirement, he still might make a comeback to box the winner. He said no, it was too late and he was happy working for a public relations firm in his home town of Brockton, Massachusetts.

Comiskey Park held 49,000 people for fights. There were 8,000 seats on the pitch area, with tickets rising from $10 at the back to $100 at ringside. Only around half would be needed. Maybe in the end fans just didn't believe they would get value for money. Pressmen filled six rows at ringside, photographers crowded together on the ring apron, and for those not allocated accommodation close to the action there was an overspill press area in the stands.

As people filed into the arena, it was a cloudy evening. A cool wind swirled around the stadium, blowing the cigar smoke from the ringside seats away from the arc lights.

12

THAT BLANKNESS OF NOT KNOWING

On the night of 25 September 1962, at Comiskey Park, home of the Chicago White Sox, Charles 'Sonny' Liston blew away world heavyweight champion Floyd Patterson in two minutes and six seconds of the first round.

Hugh Bradley of the *New York Journal-American* believed the truth of what was about to happen to him dawned on Patterson as fight time neared and he was simply unable to perform. 'He was a hollow shell,' wrote Bradley.

Before the fight, the former champions paraded in the ring – Joe Louis, Rocky Marciano, Ezzard Charles, James J. Braddock, Ingemar Johansson, Barney Ross, Gene Fullmer, Johnny Coulon – and the light-heavyweight champion Archie Moore strutted around in cape and gown, twirling a cane like a villain from the streets of Dickensian London.

Mayor Richard J. Daley was ringside with other Chicago politicians. According to the police, most of the city's hoodlums stayed away.

Grey-shirted referee Frank Sikora climbed into the ring; judges Johnny Bray and Harold Marovitz took their seats beneath the ropes. Patterson's brother-in-law, Mickey Alan, sang 'The Star Spangled Banner'. Floyd stood still, head bowed in respect. Liston ignored the etiquette, kept moving, shadow-boxing, staring.

Patterson, 25 lb the lighter man, did not use his speed to move and confuse Liston. He crouched in front of him – a tactic that appeared to be deliberate. When he did get inside, he tried to tie up Liston instead of fight with him. He threw his trademark leaping left hook and missed. Liston took his time, prodded home a couple of stiff jabs, missed with several sweeping hooks, but even when Patterson blocked right hands on his arms, he seemed to feel the impact. Liston hit air with a long left uppercut, connected with some stiff jabs, then landed the first of his heavy, thumping left hooks to the body. The effect was visible. He pounced, a left hook to the ribs was blocked, one to the head shook the champion up.

Bradley and Reg Gutteridge, whose reporting positions were near the

Patterson corner, said trainer Dan Florio kept yelling at Floyd: 'Lower, lower, lower.'

Someone was calling out: 'Eyes open, Floyd. Keep 'em open.'

The eyes were open, but there was no light, no fight, in them. Liston shook him off in the clinches, hurt him in the open. All Patterson landed in two minutes were two light jabs and a body shot that had nothing behind it. Liston just brushed him aside. Two left hooks, with Liston's right hand cupped illegally around the back of the champion's neck, spun him into the ropes. Patterson lurched off balance, and as he straightened, his legs stiffening, Liston had time to set himself and crack in another big left hook. Patterson began to stumble, a right hand seemed no more than a glancing blow, but then Liston landed a final left hook to the side of the head. Patterson crashed to the canvas on to his side. Somehow he struggled up but after referee Sikora had spread his arms to signal the completion of the count.

Liston walked over to commiserate, and they spoke briefly. As Patterson stood in his corner, he rested his head on the shoulder of Cus D'Amato. 'He didn't say anything,' said D'Amato later. 'What really was there to say?' Patterson was amazed when somebody told him he had done this. He said he had no recollection of it and tried to make light of it. 'I must have still been groggy,' he said, '. . . it couldn't have been me. It must have been somebody who looked like me. Possibly my brother . . .'

Cassius Clay, in a smart suit with black bow tie, climbed on to the apron on the far side of the ring and looked across at D'Amato and Patterson, his mouth opened slightly, just watching. Floyd's mother Annabelle clambered up the ring steps in a bright blue frock to console him.

His wife, Sandra, had made up her mind to be there at the last minute and had flown in. She admitted she didn't see any of the action. She never did. In a later interview with the *New York Journal-American*, she said:

> I'm not afraid of Floyd getting beat. But I'm very afraid he could get hurt. That's why I go to every fight even though I have to close my eyes . . .
>
> When people stood up and started screaming, I didn't stand. I didn't look. I go because I feel if Floyd is getting badly hurt – like say Kid Paret – and nobody stops it, I can. I don't want to see it. But I can do something if I'm at ringside.

(Kid Paret was Benny Paret, who was killed in a world welterweight title fight with Emile Griffith in March 1962.)

On the way from the ring, Floyd's mother told Al Coxon, who wrote a strange colour piece for the *Chicago Daily News* about gatecrashing and sitting in the $100 seats: 'He didn't get hurt, that's the main thing. He's still young and there's a next time.'

Annabelle also met reporters in the dressing-room while some were talking to Floyd. 'I'm upset,' she said, when one commented on how calm she seemed. 'But I'm keeping my emotions inside.'

Television journalism was in its infancy. Screened around the nation, the interviewer could not apparently come to terms with what he had just witnessed. As the re-run was played out, he asked Liston: 'Were you impressed by Floyd's speed?'

The new champion said: 'I sure was . . .'

At ringside, Tom Tannas, who once managed world champion Ezzard Charles and had turned down a piece of Liston in the late 1950s, said the new champion could reign a long time.

> He's a man unafraid because he's never had the imagination to be afraid of anything, to know what he should be afraid of, or why. And he could be a fine champion if they'll help him along. He'll be meeting people on a better level now.
>
> You know what they could do? Take him on an exhibition tour. Let the public see him.

Red Smith said, as people filed away from the stadium, they seemed 'bewildered, disgusted, resentful'. A peanut seller was calling out: 'Peanuts! Ten cents! Here, you get your money's worth . . .'

Meanwhile, in his dressing-room, Liston told his bodyguards to fetch Geraldine. Then he admitted reporters and was positively effusive. He said:

> Maybe this is corny. I've done things out of the ring that have been very wrong. Everybody knows that. I'm not copping a plea that I never had a chance.
>
> Being champion gives me a feeling I never have had. If the public will give me a chance to prove it, I will be a worthy champion. Like Patterson has been. And more like Joe Louis, who was one of the first to congratulate me.

Liston said he would honour the return-clause contract because that was what he was contracted to do, but also because he saw that as a promise to Patterson:

> Patterson gave me a break by fighting me. I'm ready to obey the contract.

For his sake, I wonder if he will be wise to go in against me again.

Patterson always hides away between fights. I want to be a man who can be seen and who they can be proud of. I always go to all the Golden Gloves bouts, the small club fights and anywhere else where there is a fight show. I think the champ should get around and show himself. And that's what I'm gonna do.

Liston said:

Three left hooks to the head did it. I threw one right, but it didn't do much damage . . . I hit him with one that started him on the way . . . He had been breaking clean every time the referee asked us to, but after this punch he hung on. I got the idea I must have hit him good.

When asked what words had been exchanged between them in the ring afterwards, Liston said Floyd had told him: 'If the public let bygones be bygones, you will be a good champ', adding: 'I thanked him for giving me the opportunity. Then I told him, "I'll be as much of a man toward you as you were to me. And you were a heck of a good man."'

Strangely, somebody felt it a pertinent line of enquiry to check if Patterson had hurt him at all.

'Only once,' he said, smiling. 'That was when the man said "nine", and it looked like he might get up before "ten".'

Geraldine Liston had gone to only one of Sonny's fights, back in 1954, when he had won inside two rounds, but didn't like the effect it had on her nerves. 'I couldn't stand it,' she said. On normal fight nights, she watched on television to see him introduced, then switched off. Sometimes she just tried to curl up with a book in the hotel room, sometimes simply prayed that he would be all right.

She told Georgie Anne Geyer, the Chicago journalist who was allowed to stay with her in the suite while the fight was on: 'We had hard times in those early days. He was in trouble and now he can see how bad it was. If he had had more opportunity as a boy, it would have been different.'

She had grown nervous only at 9.30 p.m., the time the fight was scheduled to start. Three minutes later, Geyer said reporters were knocking at the door, telling her Sonny had won. 'You're joking,' she said, then screamed for joy and jumped up and down. By 10 p.m. Geraldine was being driven the short distance to Comiskey Park.

The shattered Patterson spent 25 minutes in his locked dressing-room with his mother, his trainers, Cus D'Amato and a doctor, and then met the press. It took a piece of deception to get him to hurry the process along. Patterson's dressing-room turned out to be the baseball umpires' quarters, and a pressman finally hit on the idea of phoning them. He declared himself to be 'Captain Riley', who had the motorcycle escort away from the arena waiting for him.

The writer heard D'Amato, who had answered the call, tell Patterson, but the newly dethroned champion said he would not leave until he had faced the writers. The door was opened and they filed in.

Milton Gross, who had written Patterson's autobiography, had been allowed open access to Floyd's dressing-room and had actually reached it before the fallen champion. He wrote in the next day's *New York Post*: 'As he came into the room, there was a look of complete mystification on his face. He was not cut, not bruised, not in pain. There was just that blankness of not knowing.'

Sitting on a chair, Floyd told the media, barely above a whisper: 'I feel all right . . . I'll take a short rest.' He said yes, he wanted the return, then he said he hoped he would do a little better next time:

> My feelings were hurt more than my body. I never was unconscious. I did stumble getting out of the ring, but that was an accident. I could see every punch Liston threw except the last one . . . The last one hurt. I remember that one as a right. Everybody else says it was a left hook.
>
> I should have started faster. I clinched a lot because Liston was moving in on me . . . I had no plan . . . I should have started faster than I did. Liston's a fast starter. But it's usually the procedure to feel out an opponent in the first round. He surprised me . . .

Patterson wished Liston well: 'Sonny can be a nice fellow. I hope he will be a credit to all of us.'

Someone asked if he would go back into seclusion. He waited, bowed his head and nodded.

One member of the Patterson team said D'Amato wept in the dressing-room but calmed down when his old protégé arrived.

Florio said:

> Our plan was to make Liston miss. While he [Patterson] was trying to do it, he got hit behind the ear. Liston is no different than we figured. He lumbers forward with his punches.
>
> Can Floyd beat Liston in a return? The answer is yes. I am so sure that

if he doesn't do it, I don't want a dime for my work.

D'Amato sounded as if he was still trying to work it all out. 'I definitely don't think he should retire,' he said. 'It wasn't as if he took a brutal beating . . .' He admitted he hadn't seen the punch that took Patterson out.

Looking back to early in Patterson's career, D'Amato said:

> He took a punch in the gym. But if you get hit with something you get hit. Liston could be hit, too. In fact, the thing that surprised me was that Liston didn't even seem to be aggressive. I figured he'd press, press, press. He didn't.
>
> Floyd made some mistakes, though. Someone told me he was coming out of a weave with his hand down when he got hit the first hook. I don't know.

A sparring partner, Ben Skelton, said to a *Sports Illustrated* writer: 'He never did the things he trained all those months to do. It wasn't that he couldn't do them. He did them beautifully just a few days before the fight.'

Marciano still seemed surprised by what he had witnessed. 'I never realised Liston had so much power,' he said.

Cassius Clay was downbeat, appeared saddened. 'It was a disgrace to professional boxing,' he said to Leonard Shecter of the *New York Post*.

Watching from the crowd was Joseph 'Pep' Barone, Liston's old manager. 'I'm glad for Sonny,' said Barone. 'And happy he won the title. I only wish I could have been in the corner.'

The new champion took his wife out to celebrate at the Sahara Inn, where the owner, Manny Skar, had thrown a victory party. Skar has been variously described as a Mob gambling functionary and Mob associate. Three years later, he was murdered outside his Chicago apartment in a hit by Joey 'the Clown' Lombardo.

Skar invited 600 guests, including Barney Ross and the singer Patti Page, to toast the new champion in the Regency Room of his hotel. Sonny and Geraldine arrived around 1 a.m., posed for photographs behind a giant cake and took the cheers of the hand-picked well-wishers. 'The champ for the next 20 years!' Skar called out, excitedly, as he held up Liston's hand for photographers.

Sonny signed scraps of paper, ticket stubs from the fight, dollar bills. Geraldine helped with the spelling of the names of the people who asked. 'No cheques, please!' he said, soaking it up, and then he and Geraldine sat down for a meal.

He ate roast beef and had a piece of his celebration cake but did not drink alcohol, not even a celebratory glass of champagne. They stayed until 3 a.m. according to John Kuenster of the *Chicago Daily News*.

There had been a victory party prepared, too, for Patterson, at the Oxford House, with a cake waiting in the lobby and a reception organised by the manager, Leonard Trinkina. Word came through that Floyd would not be returning and that someone would call to pick up his luggage. The cake was divided between bellhops, a doorman and the elevator operator.

The next morning, a writer phoned 64-year-old Helen Liston in Forrest City, Arkansas. A neighbour had told her the news that her son was the heavyweight champion of the world. Helen said she had not expected him to win but that her son had phoned to say he would try to visit her the next month. 'I told him I was very proud,' she said. 'And I told him to be a good boy and to use the money to prepare for a nice home.'

Al Bolan, a fresh-faced, clean-cut 33 year old from Brooklyn, whose company Championship Sports Inc. promoted the fight, did not appear fazed by the one-sided finish or the half-full house. He said he wanted to arrange the contracted rematch within six months.

Bolan ran Championship Sports with his brother Tom, a Wall Street lawyer, who dealt with the legal and contractual issues; Al was the organiser, the public face. The third of the brothers, Pat, was a stockholder. Roy Cohn and Bill Fugazy were other partners, according to Dan Parker of the *New York Mirror*.

Bolan had reasons to be pleased. In spite of the fact that officials from the Internal Revenue Services temporarily seized the closed-circuit gate receipts pending further investigation, the figures broke down as follows.

Paid attendance: 18,894
Gross gate: $665,420
Net gate: $556,195
Patterson's share: (45%) $250,253
Liston's share: (12.5%) $69,515
Promoter's share: $236,351
Park rental: $40,000
Guaranteed ancillary rights: $2 million
TV firm: $300,000
Patterson's ancillary rights: (55%) $935,000
Liston's ancillary rights: (12.5%) against gross $2 million
Promoter's share: $552,550

Patterson's estimated total: $1,185,253
Liston's estimated total: $282,015
Promoter's estimated total: $788,851

The ancillary rights centred on the closed-circuit screenings in 320 cinemas, theatres and arenas around the country. The total number of seats available was 978,234. There was a planned blackout in Chicago and for a 100-mile radius, so that local people were not deterred from going to the live event. Unfortunately there was also an unscheduled blackout in St Paul, Minnesota, and another one at the Fabian Fox Theatre on Flatbush Avenue, Brooklyn, where fans missed the fight because of power cuts. The Brooklyn ticketholders were so furious that they stormed the box office, demanding their money back. The police were called in and managed to get through to them that money would be refunded. In St Paul, where 4,200 people had paid $6 a head to see a blank screen, fights broke out as the annoyed fans drifted away.

Championship Sports had actually sold off the ancillary rights for $2 million to Graff-Reiner-Smith Enterprises of Los Angeles. The Internal Revenue Services raid, to seize the closed-circuit takings, was meticulously planned and supposedly the costliest they had ever attempted. Simultaneously, agents with synchronised watches raided 260 theatres just as the show was about to begin. The IRS said local theatres were allowed to keep their share of 45 cents of each dollar. However, the other 55 per cent would remain with the IRS until the tax details had been settled. Of that 55, 15 was to go to Graff-Reiner-Smith, the rest divided between Patterson (55), Championship Sports Inc (32.5) and Liston (12.5). The *New York Times* reported that the IRS took $2,074,500 from Championship Sports and $1,710,500 from Graff-Reiner-Smith. Neither company had filed tax returns for the previous year. 'Certain aspects of the financial arrangements for this particular fight caused Internal Revenue to believe that special steps should be taken to insure the payment of all taxes due by all parties concerned,' the IRS statement read. The *New York Times* also quoted an unnamed official as saying: 'We're trying to freeze, tie up or seize this money wherever we can.'

Tom Bolan, president of Championship Sports, said the problem had been caused by a tax avoidance loophole that allowed for some payments to be made over a span of seventeen years – this fitted in with Patterson's story of how his money from the fight was to be invested over a similar time – and therefore tax on those monies would be raised at a lower rate than if the full amount had been paid in one hit. Later talks brought a settlement. The IRS had made its point. However, it dragged on more than three months. Liston, for whom all that was way too complicated, was unimpressed.

Back to the night of 25 September – Sports Programs Inc. of New York handled the job of filming the fight, with a 95-man crew under the guidance of producer-director Jack Lubell. There were two private lines, in addition to those sent to cinemas. One carried the fight live to the White House, where President John F. Kennedy sat down to watch. The other was to the Hollywood home of Frank Sinatra.

Murray Robinson watched with around 3,500 fans who had paid $6.50 each at the Academy of Music on 14th Street in New York. The broadcast was problematic. 'The picture was a Picasso,' he wrote. 'Not all the time, though. Sometimes it looked like something by Toulouse-Lautrec.' The sound, he said, was as if the whole thing was being broadcast from inside a seashell. As the customers trailed away, Robinson reported that one said: 'Well, if the picture was any better, the fight would have looked worse.'

Meanwhile, Ted Poston was in Loew's Victoria Theatre in Harlem, where 2,500 people had paid $6.75 for their seats and many others had apparently gatecrashed to stand in the aisles. The audience was almost exclusively African American, almost exclusively on Patterson's side. Poston said at the end a stocky, conservatively dressed man rose to his feet and said simply: 'God help us.' Outside, Poston reported that nobody celebrated in the streets; people just went home. 'Harlem had an early curfew last night,' he wrote.

Dan Parker took it upon himself to slaughter the character of the new champion in a general lament for the state of the fight game:

> There will be a disposition on the part of most boxing fans, moved by the American spirit of fair play, to give him [Liston] a chance to prove himself worthy of the title. Nowadays, a good prison record is an asset rather than a liability in the prizefighting business, controlled as it is by the criminal underworld which has no use for fighters and managers who won't play ball.
>
> The leopard cannot change its spots, and this Big Cat, Liston, certainly didn't impress anyone as a penitent sinner, eager to atone for his errors during his training period. He is probably the most anti-social fighter in history.

Peter Wilson wrote: 'A rogue elephant is the heavyweight champion of the world.'

Borrowing the line Jack London had used in his report of the Jack Johnson–Tommy Burns championship bout more than half a century earlier, Wilson echoed: 'Fight? There was no fight. A massacre, yes, a contemptuous display of raw power over timid defence, yes, a steamroller running over frozen peas, yes, yes, YES. But a fight – NEVER.'

Hugh Bradley of the *New York Journal-American*, wrote: 'A scowling mass of a man called Charles (Sonny) Liston today is heavyweight champion of the world.' He went on to describe Liston as 'an erstwhile Arkansas cotton picker, St Louis labour goon and resident of various jails', adding later that he 'looks as forbidding as something thought up for an Alfred Hitchcock movie'.

His colleague, Frank Graham, said Patterson couldn't bring himself to look at Liston during the referee's instructions. 'He was gone,' said Graham. 'There was nothing inside him.'

John P. Carmichael, sports editor of the *Chicago Daily News*, called it:

> plain, old-fashioned murder, so premeditated that it looked like a put-up job. Hardly anybody cheered when Sonny Liston walked down the steps from his corner, wearing the invisible crown of the ring empire. They had seen and still didn't believe.

Reg Gutteridge described Liston as 'a muscular mass of menace . . . Patterson, gentle introvert son of a Carolina dustman [he was actually a railroad worker], looked a dainty imposter by comparison. It was as one-sided as a lynching.'

Arthur Daley, commenting for the *New York Times*, felt Patterson had let down the championship's heroic legacy:

> The heavyweight champion of the world, no less, was so stricken by feelings of pacifism that he barely went through the motions of defending the title. Since he threw no punches of consequence or effectiveness, it almost could be assumed that he had sufficient time to keep up his guard and protect himself. But Liston just bulled past those feeble shields and knocked him out. It was a disgraceful exhibition . . .

Daley said the end came so suddenly that writers began arguing about the finishing punch. Afterwards, Liston was to say it was three left hooks, but referee Frank Sikora leaned over the ropes to the press rows and called out: 'That final right was the one that finished him.' Daley pointed out: 'Liston and Sikora were closest to the operation and couldn't agree. Patterson, an innocent bystander, didn't know what hit him.'

A.S. 'Doc' Young, in the first of the Liston biographies, reported one would-have-been-ringsider's irritation that he hadn't even got to his seat when the fight was over. That was his fault.

Milton Gross, in his next day report in the *New York Post*, also recorded a conversation in the Patterson corner that suggests they were struggling to take in what had happened:

'What did he get hit with?' said Cus D'Amato.

'I don't know,' said Buster Watson.

'I don't understand it,' said Dan Florio. 'I didn't see what he got hit with. It didn't seem like anything.'

One of the Championship Sports partners, Roy Cohn, said he had missed the knockdown punch because he was taking a prescribed tranquilliser at that vital moment. He looked up and Patterson was on the canvas.

Frank Butler, boxing correspondent for the *News of the World* in London, who had picked Patterson to win on points, called his performance 'the most wretched show of any world heavyweight champion in the history of boxing'.

Robert L. Teague, who had once argued for boxing to be banned on moral grounds, also in the *New York Times*, lamented: 'Nobody got their money's worth . . . with the exception of Sonny Liston.'

Budd Schulberg wrote in *Playboy* that the Chicago fans would not forget the charade they had witnessed. 'It will be a long time,' he wrote, 'before Roy Cohn and the Brothers Bolan lure them back to Comiskey, even if it's scaled down from five bucks ringside to four bits in the bleachers.'

Red Smith, meanwhile, reminded readers that it wasn't the worst heavyweight title fight Chicago had ever seen:

> It was here old J.J. Walcott sat in sad but profitable reverie while the seconds ticked away in the first round of a title match with Rocky Marciano. Floyd, at least, wasn't counting his money while he reclined on the wall-to-wall canvas. He was knocked out.

After the fight, as his team returned to the hotel and waited for him, Floyd drove away from Comiskey Park with Sandra. It was customary when a title changed hands for both fighters, not just the winner, to attend a press conference the following day.

Milton Gross was at the hotel, waiting too, along with two spiritual advisers, the Reverends Mathew Shanley and Edward McCall. Gross said nobody knew where Patterson had gone until assistant trainer Buster Watson came down a corridor with the news that the police said he had gone home to New York. It took another two hours for the lawyer, Julius November, to confirm that. Word also had it that Patterson had fled disguised in a false beard and moustache.

However, Chicago newsman Bob Smith claimed Patterson did not keep his departure a secret, telling people who stayed long enough in the dressing-room that he would return to New York. Outside, according to Smith, the deposed champion had to wait 15 minutes while his black Cadillac could be retrieved from a locked parking lot. Someone tried forcing the padlock with a hammer and a metal pipe. Eventually a hacksaw did the job.

Patterson's mother tried to explain his reaction as best she could:

> Floyd's a man that has a lot of pride, and I guess he just wants to be alone. I guess he just don't want to face the people because he always liked to give them his best. And it just didn't come out that way.

She added that she was pleased he had not beaten the count because if he had, Liston might have hurt him badly.

Sports Illustrated writer Gilbert Rogin later said Patterson also had the false beard and moustache with him in the second Johansson fight and even the mismatch against Tom McNeeley. Patterson, in acknowledging that, joked: 'If I had lost to McNeeley I would have them on in the ring . . .'

Jimmy Cannon wrote in the *New York Journal-American*: 'No bank robber ever moved faster from the scene of a crime.'

The night of the fight, with his brother so badly exposed and now on his way home, 19-year-old Ray Patterson, himself a Golden Gloves champion, felt the urge to drive the 42 miles back to Marycrest Farm, no doubt reflecting on the contrast between his return and their leaving, when Floyd was the heavyweight champion of the world and those around him were filled with optimism and pride. Ray didn't call on Mrs Widman but went straight to their training headquarters. He walked up the hill to the small white clapboard house where Floyd had lived those past weeks. Nothing, nobody was there. Even the animals that had wandered around outside had gone somewhere else.

Back at the Patterson family home at 15 East Fifth Street, Mount Vernon, New York, Floyd's father was dismayed. He had bet as big as he could afford on Floyd and could not believe the result. 'I thought he would win, I was sure he would win,' he said. Floyd's sister, Denna, reiterated what her mother had said immediately after the fight. 'The main thing is he's not hurt, that's the main thing.'

Archie Moore, 45 years young and shortly to box Cassius Clay, declared that he was sturdy enough to outpoint Liston over 15 rounds. Nobody was very interested. Clay, who would soon trounce Moore in four rounds, declared himself 'The Greatest', announced he would beat Moore in four and Liston in eight. 'What happened . . . was an embarrassment to boxing,' he said. 'The champion of the world should be able to take a beating longer than that.'

The next day, the press gathered to hear what the new champion thought, having slept on his achievement. Instead of Liston they found a somewhat dishevelled Norman Mailer at the microphone. The great novelist appeared to be in the process of creating a new fiction. He declared to his fellows of the Fourth Estate that in his opinion Patterson had won, as he himself had predicted, in the sixth round. When Liston arrived, Mailer was escorted, supported, to the exit. Liston seemed oblivious, sat down with his arms folded. He smiled and answered mostly innocuous questions, though he did seem mildly disturbed that the Internal Revenue Service had seized assets from the fight. 'From what I hear on TV this morning, I'm not gonna get paid.'

'How soon,' asked a writer, 'will you give Patterson a return bout?'

'Soon as I get paid.'

Throughout the benign questioning, Mailer, who had somehow managed to perform a U-turn at the door, was on his feet demanding to ask a question. Other hacks, wanting to hear Liston, shouted him down until eventually the new champion said: 'Leave the bum talk.'

Instead of asking a question, Mailer declared: 'I picked Patterson to win in the sixth round. By a one-punch knockout.'

Liston smiled: 'He's still drunk.'

After a few more questions, Mailer found his way to the front and said to Liston: 'You called me a bum.'

'I call you a bum and you are a bum. Everybody call me a bum. I'm a bigger bum than you, because I'm bigger. OK, bum?'

Liston, dressed in an elegant dark-grey suit, his big hands freshly manicured, said he thought he could keep the title for at least six years and, the taxman permitting, would like to box four times each year. He admitted he was contractually bound to offer Patterson the return, but it was up to Floyd whether or not he wanted it. After that, he said he would give all the contenders a chance. 'Maybe a better man can knock me off, but I don't think so. Time I get to 34, a fellow might come along and do it. Or I might get rich like Rocky Marciano and retire.'

Of his immediate plans, he said: 'Geraldine and me are going on a three weeks' vacation. We're going to relax and enjoy being champion.' He smiled when asked if he would be driving his big car himself – his driving was notoriously wayward – and said: 'No comment!'

He thought they might buy a new, big house but would wait until he was paid for the Patterson fight to decide. He was keen that he was not criticised for showing off his new wealth. He might also consider boxing exhibitions around the world. 'Geraldine would like the travelling. Me, too. I'd make some money, too.'

When he eventually emerged after a few weeks, Patterson told Gilbert Rogin: 'I definitely wasn't afraid. I wish to emphasise that.' He also insisted D'Amato had been wrong to have him avoid Liston for so long.

He also gave a stark, surprisingly candid admission:

> Boy, that was a terrible performance. I fought a fight that wasn't a fight. My mind just wasn't on the fight. It was what I call a lingering mind. Instead of forgetting everything but my opponent, my mind just lingered from here to there to the other place. The fact that my mind lingers is something I can't control.

Former heavyweight champion Gene Tunney had watched the fight in a theatre while on a business trip to Seattle. He called it a terrible hoax and blamed Patterson. 'He was so frightened he didn't even box. Can anyone imagine the champion holding on in the first clinch? And if they ever meet again the same thing will happen.'

James J. Braddock took a more sympathetic view:

> You can't say Patterson was scared to death because he kept ploughing forward, head down, right into the range of Liston's fists. The kindest thing you can say is that he fought stupidly, like an amateur.

Jimmy Cannon wrote that any boxing commission that sanctioned a rematch should be impeached:

> There is no reason for a return match. It was a disgraceful burlesque of a championship fight. But today the promoters are discussing it with a cynicism that is insulting even for the most unethical sport ever practised in this country.

Cannon said the fight had established Patterson as the worst champion 'in all the ages of boxing'. He dismissed him as an imposter who had been exposed, worse even than poor old Primo Carnera.

Cannon, in the *New York Journal-American* on 27 September 1962, went on to lambast Patterson as inadequate from the beginning of his reign, and of D'Amato he said:

[He] used the dirty statesmanship of the racket to protect this ungrateful and egotistical parody of a pug from qualified opponents.

He ducked Eddie Machen and Zora Folley when they were identified as the best in the heavyweight class. Cus the Mus selected such basket cases as Pete Rademacher, Roy Harris, Tom McNeeley and Brian London.

Cannon also claimed that D'Amato imposed an American representative, one of his cronies, on Brian London at a cost of 10 per cent. He tried the same thing with Ingemar Johansson, but the Swede complained about the 'clandestine arrangement' and, in danger of being exposed, D'Amato's man was withdrawn.

Cannon said D'Amato deliberately took the McNeeley fight out of Boston because he could not appoint his own referee. Instead, he had it moved to Toronto where the commission would allow Jersey Joe Walcott to take charge. Walcott used to be trained by Dan Florio, who was with Patterson. He said D'Amato also had another old friend, Tommy Loughran, appointed to control the Rademacher fight in Seattle.

Cannon made it plain that he believed the fights were 'on the level' but were examples of D'Amato's controlling nature, his belief in the need for insurance. He also said it was D'Amato who was responsible for underestimating Johansson in 1959. When he, Cannon, had telephoned D'Amato from Sweden to tell him Johansson had knocked out Eddie Machen in one round, Cus had replied: 'It only proves Machen can't fight.'

13

STILL THE BAD GUY

On the flight from Chicago to Philadelphia, Sonny Liston was filled to overflowing with pride. He sat next to the only journalist he ever really knew as a friend, Jack McKinney. McKinney said Liston was especially proud because he had received word before he left the Chicago-Sheraton that there was to be an official greeting and ticker-tape parade in his adopted home city. Certainly, he had received a telegram of congratulations from the Mayor, James H.J. Tate. It read:

> Your feat demonstrates that a man's past does not have to dictate his future.
> I know all Philadelphians join with me in extending best wishes for a successful reign and that you will wear the crown in the fine tradition set by Philadelphia champions before you.

The past, the past, still they couldn't say a nice thing to him without bringing up the past.

On the day of the fight, incidentally, Mayor Tate had formally entered Philadelphia's bid to host the 1968 Olympic Games.

Liston knew he had to act appropriately, say the right things, make the people glad they turned out to welcome him back. At that moment, there is absolutely no doubt that Liston wanted to show his better side, in the belief that people would like and respect him for it. He might never be able to persuade the Dan Parkers of the world, but he believed he could reach the ordinary men and women who lived out their lives as he had, often down on their luck, taking the occasional wrong turn and scrabbling to stay afloat.

On the 90-minute flight, he worked out what he would say in his speech, bouncing ideas off McKinney, who eventually wrote it down. According to McKinney's notes, Liston told him:

I want to reach my people. I want to reach them and tell them, 'You don't have to worry about me disgracing you. You won't have to worry about me stopping your progress.'

I want to go to coloured churches and coloured neighbourhoods. I know it was in the papers that the better class of coloured people were hoping I'd lose, even praying I'd lose, because they were afraid I wouldn't know how to act.

I remember one thing so clear about listening to Joe Louis fight on the radio when I was a kid. I never remember a fight the announcer didn't say about Louis: 'A great fighter and a credit to his race.' Remember? That used to make me feel real proud inside.

I don't mean to be saying I'm just going to be the champion of my own people. It says now I'm the world's champion, and that's just the way it's going to be. I want to go to a lot of places, like orphan homes and reform schools.

I'll be able to say, 'Kid, I know it's tough for you, and it might even get tougher. But don't give up on the world. Good things can happen if you let them.'

Liston also apparently answered questions on the plane ride from Gilbert Rogin of *Sports Illustrated*. When Rogin told him Patterson was being criticised as 'yellow', the new champion said: 'There's a big difference between having fear in you and being a coward…Patterson had fear in him, but he wasn't no coward.'

McKinney said as they waited for the plane door to open, Liston straightened his tie and his hat, anxious to look right for the photographs. For the people. Then he stepped outside, looked around, hesitated. All he could see were a few scattered journalists, public relations people and airport staff. McKinney said:

I watched Sonny. His eyes swept the whole scene. He was extremely intelligent, and he understood immediately what it meant. His Adam's Apple moved slightly. You could feel the deflation, see the look of hurt in his eyes. It was almost like a silent shudder went through him. He had been deliberately snubbed. Philadelphia wanted nothing to do with him.

It was going to be a whole new world. What happened in Philadelphia that day was a turning point in his life. He was still the bad guy. He was the personification of evil. And that's the way it was going to remain. He was devastated. I knew from that point on that the world would never get to know the Sonny that I knew.

Larry Merchant, later expert boxing analyst for Home Box Office, but at that time sports editor of the *Philadelphia Daily News*, had written that while a ticker-tape parade might be in order, it would be appropriate to use as confetti shredded arrest warrants. Liston was hurt by that.

> First thing I thought was, 'I'll never speak to that guy again.' Then I thought, 'No, why be as small as him? I'll make myself be nice to him.' It's guys like him I have to show, not the guys that do want to give me a chance.

However, the hurt would endure. He had the title he had always craved. He had something that should make a man respected. Yet even in the town he had been trying to call home they wouldn't begin the process of embracing him. For a brief spell, he tried to earn respect. Joan Younger Dickinson wrote a long, in-depth interview with both him and Geraldine at home in Philadelphia. Sonny was good-natured but admitted the pressure of trying to do the right thing was difficult. Dickinson wrote that Liston had two dreams, to build a gym for young people in the city and to buy a farm in the country so that he and Geraldine could have more peace. He was busy with visits to churches, hospitals and child-care institutions. 'I want to be a good champ,' he said. 'I like to go where it will be most useful to the public, but I don't think I can take it much longer at this pace.' He also said: 'At home's about the only place I can be calm any more. I figure if I can get out in the country, get a little land, maybe ten acres, I can move around a bit without getting bothered.' When asked about his ring image, he said: 'I'm not tough and I'm not scary. I'm qualified.'

Sonny and Geraldine soon decided enough was enough. The people around where they lived liked them, but he was under the spotlight all the time. And sooner or later a rejected man rejects.

In December 1962, they left to live in a 21-room mansion on Chicago's South Side, owned by jazz musician Ahmad Jamal, on a rent with an option to buy deal. They held a press conference in the living room, which had a stone fireplace, expensive curtains and carpets. Liston, positively effusive by his standards, said he liked music, especially Dave Brubeck. Jazz records were playing subtly in the background on the state-of-the-art hi-fi system. For photographers, he agreed to put up Christmas decorations, and he posed as if he was moving the furniture himself. He posed outside with passing schoolchildren and even a policeman. He was trying. He really was.

He also said that as well as himself and Geraldine, her mother Eva would live there, as well as a niece, Margie Wilhite. There was also room for a couple of his closest allies in his backroom team, Teddy King and Foneda Cox, a sparring partner he had known since they were both with Frank Mitchell in St Louis.

It didn't last. They didn't buy Jamal's house, instead moving on within a few months to Denver, where Liston, leaning on W.C. Fields, declared: 'I'd rather be a lamp post in Denver than mayor of Philadelphia.' Rejection sometimes takes time to bite deep. And it seems the void he experienced in becoming what he had dreamt of becoming for so many years was essentially destructive. His drinking, which appears to have been no more than spasmodic in the 1950s, increased. In effect, he began drowning his sorrows, began to lose perspective. There was a possibility they left Chicago in a hurry after a violent incident with the wife of a former bodyguard. At the end of September 1963, a court case would be filed in a Chicago court alleging Liston assaulted Mrs Pearl Grayson, whose husband John had been one of the security men assigned to look after him in camp before the first fight with Patterson. Mrs Grayson claimed $100,000. The case was not pursued, and the word was that the Graysons were paid off.

While they found somewhere suitable in Denver, they spent three months living in a house that belonged to the Loyola Catholic Church – in other words, the Jesuits. The deal was set up on the initiative of the priest he already knew, Father Edward Murphy. Another priest who was there at the time said Murphy organised the house, which adjoined the priest's own quarters, and made an attempt to get Liston to stop drinking.

Father Thomas Kelly said: 'You could smell him in the mornings. Oh, poor Sonny. He was just an accident waiting to happen. Murph used to say, "Pray for the poor bastard."'

It wasn't all bad, though. Liston had a fun routine with the young daughter of the priests' housekeeper. He called her 'Little Bum' and she called him 'Big Bum'. Father Murphy made another attempt to help him to read and write, and the priests had enjoyed wearing 'I Like Sonny' badges during the Patterson fight build-up.

Willie Reddish said a few years later that Sonny told him just after he won the title: 'I don't feel no different.'

A planned exhibition tour in Mexico was cancelled when the Mexican immigration department refused to allow him into the country. No official reason was given. Doc Young said the promoter of the proposed tour asked the Mexican boxing commission to help but was told that in barring Liston they were cooperating with Senator Estes Kefauver and his committee.

Some felt, when it came to it, that whatever his intentions, he just didn't have the class or the dignity required to alter people's perspective. The evidence suggests that after the Philadelphia rejection Liston did not really see the need to bother with niceties. And bad became worse.

A year on, Robert H. Boyle, for *Sports Illustrated* and best known as a fishing writer, said in the build-up to the second Patterson fight:

> Liston has had the championship for almost a year now, and in that time he has become insufferable. He is giving back all the abuse he ever had to take. He looks upon good manners as a sign of weakness, if not cowardice, and he accepts gifts and favours with all the ill humour of a sultan demanding tribute. Most of the time he is sullen. A contemptuous grunt passes for speech.
>
> He acts this way toward almost everyone. Of course, he can cop a plea with the press by claiming that he has been unfairly treated because of his past. What counts, however, is the way he deports himself with bootblacks, porters, maids, waitresses. As a onetime nonentity himself, he might be expected to know how they feel. Yet he has carried into his public life the bullying and cockiness that he uses to intimidate opponents in the ring.

Harold Conrad cited the time he took Liston to Toots Shor's famous restaurant in New York City. Shor, who prided himself on the athletes who took time to eat at his establishment, went out of his way to make people welcome. Conrad said he was excited by the prospect of having Liston as a guest, but when the publicist took Shor across to introduce him, Sonny didn't even look up. 'I don't shake hands while I'm eatin',' he said.

Shor, furious, turned away, and told Conrad: 'Don't you ever bring that bum in here again.'

Not long after winning the title, Liston had a strange public fall-out with 'businessman' Moe Dalitz, who had a 13.2 per cent interest in the Desert Inn in Las Vegas, which he had developed in the 1950s. Before he moved to Las Vegas, Dalitz was a bootlegger and racketeer in Cleveland, laundering his fortune through several legitimate businesses, including, ironically, a laundry. Dalitz was in the dining room at the Beverly Rodeo Hotel in Beverly Hills when Liston walked in and marched over to him. Words were exchanged, over what is not known, then Liston was seen to clench his fist. Dalitz said clearly: 'If you hit me, nigger, you better kill me. Because if you don't, I'll make one telephone call and you'll be dead within twenty-four hours.' Liston turned on his heels and walked out. Why he was talking to Dalitz, we don't know. Dalitz, incidentally, was in 1976 named Humanitarian of the Year by the American Cancer Research Centre and Hospital. He died in 1989, aged 89, and left his fortune to charities.

Frank Butler, boxing correspondent for the *News of the World*, suggested Liston was the most feared and controversial champion since Jack Johnson, who was champion from 1908 to 1915. 'Now one must speculate as to whether Liston's reign will last for a similar number of years and whether the new Black Prince will remain a troubleshooter like Johnson or become a great and dignified champion like Joe Louis.'

Butler said the contracted rematch should not happen for the simple reason that Patterson did not believe he could win. As to the next contenders if a Patterson return could be avoided, Butler felt there wouldn't be much interest in a fight with Eddie Machen, who back-pedalled and countered Liston for 12 rounds in Seattle in 1960. Ingemar Johansson, as a former champion, was a possibility. Cassius Clay was about to box Archie Moore, but Butler was keen on neither of them against Liston. 'Clay is too young, and Moore is too old. If garrulous Clay could fight as well as he talks, he would eat Liston alive.'

14

EVEN CLEOPATRA WAS RINGSIDE

In the lead-up to the Doug Jones fight at Madison Square Garden in March 1963, Cassius Clay was spouting off for journalists – but primarily for the television news camera. Suddenly, he was informed that the TV camera had run out of film. He stopped and called out: 'You've missed my best line!' When the new tape was installed, he began again and, like an actor on a stage, repeated it word for word.

He went too far for some in his disparagement of Jones, who was a tough, solid, respected professional:

> That ugly little man, I'll annihilate him. You know what this fight means to me? A tomato-red Cadillac Eldorado convertible with white leather upholstery, air-conditioning and hi-fi. That's what the group is giving me as a victory present. Can you picture me losing to this ugly bum Jones with that kind of swinging car waiting for me? I get sore – and Jones fall in four.

Too far or not, Madison Square Garden was sold out five days before the fight. That pleased him. He held a press conference in his room, number 1049 in the Plymouth Hotel on West 49th St, to tell the world: 'The Garden is too small for me. Where are the big places? Maybe the Los Angeles Coliseum. I was up in Harlem today, arguing with 500 people on the corner.'

Even the touts were struggling to get their paws on tickets. There were stories of people offering $75 for a $12 seat. He declared that because of him Garden staff were now employed to wipe off the seats where the pigeons used to sit. One of his odder stunts was to take a small group of newsmen to a coffee house called The Bitter End in Greenwich Village and recite his excruciating rhymes to the intelligentsia sitting around the tables. He did interview after interview for newspapers, radio and television, including the NBC *Tonight Show* with Johnny Carson.

At 6 a.m. on the morning of the show, he walked the two blocks to the Garden and stood staring at the sign – 'TONIGHT – BOXING – CLAY VS

JONES'. At the weigh-in a few hours later, even Jones had to smile when the young man turned up with a two-inch wide strip of tape across his mouth. Clay weighed 202½ lb, Jones 188 lb.

By fight time, the crowd was divided roughly into two sections: those who wanted to see what Clay was all about and those who wanted to see him knocked off his pedestal. There were exceptions: some genuine boxing fans had come down from Harlem, principally to support Jones, who was one of their own and a genuine world-title contender.

Doug Jones had been a Garden protégé – he made his debut there in 1958. He had knocked out the old middleweight champion Bobo Olson in six in 1960, had floored the 1956 Olympic gold medallist Pete Rademacher four times on the way to a win in round five, had lost his unbeaten record to Eddie Machen on a ten-round decision and had lost over fifteen for the light-heavyweight title against Harold Johnson.

He came into the Clay fight in excellent form. In October 1962, the Garden fans had seen him batter future light-heavyweight champion Bob Foster to defeat inside eight rounds. Foster, in only his tenth pro fight, had substituted for Zora Folley that night. Jones had then beaten Folley at the Garden in December 1962, recovering from a first-round knockdown to win in the seventh.

Whatever Clay said, he was not fighting a bum or a mug. Jones was a knowledgeable, experienced operator whose three defeats in twenty-five professional fights had all been on points, all in world class.

The crowd cheered Jones from the moment the spotlight caught him coming through them in his purple and gold robe. Clay, dressed in white, was booed into the ring.

The mood softened as Jack Dempsey and Gene Tunney were introduced, along with Ray Robinson and Rocky Graziano, Barney Ross and Dick Tiger. The old champions duly saluted, the fans got back to the business of booing Clay. He waved at them. He danced.

Jones made a sensational start, landing a surprise right hand that made Clay's knees dip. Cassius had to grab the top rope to regain his balance. He improved in the second, took control from the third. Jones put in a big effort in the fourth, the round Clay had called, then survived the blazing bursts of long, jarring punches. At the bell, the crowd booed some more.

After the eighth, there were those who felt Jones might even be in front. Clay had to fight harder than he ever had before and poured it out in the ninth and tenth rounds. The decision was unanimous: referee Joe Loscalzo saw it an overwhelming 8–1–1 for Clay, while the two judges had the young man ahead narrowly at 5–4–1.

As the New York crowd howled, booed, yelled 'Fix' and threw debris into the ring, including cartons of peanuts, Clay taunted them back, even picked up some peanuts and ate them. A photographer at ringside was knocked cold by something solid that hit the back of his head. The noisy protests went on for around ten minutes.

'They can boo as long as they pay,' Cassius said, back in his dressing-room. He felt Loscalzo's card was closest to the truth. 'See, I'm pretty as a girl,' he said. 'There isn't a mark on me. Doug didn't fall, that's all . . . I want Liston. He can't move as fast as Jones. Liston will go in eight.'

He left for a victory party in Harlem, at an establishment called Small's Paradise, but was too tired to stay long. He posed wearily in a tuxedo by a vast cake topped by strawberries, and returned to his hotel.

Jones' manager, Alex Koskowitz, said: 'Clay is nothing. He's a fake.' Jones himself said he didn't think much of Clay and believed he had won by at least three points. He couldn't think of anything that the young man had done well at any point in the ten rounds.

Watching on closed-circuit TV, Sonny Liston said he felt Clay had won but added: 'I'll get locked up for murder if I fight him.'

The next day, Angelo Dundee told Cassius he had fought like an amateur. Cassius admitted he had underestimated Jones. Another lesson learned.

Daily Express writer Desmond Hackett, about as spectacularly wrong as it's possible to be, believed he had witnessed the beginning of the end of Cassius Clay. In fact, he went so far as to suggest Clay was now a fallen idol who had 'arrogantly signed his own boxing death warrant' by declaring that his next fight must be against Sonny Liston.

Hackett described Clay as defiant and patronising in the wake of the hostile response to the verdict he had been given over Jones. He felt only the presence of the New York police had stopped Clay being attacked by the mob. Furthermore, Hackett believed Clay was an imposter whose victories had been achieved against a series of sparring partners and who was fortunate to be around in a time when the heavyweight division, Liston apart, was poor. 'The strutting 21-year-old pretender to the throne had been exposed,' declared Hackett. 'And the exposure could not have been more complete.'

Unless he had lost, I guess.

When Clay returned to Louisville, there wasn't a tomato-red Cadillac in the showroom. He had to go home in a rented Chevrolet. He told *Time* magazine:

> When I get that championship, then I'm going to put on my old jeans
> and get an old hat and grow a beard. And I'm going to walk down the

road until I find a little fox who just loves me for what I am.

And then I'll take her back to my $250,000 house overlooking my $1 million housing development, and I'll show her the Cadillac and the patio and the indoor pool in case it rains. And I'll tell her, 'This is all yours, honey, because you love me for what I am.'

Before leaving for London to box Henry Cooper in June 1963, Clay was virtually dismissed by Jack Dempsey, who said: 'He needs a lot of training. It would be ridiculous for him to get in there with Liston now. Johansson would probably knock Clay out. Patterson too. He needs a lot more fights.' Dempsey was one punch away from being right.

Clay's boasting and bragging upset the British nation – if not Cooper, who enjoyed the fact that Clay's insults sold tickets. The young man told everybody that Britain's favourite sporting son, who had been heavyweight champion of his country and its empire since 1959, was a bum. He walked out of a radio show because the interviewer interrupted him. He got out of his car and walked down Oxford Street just to show he could draw a crowd of complete strangers without saying anything.

On the way to the ring, dressed in a crimson gown with a gold crown, he looked around and saw 30,000 people baying for his blood. He had done his job. 'Even Cleopatra was ringside,' he said afterwards. (That was Elizabeth Taylor, who had just starred in the movie.)

In the ring, he gazed out loftily, as if he were already the champion of the world. He had said he would stop Cooper in five. For eleven minutes, three and three-quarter rounds, he danced and prodded. Cooper drew a trickle of blood from his nose, but more decisively Clay opened a cut on the Englishman's left eye. He took risk after risk, dropping his hands and inviting Cooper to hit him, then drawing back to make him miss by a fraction. In the corner after round three, Dundee warned him to stop messing around. Then with only seconds to go in round four, he made one of the worst mistakes of his career. Cooper nailed him flush with a classic left hook, and the young man slumped down backwards by the ropes. His eyes were glassy, he didn't appear to know what had happened, but somehow he dragged himself up at the count of four. The bell rang to end the round, and he weaved his way to his corner.

Dundee grabbed him, sat him down and suddenly drew the attention of referee Tommy Little to a tear in Clay's left glove. Little ordered a new pair from the Board of Control to be brought and fitted before the start of round six. There was a short delay in the start of round five, by which time smelling salts – illegal now – had been waved under Clay's nose. His fitness, his youth, his nerve, brought him up for the fifth as if nothing had happened.

Seventy-five seconds later, the fight was over. He had bounced right hands off the already damaged eye of Cooper and ripped the flesh wide open. Cooper ploughed on through a curtain of blood, but referee Little stepped between them and waved the fight over.

A month later, Liston would defend the championship in the rematch against Patterson.

15

I PITY A MAN WHO HATES

George Whiting, reflecting on the first Liston–Patterson fight in the *London Evening Standard* while contemplating the possible outcome of the second, said that in Chicago Patterson offered the feeble resistance of a mesmerised ferret: 'Patterson's only chance is to pester points off Liston and on to the scorecards of the referee and two ringside judges. Trainer Dan Florio must have his man continually moving sideways to keep Liston off balance.'

Whiting felt the rematch demonstrated why the return clause in contracts was wrong – and believed the second fight would go pretty much the same way as the first.

Whatever the writers or anyone else thought about it, however cynical and pointless an exercise it was, it was going to happen. It was originally booked for the Convention Hall in Miami on Thursday, 4 April 1963, promoted once again by the Bolan Brothers under the guise of Championship Sports Inc. However, the plan fell apart because of a stupid accident: Liston twisted his right knee while swinging a golf club for a photoshoot in Miami. He had been having fun, trying to emulate the swing of an 11-year-old local boy, Mike Zwerner, who was practising at the golf range when the cameras arrived, and the knee 'went'.

To show there were no hard feelings, he invited the lad to stay with him and Geraldine in Denver. Liston bought young Mike a scooter and together they rode around the neighbourhood. Zwerner would steer and the heavyweight champion of the world would perch himself on the pillion, helping slow it down by dropping his feet and acting as a kind of anchor. How much that helped his injured knee it's hard to say, but Liston enjoyed himself hugely. Zwerner, who later became a professional jockey, said Sonny liked setting him lateral-thinking tests. One example:

Sonny: 'If a plane crashed between Mexico and California, where would they bury the survivors?'

Mike: 'On the border.'

Sonny: 'They don't need to bury survivors.'

Mike stayed on, with the blessing of his father Jack, a Miami businessman, through the training camp and was even allowed to be a part of the corner team on the night of the fight.

A new date of 22 July was arranged, but the venue had to be switched. Las Vegas, Nevada, eventually secured it. That in itself was a piece of history – the first heavyweight championship fight to be held in 'Sin City'.

The hotel-casinos on the Strip and Downtown bought $100,000 worth of tickets up front to hand out to their regular high-rollers, which is another phrase for big-losers. The estimate was that ticket sales would eventually reach $300,000.

A fight for the championship of the world proved just the kind of attraction that Vegas would go on welcoming for the next four decades and more. To get people into the casinos, hotel owners had worked out they needed something more than gambling to attract them into town in the first place. By the start of the twenty-first century, Las Vegas had become a convention city as well as a gambling paradise, but in those early days the emphasis was on making food cheap, hotel rooms affordable and offering 'bait' like big fights, all in order to lure people into casinos for longer and longer. Some hotels even provided transport – they flew customers into town, sometimes without charge, on the assumption that they would gamble.

Not that anyone was prepared to bet on the Liston–Patterson fight. The bookmakers wouldn't offer anything on Liston, only odds against Patterson. They attracted a few wild bets from amateur chancers, but the professionals didn't want to know.

Jack Nilon said the fight was too one-sided to guarantee a huge audience, but he was not enamoured of the promotional capabilities of the Bolan brothers' Championship Sports. He said he had signed a Nevada State Athletic Commission contract but had no deal yet with the promoters. He wanted a $100,000 guarantee lodged in his bank, plus 50 per cent of the advance ticket sales, less taxes. He also said he wasn't satisfied with the financial statement from the first fight. Nilon was clearly preparing the ground for 'going it alone'.

Liston was surly and uncooperative with just about everybody in Las Vegas. Boxers can be difficult as fight time approaches, but Sonny excelled. First of all, he refused the arranged hospitality at the Dunes. (Patterson trained there instead and lived at a house out of town, eight miles from the Strip.) At the Thunderbird, where Sonny settled, there were stories that he was scornful and derisive to waiters and casino staff. Several of them, quoted in *Sports Illustrated*, said he was, among other things, mean, stupid and no good. And a woman described as a Los Angeles actress, who did not give her name but whose words carried the wounded tone of a woman scorned, said: 'Liston has no feelings. He doesn't care about anyone or anything, just himself. I hope Patterson kills him.' A blackjack dealer said Liston kicked down a barricade outside the room where he was going to work out and outside which people were lining up to pay to go in. Spectators paid to watch public workouts only to find he didn't feel like training.

The Thunderbird was the territory of Irving 'Ash' Resnick, who called himself its athletic director. Nobody was quite sure what an athletic director did in a casino. Resnick was once, allegedly, the Nevada representative of the Patriarca mafia family from Rhode Island. Resnick was in on the original deal to build Caesars Palace, and it was also whispered that he was in some way a party to the blackmailing of FBI head J. Edgar Hoover, over his long-term homosexual relationship with an FBI colleague, Clyde Tolson. Resnick stayed in the next holiday bungalow to Hoover and Tolson in Miami Beach in the 1950s.

Liston's publicist, Ben Bentley, arranged one-on-one interviews then had to make excuses when the champion didn't turn up. Bentley's frustrations sometimes spilled over in attacks at the press. He took offence when a magazine ran a photo of Liston behind bars. 'That's all you people write about. You only tell about his past, not about how he is now.' He had a point, but the tension in his reaction was plain.

Bentley's job also involved keeping a tab on Liston's car, a black Fleetwood Cadillac that carried the inscription 'This Car Was Specially Made For Sonny Liston'. The car, which came complete with telephone and television, also had a white leather roof. Sonny's initials were on the doors. He insisted it be washed only with a soap he especially liked.

Sports Illustrated writer Robert H. Boyle said the experience of trying to please Liston and keep the media happy had demoralised Bentley, who by the end was so intimidated that he worried about having to remind Liston that he had to give a press conference. Part of Bentley's role also entailed telling Liston jokes, but bit by bit he lost confidence in himself. Liston seemed to enjoy watching him suffer.

Raymond Munson was the valet – Liston liked to dress well – and also had to make sure the records Sonny wanted to train to were available. Usually it was 'Night Train', the James Brown version of the original by Jimmy Forrest, George and Ira Gershwin's classic 'It Ain't Necessarily So' or Lionel Hampton's 'Railroad Number One'.

Jack Nilon grew to dislike the man for whom he had once had a degree of sympathy. He still tried to paint a picture of a misunderstood unfortunate whose illiteracy was at the base of his problems. Once, by the pool, Nilon said: 'He's frustrated because he can't read. See that sign over there, "Please Register With Lifeguard". Now, Sonny doesn't know what that says. For all he knows, it might as well say "Free Drinks". It's embarrassing to him.'

Nilon's ulcers were playing him up, Liston was ignorant to him, and as preparations progressed he lost patience with it all. At one point he left for a week, officially to play in a golf tournament, in reality just to get away from the nonsense.

It wasn't all bad, though. After one workout, Liston did talk with a degree of relaxation and humour. No, he said, there wouldn't be a third fight with Patterson. 'It's just like marriage and divorce. Enough's enough. After Monday, I don't want to have anything to do with him.'

On Cassius Clay, he said he believed the young man's heart was not in the match, which Nilon was saying would be made once the Patterson commitment was out of the way.

'Clay's demanding great big money,' said Liston. 'Reckon he would rather take somebody else, not me. Would rather go on visiting the graveyard and digging up them bums he's had so far. What do I do then? Maybe I go to the graveyard and dig up some of them myself.'

Liston insisted he did read the newspapers – in truth he often got his helper and friend Teddy King to do it for him. He said he felt most of what was written about him was lies, but said he didn't get mad about it:

> They're just trying to stir me up. Don't pay no attention when they advise me either. They tell me I ought to get a right hand because it's slow. I pay Willie Reddish 10 per cent of my purse to give me better advice. Monday you'll see whether my hands are fast.

When somebody asked him what he made of Patterson training differently this time around, he was uninterested. 'How should I know? Don't make much sense though. It figures to be the same sort of fight.'

Someone else mentioned Patterson's claim that he had a different mental attitude this time. 'Thought people with mental problems went to places that were not bounded by the ring ropes,' he said. 'I got no mental block. I just fight.'

As he wound down, he enjoyed hurting his sparring partners. Old opponent Howard King was bludgeoned to the floor. It took handlers 20 seconds to get him on his feet. Only Foneda Cox, whose hair was now greying, sometimes benefited because Liston seemed to pull his punches a little with him. They had known each other a long time.

Of an evening, Liston liked to play craps at the Thunderbird. He was in the casino one night when Clay strode in and began sounding off. At a distance, Liston tolerated it, but the young upstart made the mistake of getting in Liston's face. That was overstepping the mark. Liston leaned close and said: 'Listen you nigger faggot, if you don't get out of here in ten seconds I'm gonna pull that big tongue out of your mouth and stick it up your ass.'

To make sure Clay understood he wasn't joking, the story goes that Liston pulled out a pistol. Clay understood.

Another time Clay was on his territory at the Thunderbird but didn't see Liston approach him. Liston tapped his shoulder and as Clay turned, he slapped his face with the back of his hand.

Clay, taken off guard, said: 'What did you do that for?'

Liston muttered: 'Because you're too fuckin' fresh.'

Clay walked away, and Liston sneered as he went: 'I got the punk's heart now.'

Clay still turned up at Liston's public workout for a bit of vaudeville fun, taunting the champion that he would fight him for a dollar a head – the price fans had paid at the door. Liston invited him into the ring; Clay instead was 'restrained' by Nilon and returned to his chair. For the amusement of the paying customers, Clay and Liston taunted each other as the workout meandered on.

Liston sneered at him: 'You can't punch hard enough to break an egg.'

Clay said: 'You just stand there and pretend you're an egg.'

From the back of the hall, Clay laughed and opened his eyes wide in mock-horror. 'Hey, Liston, you're an animal. If ever you fight me, I won't know whether to whip you or cage you.'

Arthur Daley, for the *New York Times*, also reported the day Liston formally received the championship belt provided by *Ring* magazine, whose editor, Nat Fleischer, was the self-appointed guardian of the game. Liston, for once plainly moved, stood staring at the belt that lay draped across his hands. Then, looking at Clay, he raised it above his head and said to him: 'This is something you'll never get.'

Once he was gambling in the Thunderbird when journalists watched from a distance. After he finished, they tried a few questions, which annoyed him. One facetiously asked how playing craps would help him beat Patterson. He was not amused.

You burn me up! People are always telling me how to live. They say I live high and I sure do. Way up on a hill. I mind my own business, and it's my business if I stay up till 1.30 in the morning. I'll be there when that bell rings.

Someone else asked if he might be tempted to carry Patterson a little this time in order to prolong the entertainment.

'Sure I'll carry him . . . right out!'

Jimmy Cannon talked to a man who said Liston had been playing craps in the Thunderbird at 1 a.m. a week before the fight. 'But what difference does it make?' said the man. 'Nothing will help Patterson.'

As for Floyd, he was his usual patient, gentle, reserved self. In the week of the fight, he gave British writers a few minutes at the Dunes, talking softly, with the casino's background hustle and bustle almost drowning him out. He said he felt sorry for Liston the man. 'He's a man who hates and hates hard,' he said, pausing:

> I pity a man who hates. I hated a man once. It was Ingemar, just after that first fight. I was so full of hatred when I went into the ring the second time I wanted to destroy him altogether. Then after I knocked him out and he lay there on the canvas with his right leg shaking I felt real bad. I made a promise that I would never hate another man in a fight ever again.

The *New York Journal-American* sent a reporter, Helen Sutton, to talk to Patterson's wife, Sandra, at their 11-room, limestone and redwood hilltop home in Scarsdale, New York, on the border with Yonkers. Also there were the children: Seneca (6), Trina (4), Floyd Jr (3) and Eric (18 months).

Sandra Patterson said she felt, while the strain of being made to feel responsible for the well-being of the sport got to Floyd the first time around, this time he would be boxing only for himself:

> My husband got letters from people like Estes Kefauver and Ralph Bunche saying he shouldn't fight someone with Liston's record as a hoodlum – that Liston couldn't be permitted to win. It was a terrible strain.
>
> This time Floyd is fighting just for himself – to prove to himself he's the better boxer . . . Floyd will have no excuses this time. He'll fight his best and if Liston wins, it will be because he's a better fighter. So Floyd will retire. I hate to put my husband on the line like this. But I know it's how he feels.
>
> Liston hasn't tasted any of Floyd's punches yet. I'm sure Floyd can keep away from him for one round – long enough to feel Liston out. Sonny can't box in a class with Floyd. I say within eight rounds something will happen – one way or another.

Sonny Liston – 'Some day they'll write a blues song just for fighters. It'll be for a slow guitar, soft trumpet and a bell'. (© Getty Images)

Off the beaten track – St Francis County, Arkansas, where Liston was born and raised.

'To know this and only this' – Liston, grandson of a slave, spent his early years on a farm near here.

The programme for the night Liston became champion in 1962.

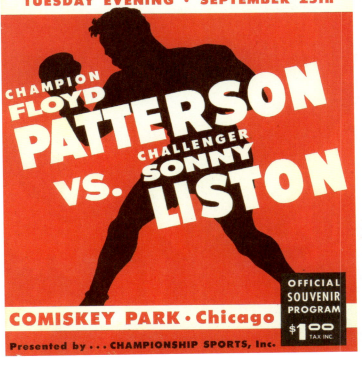

A ticket for the fight that didn't happen between Sonny Liston and Floyd Patterson in Miami in 1963.

A rare ticket for the fight between Sonny Liston and Floyd Patterson in Las Vegas in 1963.

'I told you, I told you . . .' – Cassius Clay is the new heavyweight champion of the world.
(© Getty Images)

The kit handed out to members of the world media who descended on Miami for the first fight.

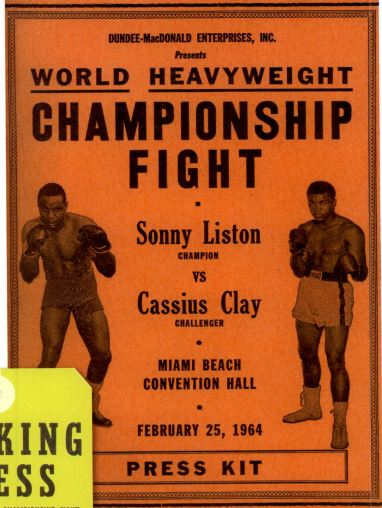

DUNDEE-MacDONALD ENTERPRISES, INC.

Presents

WORLD HEAVYWEIGHT CHAMPIONSHIP FIGHT

Sonny Liston
CHAMPION

VS

Cassius Clay
CHALLENGER

MIAMI BEACH
CONVENTION HALL

FEBRUARY 25, 1964

PRESS KIT

WORKING PRESS

WORLD'S HEAVYWEIGHT CHAMPIONSHIP FIGHT
LISTON vs. CLAY
MIAMI BEACH CONVENTION HALL
TUE., FEB. 25, 1964, 8:45 P. M.

Gutteridge
London Eve News

THIS IS YOUR ADMISSION TICKET
Non-Transferable

ENTER PRESS
No. 288   GATE No. 2
— ONLY —

(Southeast Side of Convention Hall)

SEC	ROW	SEAT
E	C	3

The ringside press pass issued to Reg Gutteridge for the fight between Liston and Clay in Miami in 1964.

Phantom punch – Ali lands the knockdown blow in Lewiston, Maine, that few saw.
(© Getty Images)

'Get up you bum!' – Ali says what audiences around the world must have thought. (© Getty Images)

HEAVYWEIGHT CHAMPIONSHIP OF THE WORLD

The programme for the rematch, originally planned for Boston, then moved to Lewiston, Maine.

Liston's modest grave in Paradise Memorial Gardens, Las Vegas.

The author with Rahaman Ali on the step where he and Muhammad sat as boys and dreamed of all they would do with their lives.

Sandra said they had no family life because her husband was in training camp 11 months a year, but they had an agreement that he would retire by the end of 1965. Then, she said, they would live a normal life in upstate New York, raising horses and children.

> I was ready for him to retire last time, but Floyd said, 'I know you're speaking from the heart, Sandra – a woman's heart. A man's heart doesn't work the same. A man's heart says you can't quit when you've been beaten, you've got to find out if you can do better.'

Floyd wasn't to quit boxing until 1972, by which time he was 37 years old. His marriage to Sandra had ended in divorce in September 1969. His refusal to retire was, it was said, at the heart of the split.

At the final press conference, Liston said he wanted to win inside the 126 seconds it took him first time around:

> The only question is how fast I catch up with him. If it takes me five rounds to knock him out I must be riding a slow train . . .
>
> Maybe Patterson has improved since then. I'm not knocking him. A guy who twice held the title has to have something . . . but I have something more.
>
> I'm the champion, and I intend to remain that. I would like to be a busy one just like Joe Louis . . . I may say some more about that as soon as this is over. Don't want to talk no more about it now.

Patterson said he was sure he was in better mental and physical shape this time around and that it wouldn't be over in one round, adding: 'That's about all the prediction I will make since I never have claimed I would win in a certain round and things like that.'

At an earlier press conversation, Floyd had said:

> I think I'm going to win. If I don't knock him out, what's wrong with a decision? I know I didn't hurt him in Chicago. I know now what he can do. But he doesn't know what I can do. How could he? I didn't show him anything in the first fight . . .

The night before the fight, Liston told a friend: 'I feel like I'm going to a dance.' On the day itself, the champion was late for the weigh-in, which cost him a $100 fine. Nilon's plan was for him to beat Patterson, take a ten-day break, then go into camp at Atlantic City with a view to fighting the 21-year-old Clay at

Philadelphia Stadium on either 23 or 30 September 1963. Nilon felt the fight could draw a live gate of 70,000 in the arena where Jack Dempsey fought Gene Tunney in 1926.

'Clay's a good fighter and a sharp monkey,' said Nilon. 'He started yelling for a guaranteed payday of $1.5 million, but he will get no guarantees. Our offer is 20 per cent of everything, but we shall probably wind up paying him around 23 per cent.' That, he said, would still give Clay $1 million if sales went as he believed they would.

Nilon said from this fight on they would be in control of the promotions. 'We control everything, all the dough goes to Liston,' he said. 'Other promoters are out – as of now.' Nilon said he believed a Liston–Clay fight could gross $7 million on the gate and closed-circuit. That was his pay-off, too, the night his investments – and his patience – would be justified.

Nobody, but nobody, had any belief that Patterson could do significantly better than he had the previous year. That in itself makes this one of the most cynical matches in heavyweight boxing history. And there are a few to choose from.

Jimmy Cannon, in the *New York Journal-American*, pointed out that Patterson had fled Comiskey Park, Chicago, in a car. This time, said Cannon, Patterson was known to have been taking flying lessons.

Publicists tried to spin the line that Liston might have got lucky first time around, that Patterson had already showed he could overturn defeat with a spectacular knockout, that the former champion might even win quickly himself this time. Nobody, but nobody, bought it.

The press conferences rarely raised themselves above the melancholy. Patterson, not one to boast at the best of times, seemed ready for his fate. If he lost badly, he said he might retire. If he lost a close fight, he would have to begin again. Of course, he also said he felt he could win, but he didn't say it very often. He did, however, promise not to run away. Especially in a beard.

16

GOD SAVE THE KING, GOD SAVE BOXING

Nearly 8,000 in the ultra-modern, carpeted, circular Las Vegas Convention Centre stood and cheered Patterson into the ring, then booed and yelled abuse at the heavyweight champion of the world. Rocky Marciano, Joe Louis and Billy Conn were announced to the crowd, then Cassius Clay shook hands with Patterson, went to cross the ring to Liston, then stopped and dashed out in mock fear – to applause and laughter.

After both had pawed out jabs, Liston landed a short right hand to the body about ten seconds into the fight. Patterson seemed to feel it, moving away as soon as he could. Liston connected with a left jab. Patterson held. It was as if he were waiting for something bad to happen. He didn't have to wait long.

A seven-punch burst, including a right uppercut that jerked Patterson's head back and almost seemed to take him off the floor, and at the fifty-second mark of round one, the challenger was down.

After the mandatory eight count from referee Harry Krause, Patterson retreated, then held and spoiled, clinging to Liston's right glove. Sonny belted him in the ribs with his free hand until Krause called break.

As soon as Liston found the room, he marched forward, this time unleashing an unanswered burst of 11 blows, a final chopping right hand sending Patterson sprawling on the canvas. He hit the floor as the clock reached 99 seconds. This time he was dazed, hurt and plainly demoralised, but he got up.

Some vestige of pride made Patterson fire a right hand, but it missed, and Liston finished him off with two rights to the side of the head and a left hook to the jaw. There was no point in another count, but referee Krause went through the formality, completing it at an official time of two minutes ten seconds. Patterson had not landed a single punch. Then again, he had only thrown five – three jabs and two right hands.

The condemnation of Patterson's pitiful challenge was pretty much universal. Lester Bromberg called him 'a mouse of a man'. A bookmaker at The Dunes in Las Vegas, Sid Wyman, may or may not have had his own agenda, but was angry when he told writers: 'If he couldn't make a better fight, he shouldn't have gone through. It was an insult to the people.'

Patterson, wrote John Gold for the *London Evening News*, went down 'beneath a raging tide of human violence. It was a fight that should have been held in an abattoir not a sports arena packed with celebrities.' At the end, Gold wrote:

> From some hole in the ring, up bobbed the irrepressible Clay, shouting and gesticulating and wrestling with the ring attendants as he tried to reach Liston. Clay gets his chance next. He will be fortunate if it isn't his comeuppance.

No deal would be signed for Liston to defend against Clay until 5 November 1963, but even in July, when Liston destroyed Patterson again, everybody knew there was no other fight that mattered, that it had to happen.

To roars of 'We Want Clay' from the back of the hall, Cassius climbed into the ring and gave an interview. 'It was a disgrace to the boxing game,' he said. 'It wasn't a heavyweight championship fight. It was just an eliminator to see who's going to fight me.' After declaring himself tired of talking, he said Liston didn't have enough experience to deal with him. 'If the bum whips me, I'll leave the country.'

Clay said he was going to New York to cut an album for Columbia Records. 'Maybe after Liston, I'll go into the movies,' he said, opening his eyes even wider. 'After all, I'm the greatest actor there is.'

He anticipated boxing Liston in front of the biggest live crowd for a boxing match anywhere, bigger even than Dempsey and Tunney, then let his imagination loose:

> I'm gonna make my entrance surrounded by beautiful queens wearing gowns that drag on the ground . . . I'll be wearing a crown on my head and a beautiful robe, like in Pharaoh's days. One queen will take the crown from my head and place it gently on a silken pillow. Another queen will help me out of my robe. The others will be rubbing me down with cocoa butter and manicuring my nails. That's what we need in boxing. Beautiful girls!

Donald Saunders, in the *Daily Telegraph*, said: 'Liston's biggest worry will not be losing the title but trying to find opponents who will be good enough to attract customers into arenas and television theatres.' Liston made a good point when he said there were no real contenders because he had beaten them all on the way up. Saunders felt American fans were missing out by refusing to accept him. 'He may not be the most likeable of world heavyweight champions but there have been, and still are, many people in boxing less deserving of sympathy and support.'

Joe Louis said: 'Nobody going to beat Liston except old age.'

Robert H. Boyle, in *Sports Illustrated*, wrote: 'Sonny Liston is still the heavyweight king. God save the king. God save boxing.'

At the post-fight press conference, Liston seemed initially reluctant, seemed to hesitate as if he wanted to leave. Willie Reddish called out: 'Ask the questions and get it over with.'

The first was a dumb one – 'Was this a better fight than the one in Chicago?'

Liston said: 'Didn't you see it?'

Liston said he would have finished Patterson even quicker but for the mandatory eight count, said it 'had me handcuffed'.

A New York columnist asked Liston, who had on a straw trilby, sports shirt and casual slacks: 'How does it feel to have made it after all these years of having nothing?'

There was a pause. 'Well,' said the champion . . . and no more.

The writer tried again: 'You know what I mean, ten years ago you were in the can and had nothing. Now you're on top of the world. Anything you want is yours. How does it feel?'

The past, the past, always the past.

Liston stared back, let loose a slow smile and said: 'It feels pretty good . . . but sometimes there are too many people bothering me.'

When writers asked him whether he thought Patterson should retire, he turned the question around. 'Would you tell a bird he can't fly?' he said.

Was Patterson afraid of him? Liston grinned. 'Yes, I think he is. He gave me that hurt look.'

On the other side of a partition in the Convention Centre's gold room, Patterson seemed like a man in a psychological trauma, like a man who was already so haunted by what had happened he wouldn't sleep for a year. He said he had no plans to retire. 'In Chicago and here, Liston showed he's a much better fighter than I am . . .'

Someone asked what he had planned to do in the fight.

'Try to make him miss and counter.'

Was Liston such a great fighter or had he developed a 'sensitivity to a punch'?

'It could be a combination of both,' said this painfully honest man. 'I wasn't afraid. Perhaps I should have been. I wasn't tense, although maybe I was a bit nervous. Liston was a better fighter than I thought he was.'

Someone asked what he planned to do now, perhaps a less direct slant on the retirement question.

'I'm not in the picture any more. I prefer to fight my way up. I eliminated myself.'

After a couple of questions about details of what punch had nailed him, Patterson was asked if he planned to put on a beard again on the way out of the building.

'I do feel disgraced terrible . . . but there will be no beard, no moustache, no nonsense this time . . . and I came here so you wouldn't say I ducked out.'

There was some applause – and it was all over.

Back in his half of the room Liston was asked about Cassius Clay.

'Who is Clay? It would take me one and a half rounds to catch him, the other to knock him out.'

Later that evening, Liston was enjoying his victory party when Clay walked in 'just to make him mad'. He made his way through the crowd to Liston's table and yelled at him: 'You're just a sucker. My brother could have beaten Floyd Patterson.'

Liston indulged him. 'Come on over here and sit on my knee and finish your orange juice!' They made as if to go for each other, were kept apart.

People speculated that during his stay in Vegas Liston lost between $900 and $20,000 shooting dice.

Financially, the breakdown of this briefest, most damning of mismatches was as follows:

Attendance: 7,816
Gross live gate: $286,180
Estimated net gate: $260,000
Estimated Liston share: (30%) $78,000
Estimated Patterson share: (30%) $78,000

Each fighter was also on 30 per cent of the theatre TV gate, which was estimated at $700,000, which meant $210,000 each.

Given the nature of the charade, it was probably more than anybody could have expected.

The lords of the Las Vegas casinos didn't care. A short fight meant punters were back on the tables sooner rather than later. Sin City's love affair with the heavyweight championship of the world had begun.

Barry Gottehrer, who was not a boxing writer but a New York political and social analyst, did his best to unravel what Liston was about:

> Servile before mobsters, he remains distrustful of most other people and feels – with good reason – that most writers are trying to crucify him. He feels secure only with his wife and, though childless, delights in the company and admiration of children.
>
> He would like to be liked, but, realistically, he is prepared to live with the boos and catcalls that greeted him when he entered and left the ring in Las Vegas.

Liston had said: 'The public is not with me, I know, but they'll just have to swing along until somebody comes to beat me.'

Jim Murray, columnist for the *Los Angeles Times*, said: '. . .the world of sport now realises it has gotten Charles (Sonny) Liston to keep. It's like finding a live bat on a string under your Christmas tree.'

In its December 1963 issue, *Esquire* magazine had a front cover photo of Sonny in a Santa Claus hat. A story circulated that for that shoot, which was in Las Vegas, Liston posed for just one photo in a room at a casino, then got up and walked away. The *Esquire* art director George Lois tried to stop him leaving and put his hand on Liston's arm. Liston stood and stared at him; Lois removed his hand. In a panic, Lois asked Joe Louis for help. Joe found Liston shooting craps and brought him back.

Two days after beating Patterson for the second time, Charles and Geraldine flew back to Denver, where they lived at 3395 Monaco Parkway, a four-bedroom house in an integrated neighbourhood. This time at the airport there were 1,500 people and the mayor and his wife. Liston was genuinely moved. 'I was thrilled,' he said later. 'It's one of the nicest things that ever happened to me.'

Geraldine was pleased with their new life. 'It's really nice, you can hear the birds sing,' she said.

Sonny said he enjoyed Denver's clean air. 'No smoke, no smog,' he said.

His home phone number was ex-directory, but the phone in his car was in the Denver telephone book. He took to cutting his grass and riding a bicycle. He felt as if he could live like that for the rest of his life.

17

I'LL BE AS GOOD AS PEOPLE
WILL LET ME BE

Liston made a promotional visit to Britain in September 1963 with manager Jack Nilon and appeared to enjoy himself hugely before leaving suddenly with commitments unfulfilled. Those around him said he flew home because of a bombing in a church in Alabama that killed four children, or because one of his children was ill. Others said he just got bored. The British Boxing Board of Control never forgave him for it. Years later when he wanted to box in Britain, they refused him a licence.

According to Mickey Duff, Geraldine arrived with him but returned to Denver after a couple of days. When he was with Geraldine, Liston was respectful and kind, but when she was out of sight, he had a wandering eye. Duff told me, for his own book: 'Those engagements went well, but his temper was uneven and his demands for female company became increasingly menacing. He had a tremendous magnetism that was quite astonishing, even to the point of taking women from their husbands.'

The Kray twins liked to think they ran London at the time – and they paid Liston £500 to visit one of their clubs and pose with them for photographs. He probably didn't know who they were and didn't care.

In Scotland, Glasgow writer John Rafferty admitted he was under the illusion that Liston was a dour, surly bear who would snarl and be unpleasant and this was shattered by the arrival at the airport of a man who was possessed of 'a fundamental honesty, native wit and sense of fun'. He was welcomed by a girls' pipe band, embraced the pipe major, put on a tartan hat and made an attempt to get a noise out of the pipes.

'I don't think I get treated right back home,' he said. 'That's why you might call me serious over there. It's different here. The people treat me like I was something. It's wonderful. I like it here . . . when I return to the States I will be cold again.'

He cracked jokes with reporters, said he had considered taking on two heavyweights at once on the same night but his manager Jack Nilon said: "'Why take one payday when you can fight them on separate nights and get two?' I think to myself, I pay you for something Mr Nilon, and this must be it. So I don't fight two at the same time.'

It was all jocular, low-key stuff, and when the name of Cassius Clay came up, he said: 'I reckon this boy has something. Don't quite know what though.'

Whereas in the United States, Liston found the press questioning intrusive and the photographers too demanding, he enjoyed the more respectful nature of the attention he received from the British media. Therefore, he was more amenable to whatever nonsense the picture-idea men came up with. In Scotland, he wore a kilt. In Newcastle, where he boxed at an exhibition at St James Hall, he rode a white horse, and even when he left at London Airport he tossed his hat into the crowd. In Glasgow, for a TV interview, he balanced promoter and former fighter Peter Keenan's son on his knee. At an Essex farm, he kept wanting to hug the niece of West Ham heavyweight Billy Walker. He signed autographs for children but not for adults, suspicious, no doubt, that the adults wanted to make money out of it. 'For kids, sure I sign, but what do big people want with my name?'

Liston and Keenan got on well in spite of a public altercation over the Scot smoking a cigar in the champion's presence. Liston told him to put it out, Keenan considered he was being ill-mannered, and they fell out, spectacularly.

It was said Keenan, unconcerned by the matter of conceding around 75 lb to the reigning world heavyweight champion, invited him outside to sort out their differences, muttering: 'I've never lost a street fight in my life.' Liston, who had the good grace not to accept, enjoyed Keenan's spirit. You didn't get promoters like that in America. Later on, he invited Keenan's son, Peter Junior, to spend Christmas with him and Geraldine in Denver. They remained in contact for a number of years.

In 2000, Peter Jr told the Scottish boxing writer Brian Donald he was invited to spend the Christmas of 1963 with the Listons in Denver. The boy was driven to the family home by Sonny in his Cadillac. As they arrived there, up in lights on the roof was a sign reading 'Happy Xmas Petesie'. After two days, they went off to Las Vegas and the Stardust Hotel, where he met Joe Louis. Young Peter remembered Liston giving Louis money, as the old champ was down on his luck. He would go off and blow it in the casino and return for another handout. Liston and Geraldine were so enamoured of the boy they cabled Keenan to ask if they could adopt him. Keenan arrived 48 hours later to take him home.

One writer asked Sonny what the future might hold if he could become, in the eyes of the world, a good man.

'I'll be as good as people will let me be,' he said:

> When you walk on top of a mountain you don't look back because you're
> gonna fall. That's me now. I keep looking forward and up. Back home, the
> writers keep trying to make me look back. When I learned to read, it didn't
> help much. I just kept reading what a big bum I was.

Liston told the British writers that being black in America was hard. He cited
the case of white writer John Howard Griffin, who in 1959 used make-up to
live as a black person as an experiment to find out 'what it's like to live our
way'. Griffin spent six weeks travelling as a black man in the Deep South,
writing down the sense of dehumanisation he felt at being harassed, insulted
and humiliated.

> Man, he couldn't wash that colour off quick enough. At times, I can tell
> you, I felt like finding out where that guy got his wash . . .
> All my life I'm taught to watch out. I guess I'm still doing it.

When Griffin broke his story in the African American magazine *Sepia*, he
received death threats in his home town of Mansfield, Texas. Local white folk
burned his effigy in the street. His family eventually left and lived in Mexico.
When Liston and Reg Gutteridge, writing in those days for the *London Evening
News*, were introduced, Liston tapped him 'below the belt'. As Reg doubled
over, Sonny said: 'Take a bow!'

Reg recalled the evening he got his own back. They were at a bar, the worse
for wear, during the Scottish stay, when Liston suddenly said: 'Why is it that
you white guys think black guys look like gorillas?'

Reg protested: 'Come on, I've never said anything like that in my life.'

'Bullshit, man,' said Sonny. 'You're just like all the other white guys, you think
us blacks are just big hairy apes.'

Unbeknown to the flustered Gutteridge this was just a wind-up.

Unbeknown to Liston he had hit on the one person in the British media corps
who could, through no fault of his own, handle what was about to happen.

'I'll bet you any money you like that you've got more hairs on your goddamn
leg than I have,' said Sonny.

The word is the general inspection of the world champion's shin revealed two
tiny hairs. Upon which Gutteridge rolled up his trousers to reveal a smooth,
shiny, hairless and entirely false leg. The real one had been blown off during an
altercation with a mine in the Second World War. Liston burst out laughing,
declared him 'a cork-legged, limey son-of-a-bitch' and paid up.

A couple of years later, they had a re-run of this episode in the States, when on a similar night, after Liston had called the British 'a bunch of faggots', Gutteridge declared himself a real tough guy – and called Liston's hard-man stuff an act. Knowing Sonny had forgotten who he was, Gutteridge took a small ice pick out of a drinks bucket on the bar and plunged it into his leg. Liston's mouth dropped open, and it was only after Reg had 'stabbed himself' a few times more that it came back to Sonny. His bad memory cost him $50.

Years on, Reg put the story in his autobiography, adding the consequence: 'I had to go to Roehampton Limb Fitting Centre to have the leg repaired. It looked as though a woodpecker had been at it . . .'

Gutteridge remembered Liston with affection:

> He was, if you can be persuaded to believe this, a bully with a soft centre. He possessed that precious gift of sometimes being able to laugh at himself, although you had to be very careful when choosing your moment.

Liston signed a deal to talk exclusively to the *Sunday Mirror* to tell his life story. The writer, Lionel Crane, said he virtually had to stalk Liston to get him to talk but eventually made something of it.

For two days, Sonny refused Crane's requests. 'He sat opposite me at dinner with his great boulder face and red-brown eyes staring at me like a bad day at Black Rock.' Crane kept at the job, parking himself next to Liston on plane journeys and in waiting rooms at airports, and eventually the story came to be written. 'It was never easy. His temper was balanced on a hairline trigger.'

Crane remembered asking him a question that provoked a violent mood swing. Liston turned on him, seething. At first, the newspaperman thought, as he said, he was 'going through the side of the plane'.

'It's no use losing your temper with me,' he said. 'You can't hit me. I'm too old and too small.'

Seconds passed, then Liston's mood swung again. He broke into a grin and said: 'Man, you don't want to live.'

The result was far superior to the previous American effort by Wendell Smith. At least Crane's pieces sounded as if Sonny had been speaking at some stage of the process:

> Ever since I been fighting, I've been a loner. I don't hardly remember anybody anywhere cheering me on to win. The crowds came to see me get licked. I know it, but it doesn't bother me none. It don't matter as long as they come . . . And when it's over and they're holding your fist in the air, what's it matter?

He told Crane he was happier now he and Geraldine had moved to Denver, where the people were friendlier and more welcoming. He was still moved by the reception he had been given at Denver airport after the Patterson rematch. He was enjoying the attention British fans were giving him, too:

> They come out to see me and cheer me just like I'm a king or something
> . . . It's great, but it don't make me feel that I got to thank anybody for it.
> I only got one man to thank for what's happened to me – me. I done it
> the hard way. Nobody never gave me nothing.

As always, the subject of Cassius Clay came up: 'Sure, he's a good boy, but the only thing that bothers me about fighting him is how I'm going to get my glove back out of his mouth.'

In another piece in Crane's series, Liston was quoted as saying:

> I've done some rough things, man, and I've had plenty rough things done
> to me, and I ain't making no excuses. You got to take the kind of life they
> hand out to you and do the best you can with it.

At one press conference, Liston felt relaxed enough to joke. A reporter asked him: 'Have you any interests outside boxing?'

Instead of glowering at him, as he would have done in America, and saying nothing, he said: 'Broad jumping.'

The reporter, knowing the American term for the long jump, walked into the trap. 'Really, what distance have you jumped?'

'From one broad to another . . .'

In general, Liston had an easy time from a press more curious and less cynical about his presence among them. One exception was Danny Blanchflower, who captained Tottenham Hotspur to the FA Cup and Football League double in 1961, and two years later was supplementing his soccer income by writing for the *Sunday Express*. During Liston's tour, he wanted to write a column loosely based on Liston and the developing Civil Rights and race issues in the United States. He admitted it was out of a morbid curiosity that he wanted to know more, after he witnessed a press conference in which television reporters threw a series of lame questions at Sonny which he used to show his lighter side. Blanchflower wanted to know what Liston thought about the way racial politics was moving in his country but had not wanted to do it at the press conference. Blanchflower wrote that he thought Liston must 'have a serious side' given that he must have experienced poverty, prejudice and police intimidation. He decided on a roundabout approach, to Jack Nilon via Harry Levene, who was promoting

Liston's tour. When he asked Levene for Nilon's number and explained what he was thinking, specifically what Sonny thought of the recent Civil Rights march to Washington DC, the result was predictably volatile to anyone who knew Levene: 'You mustn't ask him anything like that. Take my advice. Forget about that. And you mustn't mention anything about his record and the police. That's definitely out.' Blanchflower was advised to restrict himself to 'normal' questions. A few days later, he phoned Nilon, who had just spent a few days in Ireland visiting relatives. Nilon apologised but said he had no time to see him.

J.L. Manning, the *Daily Express* columnist, was for some reason unwelcome at Levene's Wembley promotion of 10 September, when Billy Walker fought Johnny Prescott and Liston sparred with Foneda Cox. The next day, Manning fired off a bitter but accurate broadside at the hypocrisies involved in the boxing business and in particular at the peculiar belief that Liston's past might do the sport harm:

> Why should there be more indignation over one Negro fighter starting out from a penitentiary than over scores of others ending up in mental asylums and mortuaries?
>
> Yet the rehabilitation of Sonny Liston became a frenzied moral issue for the United States, ever fearful of their image to the rest of the world. To want whiter than white the champion of a sport that is blacker than black is a fine little Billy Graham sermon in the Hall of Fame.

Manning suggested it should hardly surprise anybody that Liston was ill-educated, and certainly nobody should be moralistic about it when at that very moment in Alabama black children – in the rather bizarre language of the day, Manning used the word 'piccaninnies' – could only go to school with the help of federal injunctions and riot squads.

Liston simply opted out of his commitments and flew home. He gave an explanation: that he was upset by a sudden illness of eleven-year-old Eleanor, one of the two daughters who was living with Geraldine back home in Denver, and by a terrible bombing at the 16th Baptist Church Sunday School in Birmingham, Alabama, on 15 September. The bomb was left near the female restroom. When it was detonated, the blast took the lives of Denise McNair, who was 11, and Cynthia Wesley, Carole Robertson and Addie Mae Collins, all of whom were 14.

A tired, stressed Liston flew into Stapleton Field airport, Denver, around 11 p.m. on Wednesday, 18 September and declined invitations to speak to newsmen.

'You ain't going to get no words from me, I don't have to answer your questions,' he said, striding off with the gold-headed cane he had been given in Britain.

His upset at the murders of the children in Alabama seems to have been genuine and might even have bordered on grief. When asked by a girl on the plane home where he had been, for some reason he told her, 'Alabama.' He refused to give her an autograph. As he walked one block from the airport to catch a cab home, he was heard to say: 'I'm ashamed to be an American.'

At Denver airport, sparring partner Foneda Cox said: 'It's the bombing in Birmingham. That's what he's so hot about.'

Liston did at least confirm that Geraldine had called him to say Eleanor, who attended Smith elementary school, was ill.

This incident was a rare moment when Sonny appeared to react to the Civil Rights struggle. On other occasions he had refused to get involved, such as when he refused to make a donation to the NAACP, perhaps remembering when they had publicly disapproved of him before the first Patterson fight. When Liston was once asked about this, he gave the questioner his trademark stare and answered: 'I ain't got no dog-proof ass.' He avoided going back to the South because he was afraid what might happen if the police challenged him. 'They don't fight fair. Some cop puts a hose on me and I'll forget where I am.'

Back in England, events in Birmingham and Blackpool had to be cancelled, and a 'Champions In Training' feature on ITV that would have brought in £5,000 was scrapped. Harry Levene remembered: 'He was a great world champion while he was up there, but he liked the booze and women too much. He was not all bad, but after being very helpful over here, he gave me a lot of aggravation.'

Peter Keenan said:

> He had a chip on his shoulder, but being coloured and poor in the US is a terrible thing. People used him, which is why he was suspicious of them, but when you saw him with kids you realised there was a nice guy underneath it.

Two writs for breach of contract were taken out over the cancellation of the tour, but eventually the action seems to have ground to a halt in a morass of transatlantic paperwork. At one point, Joe Louis' wife, Martha, a qualified lawyer, was working on the case, representing Liston.

Early in 1965, Geraldine still said news of the Alabama bombing had certainly played on Sonny's mind but added: 'The tour wasn't set up right. Everything came too close together, and everybody was sick.' She also said questions involving the racial situation in America had put him under pressure. Sonny never returned to Britain.

18

I WANT TO MAKE A BEAUTIFUL LIFE

There is no doubt that Geraldine Liston gave Sonny more stability than anyone or anything else. He knew he could rely on her to be there, pretty much whatever he did, or how spectacularly he fell off the pedestal. She ignored what she didn't want to know about, which gave him an element of freedom – sometimes too much – and she loved what she did know about. In return, he treated her, when they were together, with complete respect. In October 1962, Geraldine described him as 'a wonderful person, the best husband you could get' to Joan Younger Dickinson.

Her mother, Eva, said: 'He's a real easy, nice person to get along with.'

Sonny helped out with the shopping, pushing a trolley round the supermarket. 'No list, no nothin',' he said to Dickinson. 'I just push that thing around and get what we need.' He was at ease if Geraldine was close by. 'I can get along anywhere so long as she's with me.'

The Liston family situation was difficult for writers to piece together and is still open to question. In London in 1963, Liston told ghostwriter Lionel Crane he had two daughters, one of whom was twelve. He implied they were from another relationship, or at least that's the way Crane understood it.

> Don't ask me a lot of questions about them because I ain't going to answer you. I'm going to tell you this and that's all. I had to leave them with their mother in St Louis. I wanted 'em but I couldn't get 'em. Now I got 'em and they're living in my home in Denver, Colorado.

Geraldine had a girl named Arletha in 1944 and may have had Eleanor around 1951. But little was, or is, known about the girls. Sonny's apparent claim to Crane that he was their father adds to the mystery and may well have been a deliberate smokescreen, perhaps to protect Geraldine's reputation. The probability that the girls were Geraldine's is also indicated by an FBI file dated 24 February 1964 (the day before Sonny fought Cassius Clay), which noted that a journalist in Honolulu named Red McQueen had written that Liston's stepdaughter had applied for a post with the FBI. Geraldine apparently told the journalist this in the presence of Joe Louis and Sonny, and at the news both fighters 'broke up the interview and howled with glee'.

However, the year before in Britain, Liston told Crane:

> I been married to my present wife Geraldine 12 years. Where I go, she goes, and I tell you that with she and the girls at home I've really got something to fight for. I want to make a beautiful life for them, the kind of life everybody dreams about. I want you to know about my wife because she's important to me.

Look magazine carried a photo of Sonny and Geraldine, with his mother Helen, and the mysterious Eleanor and Arletha in the house in Denver, published with a story headlined 'Sonny Liston: King of the Beasts' on 25 February 1964, the day of his first fight with Cassius Clay.

Having the 'daughters' around was an arrangement, however, that does not appear to have lasted long. By the second half of the 1960s, they were not being mentioned. Maybe they had simply grown up and gone.

Liston often said he was edgy if Geraldine wasn't around him. Certainly, there is evidence, from the trip to London and other misdemeanours, that if she wasn't there, he was likely to go off the rails.

> She was there when the going was rough. When I was in jail she came every visiting day. Never missed.
>
> She wears diamonds now and she's going to wear plenty more. I want her with me all the time. Apart from Geraldine there haven't been too many people that meant anything in my life . . .

In his obituary of Liston in January 1971, BBC boxing commentator Harry Carpenter, who had also worked on the *Daily Mail*, said:

> I only ever heard one person call Liston by his Christian name, Charles. That was his wife, Geraldine. She could handle him. But even she said, 'Don't be surprised if Charles doesn't say anything. Often he won't talk to me.'

Yet on another occasion, she said: 'He isn't moody. He isn't shy. He is just a person who don't talk much.'

Geraldine Liston was born Geraldine Chambers in St Louis, Missouri, on 25 January 1925. Her father Authur and mother Eva were both from Arkansas, which must have provided common ground with Sonny. Her father did odd jobs, labouring mostly, and her mother was a laundress working for a private family. Geraldine had brothers Authur and Thomas, and a sister, Mallie. She was educated to tenth grade, then left to get a job.

Sonny met Geraldine in St Louis, when they were working in John Vitale's factory, probably soon after he left prison.

Geraldine made him say grace before each meal, always the same thing: 'May the Lord bless us for the food we are about to receive, for everybody, for Christ's sake. Amen.'

She was cross when he asked for dinner at a certain time, then was late. With her he was relaxed, just a man about the house. She said he often sprawled out on a leopard skin rug on the floor to watch television. In their Denver home, he would lie down all evening and liked to watch westerns, while Geraldine preferred comedies. 'I get tired of all that killing,' she said.

Robert L. Burnes, who was involved in the start of Liston's career in St Louis, had no doubt that Geraldine was good for him. 'She manages his money,' he wrote in the *Saturday Evening Post* in 1960:

> They say proudly that they have a good balance in the bank. They won't specify how much. Geraldine keeps up his correspondence for him. For example, she writes on his behalf about four times a year to Father Stevens who, in the normal routine of diocesan changes, has been transferred from the chaplaincy at the penitentiary to a small parish in southern Missouri.

She read his mail and answered it, though she taught him how to sign his name. If anything more than 'Sonny Liston' was needed on, say a photo for a fan, she would write it. Just as in his conversations, he never saw the need to prolong things by the overuse of words. He said he had learned to read street signs but added: 'I don't have to read. I get Gerry to do it all for me.' Geraldine said: 'Sonny reads good, he just don't have any confidence in himself.'

He said another time, yes, he had learned to read a little, but he didn't enjoy the results: 'Every day I got to read what a big bum I am.'

Geraldine said her husband's enjoyment of practical jokes was a frightening feature early in their relationship. He would creep into the house and tiptoe up behind her when she was singing or humming a song and then touch her or make a sudden noise. It was something she got wise to. 'I hear a noise now and I say, "All right, Charles, come out . . ."' He also enjoyed telephoning her in a falsetto voice, asking to speak to Mr Charles Sonny Liston. Not surprising, really, that he was comfortable in the company of children! She also told Pete Hamill of the *New York Post* in 1962: 'Charles tries to play jokes and sound tougher than he really is. It's all those lies people have written about him.'

Geraldine was happy when Sonny was happy. Back before the first Patterson fight, she said, in a conversation quoted by Doc Young, that she would have preferred it if he had not boxed at all. She didn't like boxing, didn't like the people around it, didn't like the stress it brought:

> If it were up to me, I'd never have let Sonny do it. I'd take poverty over prizefighting. If we have kids, I won't let them fight, either. True, we wouldn't have the money. But if I didn't have it, I wouldn't know about it. And what you don't know, you don't miss.
>
> I'd much rather live simply without this anxiety and torment. Lots of people do things and you don't hear about it. I know he's done wrong, but if he weren't in the public eye, it would be forgotten. The sportswriters always keep bringing it up. It's like they don't ever want him to be good. How's a man going to be good, if folks don't let him? Many nights we talk it over. Sonny knows himself . . .

When he was champion, Liston gave money to ex-fighters like Johnny Saxton, the old welterweight champion who had hit hard times, and to two more who had gone blind. He also supported causes like cerebral palsy and gave his time to visit hospitals like one for disabled children in Allentown, Pennsylvania. 'You think you've got it bad,' he said. 'You go there and you know you've never had a dark day.'

Geraldine cited an example of police harassment of Liston in an interview with Barbara La Fontaine in 1965. She claimed her telephone conversation with the police, after Sonny had been arrested, went as follows:

'Well, what did he do?'

'He was driving under the influence of alcohol.'

'Was he driving?'

'Well, no, not at the time.'

Geraldine said Sonny refused to take the alcohol test, which involved picking something up off the floor after the police had thrown it down. She said he told them to pick it up themselves. 'He said, "If you want to lock me up, lock me up, stop waiting for the newspapers."' Geraldine felt it was a complete waste of time, another example of the law harassing her wayward but good husband:

> People getting killed and shot down, and they put Charles' picture on the front page! That's stupid. They ought to be worrying about the world.

He's just one little person in the world, he isn't hurting anybody. He hasn't had a wreck, he isn't beating anybody up.

I don't hold up for wrong. If he was out fighting, hurting people, I'd be the first to say, 'Now you run along.'

She said people in Denver were nice to them, but the police had actually said to him: 'We don't want you here.'

Geraldine, of course, saw the best side of Sonny, but she was also honest enough to admit his failings, or at least those she knew about:

Charles is a good man . . . I don't care what the newspapers say . . . he acts like he loves me, whether he does or not, and he takes care of his home and that's all you can ask of a man.

Charles is no preacher. I know he ought to be above reproach. I know he ought to be better than other people, but sometimes he do get into things.

On 5 November 1963, Cassius Clay rolled into Denver to sign a contract. At 1 a.m. that morning, he had pestered Liston at his house, standing outside and shouting insults until the neighbours called the police. They signed a contract in front of the media and Clay said: 'Somebody pinch me. If I'm not asleep, this is a dream come true.' After the press had what they needed Clay tucked into a plate of chicken. Liston looked at him and said: 'You eat like you headed to the electric chair.'

19

HE'S JUST A LITTLE BOY IN
THE DARK AND HE'S SCARED

William B. MacDonald Jr owned a stud farm near Delray Beach, a baseball team in Tampa, a yacht, 45 per cent of a racetrack . . . and wanted to promote the heavyweight championship of the world.

He liked to make people happy. 'You can't sell to everybody,' he said once, 'but you can be everybody's friend.'

In order to do this, he handed out cufflinks with his face engraved on them. He entertained guests on a two-hole pitch-and-putt course in the grounds of his Florida home and on a fifty-foot cruiser named *Snoozie* after his wife – 'She's still harder to wake up than a bear' – moored yards from his front door. His car of preference was a Rolls-Royce. Whoever you were, it was likely he would address you as 'coach'.

His eight-year-old daughter's treehouse contained a fridge, stove and jukebox. His son's sixth birthday present was a railway engine with 800 feet of track meandering through the gardens.

Bill MacDonald had met the President, he had met Jayne Mansfield, and he had the photographs on his wall to prove it. He was negotiating to buy Channel 10, the Miami-area television channel affiliated to the American Broadcasting Corporation. 'I've spent $165,000 in legal fees, but if I get it, it's bingo – seven or eight million right away.'

He estimated he had lost $200,000 staging golf tournaments 'but made a million friends'. And now he wanted to promote the heavyweight championship of the world.

He had bankrolled the promoters of the 1961 world championship 'decider' between Floyd Patterson and Ingemar Johansson in Miami to the tune of $400,000 but had not promoted it himself. He had enjoyed the publicity and had lost nothing. He also revealed that at one point he had been approached to act as manager for Liston. He was vague about the details but said in an interview with *Sports Illustrated*: 'Someone once approached me to manage Liston. He was looking for a front man. But it's an ugly business to begin with, and I make too much money other ways to be bothered wet-nursing those kids.'

In 1961, the city of Miami Beach had awarded him a plaque in recognition and appreciation of his 'work and accomplishments'. He was a member of the board of trustees at St Francis Hospital, a founder-member of Mount Sinai Hospital, a member of the board of Miami Heart Institute and Cedars of Lebanon Hospital, chairman of the eighth annual brotherhood dinner of the National Conference of Christians and Jews, and a member and trustee of the Eaton Foundation at the University of Miami. A publicity handout distributed with the fight media pack described him as 'a great philanthropist contributing to the betterment of his fellow man'. One stop short of a saint, it seemed.

Chris Dundee, who had promoted fights in Miami for a generation and more, suggested MacDonald spread his philanthropy to Liston–Clay. Dundee's view, or the one he offered MacDonald, was that they could make a million dollars as easily as breaking sticks. And on the back of that tip, MacDonald bought the rights to promote the fight from Inter-Continental Promotions Inc., the company Jack Nilon had set up supposedly to guarantee Liston's future. MacDonald paid Inter-Continental $625,000 for the live promotion but did not buy the theatre TV rights. That was a monumental blunder. By fight time, there were more than one million seats available for the closed-circuit screening across the United States.

MacDonald said he just went straight in with his maximum offer, didn't mess with negotiating and wasting time. 'I figure if this man Jack Nilon don't take it, he can't count. And him being in the concession business, coming up from a bag of peanuts and a hot dog, he ought to know how to count.'

MacDonald said, with other expenses, he needed to raise $800,000 from the live gate to break even. The best he could do, with a full price sell-out of all 16,448 seats, was $100,000 profit.

As, perhaps, it dawned on him that there was no chance of this happening, he accepted the probability of losses but satisfied himself that he was doing something positive for the Miami Beach area. He was in it, he said, for the kick of making it happen and making it a success. He wanted people to want to come out of their homes and queue, even sleep, in the street to be able to watch it. He said he enjoyed the 'motion' of being involved. He said moving the ringside seats at $250 would not be an issue. It was persuading the ordinary man to part with his hard-earned money to be there in the cheaper seats that was the difficult part of the job. 'This promotion is going to be as clean as possible,' he said to *Sports Illustrated*'s Gilbert Rogin. 'It's going to be a breath of fresh air.'

Surprisingly, MacDonald had a shrewd analytical take on the fight itself:

> I figure Clay wins it. He'll take the title if he stays away, jabs and runs.
> But the little jerk is so egotistical he thinks he can punch Liston's nose
> sideways. It's liable to be a stinky fight to watch, but if Clay gets by seven
> or eight he's liable to win it.

Technically, prizefighting for reward was still illegal in Florida. MacDonald
and Dundee circumvented that in the usual way by declaring that the occasion
was sponsored by the Veterans of Foreign Wars charity (VFW). For the
privilege, MacDonald and Dundee were to pay the organisation $500. They also
had about 20 VFW members at ringside. This done, the Miami Commission
licensed the fight.

In a subsequent financial wrangle between Inter-Continental and MacDonald,
Harold Conrad told the court hearing:

> Well, I think there was some kind of a handout that these guys [VFW]
> had been having for years in this town. You can't put on a fight unless they
> are at the door. I don't know what the details are.'

VFW representative Max Lenchner testified that he had received the $500
cheque and recalled the conversation he had with Chris Dundee, who told him:
'We are having a fight next week, Max. Be here with the men.' And Lenchner
said: 'That's the way it is.'

Chris Dundee had begun in boxing in 1926 when another of his brothers,
Joe, was fighting. Chris would go with him whenever he could. The family
name, incidentally, was Mirenda. They were Italian immigrants, but somewhere
along the way Joe took the name Dundee. Chris, who worked his corner, did
too. He moved from Philadelphia to New York, where he was based at the
Capitol Hotel, and looked after top-class fighters like Ken Overlin, who was
world middleweight champion, Midget Wolgast, the flyweight champion, and
contender Georgie Abrams. (Joe Dundee, incidentally, was not the fighter who
used that name and held the world welterweight title.)

Chris's younger brother Angelo, meanwhile, learned cornerwork from leading
trainers Whitey Bimstein, Chickie Ferrara, Ray Arcel and Charley Goldman.
He talked to them all, watched them all, held the bucket in corners they ran.
He watched how they wrapped hands. 'I learned how to keep my mouth shut
and my ears open,' Angelo said.

This is the way you learn. I got to be known as a dependable kid. Chris gave me some four-round fighters to handle, and I was in Stillman's Gym day and night, working with them and hustling fights for them.

Chris moved on to Miami when the small clubs in New York began to die out and the television money was controlled by the IBC. In Miami, Angelo set up his own gym on Fifth Street. 'The Cuban era came along when a lot of good fighters came to Miami to get away from the Castro regime,' he told Graham Houston in a *Boxing News* interview in 1974. 'We had Luis Rodriguez and Sugar Ramos, Doug Vaillant and Florentino Fernandez, who got robbed against Gene Fullmer for the middleweight title.'

Chris Dundee had promoted almost 400 shows by the time of his involvement with the Liston–Clay fight, including 12 at the Convention Hall. He knew the business backwards, sidewards and any other wards you could think of. The publicity pack for the promotion declared him 'a solid citizen of the ever-growing Miami Beach area', with wife Gerri, daughter Susan and son Michael.

Liston arrived in Miami four weeks before the fight. He was taken from the plane in an electric cart across the tarmac to the VIP room. Clay, who was training as usual at Angelo Dundee's Fifth Street Gym, made sure he was there to greet Liston by running after the cart across the tarmac. The girl driving the cart stalled it. Liston got out, telling MacDonald he would break Clay's arms. MacDonald pleaded and cajoled him back into the cart, and they drove away with Cassius still yelling. MacDonald's stressed-out publicist Al Taylor saw the episode as an embarrassment that did not help people believe the fight was an occasion they needed to be at.

Liston was ushered through the airport terminal, his face its usual mask, a trilby on his head, a raincoat over his arm. The only man looking grimmer than him was MacDonald, who had his arm through Liston's, guiding him. Taylor was much more animated on the other side of the champion.

Liston had hired an expensive house at 6351 Pine Tree Drive, Miami Beach, for himself and his closest associates. Among those who visited him there was Ash Resnick.

Harold Conrad was still with the Liston public relations team. He says Liston simply could not believe he could lose to Clay. Instead of training, he took life at his leisure – and pleasure. 'He thought he was invincible,' said Conrad, in an interview with Dan Hirschberg for *Boxing Today*:

He scared the shit out of Patterson just by looking at him, and here comes this big-mouth kid. He didn't train at all for that fight. He worked out a little, went to the gym. He would hang out at a beauty parlour banging on some of the chicks.

I'd tell him, 'This kid is big and strong, he's fast, he can hit.'

Sonny would just answer, 'Ah, you're kidding. I'll scare the shit out of that nigger-faggot. I'll scare the shit out of him at the weigh-in. I'll put the eye on him . . .'

Jack McKinney also felt Liston's superiority over Clay in the two incidents in the Thunderbird the year before were the worst thing that could have happened to Liston. 'Sonny thought all he had to do was take off his robe and Clay would faint,' said McKinney. 'He made that colossal misjudgement. He didn't train at all.'

Harry Carpenter remembered the only time Liston ever gave him a long quote. It was when he asked if Clay's psychological tactics were getting under his skin. Liston said:

You ever hear that saying 'whistlin' in the dark'? You know what a small boy does walking through a graveyard at night when he's scared. He whistles. Well, that's Clay. He's just a little boy in the dark, and he's scared.

Joe Louis also said Liston's preparations were not what they should have been. His sparring partners were not good enough. One of the best of them was his old friend from St Louis, Jesse Bowdry, who was a light-heavyweight. Bowdry would box on the undercard in Miami – the last bout of his long career. It would be his tenth defeat in his last twelve fights. He didn't have it any more.

Leotis Martin, a top-class amateur who would eventually turn into a world-class heavyweight – and would be the last man to beat Sonny – was another. He bobbed and weaved, moved as quickly as he could, but as imitations of Clay went, it wasn't very useful. Liston didn't look good. Louis said: 'He can't hit some of them, they're too small . . . One guy should have had his licence taken away, he was so bad.' Even so, Louis said he thought Clay stood very little chance.

In Miami, after an impromptu doorstepping job at Liston's rented house, British writer Reg Gutteridge was leaving with nothing more than a stare and rebuke from the champion, when he chanced on Louis, who was sitting on a bench outside with his wife Martha. Louis called him over and told him:

This is an angry man and he can't afford to be angry fighting Clay. I keep him cool. Cassius is a master of psychological warfare. He irritates and disturbs, and whatever Sonny may think, maybe, Clay bothers him.

I am a practical guy, and I face realities. I tell Sonny, 'Nobody saw me losing to Max Schmeling, but I did.' It curbs his over-confidence. His title is a passport to respectability. He has got to hang on to it.

Liston agreed to press workouts at the Surfside Civic Centre, afterwards answering questions. At one he was asked if he had met anyone bigger than him before. It was the kind of dumb ill-researched enquiry that on another day might have provoked him into a bitter 'yeah' and a slow, steady stare. He was relaxed, though, and offered: 'Nino Valdes, Cleveland Williams, Julio Mederos . . .'

Someone else suggested Clay might be too fast for him.

'Is he fast? Can he catch bullets or something?'

It was the same line he had used before the first Patterson fight.

'The faster he is, the faster it will be over.'

Liston felt Clay would be no faster than Patterson. 'I shouldn't have to be training all this time to go just one round.'

A large sign in front of the workout area invited fans to 'Have Your Picture Taken With Sonny Liston'. At a price, naturally.

Peter Wilson for the *Daily Mirror* enjoyed an incident outside the civic centre when Clay, with nine equally noisy friends, came to bait Liston and was threatened with being arrested for breach of the peace and blocking the sidewalk. The local police chief who almost threw Cassius into the slammer was named Wiley B. Barefoot. 'So help me, I'm not making him up,' chortled Wilson. 'I'm not that clever!'

Meanwhile, as the good Officer Barefoot was doing his duty, Clay's 'official photographer', Howard Bingham, managed to slip inside to see Liston's workout, only to be ejected by a security man, whom Wilson discovered was named Gene Buffalo. (Mr Buffalo, incidentally, had been a fighter. He was knocked out in one round by Sugar Ray Robinson in 1949.)

Liston did throw writers a few morsels every so often. 'I don't hate Cassius Clay,' he said with a week or so to go:

I love him so much I'm giving him 22½ per cent of the gate. Clay means a lot to me . . . He's my baby, my million-dollar baby. I hope he keeps well and I sure hope he turns up.

When pressed a little further, he said three rounds would be enough. 'The poor guy can't fight,' he said. 'That's why he talks so much.'

When someone brought up the question of ring-rust being a possibility, Liston seemed exasperated:

> Jeez, how good do I have to be? If I knock 'em out any quicker, the other guy won't even show up. The less I fight, the better I get. You say I've won three fights in three rounds in three years. So OK, so after next week it will be four fights in four rounds in four years.

According to George Whiting, after the question-and-answer session Liston was so irritated that he went out and took it out on sparring partner Leotis Martin. 'But for the 16 oz gloves, I feel that brother Martin might no longer be with us,' wrote Whiting, who said nobody could accuse Liston of not taking the job seriously and suggested that Clay should stick to show business.

He did have his moments of good temper. When he was late for one press conference four weeks before the fight, he actually apologised to the media and told them: 'The only way Cassius can hurt me is not to show up for the fight.'

Father Edward Murphy arrived and said he had never seen Liston so relaxed:

> Security has made a different man of him. He wants people to like him . . . Sonny has suffered frustrations all his life . . . He has no religion, but he believes in God. He comes to my church once in a while.

Willie Reddish, as trainers will, said Liston had been good to work with all the way through the camp and was in the best shape he'd been in during their four years together.

Confidence in Clay's chances did not even extend to members of the syndicate that backed him. Bill Faversham admitted he would have preferred to have given him more time, to have him fight Doug Jones again and do a better job, perhaps fight Machen and Patterson before risking everything against Liston:

> But what the hell. The guy's of age . . . All he wanted was Liston. So now he's got Liston. But we figure he can win, if the young fool doesn't get too ambitious or too impetuous in the early rounds. He's got speed, a good left hand, good enough to peck Liston to pieces after seven or eight rounds.

George Whiting quoted Faversham, and added his own incredulous rider: 'Peck Liston to pieces?'

Whiting said he and Faversham went to the Fifth Street Gym to watch Clay's workout. 'But I fear we each saw something different,' he wrote:

> The chairman of Cassius Clay Inc. enthused over the smooth dexterity with which the company's gangling asset slipped kidney punches, moved away from clinches and countered Liston's right hooks. But from where I was standing, these same manoeuvres looked remarkably amateurish.

Whiting said Clay's father was watching the workout in a pair of pea-green pants – and did not seem enamoured when his offspring was hit on the nose three times in succession by a sparring partner's left jab. When it was over, the young man declared himself satisfied. 'I believe in myself so much it's embarrassing,' he said. 'My fight will be to hit and not get hit. I can't be beat. No one can beat me.'

Jack Nilon talked up a bizarre idea he had of taking Liston to the Soviet Union after he had beaten Clay. The peanut and popcorn mogul felt a fight between his champion and a leading amateur would be huge and also helpful in terms of developing international business interests.

Liston said he would rather fight Cleveland Williams. Since the second of his defeats by Sonny in 1960, Williams had won twelve, drawn one and lost one – a split decision to a rising contender from Chicago, Ernie Terrell – in fourteen fights. He had just knocked out Roger Rischer in three. Only Liston and Terrell had beaten him in the past ten years. But Nilon wasn't interested in Williams. Liston asked:

> So why doesn't some guy fight himself into a position where I cannot ignore him? That's what I did . . . Joe Louis did all right for himself fighting the bum of the month. But times have changed. I don't think I could make a score doing that.

Betting was holding steady. It had been somewhere between 5–1 and 6–1 against Clay for weeks. Clay went on enjoying himself. 'After I finish with Liston,' he said, 'he'd rather run through hell in a gasoline sports coat than fight me again.' He also told reporters: 'If Liston beats me, I'll crawl across the ring, kiss his feet and take a jet out of the country.'

Someone called his bluff, very quietly asking: 'What would you really do?'

Clay paused for a moment, smiled and said: 'I'll go to my dressing-room, collect my money and go home . . .'

Willie Pastrano, the world light-heavyweight champion, also trained in the Fifth Street gym under the guidance of Angelo Dundee. He had seen Cassius develop and admired his talent, as well as his ability to drum up publicity. 'It's his show,' said Pastrano. 'Cassius has trouble getting off stage.'

After sparring extensively with him over the past couple of years, Pastrano also gave him a real chance of victory. 'Cassius might be scared and tense at the start, but when he finds Liston slow and easy to hit he will box like a dream.'

Pastrano also said that behind the scenes Clay was not bragging, that he admitted he was nervous, 'half-scared', but Willie worried for him that when he danced around with his hands too low and leaned away from punches, which every young amateur was taught not to do, he was wide open for a left hook. Henry Cooper had already dropped him heavily, Sonny Banks put him down too. Pastrano worried what might happen if he made those kinds of errors against Liston.

In one verbal exchange at a press conference with the television cameras rolling, Clay used the same line on the champion face to face that he had already given to the press: 'If you whup me, I'll crawl across the ring and kiss your feet.'

Liston said: 'I ain't gonna wait around all night until you're able to crawl.'

Angelo Dundee said if Clay listened, followed instructions, he had the ability to take out Liston late in the fight. 'We have many assets,' said Dundee to Tex Maule of *Sports Illustrated*:

> Clay has a style Liston has never seen before. He is much faster than Liston. He has the faculty of getting under Liston's skin, and he will not be browbeaten by him.
>
> Cassius respects the champion, but really, deep down inside himself, Clay thinks he is unbeatable. And he can hit Sonny with every punch he has. Sonny isn't hard to hit . . .
>
> We can hit him with uppercuts. Left and right. Cassius is the only heavyweight in the world with a good left uppercut . . . If you built a prototype of what kind of fighter can whip Liston, you couldn't improve on Clay. He hits hard, he moves, he has every punch in the book.
>
> We can knock Liston out in the 11th or 12th round by wearing him down with the quantity of punches. If Cassius will do what he's told.

Solomon McTier, who helped Dundee after his own career had been ended by a detached retina in 1961, was a quiet member of the team but saw in Clay a touch of greatness that many still overlooked:

You see this kid, the way he can go, the things he can do. He can be a great man if he only does what he is told. All he needs to be afraid of is Clay.

If he keeps his cool and outboxes and outfoxes Liston – which he can do with ease – he can win without any trouble. He's the most wonderful boxer there is. Liston could be just another sparring partner for him. But he gets carried away. He's young and restless and foolish sometime . . .

Another time Clay said:

Maybe I can be beat. I doubt it. But the man is going to have to knock me down and then I'll get up and he'll have to knock me down again and I'll get up and he'll have to knock me down and I'll still get up. I've worked too hard and too long to get this chance. I'm gonna have to be killed before I lose, and I ain't going to die easy.

And he said: 'I'll uppercut him stupid. I'll upset the world. I talk too much to lose.'

Once while on his back having his Cuban conditioner, Luis Sarria, work on him, he talked quietly as the press gathered round in chairs; sometimes it seemed he was talking to them, sometimes perhaps to his handler, or even to himself:

I'm a pretty fighter. I don't get hit. I'm pretty and smooth. I don't get cut. I'm not marked. I'm something new. The game is alive. Before I came it was dead. The reporters have got something to write about now.

The peanut man is going to make money, the popcorn man is going to make money, the beer man's going to make money. The town is alive.

This is the biggest sport. I am participating in the biggest sport that ever took place in the whole wide world. Nothing is as great as me. The biggest thing in the world is the heavyweight champion. And I'm not going to be just an ordinary heavyweight champion. I'm going to be the greatest of all time.

20

RUMBLE, YOUNG MAN, RUMBLE

Chris Dundee and Bill MacDonald set the tickets in the 16,448-seat Miami Beach Convention Hall, a pink and blue building surrounded by fountains, from $20 to $250, the latter price 'for the Golden Circle – Distinguished Sportsmen Only'. They had guaranteed the fighters $625,000 and needed $800,000 from the live gate to break even. Theatre Network Television (TNT) had the closed-circuit rights.

An interesting, perhaps revealing twist was that Liston refused to sign the deal unless TNT guaranteed there would be no segregation in seating in any of their venues. This meant that three cinemas who had intended 'whites only' audiences actually cancelled plans to screen the fight. They were in Jackson, Mississippi; Waco, Texas; and Montgomery, Alabama. James Farmer, the national director of the Congress On Racial Equality, praised Liston for taking a stand. The *New York Herald Tribune* reported that the champion's legal advisers were investigating a New Orleans theatre where three black men had refused to leave the box-office area after being refused tickets. It provides the first firm piece of evidence that Liston, while primarily concerned with the well-being of himself and his wife, was not entirely apolitical, that his anger and grief at the deaths of the youngsters in the Baptist church in Alabama the previous year was not simply indicative of the warmth and empathy he felt for children.

In New Orleans, there was a row because the Municipal Auditorium rented half of the building to the promoter of the closed-circuit screening of the fight, at which the potential for noise or even rowdiness was high, and the other half to the local philharmonic society, which apparently had a contract that guaranteed them a quiet, peaceful performance. The classical music fans were not amused, but the show went ahead when the fight promoter insisted he would make sure his customers did not become unduly boisterous. Liston's Inter-Continental Promotions concentrated its energies on pushing the closed-circuit sales, which would drive its profits higher. It was, inevitably, less interested in helping with the live tickets, as if Dundee and MacDonald took a financial bath it was not Inter-Continental's concern. One of the Theatre Network Television publicists went so far as to fire a broadside at the live ticket price, suggesting it made more sense to watch in a theatre for $10.

MacDonald's publicist Al Taylor later admitted the whole experience of trying to promote the fight was a nightmare. For seven and a half weeks, crisis piled atop crisis until it didn't seem possible the bad luck could continue. One of Taylor's headaches was how to cram more than 500 members of the world's press, including radio broadcasters, all of whom had been given written approval to attend, into 396 seats. Altogether the fight would be relayed live to listeners in Japan, Italy, France, Germany, South America, Sweden, the Philippines, Canada and the British Isles. In the end, Taylor had to put some no doubt disgruntled writers into an auxiliary section. Even then, he and his wife, Claire, had to redraw the whole seating plan when they realised someone had omitted to allow room for the steps in the ring corners. More chaos ensued when it was discovered that only 16 inches had been allowed between press rows – no room for a table that would accommodate the essential typewriters.

Taylor was happy with the coverage afforded the fight by the *Miami News* but was exasperated by what seemed to him deliberate opposition from the larger, influential *Miami Herald*. He had problems setting up photo shoots as well. Astonishingly, as well as Liston, Clay, who was as media-friendly an athlete as there has ever been, refused to have photographers along for roadwork sessions. Clay let writers and cameramen talk to him at home, but Liston refused. The champion also declined requests for photographs in the ring at the Surfside Country Club where he was winding down his preparations.

It didn't help much either when Clay had an off day in the gym while the cameras were there. Harvey aka Cody Jones, a 6 ft 1 in. 210 lb sparring partner from Detroit, repeatedly nailed him with left hooks, both to head and body. On other days, however, he handed his sparring partners, mostly Jones and Dave Bailey, a boxing lesson. And he was always bubbly, with the bright-eyed intensity of a child playing his favourite game.

'Ain't no light-heavyweight fast enough to catch me,' he would yell. 'I'm the fastest heavyweight who ever lived . . . I am the Greatest.' And with Bundini Brown, he would chant, in perfect unison: 'Float like a butterfly, sting like a bee' and 'Rumble, young man, rumble' – then, staring at each other, they would roar. And so on, and so on. (Brown's real name was Drew, but everyone called him Bundini. After years in the US and merchant navies, he had joined the Clay entourage as a motivator, helping hand and court jester shortly before the Doug Jones fight in New York.)

...t setback of all, said Taylor, was the constant rumour that Clay was ... sympathetic to the Nation of Islam. At one point, Cassius was ...ed by the promoters to keep his beliefs private until after the fight, ...e was young and self-righteous. Instead of compromising, he broke camp and flew to New York for a Black Muslim meeting. The *Miami Herald*, quite rightly, ran the story. Taylor said MacDonald was furious that by paying Clay for his services he was helping finance the Nation of Islam and very nearly called the fight off. In the end, the collective brains around Cassius made him see sense. When a story was put out that in the wake of the revelations somebody had tried to burn the ring in the Fifth Street Gym, Liston's publicist Harold Conrad, who was not incapable of tinkering with the exact truth, denied all knowledge. 'Publicity stunt?' he roared. 'Man, that's arson. I draw the line at arson!'

Conrad did, however, fly in newsworthy sources like Cus D'Amato, who always had something to say, Marty Marshall, who had broken Liston's jaw back in 1954, and Eddie Machen, who had extended Liston for the full 12 rounds in Seattle in 1960. Barely anyone took up the opportunity to conduct interviews.

Liston was furious at the arrival of Eddie Machen. 'You trying to shame me, or something?' he yelled at one of the public relations team. Liston and Machen met once and exchanged abuse. Liston said at a press conference that when they fought it was a foot race; Machen challenged him to a return, they shouted, and Machen's friends led him away from the room.

Father Stevens arrived and was introduced at a Liston workout as the man who gave Sonny his start in boxing. Liston nodded. The priest said that whatever he did all those years ago it would have had no effect if Sonny had not been the man and fighter he was. 'Sonny demonstrated what a man can do when he has the opportunity – and takes it.'

Another day they brought The Beatles into the gym to meet Clay, who happily played around with them for the cameras. 'You ain't as dumb as you look,' said Cassius.

'No, but you are,' said John Lennon, with the smart-ass style of a would-be rock god. The joke fell flat.

Liston, who liked jazz and blues, was taken to see The Beatles play and was some way less than impressed, asking: 'Is this what all the people are screaming about? My dog plays drums better than that kid with the big nose.'

An artist, Douglas Gorsline, arrived to paint both fighters for *Sports Illustrated*. Liston said no, but Gorsline did spend an afternoon with Clay at the challenger's home, working while he talked on the phone, lay on the couch and lounged around. Gorsline liked him: 'Basically he is a sweet man, and serious-minded, but naive. He can't figure himself out.' Gorsline also drew the scene in the gym as Luis Sarria rubbed Clay down. 'He was talking about building some sort of utopian community, with pretty buildings and clean streets and everybody happy. That's how he thinks. That's what I mean by naive.'

Cassius enjoyed himself when Jim Jacobs came into the gym with a TV camera. Jacobs introduced the challenger to his viewers: 'Ladies and gentlemen, this is Cassius Marcellus Clay. He's young, he's handsome . . .'

'They know it,' interrupted Clay.

Jacobs ploughed on: 'He's a poet and a prophet and many people think he will be the next heavyweight champion of the world.'

At one point he began to make a point by explaining: 'I saw Sonny Liston a few days ago, Cassius, and . . .'

'Ain't he ugly!' interrupted Clay again, this time taking over: 'He's too ugly to be champ. The champ should be pretty like me . . .'

Jacobs never did get to make that particular point, as Cassius and Bundini Brown took off on one of their rants. He declared that 100 per cent of the people in the crowd were coming to see him and 99 per cent wanted to see him beaten. 'They think I talk too much,' he said. 'I am the resurrector, I am the saviour of the boxing world, if it weren't for me boxing would be dead!'

When Liston was working out, Clay paid a visit in a sports jacket and bow tie. He took the jacket off and began deriding the champion, then climbed into the roped-off area where Liston was working out. Liston chased after him, Jack Nilon threw himself between them, and Cassius scrambled through the ropes. Everybody was laughing. Even Liston allowed a grim smile to play on his face for a second or two. Liston gave the interviews he had to give. He said no, he wasn't edgy. No, he wasn't stale. No, he hadn't underestimated Clay.

Clay's rhymes were in full flow, of course. Once he called out to Liston in a prearranged microphone exchange: 'You are 40 if you are a day / And you don't belong in a ring with Cassius Clay . . .'

Another television interview saw the airing of the inspired rhyme in which he described the end of the fight in round eight. It began: 'Clay comes out to meet Liston and Liston starts to retreat / If he goes back any further he'll be in a ringside seat . . .' And it ended with Liston being knocked out by a punch that lifted him out of the arena and out over the Atlantic:

> Who would have thought when they came to the fight
> That they would witness the launching of a human satellite.
> They did not dream when they put down their money
> That they would see a total eclipse of the Sonny.

Clay's sense of fun could not turn the fight into a financial success, however. In a country so suspicious, so traumatised, as this, the publicity about his link to the Nation of Islam had killed interest. Los Angeles columnist Jim Murray highlighted the increasingly unattractive proposition the match presented – a man with 'a record of armed robbery, women-scaring and cop-beating is the sentimental favourite. . . The villain is the pretty one for a change. Liston gets the white hat.' Murray said the open secret that Clay was embracing what he described as the Black Muslims had turned people off him. 'Black supremacists are just as big an affront to humanity as white supremacists.' Clay, he said, was about as popular as a barracuda.

With a couple of days to go, Chris Dundee, who had told Bill MacDonald they would make a million dollars as easy as breaking sticks, admitted any idea of making a profit was out but felt optimistic they might still cover the guarantee. For some reason best known to themselves, only three ticket agencies were set up for sales in south Florida, apart from the arena itself, and all three were relatively inaccessible to most Miami residents or visitors. The organisation could not have been less successful if they had been laundering money.

Dundee's neck, ricked some weeks earlier, was paining him again. He took to wearing a neck brace. Columnist Tommy Fitzgerald wrote unkindly that tickets were moving only slightly faster than Dundee's head.

Someone also started rumours that MacDonald and Dundee would cut the prices nearer the fight, which had the effect of putting people off from buying in advance. Al Taylor said that in spite of MacDonald's constant denials that this was the case, around 3,000 people stood in the rain outside the arena waiting for the price cut. They were still there only ten minutes before the fight began. With $800,000 needed to break even, the take was said in a later court hearing to be $225,000.

Taylor said the final twist came when the rain, in the shape of a prolonged, heavy storm, washed out any hopes of a 'walk-up' at the gate. Taylor said: 'I was frazzled and crushed. All day long I had been running around like a madman, attempting to juggle a thousand details . . . But nothing worked.'

21

THIS KID IS OUT OF HIS MIND

It was Jack Nilon who asked the Miami Commission for the fighters to weigh in separately. Nilon's worry concerned what his man might do to the challenger before the time came for violence to turn legal. 'Liston is angry and might knock out the kid when they get to the scales,' he said. While the commissioners felt something unpredictable might happen, they could not have been prepared for the scale of it. They said there was no reason to change tradition. The boxers would weigh in, one after the other, in the same room beginning at 10.30 a.m. Each boxer would have a chair, and medical officers would examine them on the stage.

There was an audience, too. One estimate was that about 500 people were there, only a small proportion of whom were on official business. Among them, the 1930s heavyweight Kingfish Levinsky was apparently attempting to sell ties. (Kingfish had once lasted less than a round with Joe Louis and was so traumatised that as the fight ended he urged the referee: 'Please don't let him hit me again.')

Clay and Bundini Brown walked in – Cassius had on his blue denim 'Bear-Huntin' jacket – hollering: 'Ready to rumble.' Eventually, they were shown to a dressing-room. Faversham sent Gordon Davidson, a lawyer for the syndicate, to warn Clay that if he misbehaved the Miami commission would fine him. Davidson recalled that Brown shouted that they couldn't fine Cassius because he was the greatest . . . logic and common sense seemed to have broken down, and Davidson explained: 'Yes, they can, and he can pay.' Faversham admitted he was perspiring freely as they waited for proceedings to begin.

There was a delay when neither man would leave their dressing-room first. Faversham sorted it out by pointing out to his man that he wasn't champion quite yet and when he was, then he could come out last. 'I tell you,' he said, 'it was worse than handling Caruso!'

Davidson led them out, and once they saw the crowd again, Clay and Brown set off on their choreographed rants. Clay was advised by a commissioner to control himself and conduct himself in accordance with the rules. Flanked by Angelo Dundee and Ray Robinson, he stared back.

The moment Liston appeared, Clay went into verbal overdrive, pointing and screeching:

> I'll take you on right now. I can beat you any time, you chump . . . You're a sucker, you don't have a chance . . . You think you're something and I'm nothing . . . I am the greatest, I am the king. I can whup any man in the world. I float like a butterfly, sting like a bee.

Looking on, it was Madison Square Garden matchmaker Teddy Brenner who said: 'My God, he's scared to death. This kid is out of his mind. He might not show up for the fight.'

Faversham held him around the waist. Ray Robinson had an arm. When Bundini set off again, repeating into Clay's ear, 'Float like a butterfly, sting like a bee', Faversham snapped at him: 'For Christ's sake, Drew, shut up, will you?'

Liston had believed he would destroy Clay psychologically at the weigh-in, almost from the moment he looked at him. When he gave Clay the stare, the young man said: 'Who are you looking at, you big ugly bear?'

Harold Conrad, who was working with Sonny's publicity team, said: 'He [Liston] lost the fight right there.'

As Clay stepped up to the scales and took off his gown he shouted across to Liston: 'You ain't got a chance. There is no way you can win and you know it.' Liston came closer, but Clay pointed at him over the top of the heads of officials: 'You ain't nothing. You ain't nothing.'

Clay's weight was announced: 'Two hundred and ten and a half pounds.'

As Liston stepped to the scales, someone – probably a press photographer – called out: 'Bring Clay over, bring Clay over.'

Liston's weight was announced: 'Two hundred and eighteen pounds.'

Once his pulse had been taken, Clay launched a tirade of abuse at Liston. 'I'm gonna eat you alive!' he screamed.

Liston walked over to where Clay was being examined, sitting down. Clay reached out, even as the doctor's stethoscope was on his chest, to prod Liston, but police moved between them. As the champion moved away, Clay called him a chump and a jailbird.

People laughed as Liston raised two fingers to photographers in the traditional victory salute – which might also be interpreted as a two-round prediction. Clay pronounced: 'I predict that tonight somebody will die at ringside from shock . . .'

A member of the Miami Commission announced over the microphone: 'Clay is fined two thousand five hundred dollars.'

Dr Alexander Robbins, examining the boxers for the commission, took it upon himself to declare that Clay was 'in an extreme state of excitement amounting to fear'. He said: 'He is emotionally unbalanced and in a severely nervous state.'

After Robbins' assessment of Clay, rumours spread through the city that, never mind price cuts, the fight would not even happen. Ray Robinson didn't help. He told English journalists that Clay's heart and pulse were in overdrive. Apparently, Dr Robbins had said that.

The writers found Angelo Dundee, who denied any suggestion that Clay was in trouble. 'Maybe you think he's nuts but he's really being smart,' he said. Of course the fight was on, he said. No, Clay wasn't afraid, he said. 'With that kind of fear I'd face a cage of lions. Cassius will win. Liston was so shook up he couldn't talk. He just didn't know what to make of the kid.' They found Clay's personal physician, Ferdie Pacheco, who said yes, the heartbeat was fast, but that it was nothing to worry about. A journalist asked the doctor if he had given Clay anything before the weigh-in that might have induced his behaviour. The doctor said he had not. The rumours went on.

When Gordon Davidson followed Cassius and the team into the dressing-room, he found him sitting on a chair, smiling. 'How about that!' he said.

Davidson pointed out that his antics had just cost him $2,500.

'Oh, don't worry about that,' he said.

Faversham and Davidson were having lunch in their hotel when the British writers arrived and questioned them about the rumours that the fight was off. They in turn found Dundee and Pacheco, and asked them to go and check him out at the house where he was staying. In three-quarters of an hour, the news came back to them from Pacheco that Clay was at the house, sprawled out on the floor, watching television. His blood pressure and temperature were normal. Faversham told Pacheco to stay with him and keep on checking him.

Pacheco, by the way, knew the fight business. He had worked with Dundee's fighters for some time, including world champion Luis Rodriguez and contenders Florentino Fernandez and Doug Vaillant. He didn't charge them, preferring to make his living from his ordinary medical practice in Miami.

Pacheco and Dundee have always insisted Clay's behaviour was 100 per cent deliberate, that just by getting himself so excited he caused his blood pressure to rise, but as soon as the act was over it returned to normal. In the afternoon, Pacheco said, Cassius went off and had a sleep, even though the house was crammed with people making a fair amount of noise. Later on, nerves showed in that he suddenly seemed to lack trust in anyone around him apart from his brother. As they waited on the lawn outside the house for the cars to arrive to take them to the fight, Pacheco said Cassius told him: 'I don't trust you. You want Liston to win. You bet with gangsters.'

Pacheco said: 'Cassius, I'm here as a doctor. I'm not interested in betting.'

Angelo Dundee and Luis Sarria also came under suspicion. In the dressing-room, Cassius refilled the water bottle several times, worrying that someone in the team was tampering with it. Pacheco later said Clay's problems on the day were merely an exacerbation of general anxiety problems he had. Because he was so desperate to win at anything he did, and because fighting was such a high-risk, high-profile activity, in effect every time he did it he took himself to the brink of an abyss, and when he stood there, he was afraid that someone, even a purported friend or supporter, might be secretly hoping for him to fail and would therefore be prepared to push him over the edge.

Clay admitted to stressful dreams – of flying off tall buildings, of driving fast cars towards head-on accidents with trucks. His old mentor, Joe Martin, always believed his verbal assaults on opponents were his way of getting his courage up. He told Jack Olsen:

> He's just overcoming that cowardice that's in him. And I'm not saying that to knock the boy either, because I had a very enjoyable time with Cassius, and I have no animosity towards him. We're all afraid of one thing or another, and it takes a brave man to fight to overcome his fear. Cassius's way is to make a lot of noise and commotion.

The Louisville Syndicate's investment was safer than they knew. Eventually, they were so pleased with their return that, after the Commission had cut the fine to $1,000, they paid it.

On the afternoon of 25 February 1964, anybody looking for an omen might have taken notice of the race results at Hialeah, Florida. The winner of the fourth race was a 19–2 shot . . . called Cassius.

22

A DANCING BEAR AND A FREAK WHO NEVER STOPS TALKING

Everybody who was there had an opinion, of course. Eddie Machen, flown in to help provide a news angle, said of Liston: 'He's a murderous puncher. I was smart enough to nullify it, but Sonny beat me fair and square. Maybe Clay can do the same, but I have to go along with Liston . . .' However, Machen also knew Liston might be vulnerable because of his inactivity and covered himself: 'If the fight goes more than five rounds, you may be in for a surprise. Clay is a good fighter. He's strong, big and fast, and his awkward style makes him hard to fight.'

Machen, who had suffered a mental breakdown following a ten-round draw with Cleveland Williams in 1962, but who was now on the comeback trail, knew the psychological side of the business of fighting at the highest level better than most.

> He [Liston] moves like a train – one track all the time. When he finds a sitting duck like Patterson or Williams, he knocks them off the track. I think of my fight with him, and I know I can beat him. He jabs, puts everything behind it, then he drops his left hand. No man can get away with that forever.

Marty Marshall, up to then the only man to have beaten Liston, said: 'You've got to confuse him, keep him off balance. And don't let him tag you with that left hook. Liston is a much better fighter than when I fought him. He snaps that left a lot faster and he has shortened the right. But he's still no ballet dancer. He can still be whipped by a man who is smart, patient and uses the right strategy.'

Cus D'Amato said: 'If Clay moves, he has a chance.'

Mike DeJohn, who had said, with a beaten man's illogical pride, that Liston couldn't fight after Sonny had beaten him in 1959, appeared to have changed his perspective. DeJohn, who had also sparred with Clay, said:

I don't see the kid going more than one, two rounds. Maybe in a year, two years, but he isn't ready now. Liston is too strong. He can take a big punch. He doesn't blink or flinch. He just fights harder. I hit him with my Sunday punch. I thought I hurt him, but he covers up so well with those big arms I never got another shot. Clay can't take that kind of punch.

Rocky Marciano, perhaps predictably in view of his own march-forward style, could not see Cassius handling Liston's aggression. 'I think Sonny Liston will put him away before the fifth round,' he said in a column published in the *Daily Sketch* in London. The day before, however, his ghostwriter had credited him with the following analysis, pointing out that it was impossible to know how good Sonny was because nobody had pushed him close in recent years:

> In two years, he has had about eight minutes of fighting. Liston has never been hurt. I don't suppose Liston has even taken a real punch in his life, because there's nobody to hand it out.
>
> Clay has the same assets as Ray Robinson – magnificent legs. He'll need them to keep away. If Liston should hurt Clay in the first minute, the fight could become a one-round farce. Folks are feeling a bit flat because everyone is fed up with Cassius Clay and his non-stop yapping . . . he has lost that knight-in-shining-armour image, and folks want to see him well and truly licked.

Joe Louis agreed: 'Liston has the killer instinct and Clay has only to make that one mistake Sonny needs.' Louis had watched one Clay workout and had said: 'I don't know what Cassius has got to win with. He just runs round in circles. Cassius has got to be kidding. If he fights like that, pulling away the way he does, Sonny will knock him through the front door.'

In a syndicated piece for the North American Newspaper Alliance, Manny Seamon, a veteran who had trained world lightweight champion Benny Leonard and had worked with Joe Louis too, said Clay was capable of winning if he took the job seriously and did not fall into the trap of believing the hype that was spouting from his mouth. That said, Seamon acknowledged: 'My friends may be apprehensive of my sanity.' He just felt Clay had the style and speed to win.

Billy Conn, who had held the light-heavyweight title and almost danced his way to an upset victory over Louis for the heavyweight crown, said:

> Liston has got to kill Clay as soon as he touches him. He [Clay] is a freak, just an amateur. But Cassius can laugh all the way back to the Black Muslim meeting, only he won't feel so good for a few days.

Ray Robinson, who was close to the young challenger, was in no doubt. 'Clay will win by a knockout,' he said. 'His speed will be the decisive factor.'

Willie Pastrano, who knew Clay as well as most, agreed with Sugar Ray. 'Cassius is my pick,' he said. 'He'll stay away from Sonny until he has him winded and then move in for the kill. I have been his sparring partner but honestly that hasn't affected my judgement in the least.'

Former welterweight title challenger Vince Martinez saw it the same way:

> I like Clay's chances. If he can stay out of range for two or three rounds, he'll
> be a cinch. My beloved manager, Honest Bill Daly, I'm sure, feels the same
> way about it, although he didn't confide in me. Actually, he never did!

Mickey Genaro and Rocky Graziano teased writers. Genaro said: 'Sonny can name the punch or my name isn't Mickey Genaro. As a matter of fact it was Leo Manganaro before I started boxing . . .'

Graziano, former world middleweight champion who by then was a successful stand-up comedian, said:

> This Liston is just a baby. He was overmatched twice with Floyd Patterson.
> Irving Cohen, my manager, would never make the mistake of putting him
> in with a fellow as ferocious as Cassius . . .

It was almost 25 years since Two-Ton Tony Galento floored Joe Louis in a heavyweight championship fight – Louis got up to slice him to pieces in the fourth round. Galento, still running his bar in New Jersey, had not changed at all. He declared he could murder both of the bums in the same ring with his left hand tied behind his back.

Jack Dempsey wasn't listening to any of the press hype. 'I think Clay is a much better fighter than people think,' he said. 'I give him a good chance to win.'

Another old heavyweight champion, James J. Braddock, said: 'They each have two legs and two arms and anything can happen. Those 7–1 odds are ridiculous. Clay has a good chance.'

Floyd Patterson appeared indecisive unless you paid attention to the punchline: 'Who's my choice? Now, that's a hard one to figure out. But I'd like to meet the winner in a third bout.'

Jimmy Ellis, Clay's boyhood friend from Louisville and now rising through the light-heavyweight ranks, picked Liston in three or four:

> I boxed with Clay more rounds than anybody he ever had in the ring with
> him. He'll get knocked out for two big reasons. First, he doesn't have the

experience he needs to fight a guy like Liston. Second, he's too easy to hit with a left hook.

Of sixty-two writers polled, only three went for a Clay win. Only Bob Waters of *Newsday* picked him to win inside the distance. He said it would be inside 13 rounds. Even his own newspaper ran his prediction under the headline: 'Our Man Picks Clay . . . Clay? Clay!' Leonard Koppett of the *New York Times* and Bill Wise of *True* magazine both said Clay on points.

Tex Maule of *Sports Illustrated* felt the key lay in the quality of each man's jab: 'Where Clay's jab stings, Liston's wounds. His arms are massively muscled, and the left jab is more than a jab. It hits with true shock power.' Maule also felt Liston could hook off the jab better than Clay, said Liston was cleverer defensively than he seemed:

> He is an expert at moving his head ever so slightly to let a punch slide by, or at picking off a punch with his big hands and arms, always keeping his balance, always ready to hit back from a solid base.

However, he got it right when he said that for all his skills, Clay's best weapon could be his mindset . . .

> His very arrogance, his youthful, absurd confidence. He has a chance if he fights his fight – or Angelo Dundee's version of his fight. If he pops and runs and pops and runs and forces Liston to come after him, he may last. He might even win.
>
> But he has to come within arm's length of Liston every time he hits him. He must concentrate for 15 rounds. He cannot afford a mistake.
>
> Unfortunately, the arrogance which could give him the confidence to fight Liston as though he were another sparring partner could also push him past the edge of discretion into disaster.

Peter Wilson called Clay a 'comparative greenhorn' and said he would be surprised if he could go more than three rounds.

Sam Leitch, for the *Sunday Mirror*, said: 'I take Liston to freeze his challenger before the end of the third round.'

Peter Lorenzo, another British writer, said: 'Clay won't be around after the third round.'

Donald Saunders, for the *Daily Telegraph*, joined the consensus. 'If Clay is still there when the fourth round begins, he will have done better than expected.'

For the *Daily Express*, Desmond Hackett was slightly more cautious: 'I take Liston to win in the fifth round.

Frank Butler, for the *News of the World*, said: 'His [Clay's] only chance of a sensational win would be to jab and run in the hope of tiring the champ.'

Reg Gutteridge, for the *London Evening News*, wrote: 'Liston should make certain . . . surely before the eighth round.'

George Whiting, Gutteridge's rival on the *London Evening Standard*, said, somewhat strangely: 'I see Liston swinging an axe on a Clay pigeon no later than round four.'

Most of the American writers were thinking along the similar lines as their British counterparts. 'Sonny inside of three,' said Lester Bromberg, while his colleagues at the *New York World-Telegram*, Joe Williams and Bob Stewart, said respectively: 'Clay will fall early' and 'Liston in the sixth'.

Yet more *World-Telegram* opinions came from Willard Mullin and Phil Pepe. Mullin said: 'The champ in two.' Pepe's call was: 'Liston in four (minutes).'

Jack Cuddy of *United Press International* said Liston in four [rounds], while Murray Rose for *Associated Press* said: 'Sonny does it in three.'

The *New York Herald Tribune* writers Jesse Abramson, Red Smith, Jack Mann, Tommy Holmes and Irving Marsh – yes, they had five reporting it, four on site and Marsh at a theatre broadcast – all went for Liston between rounds three and six.

Jimmy Cannon wrote in his preview for the *New York Journal-American* published on 25 February:

> The Sonny Liston–Cassius Clay troupe plays a one-night stand here, a one-ring circus featuring a dancing bear and a freak who never stops talking but says nothing . . . Once sports events had a thrilling privacy of a sort. The stub of a ticket to a big fight granted a man saloon prestige. People bragged they were there, and travelled long ways to see it. Now the guy who pays a fin for a theatre seat has no respect for the one getting up two hundred and fifty to occupy a chair in Convention Hall tonight.

Cannon's sourness towards the event – 'this fight has the morbid appeal of a street accident' – did not prevent him from making a prediction. 'The majority of the spectators feel it won't last the three minutes of the first round. But I think Clay will keep out of Liston's way for five, before silence engulfs him for at least ten seconds.'

Murray Robinson, also for the *New York Journal-American*, cynically believed the match was so bad, and boxing so desperately needed the night to be a success, that Liston would carry the challenger for a few rounds in order to make him look better than he was. And he might even carry him long enough for people to believe a rematch would be in order.

> If Sonny Boy lets him run long enough, a rerun and another vast payday are inevitable . . . Liston should bring him down in the eighth, the same round in which Clay used to brag, in lousy rhyme, that he'd kayo Sonny. That would be poetic justice.

Cannon and Robinson had colleagues Dan Parker, Hugh Bradley, Max Kase and Frank Graham covering it in some form. Their collective pick was Liston from rounds two to four. Others ran along similar lines: Al Buck of the *New York Post* – Liston in five; Robert Lipsyte, *New York Times* – Liston in four; Barney Nagler, *New York Telegraph* – Liston in three; Marshall Reed, *Long Island Star-Journal* – Liston in four; Stan Isaacs, *Newsday* – Liston in twelve; Hy Goldberg, *Newark News* – Liston in four.

Jack Nilon answered the point about the possibility of Liston carrying Clay: 'Not only is that illegal, but it's downright impossible. Not even God could suggest that to Sonny.'

And so the writers descended on the Convention Hall at 1700 Washington Avenue. Over the front entrance were the words 'Dedicated to Peace, Achievement and Progress'. The journalists collected credentials that included the polite request: 'Please do not jump on apron or into the ring either before or after the fight.'

The media were urged not to congregate outside the dressing-rooms before or after the fight, and instead informed that after the fighters had been given a chance to 'cool out' they would be escorted to the press conferences: Liston to the Cyprus Room, Clay to the Veterans Memorial Room. Still-photographers were to be given two minutes to take photos before the sessions were opened up to questions.

The police and ushers had been asked to keep staff to a minimum in the ring afterwards when the fight ended. The instructions continued:

> This will enable photographers and newsmen to see and, of course, photograph the hysteria. There will be, however, a closed-circuit cameraman and an ABC radio man in the ring as previously authorised and previously agreed to in the photographers' meeting held on Friday, February 21st.

The main press lounge was in the Coral Room, with a second working press room in the Tropical Room, and Western Union facilities were in the Flamingo

Room. 'There are approximately 25 typewriters for your use in the Coral Room, and we suggest that you bring your own typewriter to be used either at ringside or in the press rooms.'

Theatre Network Television Inc. put out a press release, announcing: 'Even the referee will be wired for sound.' TNT were also proud of a side-view camera and an overhead camera, both, it was claimed, firsts for the broadcast of boxing. Nathan L. Halpern, president of TNT, declared the innovations an electronic marvel. TNT also purchased the referees' shirts (three because the identity of the official would be kept secret until shortly before the bout). Tiny microphones would appear as a button on the shirt with the transmitter carried in the referee's pocket. 'A so-called creepy-peepy TV camera will also be at ringside for close-up views of the fighters from the ring apron.'

TNT's preparations took six weeks. They constructed a model of the Convention Hall in order to plan the position of the lights and cameras properly. They hired a director, Marshall 'Sonny' Diskin, who had a long history of covering boxing promotions, and installed Steve Ellis as blow-by-blow commentator, with Joe Louis adding analysis.

The pictures were to be monitored at a technical centre at Woodside, Long Island, and transmitted to 355 locations in the United States and Canada. The total number of available seats had settled at 1,103,451, by far exceeding the previous largest of around 700,000 for the first Liston–Patterson fight. Admission prices in the closed-circuit venues ranged from $4 to $10. In addition, there were 84 locations for subscribers to community antenna television systems, which paid rights fees, a total of 246 cities in 46 US states and 16 cities in 5 Canadian provinces. There was, however, no theatre or home television in the South Florida area because it was felt that would affect the live gate.

Murray Robinson, in the *New York Journal-American*, was distinctly unimpressed by all this technical wizardry:

> Boxing, owned by hoods until the fuzz chased most of them in recent years, has now hocked its shabby little soul to television . . . old-style promotion of heavyweight title fights is about to expire.
>
> Bill MacDonald, staging tonight's Sonny Liston–Cassius Clay mismatch in Miami Beach, is due for a blood-red-ink bath, perhaps to the extent of $300,000. Meanwhile, the fighters and TV people, including theatre operators remote from Florida, will cut up closed-circuit television millions.
>
> What would-be promoter in his right mind will ever again bankroll a fight sure to cost him his pants while others cash in on his sweat, tears, ulcers?

Robinson saw a gloomy future, with fights fixed to suit television requirements – something that had happened before, of course: Jack Johnson, for one, was not averse to the idea of prolonging contests in order to make a better product for movie goers.

'And so,' continued the irritable but prophetic Mr Robinson:

> Theatre-TV and, not too far in the future, pay-TV, will complete the takeover of the fight racket begun by 'free' television. As Mike Jacobs predicted long ago, big fights will be staged in studios and only the elite of suckerdom allowed to view them 'live' at outrageous, statue-building prices.

23

WHAT THE HELL IS THIS?
WHAT DID THEY DO?

Before the fight, the dignitaries in the 20-foot-square ring included Jake LaMotta, the middleweight champion who had admitted to the Kefauver Committee that he had taken a dive on Mob orders against Billy Fox in 1947. A long-time Miami resident, the legendary Bronx Bull was now largely ostracised by the boxing community. He took his bow anyway.

Sugar Ray Robinson stepped into the ring as immaculate as ever. He had lost his unbeaten record to LaMotta in Detroit in 1943 but had won four out of four meetings with him after that. Their last fight, in Chicago on 14 February 1951, was remembered as the St Valentine's Day Massacre. 'We fought so often I got diabetes,' said LaMotta.

Angelo Dundee's world champions Willie Pastrano and Luis Rodriguez were called in, too, as was Eddie Machen, who had taken Liston 12 rounds in 1960.

As challenger, Clay was first into the arena and, according to New York Yankees legend Yogi Berra, had to wait seven or eight minutes in the ring for Liston to appear. If it was deliberate, it was an old trick. If Clay had been feeling the tension, the wait could have all but destroyed his mind.

Ring announcer Frank Freeman introduced Liston as from Denver, Colorado, as if Sonny wanted to embrace publicly his new home town. Willie Reddish, though, wore a T-shirt advertising the Thunderbird Hotel, Las Vegas. Athletic director of the Thunderbird, Ash Resnick, was in the corner team, for no reason anybody could guess. Years on, when the fix theories were discussed, Resnick's presence was used in the argument that Sonny quit to order.

When the referee, Barney Felix, drew them together in the centre of the ring, Cassius met Liston's stare with one of his own. As they waited in their corners for the first bell, Clay danced around, ready to go. Liston shifted his weight ponderously, foot to foot.

The first round saw Clay moving and Liston trying to press, but too quickly, missing with one huge left swing. Clay was first to land with his left jab. He concentrated on movement, then towards the end of the session a sharp right hand connected solidly and he let go a barrage of shots that had the crowd roaring. Reddish was calling to Liston to shorten his punches, to narrow his stance.

The second was quieter. Liston landed a good left hook, but Clay rode it and kept dancing.

The third saw Liston rock from a right hand. He was having trouble with Clay's speed and long, raking blows. The jab was bothering him. Suddenly, Liston was leaking blood from a gash beneath his left eye. Over the second half, though, Liston came back with body punches, his own jab and some clubbing rights. Clay concentrated on damage limitation.

By the fourth, however, the challenger was blinking. Mostly he kept on the move, reluctant to get involved at all. Liston plodded after him, unable to cut the ring down but landing most of what punches there were.

In the corner at the end of the round, an agitated Clay told Angelo Dundee: 'Cut the gloves off.' He wanted the world to know that somebody had pulled a stunt, that something was fixed – his right eye, especially, was stinging from some kind of solution. Dundee was always convinced it was simply some solution Joe Polino was using on Liston's cut that had somehow got into Cassius's eyes. The young challenger was close to panic, insisted he couldn't see, but Dundee got him up for the next round, told him to run. One story emanating from, among others, the Cubans in the Fifth Street Gym, was that Dundee actually hesitated and it was the Cuban, Luis Sarria, who decisively told him to push Cassius back out because it was 'for the big one'. Barney Felix said, as they stood in the corner, still trying to put Clay's mouthpiece in, he was a second or two away from stopping the fight.

Liston ploughed forward, chasing, missing mostly, but landing sometimes, and Clay kept wheeling around the ring, buying himself recovery time. He did it.

By the sixth, his eyes had cleared, his jab was working again, and Liston looked terribly tired. Not to mention old. The champion was painfully slow on his feet and slow to react. A barrage of seven unanswered punches peppered Liston, but he continued to stand off. He took jab after biting jab as Clay picked him off in his own time. At the bell, Clay had the jaunty swagger back; Liston trudged to his corner, a ridge of flesh under his right eye, the cut on his left still visible.

In the corner, he said something to Willie Reddish. Jack Nilon was leaning through the ropes, and it became clear something serious was happening. Reddish touched Liston's shoulder. Sonny seemed uninterested, but his facial expressions were never a reliable guide to what was going on in his head. Then referee Felix was called over to the huddled group and after some discussion he turned and spread his arms to signal the end.

By then, Clay was already on his feet, early for the seventh that would never come, and spotted what was happening before anyone else in his corner – and probably before most in the hall. He raised his arms and shuffled and danced, then as his people dived between the ropes to congratulate him, he opened his mouth and eyes wide, almost in disbelief, and raced to the ropes to celebrate. 'I told you, I told you,' he yelled at ringside reporters. 'I shocked the world, I shocked the world.'

Liston just sat forlornly in his corner, the first world heavyweight champion since Jess Willard in 1919 to lose his title while sitting on his stool. Willard had a little more excuse: he had been floored seven times by Jack Dempsey, had his cheekbone and orbital eye socket fractured and swollen, and had lost some teeth. Liston had what amounted to a sore arm.

The *Miami News* reported that when Barney Felix raised Clay's hand in victory it began to dawn on the audience that Liston had quit. Muttering could be heard around the hall but no cheers or wild screams. It was five minutes before it was announced that the cause of Liston's retirement was a shoulder injury.

Dan Parker, in the *New York Journal-American*, described what it was like in the minute or so immediately after Liston's surrender became apparent:

> Clay's supporters stormed the press section, climbed over the broadcaster's bench and broke the plant supporting their instruments, scattering them in all directions . . . A doctor appeared from somewhere, equipped with heavy bandaging tape with which he plastered the fallen champion's shoulder – the one on the same side as his heart.
>
> The crowd booed its lungs out as Sonny Boy, the tame bogeyman, arose and, with shoulder bared to show the bandage, lumbered down the aisle . . .

In a ringside seat, Rocky Marciano slapped his head in astonishment. 'What the hell is this?' he said. 'What did they do?'

On his way from the ring, Clay paused long enough to call out to writers: 'I came, I saw, I conquered.' He pulled an angry scowl, then winked at them. 'I borrowed the line from Caesar,' he said, pointing out helpfully that in his day Caesar was the greatest, too. He was kissed by his mother and hugged by his brother. He shook hands with his father. Sugar Ray Robinson and the pro footballer Jim Brown walked alongside him.

Yogi Berra, who like Liston had grown up in St Louis, sat with Yankees manager Ralph Houk and the long-retired Joe DiMaggio, who had once been married to Marilyn Monroe. Berra was impressed by Clay. 'He's a big guy, and he surprised me how good he could move.'

As Liston was led away from the arena with two strips of tape patching up his cut eye, it was claimed he said in a voice scarcely above a whisper: 'I tried to throw a left hook. It missed. I felt something snap. I just couldn't throw a punch. Not the jab anyway. My arm was killing me.'

Maybe he said it, maybe he didn't.

There was an unsubstantiated suggestion that Clay's agony in round four was the result of skulduggery ordered by Liston himself. The word was that, in case of emergency – that is, the fight lasting more than three rounds – cutman Joe Polino was to smear a caustic solution, which Clay later described as carbolated Vaseline, onto Liston's gloves and shoulders. Like so many other possibilities, it's just a rumour, but Polino allegedly confessed to it many years later in a conversation with Jack McKinney. Maybe he was telling the truth, maybe he had other reasons for saying what he said. Nobody will ever know.

Liston was ferried to St Francis Hospital, from which he would eventually emerge with his left arm in a sling attached at the shoulder and hip. Eight doctors had consulted and come to the conclusion that the injury was genuine and debilitating. The shoulder muscle was torn. Dr Alexander Robbins, the chief physician of the Miami Beach Boxing Commission, who had been in charge of the pre-fight medicals, read out a statement to say that Liston had been with doctors for three and a half hours:

> We came to the conclusion that Sonny Liston suffered an injury to the long head to the biceps tendon of the left shoulder with the result there is separation and tear of muscle fibres with some haemorrhage into the muscle belly. This condition would be sufficient to incapacitate him and prevent him from defending himself.

Robbins also said: 'There is no doubt in my mind that the fight should have been stopped.'

Jack Nilon, standing to the side of Robbins, asked writers: 'Please make this positively accurate.' He also said six stitches were inserted in the cut below Sonny's left eye, which would need plastic surgery. Nilon also said: 'Put a Bible before me and I'll swear this was on the level.'

When the scorecards were revealed, they showed the fight was even at the time it ended, the officials split three ways. Referee Barney Felix scored 57–57, judge William Lovett 58–56 Liston, judge Gus Jacobsen 58–56 Clay. The scoring system was not as it is today. The points gap between the fighters in a round was more liberally applied, while today 10–8 rounds are given only if one fighter is knocked down or a round is particularly one-sided and gruelling.

The scorecards in terms of rounds were as follows (C for Clay, L for Liston, E for Even):

	1	2	3	4	5	6	Total
Barney Felix	C	L	C	L	L	C	3-3
William Lovett	C	L	E	L	L	C	3-2-1
Gus Jacobsen	C	E	C	C	L	C	1-4-1

For what it's worth, under today's rules, the scores would have been: Felix 57–57, Lovett 58–57 Liston, Jacobsen 59–56 Clay.

After six rounds, Peter Wilson said he had Liston ahead by one point.

Bill MacDonald joked that boxing writers were as bad as political commentators in their lack of ability to predict outcomes. 'We had over 400 sportswriters from many parts of the world and only three or four gave Clay a chance,' he said.

In Britain, the *Daily Mirror* would run a front-page piece headlined 'The Men With Red Faces', followed by nine photos of British boxing writers with their wrong predictions. In that hall of shame were the *Mirror*'s own Peter Wilson, Sam Leitch, Peter Lorenzo, J.L. Manning, Desmond Hackett, Donald Saunders, Reg Gutteridge and George Whiting, along with Rocky Marciano, who had done a ghostwritten prediction in the *Daily Sketch*. The scandal of the ineptitude of the British boxing press relegated the latest in the Jack Ruby trial to page two and news that nine Russian Jews were to be shot for running a knitted goods racket to the back page.

Harold Conrad said Liston's woeful preparation was to blame, nothing else:

> He was there for just three rounds. His tongue was hanging out. He aged twenty years in four rounds. Even though he was chasing the guy, he was way behind on points, and I could see he looked like an old man by the way he sat there on his stool.
>
> He was cut for the first time in his life, and it was a bad one. He was bleeding, and he had never bled before, not in all of his tough fights. When it came to the seventh round, he just couldn't get off his damned stool. He just couldn't catch him, and he just . . . well, don't forget he was no kid any more.

Clay had to be persuaded by Angelo Dundee to give the traditional post-fight interview to writers. 'Hypocrites,' he said. 'I shouldn't be talking to you.' Then he eased into full flow, taunting writers that they had criticised him for holding his hands too low, pulled away from punches, couldn't take a punch:

> Well, I'm still pretty, and he's in the hospital. I'll fight anybody the public wants me to fight now. Boy, I whipped him bad. I tried to tell the world it was going to happen, but you didn't listen. Hypocrites, hypocrites, hypocrites . . .
>
> I don't know what happened to Liston. All I know was he was floundering around, and I was flying like a bird. They tell me he had to stop because of shoulder trouble. All I know is he kept throwing lefts and was still throwing them in the fifth when my eyes were troubling me.
>
> Wasn't the old man the one who said last week he could fight with one leg and one arm and still beat me? Hail the champion! Look at me! Not a mark on me. The old man was cut up around the left eye from the third round on. They made Liston the 7–1 favourite. That was a foolish thing to do. I never could be an underdog. I am too great.

Bundini Brown laughed and sang out: 'Hail the champion!'

'Say it again,' said the champion, and together they yelled: 'Hail the champion!' He said he would fight Liston again, or Eddie Machen or Doug Jones. 'Anybody,' he said.

Angelo Dundee defused any suggestion that they were accusing Liston and his team of deliberately attempting to blind Clay. 'It was just an unfortunate accident,' said the victorious trainer. 'They are too nice and too fair to resort to such tactics.' Dundee also said:

> I've been telling everybody that this kid is a great fighter. The talk's only an act. The kid's different, that's all . . . He did exactly what he had to do . . . So what if he fights with his hands down. So what if he pulls back to evade punches. He does everything different.

Liston would never again intimidate a world-class fighter and therefore would never again be the fighter he used to be. He understood that as well as by his power and ability he had beaten opponents by dominating them psychologically. He would not be able to do that to world-class opponents from then on.

It happened a couple of generations later with Mike Tyson. When he was taken apart by Buster Douglas, the aura of invincibility that had surrounded him for more than three years simply evaporated. After that, even fighters of ordinary talent, for that's all Douglas was for most of his career, knew they could beat Tyson.

Harold Conrad and his wife went to see Liston. He was propped up on the pillows in his bed, hazy from medication. 'What are they saying out there? What are they saying?' he said.

Conrad told him the people felt he 'dumped' the fight.

Liston threw a glass against the wall and yelled out: 'Don't they know what that title meant to me?'

Conrad believed Liston was being honest. 'He said, "You see me, you know what it means to me to hear a kid say, 'Hello, champ'?"'

Johnny Tocco, the Las Vegas gym owner who knew Liston and the ways of the Mob well, didn't subscribe to a fix theory. 'Sonny was tired, so he quit,' said Tocco.

Jimmy Cannon said the fight was 'peculiar even by the standards of this mean racket'.

Dan Parker was scathing:

> Real champions don't quit, even for dislocated or broken limbs, as many of them, much less fearsome looking than this straw bogeyman, have proved down the years . . .
>
> Sonny the Bullyboy, realising that the phony image created by his press agents that represented him as a creature so awesome no human being could stand up against him was about to be revealed as a colossal fraud, lost heart and decided to chuck it . . .
>
> The climax to this strange promotion, which, from the start, seemed like something out of Alice in Wonderland, came without warning at a time when the judges' cards showed they had it scored evenly.

An angry Parker suggested Liston 'should be sent back into the oblivion from which he was rescued by that great American patriot, Blinky Palermo' and suggested that while Liston's purse was held temporarily by the Miami Commission 'you can bet that the boys who split it up behind the scenes will get theirs'. As to Clay, Parker said the victory had effectively made Elijah Muhammad, leader of the Nation of Islam, the new ruler of boxing. The *New York Journal-American* also reported that complaints had flooded in to the office of Governor Bryant. An aide to Bryant tried to calm things down: 'I think it was an honest fight and I am sure the Governor feels the same.'

George Whiting's ringside report, sent back to London for the *Evening Standard* front page, said: 'Cassius Marcellus Clay, the lissome Kentucky kid the world derided as a shrill and raucous false alarm, is now heavyweight champion of that same world. The horizon is his, and all its rainbows.'

Clay moved on from the Convention Centre to Hampton House, a Miami hotel, for what he termed 'a private party with some friends'. Among them, to nobody's surprise, was Malcolm X. Even the most blinkered of Clay apologists realised the truth: the new heavyweight champion of the world belonged to a religious group that preached its own form of segregation.

The day after Cassius Clay beat Sonny Liston, it was announced by Elijah Muhammad before a gathering of 5,000 followers in Chicago that the new heavyweight champion of the world was a member of the Nation of Islam. On 6 March, Elijah renamed him Muhammad Ali.

The public acknowledgement of his change of faith hurt his bank balance. Bill Faversham told Joe Williams: 'We had a choice of two national product endorsements, each guaranteeing him $500,000 spread over three years, and both were withdrawn the day after the story broke.'

Cassius was unrepentant:

> I go to a Muslim meeting and what do I see? I see there is no smoking and no drinking, and the women wear their dresses down to the floor. I come out and you tell me I shouldn't go in there. Well, there must be something in there . . . I know the truth and I don't have to be what you want me to be.

The Temple of Islam in Detroit was opened by Wallace Fard Muhammad around the end of 1929 or the beginning of 1930. He preached there until his disappearance in 1934, a mystery that has not been solved. According to the FBI, he was born Wallace Dodd Fard on 25 February 1891. The Nation of Islam said the FBI had the wrong man, that their founder was born in the 1870s and arrived alone in Detroit from Mecca in 1930. There is a First World War draft registration card for a Wallie Dodd Fard from 1917. At that time he was in Los Angeles working as a restaurant owner, claiming to be born in Shinka, Afghanistan. By the 1920 census, he was still in Los Angeles with a wife named Hazel, still running a restaurant, but by now claiming to have been born in New Zealand. The date of his immigration was left blank, as was the space for the birth country or US state of his parents. After this, the historical record becomes darker: in 1926, Wallie Dodd was sentenced to jail on drug offences, and he spent the next three years in San Quentin prison. In 1932, two years after the opening of the Detroit temple, a Wallace Fard was arrested. His fingerprints matched those of Wallie Dodd. However, the Nation of Islam claim a smear campaign, that this was not their man. There are two known photographs, one provided by the FBI, one by the Nation of Islam. Aside from the hairstyle, the men look similar.

Upon his disappearance, Fard, by then Fard Muhammad, was replaced by Elijah Muhammad, who presided over the faith for the next 40 years. Elijah was born Elijah Poole, one of thirteen children in a family of sharecroppers in Georgia. By 1917, he was married and by 1923 had settled into life as a car worker in Detroit. When he took over the temple, he took on Fard's theories and developed them. His view was that black people needed to be politicised under the moral code supplied by Islam. He denounced drinking, gambling, the physical abuse of women, and believed black men should enable themselves to stand up physically against the violent element in white America. Beyond that, he felt that if equality for the black race could not be established within America, it made sense to work towards a separate territory and nation. Like many religious zealots, he decided they were living in the last age before a righteous tumult devastated and rearranged the world. Astonishing as it sounds, he allowed the leader of the American Nazi Party, George Rockwell, to address the Nation of Islam, on the grounds that both were separatist organisations. In 1943, Elijah was arrested in Washington DC for preaching a message of non-cooperation with the draft. He was cleared of sedition but jailed for four years for instructing his followers not to serve in the US Armed Forces during a time of war.

By 1952, the organisation was still tiny, with about 500 members, but a decade later it had 30,000. A major factor in its increased popularity was the arrival of the charismatic, enigmatic Malcolm X, who had taken on the Harlem temple in 1954. He was born Malcolm Little in Nebraska in 1925. His father, a Baptist named Earl Little, supported Marcus Garvey's Universal Negro Improvement Association. Earl was run over by a streetcar in 1931, when Malcolm was six. The official verdict was suicide. The same year the family home was burned down. Malcolm's mother, Louise, went insane and by 1938 was housed in a state psychiatric unit. Eight years later, in Massachusetts, Malcolm was sentenced to eight to ten years for grand larceny and breaking and entering. It was around 1948 that he heard of the Nation of Islam, and when he was paroled in 1952 he changed his name to Malcolm X. The FBI had a file on him that eventually concluded he showed the symptoms of a pre-psychotic paranoid schizophrenic. His influence was huge, and he became an increasingly high-profile figure. However, he upset Elijah Muhammad first with a tactless attack on the Civil Rights march on Washington and then on the death of President John F. Kennedy when he said he could not be sad about chickens coming home to roost. Elijah banned him from public speaking.

Mary Turner Clay, Cassius' aunt, insisted her nephew's first contact with the Nation of Islam came when he boxed in the Golden Gloves in Chicago when he was 16 but said he was really drawn into full involvement with them when he was in Miami and in contact with both Malcolm X and a Muslim called Sam Saxon, who changed his name to Abdurrahman. Abdurrahman said:

> I started to teach Cassius the tricks of the white man and how we, as blacks, became slaves and were skilfully deceived by the white man in this country. I started to talk to him about the African empires and how great these empires were in their heyday when the whites were still living in caves.

In September 1963, Cassius had attended a rally in Philadelphia when in a three-hour sermon before 5,000 followers Elijah Muhammad called white Americans the most evil people on earth. During the weeks leading to the fight, Clay's house filled with Muslim brothers to the point where his father, who had been staying with him and attending his training sessions, found somewhere else to live. Cassius Sr was exasperated. He told Pat Putnam for the *Miami Herald* when everything became public:

> They've ruined my two boys. They should run these Black Muslims out of the country before they ruin other fine young people. The Muslims tell my boys to hate white people, to hate women, to hate their mother . . . I told Malcolm X that my grandparents were Christians, that my parents were Christians, that my wife is a Christian and that I was a Christian. And that we would all die Christians . . . They wanted me to change our last name to X. I laughed at them. I told them I had a good Christian name and it would stay that way. I told them that after a person learns to read and write he don't have to use any X.

Cassius was to reiterate the theory that the black man was damaged by the presence of white blood inflicted on him through slavery: 'My white blood came from the slave-masters, from raping. When we were darker, we were stronger, we were pure.'

He explained he felt more comfortable in the company of black people. He trusted them, could be himself:

> If I see a girl I want to wink at, I don't have to worry about getting strung up to a tree . . . I just want to be with my own. I'm no longer a Negro. I'm no longer a slave. I am with myself and my own kind.

The day after the fight, press conferences were held in a room in the Convention Hall. Clay said he felt sorry for Liston because he had been built up into something he wasn't. 'He's an old man. He's beat up, and he's overrated. They called Liston the equal of Joe Louis and Rocky Marciano. This must mean that I'm the greatest!' This time he didn't shout, just quietly, thoughtfully made his point. He was planning to return to Louisville for a victory party.

Clay explained his problems at the beginning of the fifth round:

> It happened in the middle of the fourth round. I felt something burn my eyes and my face. It came off Liston's glove or head, I don't know which. I couldn't see. My eyes were on fire. My face was burning . . . There was something hot in my eyes, and I couldn't even see where I was. Angelo pushed me out. And then it made sense to go on.

Dundee said: 'I told him this was the big apple, that this fight was for everything. He only had his mouthpiece halfway in his mouth when he went out for the start of the round.'

Clay said he had been warned before the fight 'by a wise, wise person' that somebody might try something. He said he was watching out for it, even from Dundee himself. Dundee took the apparent insult calmly. He knew that fighters are complex, sometimes paranoid souls, especially in a situation as tense as a world championship fight – and Cassius Clay was more complex than most.

Liston appeared in sunglasses, with his left arm in a sling, half an hour late at 1.30 p.m. He felt his defeat was an accident, plain and simple. 'After a hook in the first round, I knew it went out.' He said he did not have the injury going in and didn't ask for the fight to be stopped. That decision, he said, was taken by Reddish and Nilon. He said Reddish told him in the corner after round six that he had to double up the left hook. He told Reddish he couldn't do that because he could not lift his arm. 'He told the referee, the referee stopped it,' he said. Liston said the arm injury had prevented him carrying out his plan of working Clay's body, and his left hooks didn't have their normal power.

When asked how good Clay was, Liston's response was odd, as if the tactics of boxing on the move and using his speed disqualified Clay from any right to the usual respect one fighter has for another. Because he fought on the 'run', he somehow wasn't real.

'He's not as good as Machen or Folley or Williams,' said Liston. 'They came to fight. He's not as good as Patterson either. He came to fight, too. I was never tired. And he didn't hurt me either. I thought I could make it. Even 15 rounds. Even with one hand.'

The questions were soft, as if everyone knew they had in front of them a broken, demoralised man who couldn't be expected to give proportionate answers because he could not come to terms with the catastrophe that had struck.

'Sure, I want to fight him again,' said Liston.

Asked how he felt at losing his title, he said: 'Like I did when the President got shot. I never wanted to quit . . .'

Liston's physician, Dr Robert C. Bennett, intervened to show an enlargement of the X-ray of Liston's arm. He said there had been a 'direct trauma', a torn muscle. Contrary to what Liston had said, Bennett said there had been a problem in training:

> Sonny felt a little pain in his left arm during training, but we let it go. The first time he threw a left hook last night, he got a pain in his left shoulder, which got progressively worse. By the time the seventh round began, his hand was completely numb.

After Liston's death, Geraldine was to say to *Esquire* magazine that Sonny had hurt the shoulder before the fight but was afraid to pull out because of the bad press it would cause him. Nilon was more specific: Sonny had not sparred between 3 and 5 February, nor again on the 14th, because of soreness in the shoulder. 'We thought we could get away with it,' he said.

Nilon, who once declared that the amount he knew about boxing could be written on a postage stamp, said he had stopped the fight, Liston had not retired. 'I was the one who made the decision,' he said:

> Sonny wasn't tired. He simply lost all sensation in his left hand after being hit in the left shoulder at the tail end of the first round. He got hurt when he tried to throw a punch and block one at the same time. He kept complaining about it, but we didn't pay much attention to it.

Willie Reddish said Liston had told him he had no feeling in his left arm, that it was like a paralysing sensation.

Liston said he wanted to go home to Denver and would then see a preferred specialist in Philadelphia. 'I don't want any surgery,' he said, evidence perhaps of his reluctance to undergo any kind of needle-induced anaesthetic. 'Last year I had trouble with my right knee. I wouldn't let anybody cut me. I figured nature would cure me. So it did.'

Morris Klein, for the Miami Commission, said he was happy that the fight had been 'clean, well run and well ordered' and that the public had been given a 'good run for their money'. He said he was satisfied that Liston had not gone into the fight carrying the injury. Ed Lassman, president of the World Boxing Association, said the medical report was satisfactory. However, Florida State attorney Richard Gerstein was more inquisitive. He asked the commission for records and medical papers dealing with Liston's situation and helpfully reminded those involved that, under Florida law, 'altering the outcome of an athletic event' carried a maximum sentence of ten years in jail. He did say he had received no public complaint, and no apparent evidence had been presented before him, but he wanted to see the reports because the conclusion to the fight had, in his words, 'left me wondering whether what I had seen happen actually did happen'.

Gerstein said he wanted further opinions on the medical report and X-rays, both from the Dale County medical examiner, Dr Joe Davis, and from the medical-legal adviser to the Attorney's office, Dr Franklin J. Evans. Klein also ordered reports from two orthopaedic surgeons to examine Liston the day after the fight and temporarily withheld his purse, or at least the 'live gate' part of it – $367,000.

It was also disclosed by the Inter-Continental attorney, Garland 'Bill' Cherry, in an article by Hugh Bradley, in the *New York Journal-American*, that $50,000 had been paid by the promoter to Clay's lawyers in the 24 hours before the fight as part of the contract relating to their rights over Clay's next fight should he win. 'We have the right to name the opponent, the site and the date. I would guess it would be Liston as his opponent.' As Liston was president of Inter-Continental, he might therefore be said to have had a financial interest in the outcome. While technically true, this does not mean he threw the fight. Fighters having a piece of a promotion is more prevalent 50 years on. It has also become common practice for the promoter of a world champion to secure options on the services of a challenger (except in the case of a mandatory defence, where the rules of most organisations prevent it).

There was also at least one heavyweight championship precedent. When James J. Braddock defended against Joe Louis, his manager Joe Gould negotiated a deal whereby, in the event of his losing, he would be entitled to a percentage of Louis's promotional profits for the next ten years. Braddock, it should be said, was managed by Joe Gould, who had, according to legend, sold part of the contract to Pete 'The Goat' Stone, who worked for Bill Duffy, and Owney 'The Killer' Madden, who ran Hell's Kitchen.

Compared to the deal Gould was accredited with striking with Louis's promoter Mike Jacobs, this one involving Liston and Clay was clean as fresh snow. In 1964, however, given the general atmosphere of mistrust and suspicion, and given Liston's connections – and for that matter Clay's – the questions seemed to carry great pertinence.

Bill Faversham, the Louisville businessman whose syndicate had hit the jackpot, said there was a moral obligation to give Liston a rematch, but 'I don't think he'll want it.'

'We'll grab a return bout if they are good enough to give us one,' said Jack Nilon. He knew about the return clause, so was playing the part of humble loser for public consumption. 'We're out of business. Sonny will keep fighting, of course – if he wants to.'

The financial breakdown shows just how badly MacDonald was burned:

Bill MacDonald: staked $625,000 plus another $140,000 in expenses
   Receipts at gate $402,000; loss $363,000
Sonny Liston: received $1,360,500 (gross, including 22.5% share in
   Inter-Continental Promotions receipt)
Inter-Continental Promotions: received $813,000, broken down between Jim
   and Bob Nilon (72.5%, $589,425), Liston as above (22.5%),
   Garland Cherry, Inter-Continental lawyer (5%, $40,650)
Cassius Clay: received $315,000
Louisville Syndicate: received $315,000
Theatre Network Television Inc: received $362,000
Closed-circuit exhibitors: received $1,750,000

By the day after the fight, Rocky Marciano had gathered his thoughts. 'I thought Clay fought a real good fight,' he said. Cus D'Amato went further. 'He fought the perfect fight. He did everything right.'

Jimmy Cannon wrote:

Clay was not intimidated by the thug who learned his mean business breaking heads for the mobs of St Louis. He came to Clay in the first round in heavily clumsy hops, like an aged chophouse waiter with bad feet carrying a heavy tray. The laughter of the multitude rose to mock Liston, as the kid moved nimbly out of range. Liston heaved punches as if they were cobblestones.

Clay impressed Cannon: 'He ran, but he paused long enough to bust up Liston. It was the tough guy who folded up.'

Reg Gutteridge, in the *London Evening News*, called it the biggest upset since Sitting Bull slaughtered General Custer. 'Sonny Liston,' he wrote, 'was exposed as a fumbling automaton.'

Sam Leitch, for the *Sunday Mirror*, wrote:

A smell has gone round the world since Sonny Liston sat on his backside and spat away, along with his gumshield, the title for which any man would give his left arm – the world heavyweight boxing championship . . .

Clay, the challenger, wanted to quit; his corner said No.

Liston, the champion, didn't want to quit; his corner said Yes.

I was one of the last of the red-faced writers to leave the bizarre atmosphere of Miami Beach. But the longer I stayed, the less sense it made . . .

Jimmy Cannon pointed out that the only man in the ring whose courage wasn't questioned was the referee.

Joe Louis didn't buy the shoulder story. 'I don't think the shoulder made him quit,' said the old champion.

'What did?' asked Cannon.

'I'm not sure. I don't want to say what I think unless I'm sure . . .'

Louis tried to explain more precisely: 'He definitely hurt his shoulder. I don't want to say no different. He told me he hurt his shoulder. But a guy as tough as Liston, I don't figure it hurt him that much.'

Louis, who went into the Liston corner straight after the fight was stopped, was insistent that manager Jack Nilon was telling the truth when he said he stopped the fight. In the *New York Journal-American* on 4 November 1964, during the lead-up to the ill-fated rematch, Jimmy Cannon revealed a conversation he had with Louis. Surprisingly, given that Cannon was a wise man with a strong news sense, this information was way down in paragraph 18 of a 28-paragraph column.

I was the first one in Liston's corner Nilon say he stopped the fight. I looked at Liston. He don't say nothing, just smooth and calm sitting in the corner. Liston wasn't mad. He didn't say nothing. Nilon was doing all the talking.

Louis accompanied Liston to the rented house where he had been living at 6351 Pine Tree Drive, Miami Beach. Again, contrary to what Harold Conrad said, the deposed champion seemed to be a little too short on despondency for Joe's liking. 'At home he wasn't too upset,' said Louis. 'He told me his arm was hurt . . . I didn't see no sign that he was mad at what Nilon did.'

Doug Jones, who had taken Clay ten hard rounds eleven months earlier, said: 'I was shocked because I saw things that Liston could have done, but he didn't do them. I don't know why . . . I should be next in line.'

Whenever a big upset happens in boxing, there will be those who will claim the loser took a dive, or deliberately did not perform at his best, or a fix was in. It's in the nature of things: people like to have an opinion on what will happen in big sporting events, like the satisfaction of knowing their opinions are proved right, that 'here, look, there is evidence that I know what I'm talking about'. Picking the right horse, picking the right fighter, bolsters the ego. Getting it wrong – getting it as wrong as so many people got Liston v. Clay wrong – makes people look as if they don't know what they're talking about, makes them feel angry. Therefore, they look for reasons.

And when the fighter who should have won but somehow didn't is known to have been involved with the Mob, then the 'fix' is an easy answer. How could they have picked right when, unknown to anybody, 'the fix was in'? By whispering 'fix', 'scandal', 'corruption', all those people who got it wrong get themselves off the hook. They're not stupid after all; they can still talk about boxing as if they know something about it. And then again . . . there were those who said the word was out before the fight that something was wrong. Some felt that it was not the Mob but the Nation of Islam that had applied pressure to Liston himself. Nobody will ever know.

Former champion Ingemar Johansson said that rather than Clay winning the title it was a case of Liston losing it. He said he didn't think Clay would be champion for long: 'I don't regard Cassius Clay as a worthy champion.'

Nilon said they would have Liston's injury treated in Philadelphia and then look at working for the rematch. 'We'll win it back,' said Nilon. 'I know it. This guy has pride – you can't imagine such pride. This thing is killing him. For the next one, I'll take him up to the woods, and when he comes down he'll be hungry.' Nilon talked well but was on his way out and knew it.

A month after the fight, on 24 March 1964, in the investigation into the outcome, District Attorney Richard Gerstein recommended that boxers 'should be compelled to disclose prior injuries – and that medical examinations should be clinical, rather than cursory, made routinely for the benefit of photographers'.

On 29 May, in Denver, Liston was fined a total of $600 for speeding and possessing a firearm soon after returning home upon losing his title. It seemed a surprisingly lenient sentence given that according to police he was driving at 70 miles per hour in a zone restricted to 30, he was drunk when arrested and was, according to police, aggressive in the police car as he was driven to the station. Colorado laws ruled it an offence for an ex-con to be carrying a gun. An unknown woman who was in the car with him was let go. It seems when Liston got home, he went off the rails again.

24

I AM HIS BEST FRIEND, AT LEAST IN PHILADELPHIA

The rumours that Liston was still controlled by underworld forces just would not go away. In early April 1964, the Senate subcommittee on Antitrust and Monopoly wanted to interview Liston's business associates once again. It appeared that Pep Barone had been seen around the camp before the Clay fight and for some strange reason Irving 'Ash' Resnick had been a minor part of the corner team. Sonny had also been seeing a lot of a Philadelphia 'character', Sam Margolis. While not his manager of licence, Margolis had apparently taken over from Jack Nilon as the man in control of Liston's business arrangements.

Time described Margolis as 'a pudgy and pious Philadelphian, who freely admitted his friendship with Blinky Palermo, who as everyone knows is a friend of Frankie Carbo'. Margolis, it transpired, had 45 per cent of Liston's 50 per cent share of the promotional company Inter-Continental, which Nilon had set up supposedly to benefit Liston. Of Sonny's 500 shares, Margolis now had 225, and a lawyer from Camden, New Jersey, just outside Philadelphia, Salvatore J. Avena, had another 50.

Avena said he had represented Liston at his initial meeting with Nilon in 1961, which had been set up by Margolis and which led to the deal being agreed that Jack would take over the management of Sonny, and the 50 shares were Avena's fee for doing that. As good deals go, that seemed spectacularly good. Margolis explained that Liston had run up a tab of thousands of dollars in his restaurant, where the champion liked to sit and play checkers with local students from the University of Pennsylvania, and the percentage cut to him was volunteered by Liston 'out of gratitude' for his help. The restaurant was the Sansom Delicatessen at 111 South 39th Street, ownership of which Margolis had shared 50–50 with Palermo up until 1961. He said Liston also knew that if ever he needed advice he only had to call. 'I am his best friend, at least in Philadelphia,' said Margolis. With friends like that . . .

'It sounds to me like Liston was fleeced,' said Senator John McClellan. Garland

Cherry, for Inter-Continental, denied this emphatically and declared Liston's deal to be the best in the history of boxing. However, when pressed, Cherry had to agree that the fee paid to Margolis for 'finding' Nilon was, as the senator put it, rather large.

In 1937, Sam Margolis had pleaded guilty to operating a gambling house in Chester, Pennsylvania (Jack Nilon's home town). He received a minimal jail sentence – one to three months. In the 1940s, he was twice charged with illegal gambling in the same area – Delaware County, Pennsylvania – but acquitted. In 1950, a charge of assault and battery in Philadelphia didn't stick.

The senate hearings into the state of boxing, headed by Estes Kefauver in 1960–1, included testimony from an undercover New York police officer, Anthony Bernhard, that Margolis was present at a meeting – as was, intriguingly, Angelo Dundee – between Frankie Carbo and Blinky Palermo in 1958 in Washington DC. Margolis had also been present, sitting in the public gallery, at the trial of Carbo and Palermo in Los Angeles in 1961. He repeatedly visited Palermo in jail during the days the proceedings lasted. Under oath, Margolis denied Palermo and Carbo had any business interests in Liston.

Jack Nilon said at the subcommittee hearing he expected his personal share of the proceeds from the Clay fight to come to $400,000, then, as if that were nothing, added: 'There's a lot more to life than bread.'

Senator Philip Hart, from Michigan, responded quickly: 'There's a lot of bread in that life . . .'

Nilon said Liston still liked having Barone around because he felt he brought him luck. 'Sonny,' he said, 'thinks an awful lot of Pep Barone.'

While they were in Miami just before the fight, Barone complained that he was still owed $42,000 of the $75,000 Sonny was supposed to have paid him for his contract in 1961. After the fight, Nilon said Barone was so broke he didn't have enough money to leave Miami and so charged Liston's account either $3,000 or $4,000 – he couldn't recall which.

Nilon told the subcommittee he had done his best with Liston but had never been able to get him to see the world in what he described as a clear light. When Liston had done the deal with Margolis, Nilon insisted that he had taken a dollar bill and ripped it into pieces to represent what he was signing away and tried to explain it to him. The champion of the world was not interested, he said.

Nilon also said he did not feel Margolis was overcompensated for the attention he had given Liston. At the end of his tether with the whole thing, Nilon said: 'Personally, I feel that anyone who can put up with Mr Liston's antics, even if he got the whole thing, would be underpaid.' He also said he was so exasperated by having to represent Liston that he had planned to quit as his manager after the Clay fight, win or lose. Liston, according to Nilon, had behaved like a hypochondriac – 'if he caught a cold, he thought he was dying' – and had not trained properly because he had believed what everybody was saying that Clay stood no chance. Neither did he get his proper rest, because his house was full of hangers-on. 'It was like a ballroom,' he said.

Would Nilon have said that if Liston had won and was still a viable asset?

Outside the hearing, a reporter asked Nilon why he believed Liston had given Margolis and Avena large chunks of his earnings. 'I don't need to answer questions,' he said, adding, 'I've got an imagination.'

Prior to the Liston–Ali rematch in Lewiston, Maine, in 1965, Jimmy Cannon interviewed Sam Margolis. 'I'm a front man for nobody,' Margolis told the man from the *New York Journal-American* in respect of his role with Liston and his relationship with the incarcerated Blinky Palermo. 'I'm representing myself. I know Blinky but only as a friend. I love fights. I've been around them all my life.'

Cannon said people in the boxing business believed there had been a fall-out between Margolis and Palermo over Liston.

'Blinky was a friend of mine. Let it go at that. But I want to make it clear. I'm in this for myself, and I'm entitled to it because I put Inter-Continental together with the Nilon brothers.'

This was the first time Margolis had admitted being involved in Inter-Continental from its inception, when it had seemed Jack Nilon was attempting to set up the business in Liston's interests. Margolis had taken a cut of Liston's percentage for supposedly arranging the initial meeting with Nilon, but here he was now implying that he actually set up the company as well and was in effect a sleeping partner. Margolis said he was not Liston's manager, that Sonny didn't have one. His interests were handled by his lawyer, J.K. Murphy. Margolis, grey-haired, cigar-smoking, told his side of the story:

> Look, I'm not scholarly. I didn't go far in school. I was out scuffling, selling newspapers when I was six years old. But I know the penalty for perjury. I testified before Congress that I wasn't fronting for Blinky.

Margolis said negotiations went on for months, with him visiting the Nilons in Chester. He wanted to bring the lawyer, Salvatore Avena, into the deal because that was how the Nilons were working their end. Liston was reluctant but then agreed to pay Avena in shares.

> The lawyers made a mistake. They put all the shares in Liston's name. They

put the stock away. Half of the stock belonged to me. I put this deal together. I've read in the papers where Sonny just gave me the stock. It was mine all the time. The lawyer just forgot to put it in my name.

Margolis also said Sonny's share was no longer in his name but in that of his father-in-law.

Back in 1964, another interesting exchange came between Senator Jerry Cohen and Garland Cherry. Cohen established that Inter-Continental might have been built around Liston, but it stood to gain more if he lost to Clay because it held the rights to the return:

Cohen: So actually, Inter-Continental as a corporation will stand to make more on its promotion of Clay than it did on its promotion of Liston. Isn't that correct?

Cherry: That is right.

Senator Kenneth Keating of New York chipped in: So that the rematch here was a rematch run by the same promoter who stood to gain, perhaps gain more, if the champion lost.

As the hearing drew to a close, Keating called for a bill to be passed immediately that would place an individual selected by federal government in control of boxing in the United States in order to remove 'the leeches who monopolise the faith and confidence of the untutored boxer'. More than 40 years on, nothing had been done, and the question of federal control of a notoriously maverick sport was still raised sporadically, without any decisions ever being made.

However close to the mark the subcommittee's investigations were and whatever their intention, the perception was that it wasn't just the ordinary Joe in the street who suspected a fix might have been in, the people in high places had an inkling of it, too. Senator Keating was certainly suspicious and 'wondered aloud' if Carbo, in spite of being locked up in a jail cell, did not have influence over what happened to both Liston and Clay. Dundee, of course, was paid by the group of 11 Louisville businessmen who backed Clay, and they had no known Mob connections.

It is also easy to add two to two and make five. In ensuring the company was in a position to promote any return, those guiding Inter-Continental were safeguarding their own interests. Anything less than that could leave them accused of a naive negligence. When all the sums were in, Bill MacDonald was the big loser. Even the most stoical of investors might have felt that one financial bath that deep was ill-advised and two would be plain stupid. For MacDonald, who had initially voiced an interest in staging a rematch in Shea Stadium, New York, during the World's Fair later that year, the boxing adventure was over.

25

TO BOSTON AND SUITCASE SAM

In 1960, when Cassius Clay was 18, he had registered, as required, with the local draft board in Louisville. Two years later, he had been classified 1-A, which meant he could be called up at any time. That probably meant little at the time, but after the assassination of John F. Kennedy, the war in Vietnam was stepped up. In January 1964, the month before the Liston fight, he had been called to the US Armed Forces Induction Centre at Coral Gables – south of downtown Miami – to take a mental aptitude test to assess his capacity for military service. He messed up. He couldn't understand some of the questions, let alone pick answers. The test revealed he had an IQ of 78. They re-classified him as 1-Y, or fit for induction only in time of national emergency. He was embarrassed and tried to laugh it off. 'I said I was the greatest, not the smartest.' There were questions over whether or not he had been given privileged exemption, but the Army said he had not.

In March 1964, Malcolm X's increasingly strained relationship with the Nation of Islam in general and Elijah Muhammad in particular snapped altogether. He labelled Elijah Muhammad a hypocrite. Elijah had, it seemed, been sleeping with young female members of his staff and, when questioned about it, justified it on the grounds that even Biblical prophets had concubines. Malcolm felt the time was right for black political consciousness to be organised and believed the Nation of Islam was too bound by its religious theorising to achieve more than it had already accomplished. They parted company. 'I am probably dead already,' said Malcolm.

In May that year, Ali and Malcolm were in Ghana at the same time: Ali for a visit to the continent of his roots, Malcolm for political meetings with heads of governments following a personal pilgrimage to Mecca. Ali appears to have followed the Nation of Islam party line with him. If you were in, you were in, if you were out, you were nobody. 'Nobody listens to that Malcolm any more,' Ali said. As Malcolm X was pushed away from the movement, Ali spent more and more time with Herbert Muhammad, Elijah's son.

Time alters our perspective, of course. In a 1998 interview for a magazine called *Lifestyle*, Ali said his favourite photograph of himself was one with Malcolm X walking in Harlem. 'He was so controversial, so bold, so courageous.'

When he returned to the USA in June 1964, Ali was fat, between 20 and 30 lb above his fight weight. He needed to get back to work. He described his excess as 'health fat'. Whatever it was it had to be removed. It wasn't easy. Chip Johnson knocked him down in sparring with a short right hand. 'I froze on the spot,' said Johnson. '"Chip Johnson," I said to myself, "you know you just dropped the champ."' Johnson told him to get up, to stop jivin'. Ali said he wasn't, the punch was true.

Ali had found himself a serious relationship, too. Perhaps it was a distraction, perhaps not. On 14 August 1964, six weeks after they first met, Muhammad Ali married Sonji Roi, a Chicago girl who had been working as a cocktail waitress. He had already married her according to the rules of Islam before members of the movement and then completed the state marriage requirements before a justice of the peace in Gary, Indiana.

Sonji's father had been killed over a game of cards when she was two, and her mother was dead by the time she was eight. She had given birth to a child when still at school. She had been looking after herself and paying her way in life ever since. The evidence suggests that, yes, it was a whirlwind romance, but Ali was smitten.

It seems they were introduced by Herbert Muhammad, who, as well as being the son of Elijah, was a photographer and producer of the Nation of Islam newspaper, *Muhammad Speaks*. Herbert may have planned no more than a good time for the young champion, but he and Sonji became inseparable.

Herbert didn't like the idea. 'Man, you don't marry this girl,' he said. 'She works as a cocktail waitress wearing one of those little bunny things on her behind. You don't want to marry no girl like this.'

Sonji said Ali asked her to marry him on the first night they met. 'I didn't know anything about him. But I was alone in the world. I didn't have a mother to go home and ask . . .' She took time to think. 'I said to myself, there's nothing else I'm doing with my life. I can do this. I can be a good wife to this man.'

With his love life and faith sorted out, it was time to return to his job: the roadwork in heavy boots, the gym sessions, the hard sparring. The Liston fight was three months away. He knew it, and Dundee said he did not have to motivate him: 'He wants to work, that's his biggest asset. He wants to train. No one has to push him. This is everything he wants.'

But the build-up to the rematch was not without controversy. The World Boxing Association had been formed by a combination of state commissions and national federations and control boards in the summer of 1962 in a response to the Kefauver Commission's damning findings on the way boxing was run. Unfortunately, within six months it had a rival: the World Boxing Council, formed by other administrators not allied to the WBA. Boxing administrators proved they could not be trusted to police themselves. After the first Ali–Liston fight, the WBA objected to a return and so declared the title vacant when Ali signed the contract to meet Liston again. WBA president Ed Lassman had also called Ali a bad role model to the country's youth, presumably by rejecting Christianity. At the time, the concept of a world governing body was so new that only other administrators took any notice. It was generally understood that the heavyweight champion of the world won the title in the ring – and lost it there. Jimmy Cannon dismissed the WBA: 'One word from them, and the fight mob does as it pleases.'

The WBA were insistent that its member states bar the fight. They garnered support in Britain, the Commonwealth, Europe, the Far East and Latin America, too. The British Boxing Board of Control were only too pleased to help. They hadn't forgotten that less than 12 months earlier Liston had gone home early from his tour of Britain with commitments unfulfilled. The president of the BBBofC, J. Onslow Fane, wrote on 5 August to the WBA, saying:

> My Board have very strong views and I feel immeasurable harm would be done to the sport if such a bout is permitted.
>
> It follows that if all your members agreed the contest could not be held in their territory, it would be impossible for it to take place . . . and thus a great service would be rendered.

Britain's objection was officially based on the contract Inter-Continental held on Ali's services, thanks to the rematch clause from the first fight, and the unsatisfactory finish. As smokescreens go, that's about as flimsy as it gets.

The WBA representative Abe Green declared: 'A return bout would make suckers out of millions of boxing followers and a mockery of boxing administration.'

When Boston was proposed as a venue the WBA, which had been in existence less than two years, tried to influence the Massachusetts Commission, which was affiliated to it, against allowing the event to be held in the state. The Massachusetts commissioners gave some kind of verbal pledge to the WBA, but they sanctioned the fight anyway.

Cannon was scathing about the whole episode: 'The promoters claim Boston outbid ten other cities to get this gag. The only town I ever heard of that wanted Liston is Jefferson City, Missouri . . .'

Jack Nilon had gone, his patience worn out, but his brothers continued to hold promotional rights through the company Jack set up, Inter-Continental. Sam Margolis was with Liston when the rematch was announced to the press in Boston. He denied having any official involvement, and Liston said he no longer needed a manager.

Boston promoter 'Suitcase' Sam Silverman would be the man on the ground, responsible, as Chris Dundee had been in Miami, for the day-to-day workings of the event. Suitcase Sam earned his nickname by carrying around details of his entire business in a suitcase. Most of it consisted of cash. He had an office next to his gym on Friend Street in Boston. In the old days, he had worked on most of Rocky Marciano's early career fights in Massachusetts.

They had a press conference to launch the fight in a ballroom at the Logan Airport Motel, Boston, on 14 September 1964. Leonard Shecter, for the *New York Post*, reported that it was somewhat chaotic, with everybody trying to talk at once – including Sam Margolis, whom Shecter described as 'sneaking into the back of the pictures'.

Liston, in a blue suit, brought it to order himself. 'Ain't no use of my trying to answer questions if everybody is talking,' he said.

He tried to explain why he had gone on throwing punches with his left hand in the first fight even after it was hurt: 'When you go out and your feet start hurting, you ain't gonna quit walking, are you, until you get home and lay down in bed? So that's the way it was with the fight.'

Liston said he would have to hunt Clay down: 'There ain't but one way to catch a 'coon [raccoon]. You got to trick him and trap him.'

Ali, for once, wasn't in a good mood. When asked about his involvement with the Nation of Islam, he said: 'Why you ask about my faith? You ask [Barry] Goldwater about his faith?'

Liston made a mess of Ali's new name. 'I'm not fighting no Ali Millamed,' he said. 'I met him as Cassius Clay and I'm gonna leave him as Cassius Clay.'

Someone asked Ali if he found that insulting.

'No sir,' he said. 'He don't understand.'

Liston was asked why he was cheerful and Ali wasn't.

'He knows what he's in for and you don't,' he said.

Ali sucked on a sweet and tore the wrapper into pieces, dropping it absent-mindedly into a glass of water. He closed his eyes and snored.

Liston said: 'He's getting used to doing that.'

As the writers laughed, Ali opened his eyes and said: 'Please, call me Muhammad Ali.'

It was one of the odder moments in one of the oddest of boxing stories.

26

EVERY GANGSTER WANTS
TO BE AL CAPONE

The WBA stood by its threat to declare the title vacant the moment the Ali–Liston fight was signed and announced an elimination series between Ernie Terrell, Cleveland Williams, Doug Jones and Floyd Patterson. Most people, however, agreed with the stance the Massachusetts Commission took. Its head, Ed Urbec, said: 'I can't visualise the public not accepting Clay as the champion. Titles are won or lost in the ring.'

Liston trained in Denver. Like Ali, he was around 235 lb when he began and looked to take off around 20 lb in a three-month period. He would run in the mountains, sometimes up the 373 steps to the Statue of the Sacred Heart, the 33-foot high shrine that overlooks Denver, and for three months he did his daily gym routines at the Amid Karate and Judo Club in the south of the city. Mostly, people left him alone. Even the Denver press weren't particularly inquisitive. There were rumours that Liston was keeping bad hours, drinking and driving his black Cadillac around the town, but nobody substantiated any of it. If so, however, it seems his drinking, once an occasional difficulty, was more of a habit. Whereas in the old days a couple of beers might make him the worse for wear, now he was drinking vodka. And he could take a lot of it.

When he first moved across from Denver, Liston worked at the White Cliffs Golf and Country Club in Plymouth, Massachusetts, overlooking the shores of Cape Cod. His gym was in a room at the clubhouse. Somebody dreamt up an invitation for 24 of the better-behaved inmates of the Massachusetts Correctional Institution at Concord to go to the golf club and watch a training session. Doug Ibbotson, from the *London Evening News*, said the inmates were criminally insane. Somebody also felt it was safe to put them in the same room as around 250 members of the public also there to witness Liston's training session. The reaction of the members of the exclusive club at seeing, if Ibbotson was correct, two dozen insane convicts and a former world champion prizefighter, himself a former hood with Mafia links, inhabiting their multi-million dollar premises, is not recorded.

He did 90 minutes, which was good value, then after a shower emerged for the routine question-and-answer session.

'Do Clay's insults bother you?'

'Nope.'

'What do you think of Clay's chances?'

'Poor.'

'What difference do you find between being challenger and being champion?'

'Even the push-button elevators don't stop for me now . . .'

'How do you plan to fight Clay this time?'

'I don't. When you go to a house you don't walk in, you knock at the door. When the door opens you walk in. I plan to do just that.'

Gilbert Rogin managed to get a better reaction from Liston when he found him returning from a store with Geraldine, in the unlikely act of carrying a bag of groceries back to White Cliffs:

> One day you're the champ and your friends say, 'Yes, champ, no one in the world can beat you, champ.' Then you are no longer the champ and you are all alone. After that, your friends and the people who have been making a big payday off of you aren't talking to you but about you, and what they say isn't what they said the day before.

Rogin said Liston suddenly stopped, broke off and pointed at the sunset. 'Look at there. Isn't that the most beautifullest sight you've ever seen? When I first came here, the moon was so full and all the men kept going outside to see the moon on the water . . .'

Liston also did some workouts in a gym in the Boston suburb of Dedham. He looked old in that his cheek muscles sagged more than they had done, but he was fit. He had lost bulk in his backside and off his hips. Word had it that, never mind 215 lb, he was down below 210.

He still charged the public $1 a head to watch him work out. This time it was in a stifling gym on the second floor of a new, partly finished, partly occupied three-storey office building opposite the Towers Motel, where he had taken rooms. The hour-long workouts would attract around 100 people. Then one day a local police chief, Walter Carroll, put his head around the door and brought the programme to a halt. Carroll said that as admission fees had been charged even a sparring session constituted a public prizefight, and as the sparring partners were not licensed in the State of Massachusetts they could not take part – at which point one of the promotional aides had to walk along the rows of seats handing back $1 bills. Liston, who liked charging for his workouts, was not amused.

Willie Reddish was talking to a TV interviewer on the floor at the edge of the ring when Liston wanted to get down to the business of sparring. Three times he called out 'Willa!', but Reddish, or the interviewer, hadn't finished. Liston cut the session off in charmless style. He walked across the ring and kicked Reddish in the back. Reddish put down the microphone and got on with what he was paid to do.

Al Braverman, described by writer Robert Lipsyte as a New York art gallery owner, was sharing organisation of the camp with Archie Pirolli. On that day, for the benefit of the press and public, Braverman gave a running commentary on what was happening. Liston sparred with Amos 'Big Train' Lincoln, Foneda Cox, Curtis 'Honey Boy' Bruce and Leroy Green. There had been reports that Liston had been putting sparring partners in hospital with a grim regularity, but Lincoln and Cox (who was also in charge of the record player) had been through most, if not all, of the camp.

Cox, Liston's old friend from St Louis, was there to run, to give Liston speed. He wasn't a good fighter, and his own career, or what there was of it, had long been over. Cox had one fight in 1962 but apart from that had not boxed competitively since 1958. He was older than Liston.

The tall, wiry Lincoln had his own agenda. He was learning and nurturing his own dreams of becoming champion of the world. It wasn't to happen. (When they fought for real in 1968, Liston knocked him out in two rounds.)

Green prided himself on being near-impossible to hit. 'I'm kinda special,' he told Mark Kram. 'Ain't nobody hits me. But Sonny'll kill Clay after working with me.' (Unfortunately for Leroy, as good as he was at not being hit, too often he forgot to throw his own punches as well. By the time he was sparring with Liston, he had won only one of his last nine fights.)

The non-paying customers of Massachusetts were reportedly disappointed that Sonny didn't inflict violent abuse on the sparring partners or even skip to 'Night Train'. Stan Zimmering, a new camp aide, explained that the beat of 'Night Train' was considered too slow. Instead they used a track called 'Railroad Train No. 1'. Reddish, as usual, stood over Liston and threw a 16 lb medicine ball into his stomach. Braverman told the crowd it was 25 lb.

Liston gave interviews and said in the first fight he just wasn't good enough: 'I fought a stupid fight. I shouldn't have run after him. I had something he wanted, and I should have waited for him to come to me.'

Of the commotion caused by the police chief, he said: 'I thought it was Cassius Clay . . .' Then he offered his opinion that there were similarities between the police and hoods: 'The polices [sic] are just like gangsters. Every gangster wants to be Al Capone. Every police wants to be Eliot Ness.'

Liston curtailed the press conference by looking at his pocket watch. 'Time to go,' he said, and walked out.

Liston was annoyed, too, when he had to leave his hotel for a fire alarm that turned out to be false. Then there was the night two police cars parked outside his window with their windows open and radios blaring. And the story that somebody had found a snake in the corridor near his room.

Jimmy Cannon asked Joe Louis if he thought Liston could win.

'He get his mental attitude into condition, he'll win,' said the old Brown Bomber.

'You think he can?' said Cannon.

'I don't know,' said Louis. 'I don't know.'

Cannon was not convinced. He did not like the way Liston seemed to have trained himself down too far and felt that in shedding his bulk he had lost something far more relevant: his self-belief and his capacity to dictate psychologically. Perhaps this is why, as well as to convey to the public and press the image of Liston the Monster, sparring partners who had apparently stood up to him well enough before tended to go down as training drew to its close.

Meanwhile, Ali was installed in a ten-room suite in the Sherry Biltmore Hotel with an entourage that included his brother Rudolph (now Rahaman Ali), Angelo Dundee, Bundini Brown, Luis Sarria, a valet, a social secretary, four sparring partners, three cooks named Bertha Bell, Mildred Saxon and Ruth Bryan, and a chauffeur, whose sole responsibility was the safekeeping and provision when required of the champion's $14,000 black Cadillac, which came equipped with telephones, television and record player – just as he dreamt it would be all those years ago in Louisville. And of course representatives of the Nation of Islam were ever present, with their black suits, white shirts and narrow ties.

Ali still cracked jokes from time to time, once declaring he was going into business selling Sonny Liston sit-down stools, but was noticeably growing up, growing into his role as heavyweight champion of the world, devotee of Islam and married man.

Before leaving for Boston, Ali had repeatedly watched the movie of the first fight. According to Gilbert Rogin, once he had even had a broadcast by Elijah Muhammad turned off so that he could go over the tape again. It was projected on to a wall of the room below a handwritten sign that read: 'Allah is the Greatest'. He took the film to Boston and played it when he felt like it in his room at the Sherry Biltmore. Rogin, who watched it with the champion once, said at one point when Liston was being backed up Rahaman got excited and called out, 'Cook on him, Brother Muhammad.'

Luis Sarria suggested Ali had fought on fear in the first round of the first fight.

'I was a little nervous,' agreed the champion. 'In Miami, I was Columbus. I was travelling into the unknown. I had to be cautious because I didn't know what to expect. Now I know.'

British writer J.L. Manning got himself steamed up about a statement made by Ali that might seem to us, 40-odd years on, fairly innocuous. Ali had said he believed the result of the fight was God's will, therefore implying that he would cope with victory and defeat equally. Manning, who wasn't too keen on the presence of priests in Liston's entourage either, felt it was out of order to bring religion into boxing. He declared the whole thing blasphemous. 'The event is hardly a job for a sportswriter,' he complained. 'It calls for a psychologist, a moralist or a criminologist. Even a humorist would do.'

Ali trained at Santo's Wrestling Emporium, adjacent to the old Boston Arena. London writer Doug Ibbotson felt Ali had grown physically since the first fight and was impressed by the unorthodoxy and speed of his gym work. He looked in perfect shape.

In spite of the arrival of Braverman, the self-regarding, cigar-smoking Pirolli was still Liston's 'camp manager', through whom anybody who wanted to see Sonny had to go. Pirolli, wrote Mark Kram, had a habit of 'pacing up and down like the "brains" awaiting the outcome of a bank robbery in some old movie'. He kept muttering: 'I know his moods, I know his moods.'

Reddish looked sad even when he smiled, while Teddy King said next to nothing. Stan Zimmering, a US Air Force physical education instructor from Denver, was young and softly spoken and that rarest of creatures, Liston's confidant. It was also said he was working for nothing beyond the privilege of being there.

Pirolli didn't like giving answers to any questions himself, didn't like allowing what he saw as the privilege to ask Liston a question. Zimmering didn't mind sharing a little of what he knew. He reported faithfully that Liston, in spite of no fighter liking roadwork, was pounding out five and a half miles every morning. In their conversations, he said Liston never once mentioned Cassius Clay, preferring to talk about his dog, Jackie. He spent his rest time watching cowboy films on television. The shoulder was perfect.

Kram was permitted, on one day, to talk to Liston for five minutes, but didn't get anywhere. Pirolli was listening in anyway and had, true to form, warned him 'don't come on like a cop'. The next day Pirolli claimed Liston had phoned him later on to tell him to keep Kram and everybody else away from him, that he only wanted to think about the fight. Pirolli told Kram: 'I'll tell ya, the man is vicious. All he wants to do is fight and think about fighting.'

Liston saw Kram, walked over and accused him of going to city hall to do some background research on his past. He was extraordinarily agitated: 'Oh, man, someday I'm gonna write a book and I'm gonna talk about some people.'

Mostly, when he absolutely had to, Liston dealt with the press interrogations by mumbling nothing in particular. It seemed as if anything vaguely connected to the question would do. The shorter the answer, the sooner it would be over. When asked how much he weighed, Liston grunted: 'Lightest in three years.' He declined to offer any suggestion how he might approach the rematch differently. Somebody tried to pursue the size angle, suggesting that Ali might even be the heavier of the two this time around. 'Could be,' said Sonny.

With a week to go, the medicals were held at the public safety department. For the ease of routine, the boxers were scheduled to arrive well apart. Ali ignored that, striding about Commonwealth Avenue, brandishing a bear-collar and a substantial jar of honey, bringing traffic to a standstill, checking cars to see if he, or his equally noisy cohorts, could find Liston. Eventually he did and jumped on to the running board of the grey saloon car, screaming mock abuse. Liston, in a flat fawn cap and yellow sweater, stared at him until the police eventually prised the vehicle out of the traffic jam and ushered the party into the hall.

Needless to say, both men passed the preliminary medical inspection carried out by Dr Nathan Shapiro of the Massachusetts Department of Public Security. Curiously, one of the examinations he made involved removing Liston's false teeth. No such problems for the champion. 'Cassius Clay,' wrote George Whiting, 'is healthy, well-fed and sound in wind and limb – especially wind.'

Peter Wilson said that in spite of the outcome of the first fight, he could not make up his mind who would win the rematch: 'One thing is sure. Liston won't be able to quit in his corner because of a damaged shoulder this time, for he has said again and again that it's now perfect.' Wilson said he was sure of only one thing, that the fight wouldn't go 15 rounds.

Clay acknowledged in one post-training interview, on the Wednesday before the fight, that the heat over his change of faith was annoying him. 'They are trying to take my title away,' he complained, 'because they say I am a bad example. Well, I don't smoke and I don't drink and I'm happily married.'

As ever, when he had a large audience, he was more than ready for some extravagance. 'I ain't making any exact predictions,' he said, 'but Liston ain't going to be around no place after one minute and forty-nine seconds. His big, ugly face will be gushing with blood. It will be a shocking and dreadful sight.'

The madness of his act was given extra impetus – as if it needed any – by the arrival of the comedian Stepin Fetchit and a woman who claimed to be a 'physiognamist'. As writers approached the gym, she was hovering by the door offering to give them a personal reading. Fetchit would plead with visitors not to spit on the carpet or smoke. George Whiting saw the whole thing as a weird pantomime that might have been produced by a combination of the Marx Brothers and Josef Goebbels. However, when Whiting was taken by Angelo Dundee to meet Ali in the dressing-room, he found an altogether more serious young man.

'Liston will be harder to lick this time,' said the champion.

> If I can get to him in 11 or 12 rounds I shall have done well, but it might even go to a decision over 15. Why else do you think I did 13 miles on the road this morning?
>
> I've boxed nearly 150 [rounds of sparring] and the brash kid you saw beat Liston last time has become a grown man. I'm not saying he won't hit me, but he's got to set me up before he can hurt me with any kind of combinations, and I ain't stalling around for that kind of stuff.

Jersey Joe Walcott offered his own succinct take on the champion's ability. 'Clay may be nuts,' he said. 'But he moves around like a jumping bean – and I ain't seen beans get hit too often.'

The most important tactical issue Ali had gleaned from the first fight was that Liston's jab was too slow to hit him, as it had done others. To nail him, Liston was going to need the left hook, perhaps as a lead, but he had hit Ali in the first fight with left hooks, and the young, nervous challenger had taken them. It was going to take either a crazy mistake from Ali, for example walking into the punch (as he had done years before against Sonny Banks), or for Liston to land three or four of them in a row.

'Liston's going to try to grab my jab,' he said. 'Pull me to him with his left and chop me in close with his right. My strategy is to dance, stick and move. In the clinch, spin, grab and hold, I'll be hitting harder. I'll be more confident and determined.'

'In Miami,' said Bundini Brown, 'you only seen one quarter of the things this kid can do.'

27

HE COULD HAVE DIED

On the Friday afternoon, before he was to box Liston on the Monday, Ali walked with *Boston Globe* writer Bud Collins from the hotel to an art gallery on Newbury Street to view a portrait of himself.

A few hours later, Ali was in hospital with a hernia that required immediate surgery. The fight was off.

Around 7 p.m. in Room 614 of the Sherry Biltmore Hotel in Back Bay, Boston, as the champion and his close entourage watched the Edward G. Robinson movie *Little Caesar*, he doubled over in agony.

'We were so happy,' said Bundini Brown, 'then it all happened so suddenly. The champ had just finished a large steak with some spinach, salad and coffee and . . . he rushed to the bathroom and was sick.' Brown said the swelling in his abdomen was as large as a lemon. 'He asked us to send for an ambulance.'

Sonny McDonough, a Boston city official, answered the phone in the press room, listened, dropped the receiver and announced in disbelief: 'Clay's been taken to hospital with a suspected hernia.' He phoned his bosses, and Governor Endicott Peabody sent him to the hospital to keep up to date with events as they unfolded.

The initial media reaction in the press room was to suspect some kind of bad-taste prank. Bill Faversham, at a basketball game with Angelo Dundee, admitted his immediate response to the phone call he received was: 'What fun and games is Cassius up to now?'

The briefest of investigations revealed the truth. The world champion had been taken with Sonji in a police ambulance to Boston City Hospital where, on the fifth floor, Dr Charles Averill had diagnosed the hernia. A press conference was called at the hospital, with Dr Averill and Dr Morris Prizer, who confirmed the diagnosis, both present. Ali would be in hospital for ten days. A nurse found the time to tell him: 'You're the greatest.'

He smiled and said: 'Not tonight . . .'

More than a hundred writers, photographers, cameramen, soundmen and television newsmen crammed into the hospital lobby, mingling with outpatients who had their own problems. The police appealed to the media to leave.

Dr William McDermott, who was in charge of the hour-long procedure, emerged to say it had been a complete success. The hernia was, he said, in the lower right bowel wall. Contrary to some reports, he said it had not strangulated. Dr George Starkey, another of the five-man team who performed the surgery, said the hernia had been present for some time but had been masked because of Ali's physical condition. A third surgeon, Dr Thomas O'Brien, said: 'He is very lucky this happened when it did. If it had happened in the ring, it would have been the end of the fight. There would have been so much pain he would have collapsed.'

And Dr James Sacchetti said: 'Without immediate surgery, gangrene or peritonitis could have set in. He could have died.'

Nathan Shapiro, the doctor who had carried out the pre-fight medicals on behalf of the Massachusetts Commission, said; 'Thank God it did not happen in the ring . . .' and added, 'Had Clay collapsed during the bout and retired, everybody would have screamed that it was a fix. And that would have killed boxing for all time.'

One commissioner earnestly suggested that had Ali suffered the hernia in the ring he would also have lost by a technical knockout.

Peter Wilson reported the early rumour-mongering: that people were saying he had been 'slipped a Mickey Finn' and that it was the violence of his physical reaction that caused the hernia.

Harold Conrad broke the news to Liston. 'Sonny really worked his ass off . . . was really ready. I had to call him and tell him it was off. He said, "Holy shit, I'd better start washing dishes 'cause I'm busted. What am I going to do for money?"'

On the Monday, the day he should have fought for the championship, Liston received notice in Denver of a $70,000 lawsuit from the Associated Booking Corporation over his failure to complete his 1963 British commitments.

Milton Gross knew the impact the postponement could have on Sonny: 'Clay may have thought he was dying when he felt the abdominal pain that the incarcerated hernia produced as his bowel came through his stomach wall, but it was a tear that more likely killed Liston.'

Gross again brought up the subject of Liston's age: 'He says he is 30, but his handlers believe he is 37, and there are some non-believers who are convinced he is closer to 40.' The point being that Sonny might have had the inner resolve to get himself properly prepared just one last time, but all the tension and adrenalin that had been building, ready to drive him into a big enough performance to beat Ali, now evaporated. He would have to begin all over again. Whatever the exact number of his age, in life-years he was old. There is only so much resilience in any man. The people around Liston suspected that the moment this fight was postponed his chance had gone.

Joe Louis said in a ghosted, syndicated column:

> I was getting ready to pick Sonny. I figured he would KO Clay around the tenth round. I had talked to him man to man. I knew his frame of mind. He was serious-minded like I'd never seen him, more determined than before his first fight with Floyd Patterson. And he was in amazing condition. Sonny hit a peak, a real peak. Now, of course, he's a tiger with nobody to chew up. He's got to feel cheated. Got to feel he worked his heart out for nothing. Got to be down.

For public consumption, Liston snapped: 'I knew he'd hurt his-self . . . talking so much.' He also muttered: 'Could have been worse. Could have been me.' Once alone, he retired to a bar where he knocked back Screwdrivers – vodka and orange juice – to numb the misery.

SportsVision, the company that held the closed-circuit rights, had not insured the show, and the hernia meant, instead of making a gross $5 million, they had blown $250,000. Fred Brooks, the 29-year-old boss of SportsVision, was still working out what to do as he returned to his hotel. When he got out of his car, a nickel fell out of his pocket. He picked it up. 'I can do with all the nickels going right now,' he said as reporters came towards him to ask for his reaction.

One of Ali's visitors at the Boston City hospital when he was recuperating was a schoolboy from Brighton, Massachusetts, Mike Marley, who had boldly declared himself president of the International Muhammad Ali Club and the 'world's youngest sportswriter'. Ali, in return, called him 'my greatest fan' and introduced him at the press conference when he left hospital. Marley would spend his life around boxing. He remembered years later that in hospital Ali was surrounded by Nation of Islam bodyguards.

The backroom teams for each man knew the fight must still go on if at all possible. That is, assuming Ali recovered and Liston, while kicking his heels wasting time he didn't have, didn't do something crazy and lose his liberty.

The promotional contract was valid only until 15 May 1965. Up to that point, the fight belonged to Boston. After that date, it could be taken anywhere. Boston promoter Sam Silverman still hoped it was possible to hold it at the Garden. Initially, Herman Greenberg, the Massachusetts Commission chairman, decided that if an investigation showed any connection between Liston and Inter-Continental Promotions Inc. then he would not be allowed to box in the state. Then they changed their minds, ruling that as Inter-Continental were not 'licensees' of the fight, Liston's relationship with them was irrelevant. However, the momentum had swung and whatever Greenberg said about the fight still happening in Boston, the city didn't really want to know.

28

SONNY? YOU OUT THERE?

At the end of their elimination series, the WBA decided Ernie Terrell would box long-time contender Eddie Machen for the vacant 'heavyweight championship of the world' in Chicago on 5 March 1965. It was a test case in which they must have been supremely confident. They must have believed the sporting world would approve of the idea of sweeping aside the tired, worn out Liston–Ali saga and welcome the attempt to introduce new championship blood.

They misread public opinion. To the man in the street, Ali may have been a Black Muslim, he may have been handed the championship when Liston quit, he may have come across as a brash young pain-in-the-ass. He may have been all of these things, but until he lost, retired or died, he was the champion. Consequently, when Terrell outpointed Machen, few cared.

The writer, Barbara La Fontaine, was in Denver researching a fine piece she eventually wrote on Liston and was at the home of Teddy King, Liston's co-trainer, when Sonny announced his unexpected arrival by letting off a firecracker outside the living room. He had not known La Fontaine would be there. She described the chaos:

> There was an explosion in the dining alcove . . . Plaster sprayed across the table and smoke still hung in the air when Teddy got to the door.
>
> 'Sonny? You out there?'
>
> Sonny came in, immense, unimaginable, looking pleased and happy with his firecracker. He did not look so pleased and happy when he saw me.

La Fontaine analysed the aura Liston gave off when he was socialising away from Geraldine: 'Sonny gives people, except for Geraldine, the feeling that they had better please him, but he offers no clue as to how he is to be pleased. It is disconcerting.'

She was also in his car with him when he was in a good mood – and leaned out of the open window to bark at a dog. Two policemen in a patrol car saw him do it and laughed. He saw them laughing and his defences immediately came up. La Fontaine said: 'Oh, come on, they were smiling.'

Liston said: 'Yeah, smiling. They smile with one hand and write you a ticket with the other.'

Liston was arrested again on Christmas Day 1964 for driving under the influence of alcohol after police officers saw him stagger out of a restaurant to his car, a new Cadillac. He remonstrated with them and shoved one or two, so spent half the day in a jail cell. A month later, he was cleared after claiming he was dancing not staggering.

Around the turn of 1965, Liston had a bit part in the movie *Harlow*. At a press conference in Beverly Hills, everything was running along without much incident when a reporter shot him an unwise question, claiming that his sparring partner, Amos Lincoln, had said by the time he got a real fight with Liston, Sonny would be in jail.

Liston didn't answer. The room fell quiet.

The writer said sheepishly: 'I was kidding. Amos didn't say that.'

Liston said: 'I didn't think Amos would say that.'

From there it descended further: 'Sonny, how old are you?'

'Thirty-one.'

'When did you stop counting?'

And then: 'How old's your daughter, Sonny?'

'Thirteen.'

'The oldest one?'

When another writer asked if he felt the press had been fair to him, he said he didn't think they had, citing the fact that he had sold the gloves he wore in the first Patterson fight for $800 and gave the money to cerebral palsy, and that when there was food left over from his wife's birthday party he drove it himself to the local skid row and gave it to the homeless. 'There's two sides to everything,' he said. 'If I do anything good, you never hear about it.'

He was asked about his motivation for the rematch, in other words whether he was taking it for the money or whether he really wanted to redeem himself in the eyes of the fans.

'Yes, I do,' he said. 'It isn't the money. The money means more to the Government.' He had kept calm throughout.

Barbara La Fontaine, who was there to observe as a part of the background for the piece she was writing, was then surprised to read the next morning's newspapers, which talked of him snarling, sneering and snapping. The *Los Angeles Herald Examiner* writer also twisted the reference to his giving away food after Geraldine's party: 'Following a dinner party thrown by his wife he distributed the extra food to residents of skid row in Denver. Much to Liston's sorrow, there were no members of the press in the area to write of his generosity.'

Liston's answer when this kind of accusation happened was that he didn't need sympathy from anybody. He visited children's homes in Anchorage, Boston and in Denver. 'I picked up a little boy, who hugged me and wouldn't let go for nothing,' he said. 'I had to rock him to sleep.' He added: 'I don't care if my heart is as hard as a rock. When I see those kids – some can't walk and some can't hear or talk – well, every man has a tender spot somewhere . . .'

When the date for the rematch was set for 25 May in Boston, he began training again in earnest, first in Denver and then in Dedham, Massachusetts, where, once again, Al Braverman was in control of operations. 'I never had a problem with the son of a bitch . . .' said Braverman:

> He had a great sense of humour, but at other times you wouldn't know what to think because he'd always be glowering at you. He could give you a glare so baleful you'd just wanna fold up. Like a child, like a baby. He was very suspicious, very self-conscious. He didn't get on a platform for the blacks because the only things he cared about were Sonny Liston and his wife. And children. He loved children, trusted 'em. Didn't trust adults.

Liston tended to drift down to a store in Dedham in the evenings where teenagers drank soda and played records on the jukebox. He would chat to them, just generally hang out. He liked to play 'My Girl' by The Temptations. Repeatedly. On his last evening in town, the youngsters made him a presentation of a gift and a card, which read: 'Win, lose or draw, you will always be our champ.'

29

YES, IT'S ME IN YOUR TOWN

Ali was booked into the Schine Inn, which might have sounded a modest establishment but actually covered some 1,500 acres in a place called Chicopee Falls, just off Exit 6 of the Massachusetts Turnpike. Ali decided not to fly but to travel in his new toy, a ten-year-old, twenty-two-seat team bus known as Big Red. He had attempted to drive it but put it into a ditch, so was forced to pay a driver, a brother from the Nation of Islam. His name was Otis 5X. (Apparently he was the fifth Otis on the books.)

The champ wanted 'Muhammad Ali' painted on the side of Big Red, but, fearing reprisals as they drove through the South, his management persuaded him to be content with 'World's Heavyweight Champion'. He invited four writers to share the momentous journey: Mort Sharnik of *Sports Illustrated*, Bud Collins of the *Boston Globe*, Ed Pope from the *Miami Herald* and George Plimpton.

Ali decided it would be fun to drive along the back roads, calling in at sleepy towns where they didn't get to see the heavyweight champion of the world every day. He had a routine. When the bus rolled into town, they found the black, poor neighbourhood, and Ali would get out, beaming and crying out: 'Yes, it's me in your town!' As the crowd gathered, he would shake hands, kiss old ladies, make a noise, give the people something to remember. Then, after exuberant farewells, the vehicle Ali labelled 'the most famousest bus in the world' would slide away in search of the next audience.

At two in the morning, they pulled into Yulee, a Florida town near the Georgia border, and found an all-night diner. The four writers walked in, all of them white, with Bundini Brown.

Collins recalled in the *Globe* in a 2005 memory piece that the waitresses ignored them and the patrons glared at them. Eventually, he walked up to the manager, who was behind the cash till, and said they wanted to be served. Collins remembered the conversation thus, beginning with the manager's response.

'Not with that boy with you.'

'Isn't that against the law, sir?'

'Not here.'

'But isn't this the United States?'

'Not yet.'

Plimpton described it with different details in a *Sports Illustrated* piece, but the gist was the same. He said they were offered separate facilities. 'Out the back. Food's just the same,' said the manager.

Ali, who had also got off the bus to stand with the sparring partners, launched into a tirade against Brown: 'You fool, what's the matter with you, you damned fool . . . nigger, they don't want you here, you ain't wanted, nigger . . .' On the bus, Ali carried on his taunts – 'Uncle Tom! Tom! Tom! Tom!' Brown refused to give ground. 'Leave me alone,' he said. 'My head don't belong between my knees. It's up in the stars. I'm free. I keep trying. If I find a water hole is dry, I go on and find another.'

Further on, on a remote road in Cumberland County, North Carolina, Big Red broke down. Somebody suggested it had a hernia in its rear axle. Pope and Collins hitched a ride to Fayetteville and sent stories from a Western Union office about being stranded with the champ. It took nine hours for a replacement – described by Collins as 'an ordinary, civilised Trailways bus' – to be brought out. It came with its own driver. Otis 5X, blamed for the breakdown, was dismissed to a seat at the back.

Once settled into the Schine Inn, Ali trained in an adjacent building, above a bowling alley. The Knights of Columbus, a Roman Catholic business and charity organisation based in Massachusetts, held a convention at the hotel at the same time. Ali signed autographs. At one point he took a day off to go to Bradley Airport, across the state line in Connecticut, to pick up a newspaperman, who had arrived on his own.

Things livened up a little with the appearance of world light-heavyweight champion Jose Torres, who had apparently issued a challenge to Ali, who in turn decided he was to be called Squirrel.

'What you mean challenging me?' demanded Ali, when he saw him. 'You too little. You fight my sparring partner, James Ellis. He's grown into a light-heavyweight. Squirrel, you fight Ellis, and then I'll fight you.'

At a meeting of the Organization of Afro-American Unity at the Audubon Ballroom in Harlem on 21 February 1965, Malcolm X was shot dead by three gunmen. He had assessed his precarious situation upon his expulsion from the Nation of Islam with chilling accuracy. There was anger among those who still followed him. The situation was unstable. Nobody knew if vengeance would be taken and, if it were, what form it would take or who would be the target. Five days after Malcolm's death, Elijah Muhammad said at a convention: 'Malcolm X got just what he preached.'

By the spring of 1965, Boston's powerbrokers had decided the Liston–Ali story had become an embarrassment and wanted done with it. Sam Silverman kept on pushing, but in April, the district attorney, Garrett H. Byrne, filed a case before Superior Court judge Felix Forte, citing technical irregularities connected with the organisation of the event. According to Byrne, Silverman was no more than a front man for Inter-Continental Promotions Inc., which was not licensed in Massachusetts, and the papers for the licensing of the event were not in order. He called it a public nuisance. Instead of wasting money in fighting Byrne, Silverman capitulated. Perhaps he took the pragmatic view that he wouldn't win anyway and had no time to waste.

After driving the promotion out, Byrne went further, alleging the fight had been permitted in Boston in the first place only because of pressure put on the Massachusetts State Athletic Commission by a prominent politician and a high-powered lawyer. By accepting the fight, Massachusetts had reneged on a promise made to the World Boxing Association, to whom it was affiliated and which did not recognise the fight as a championship bout. This, according to Byrne's argument, made the event illegal. 'I don't see how any DA could stand by and let an illegal fight go on in his district,' he said, also announcing the possibility of a grand jury investigation. Who, if anyone, was influencing Byrne, was anybody's guess.

As compensation, Silverman got to run the fight on closed circuit in Boston Arena and Boston Garden. He did well out of it.

Silverman was of the opinion that Liston's chance went with the hernia operation:

> Liston was under-trained the first time . . . was just right when their second fight was supposed to happen, and this time I think he's overworked himself to get perfect.
>
> In the time since their first fight, Clay has grown up. In the same time, Liston has grown old.

'Suitcase Sam', like most cash hustlers, always had a pay-off line: 'Sonny has a very old face . . . like somebody's wife.'

30

OF MOOSE AND MEN

Ali remained happily in Chicopee, even after Boston was rejected as the venue and the whole project had been transplanted 250 miles away to the century-old mill town of Lewiston, Maine, where they had an ice rink available on the 25th – and probably on most other dates. It was noted by the more cynical hacks that the St Dominic's Arena was at the foot of a ridge locals knew as Skunk Hill.

The Mayor of Lewiston, a 24-year-old political baby named Robert Couturier, admitted he disliked boxing on moral grounds but felt his town of around 40,000 inhabitants could benefit from the publicity. 'I'm stunned,' he said, 'but I'm beginning to recover.' He would not, however, attend the event, which he called brutal.

A reporter from the local paper, Paul Marcotte, had broken the news to him that, having tried and failed to relocate to Cleveland, the promotion could be on its way to them. Mayor Couturier said:

> There's no question it will mean millions in publicity for the state. As for the impact on our town, it will create some problems for us, the problems always created by a rush of visitors – traffic, accommodation and so on – but we'll cope with them.
>
> Lewiston has been the capital of schoolboy hockey and now we're moving from hockey to fighting.

The Mayor, incidentally, was part time. The rest of his week he earned a living teaching some classes, selling advertising and hosting a French-language radio show.

The Governor of Maine, John Reed, had no objections. In fact, he said, he was happy that the 'Pine Tree State' had been selected, promised full cooperation and traditional hospitality.

Lewiston's director of economic development, Sam Michael, who had promoted fights before, did the groundwork. And he moved fast. It took him two days to get the whole enterprise signed and sealed.

They learned as they went along. The first ring, hired from the Brunswick Naval Air Station, was too small – 16-feet square. Angelo Dundee, who drove up from Boston for the specific purpose of checking arrangements were as per contract, rejected that. Dundee said the ring must be 20-feet square inside the ropes. 'The smaller the ring the more it favours Liston,' he said. 'My man likes plenty of room to manoeuvre.'

Dave Anderson did a little point-scoring by suggesting he spotted the 16-foot ring before Dundee even arrived. And, he said, he mentioned it to Bob Nilon, who took it in his stride: 'Is that so? Well, we'll just have to put in a new one.' Anderson suggested they waited for Dundee to arrive in order to get a little publicity from his inevitably loud and public protests.

For some reason, the replacement brought from Portland turned out to be a worn-out relic used for small-hall wrestling. Its ropes were sagging and frayed, its canvas horsehair. A third ring was transported all the way from Baltimore. The tickets had to be ordered from Wilkes-Barre, Pennsylvania.

There had been three hotels in Lewiston, but one had just been demolished. There were a couple of motels. Fight fans would probably have to stay in Portland, Augusta or Brunswick and get to Lewiston as best they could. It didn't have a railway station. An Associated Press report quoted two unnamed local residents as saying: 'It's the most wonderful thing that ever happened in Maine. But where the heck are we going to put all the people?'

It was the smallest town to stage a heavyweight championship since the deluded burghers of Shelby, Montana, dreamt up the Jack Dempsey–Tom Gibbons fight in 1923. In Shelby, when they ran out of money they attempted to pay Dempsey in sheep.

As the hacks, gloomy and uneasy out of their natural habitat, rode towards Lewiston, they were confronted by a sign that read: 'Moose Area Next Eighteen Miles'.

On a storefront at 32 Ash Street, Lewiston, they had a 30-foot sign that advertised the coming of an evangelist: 'Hear John Wesley White – Billy Graham Associate – Central Area Crusade'. When he arrived in town, Bob Nilon felt that seemed a good place to have a poster and so induced the storeowner, ironically on a Sunday morning, to replace it with one advertising the heavyweight championship of the world. 'We took Billy Graham down and put Sonny Liston up,' said Nilon.

Arthur Daley of the *New York Times* took a wry view of the proceedings:

The Cassius Clay–Sonny Liston fight is now in the same category as *Lady Chatterley's Lover* and other works of dubious distinction: it has been banned in Boston.

Like fugitive fighters of ancient days, they've taken it on the lam across a state line and will set up their tent in Lewiston, Maine, 130 miles to the north. It isn't far enough. Labrador would have been better. Then it could have been placed in a deep-freeze.

Daley felt the two protagonists were responsible for the mess: Liston because of who he had always been, Ali because of who he had become.

George Russo, chairman of the Maine Boxing Commission, was asked if his organisation was still affiliated to the World Boxing Association, who no longer recognised Ali as champion and instead had installed Ernie Terrell of Chicago. 'We were the last I knew, but I rather doubt it now,' he said. Duncan MacDonald, another Commissioner, made it plain that Maine did not support the WBA's stance on the heavyweight situation. 'A man wins his title in the ring and you can't take it and put it where you want,' said MacDonald.

Liston and most of the visiting writers were billeted at Poland Springs, where Gene Tunney had trained for one of his fights with Harry Greb in the 1920s. More important to the hacks than boxing history was that it was 14 miles out of Lewiston. Also at the hotel, apparently for a retreat booked some time before, were 235 Catholic priests belonging to the State of Maine Diocese. Somebody had given them 'I Like Sonny' badges to wear. During a no-doubt well-earned break from contemplation and reflection, they milled around the lobby and then formed an orderly queue to shake the hand of Jersey Joe Walcott, the former heavyweight champion who had taken time off from his job as a deputy police commissioner in Camden, New Jersey. This surreal vision was enough to send some of the hacks off in search of more earthly pursuits.

Sam Leitch, of the *Sunday Mirror*, managed to get a quote from an artiste named Sonny Mitchell at the town's strip joint. He faithfully reported her analysis of the fight: 'Liston will win because it's his turn to take the title,' she said. Allegedly.

Milton Gross, of the *New York Post*, appears to have taken similar refuge, although he didn't stoop to quoting Ms Mitchell. He took a more pompous, unkind line, declaring her as a 'sleazy stripper going to flesh'. George Whiting decided to rename her 'Miss Misty Knight' for the readers of the *London Evening Standard* and solemnly informed them that one of the local bones of contention was how much of her clothing she was actually permitted to remove. Gross also found a shop called Mac's, which claimed to have the largest selection of memorial wreaths in Maine. Mac, said Gross, also sold hearing aids.

A 65-year-old shopkeeper named Bill Davis ran The Smoke Shop, at the back of which local youths played pinball machines. Davis said:

> People were saying that our town will be filled with thieves and thugs because of the fight, but that's not true. It's created a regular holiday spirit in town. Before this, all you had to talk about was the snowshoe clubs we have here, like the Pastime and Le Montagnard. From now on, we'll always be able to talk about the fight.

Peter Wilson lamented being 'stuck out in the wilds of Maine'. He could barely believe what he was having to go through in the name of work: 'A chapel in the grounds is said to be the only "hotel-owned and operated chapel in America".'

After explaining the incongruity of seeing Liston, who was accommodated in the historic Mansion House a short walk from the main hotel, trudging around the grounds one minute, and the next, the group of priests, Wilson seemed close to snapping point: 'The truth is that big fights belong in big cities – not tucked away in rural solitude.'

Then he gloomily forecast that this might be the way of things from now on because the real money was no longer in the live gate but in the closed-circuit theatres. And if a promotion were held in a major city, the local signal blackout required to pull in the on-site gate would carry in its wake the loss of a large number of closed-circuit sales. The key to financial success, he felt, was to put the fight in the middle of nowhere, price it well enough to get curious locals to pay up to be there and milk the closed-circuit market in every major city in the country.

Red Smith took things more lightly than Wilson. He enjoyed comparing Poland Springs with Rocky Marciano's old training camp in upstate New York. 'It is the Grossingers of the North,' he wrote, 'with Sunday Mass. And moose.'

About Poland Springs, Leonard Shecter was positively exuberant:

> There are buildings on the grounds the new owners, who have been here three years, have not yet explored. There are paintings on the walls and ghosts in the attics. It's the kind of place that used to have a chamber orchestra in the lobby, and if you stop for a moment you can hear it still.

George Whiting, considerably less enthusiastic, bemoaned the fact that nobody had persuaded Ali to raise himself and join them all in Maine, and pointed out that among the curious local rules was one that demanded a man 'sit down while drinking intoxicants'.

Liston added to the holy element by inviting his early mentors, Father Alois Stevens and Father Edward Schlattmann, to stay with him, alongside more recent supporters, Father James Moynihan and Father Edward Murphy.

Father Schlattmann told Herb Ralby of the *Boston Globe*: 'Sonny is more sinned against than sinner. He's not the kind of man who wants to hurt anybody except in the ring. That's his business.'

Father Moynihan said: 'Any man who likes children as much as he does, and priests, can't be too bad. But he doesn't like being picked on. Who does? That's when he becomes insolent and fights back.'

From Liston's room, according to Bud Collins, he had a view of a cemetery. 'Liston does not look quite as old as the Mansion House,' was Collins' considered opinion. 'The Mansion House was built in 1794 and Sonny probably did not appear before 1920.'

A bus was hired to take the working journalists from Poland Springs to Lewiston. Along its side somebody had taken the time to have a sign painted on that read: 'Maine Welcomes the Sportswriters'. It might have done, but those hoping to use the arena facilities to file their pieces for Monday's newspapers were made to feel less than welcome. The Dominican Fathers who ran the premises refused to allow it to be opened for business on a Sunday. That included the ticket office.

Boston Traveler sportswriter Bucky Yardume phoned Rocky Marciano for his opinion and found the former champion in disenchanted mood:

> Boxing is dead. Imagine a world heavyweight title fight in front of 4,600 . . . I don't care who sees what on TV. Nobody can make a living at boxing. Not fighters, promoters, managers, nobody, TV hasn't helped. It's killed the game.

In response to that, a writer named Joe O'Day talked to Dick Tiger and Rubin 'Hurricane' Carter as they prepared for a ten-round fight at Madison Square Garden. Both turned on Marciano. 'Marciano still makes a pretty good living from boxing; everything he has he owes to boxing,' said Tiger. 'The bulk of his earnings, even now, come from the fact that he was once heavyweight champion of the world.'

Carter said: 'Marciano would probably be a fat, bald-headed guy making shoes in Brockton if it hadn't been for boxing.'

At least the Tiger–Carter fight provided some relief for the British press, some of whom made the trip to Madison Square Garden to cover it. In the *London Evening News*, Reg Gutteridge got a long front-page piece complete with photo of one of the four knockdowns Tiger scored on the way to a points win. Boxing was far from dead, according to British sports editors, at least.

Red Smith preferred to write his copy in an office in St Dominic's Arena itself, his typewriter next to piles of unused tickets from a New England prep school hockey match. He got interested in the town: it consisted of textile mills, frame houses and towering Catholic churches beside the Androscoggin River. Seventy-five percent of the population, he said, was of French-Canadian origin. The arena had been built in 1958 to replace one that had burned down. He said it looked like an aircraft hangar:

> It is light, airy and immaculate under the arched ceiling, with 2,803 permanent seats surrounding the rink – ten rows along the sides, eleven rows at each end. The floor measures 200 feet by 85, and the poorest seats, a few tucked up on shelves in the four corners, will be 140 feet from the centre of the ring.

Bob Nilon had checked and planned the seating capacity before getting the tickets printed. As he worked, stray members of the public wandered about the rink. One called across to him that he might allocate a ticket for Garrett Byrne in the 'sin-bin' box. Meanwhile, outside, Nilon's Cadillac was considered by a local police officer to have been parked illegally. He got a different kind of ticket to the bundles he was trying to sell.

Frank Butler, for the *News of the World*, suggested the Liston camp were so worried about Sonny's mental and physical condition as the fight drew near that, in the last public workout in the Mansion House, they paid a sparring partner, Amos Lincoln, an extra $100 to fake a knockdown. It was the price of a ringside ticket, many of which were still unsold.

Alan Hoby saw him train and could barely believe how bad he was: 'Maybe Liston's camp are staging some outrageous confidence trick to deceive Clay, to deceive all of us, but on the evidence of my own eyes, Liston looked at times like an old bull moose who has strayed far from home.'

Moose again . . .

> Sparring in the 200-year-old ballroom of the Mansion House, an elegant, colonial clapper-board structure of decaying gentility, Liston led off with swinging rights to the body. He also flung clobbering telegraphed rights over a left lead. But he was often flat-footed and clumsy . . .

Although Sonny can punch harder than Clay in single shots, he has provided no evidence in training that he can either nail a shifting target or move side to side himself.

Hoby also reported that Liston had been telling acquaintances that he planned a 'waiting game' this time, stalking until the right moment came to let his big shots go.

Sonny's makeshift gym had stained-glass windows and floral curtains. As the local folk who wanted to see Liston train waited for him to arrive, Al Braverman would conduct a question-and-answer session. On one occasion, a lady asked him if Liston had been 'to see our arena', meaning St Dominic's.

Braverman was effusive: 'He's not only been there, but he thinks it's the cleanest and most beautiful arena in the whole country.' At which the audience applauded as one.

Liston would arrive, as always shadowed by three State troopers, presumably in case there was an assassin waiting among the curious locals, and his new fans would clap and cheer whatever exercise he did. They particularly liked the rope-skipping and the bit where Willie Reddish pounded the medicine ball into Sonny's belly. Always there were more people wanting to watch than could be accommodated, so the remainder milled around outside, some of them pressing their noses against the windows to get a glimpse of what was happening.

On the Sunday before the fight, Liston was serenaded outside the Mansion House by a drum and bugle club, the Pine Tree Warriors, as a crowd of 300 people stood and watched. Liston accepted the salute gracefully from his porch. It seems the people of Maine genuinely took to Liston, possibly because he moved there earlier than Ali, possibly because he did not boast or make a lot of noise. As the columnist Gene Ward put it: 'Sonny Liston is a man of few words; in Maine, that's the kind of man they understand.'

Sam Leitch said he had changed his mind since Boston the previous November, when he felt Liston could regain the title. Now, he said, he just seemed so old: 'The stony face has a wizened scowl. Age takes the discipline from a big man's muscles. Liston boxes as he has always boxed – ponderous and as predictable as a pendulum.' Leitch did not write Liston off – whatever else, Sonny could still hit very hard indeed – but felt Ali's combination punching on the move would bring him through.

Frank Butler took much the same line. He noted how easy Liston was to hit with the left jab, how few punches he landed when his sparring partners boxed on the move, how menacing he was when they stood flat-footed in front of him:

His tree-trunk-like left jab almost sends heads rolling off shoulders, and his short left hook could put any living man to sleep. But it's got to land before his own legs grow weary, as they seemed to do in Miami.

By contrast, Butler said Ali, whom of course he called Clay, looked bigger and even younger than before:

The hernia operation has not troubled him, and he's striving to keep up the new image of being a more serious young man who only screams 'I am the greatest!' as a publicity gimmick . . .

Clay at twenty-three is more mature than even six months ago. This good-looking young Negro has a captivating smile, a quick sense of humour and a friendly wink. When he controls his boasting, he's even likeable. And make no mistake, he has a great deal of natural boxing ability.

After his last training session, Liston gave the hacks a few words to fill out a column inch or two.

On why he felt he was better prepared this time around: 'Bigger sparring partners and working harder.'

On whether or not he had done more roadwork: 'Sixty miles more.'

On why he had treated Ali so lightly first time around: 'Well, I couldn't say.'

When Reg Gutteridge came across Sonny on his own in the Mansion House, he took the chance to get a few quotes for himself and returned to the horny old subject of Liston's age. Sonny answered that he was 33 'last May', presumably forgetting it was still May . . . 'Anyone who says I'm older better not tell my mother . . . That would mean I'm catching up to her age. My wife has got the birth records.'

Gutteridge said he had also heard Liston was quietly paying the bills for two broke old fighters. 'Despite his growls and moods, I seem to be the only guy around here who can stomach Sonny,' he wrote. 'I have been around fighters long enough not to expect gentility.'

He asked Liston about the reason he had wanted the rematch.

'It ain't the money this time, because that means more to Uncle Sam than me. It's getting the title back and the respect. Clay is a coward cos he's gonna run. Only cowards run.'

Liston, quoted this time by George Whiting, also said: 'Don't tell me I'm afraid of Clay. All I'm afraid of is if he opens his big mouth wide enough I'll lose an arm.'

Liston also said the champion would be well advised to stay away from Poland Springs and not to repeat the 'bear-huntin' taunts of Miami: 'If he shows up here he'd better have padding on his behind because we got a couple of police dogs waiting for him.'

Leonard Shecter, for the *New York Post*, said locals were already comparing the impact of the fight to the 1960 visit of President Kennedy, to the time Lewiston was cut off when the Androscoggin River flooded in 1936 and even something known as 'the Great Auburn Fire' of 1933. He was among the few who appreciated the change of scenery:

> Lewiston is surrounded by breathtakingly beautiful countryside, hills and lakes and stands of oak and pine. In the evening, visitors can pick out a large lobster at Steckino's on Middle Street, watch a strip teaser in the Leopard Room of the Holly Hotel, lose money on harness racing at Lewiston Fairgrounds and plan how to drink enough whiskey to be drunk by closing time, which is midnight . . .
>
> The town itself is not exactly picturebook New England. It's mill town and shoe factory and old and just a little run down. But the streets, many of them, are cobblestoned, narrow and quaint and no one would ever mistake them for Los Angeles.

Back at the Schine Inn with a week to go, members of the Maine Commission arrived to give Ali his preliminary medical. It was usually the fighter's job to go to the commission headquarters. The Maine commissioners, and the necessary physician, were so grateful for the task of administering to the heavyweight championship of the world they were only too pleased to drive for hours to Chicopee.

When the Maine men visited Liston at Poland Springs, they found the challenger galloping around on a horse. After Clay's hernia in Boston, the last thing anybody needed was Liston hurting himself. Harold Conrad eventually persuaded him down with one of his acidic lines: 'You've got to get off the horse to meet the Governor. He's the one who gives out pardons in this State.'

Liston was in a good mood. On another day, a wisecrack like that might have earned Conrad a free ticket out of town. This time, Liston brought out one of his favourite tricks to play on the commissioners – a box of candy that gave off an electric shock. In spite of this, Dr Ralph Turgeon declared Liston to be in superb physical condition. 'The fittest man I ever examined,' he said.

Meanwhile, in Chicopee, Dr Leo Lemieux had declared Ali 'the most perfect physical specimen I have seen in 32 years of examining athletes'.

As Bud Collins said, without statements like this from doctors a big fight just wouldn't be a big fight: 'I keep waiting for the day when one of the physicians will say, "This bum belongs in an oxygen tent."'

Ali took the prospect of boxing in Maine lightly. 'Maine is the land of the bear,' he said. 'How am I going to recognise the ugly one?'

He decided to stay at the Schine Inn right up to fight weekend. Accordingly, the journalists had to be bussed back from Maine to watch him train.

By now the astute Alan Hoby for the *Sunday Express* was convinced Ali would win. After the light sparring session with Ellis, Hoby wrote: 'He has developed into one of the most beautiful fighting machines I have seen. As the champion pranced and danced across the canvas, his feet moved at staggering speed for a heavyweight.'

Hoby said Ali displayed 'a really cracking right cross – a weapon Clay has deliberately developed in training to whip home when Liston, as so often happens, drops his hands in front of his chest after being hit by a jab.' As it turned out, that was a more expert piece of analysis than even Hoby probably realised.

He knocked back claims that the champion was, psychologically, an artless man-child. 'The truth is that the champion is a likeable actor who switches the moods on and off like flipping a switch.'

Ali was already talking of defending against Floyd Patterson once he had dealt with Liston: 'The money, I want the money, honey . . . I want to be able to open up a trunk and count out one million dollars.'

Reg Gutteridge felt Ali had grown up and calmed down since the first fight – except when the need for the 'act' was just too tempting.

Joe Louis, Jersey Joe Walcott and James J. Braddock came down for the day, too. Braddock watched and said: 'All you can see is if they're in shape. And this guy is.'

With an eye on the old champions, Ali declared: 'I am a great artist. There has been no one like me before and there will be no one like me afterwards.'

Of Liston, he said: 'Liston's body is too big. His brain cells are too small.' Ali also called Liston a dirty fighter:

> He's planning punches at the body and to certain spots, hernial punches. He wants to work on certain weaknesses he thinks I've got. I don't want no dirty mess. Seventeen million people will be watching . . . The forces of evil are still at work.

It was not to everyone's taste that Ali went off on a rant, shadow-boxing, explaining to Louis how he would have knocked him out in one round. He mimicked his style and Walcott's, too.

'There'll never be another me,' he said. 'I'm the onliest fighter in the history of boxing to name the round the clown goes down. Ain't I the fastest you ever saw, Joe? The fastest in all history?'

Ali had heard Louis's commentary on the first Liston fight in Miami when the boxing legend had said at the end of round one that he had surprised a lot of people by getting through even that session. It was fair comment at the time, but Ali saw it as a slight from a non-believer, a friend of Liston: 'Cassius has got through into the second round. He's surprising the world, surprising the world. How's the Bear lookin', Joe? Is he fast?'

Louis said: 'You know he ain't fast.'

Ali ripped straight back: 'Then he's whupped, Joe. If that man even dreamed he'd beat me, he'd apologise. He'd rather attack a lion with a dull razor, Joe . . .'

Louis enjoyed the show, too, but when Ali looked at him and said: 'You know I'd whup you when you were in your prime,' Louis looked straight back and said: 'I'll use your own words. If you even dream it, you should apologise.'

Angelo Dundee acknowledged the press workout was for show and said Ali had sparred 148 proper rounds, with Jimmy Ellis, his brother Rahaman, Cody Jones and Dave Bailey. 'He's as ready as he'll ever be,' said the trainer.

Some wondered. Ellis knew his job but was a light-heavyweight. Ali's sessions with his brother were hard enough, surprisingly hard given their relationship. He had to ease back several times when Rahaman was struggling. It was said Bailey, a second-rate pro, had a back injury, and Jones had been in hospital for some treatment on an eye problem. Ali didn't seem too inclined to hit either of them.

Ali had a way of making writers feel included, a part of his inner sanctum, if only for an hour or so. As Liston alienated, Ali engaged. 'I don't usually tell people this,' he said, while posing for photos slugging a tree trunk with an axe:

> I don't really have no fight plan. Angelo, he got a fight plan, and I do it when I can. But it would be the worst thing I could do to go in there with my mind all made up what to do.
>
> I been fighting since I was a child, and I do everything on instinct. Sometimes I wonder at myself when I see a big fist coming at my head, and my head move without me thinking, and the big fist go by. I wonder how I did it.

One thing gonna be very different this time. Now, last time I was ducking just to not get hit. Ducking to get away. This time, every move I make, it's gonna be to set him up.

State police patrolled the grounds of the Schine Inn. One cop, usually Officer Robert Erhardt, was stationed outside Ali's window at night. He told Ali: 'The chief don't want anything to happen to you here, and we can't let it. If you so much as cut yourself, I'll have to bleed.'

The champion did his road runs through Blunt Park, two blocks from the Smith & Wesson gun factory. The camp seemed relaxed. Sonji passed the time with a James Bond book.

Although he was happy having Sonji with him, Ali did not want the media to pay her attention. Sonji agreed to an interview with Tim Moriarty in the lobby of the Schine Inn only 'if we keep it short'. She had not watched a fight live before and said she did not know how she would react, especially if Ali was hurt: 'I hate to see anybody get hit or hurt . . . My husband keeps telling me not to worry. He says, "I'll be dancing, honey, just dancing and punching." But I can't help worrying.'

She said when they were together Ali hardly ever spoke about boxing: 'We just talk about us mainly, you know our future plans for a home and a family, things like that.'

They had been living in a small apartment in Chicago, but now she wanted more peaceful surroundings: 'I'm tired of the big cities and all the bustle . . . I want a nice home, not an apartment . . . away from people. And I want a big house with a lot of land all around, and a swimming pool, and a swing and a hammock under a tree . . . things like that.'

Before she ended the conversation, she said: 'I can't wait for this fight, and all the worrying, to end. Then I'm going to steal my man and run away with him and hide somewhere.'

31

THE BOY IS GONE

Ali, as he said he would, left it until Sunday, the 23rd, with only 48 hours to go to move north.

Otis 5X got his job back. It was a five-hour ride on Big Red. 'Allah will protect me,' pronounced the champ, who had shelled out $1,100 for the repair bill.

On the way out of the Schine Inn, Ali shadow-boxed in the lobby, chanting: 'Fall, Bear, fall!'

Packing everything into the revitalised, repainted Big Red took a while, and as he waited Ali signed autographs and chatted with people who had come to see them off. When an ice tank wouldn't fit into the luggage space, he asked who wanted 'a gift from the champ'. It was duly recorded by Steve Cady of the *New York Times* that one E.J. Cogut of Springfield said, yes, he did, and wandered off, presumably with a degree of pride as well as his second-hand cold box.

Then the departure was delayed a while longer because Sonji and her sister-in-law Lentoy Roi were still eating a meal in the hotel restaurant. Ali was patient and spent time talking and shaking hands with Harold Bennett from Ludlow, Massachusetts, the man who had given Big Red a new coat of paint. It had taken him four days.

The passengers included a few reporters, immediate members of the entourage and, according to reports, 14-year-old Mike Marley, who had taken three days off from his studies at Tamp Junior High in Brighton. Ali had kept the promise he had made to the self-styled 'world's youngest sportswriter' by inviting him to the fight as his guest. Marley shared a room in Maine with one of the sparring partners and was given a ringside ticket to the fight.

'What a guy the champ is!' said the excited youngster, to the *Boston Traveler*. Marley would go on to be a lawyer but stayed with boxing as a newspaper, television and eventually Internet journalist – and had a lengthy spell in the 1990s as Don King's publicist. (In fact, Marley contradicted this story years later, saying Angelo Dundee forbade him to travel to Lewiston because of the fear that there would be trouble. Instead, according to Marley, after being found crying in the lobby of a hotel, a local pimp who was travelling to the fight gave him a lift, then forgot about him afterwards. He said he was treated kindly by Canadian heavyweight George Chuvalo, who took him to meet Rocky Marciano.)

Someone had spun a ridiculous, desperately bad-taste line that some supporters of Malcolm X had identified Ali as a suitable target for revenge. The word was that they had stolen an anti-tank gun from a National Guard weapons department and were planning to blast Big Red and all who travelled in it to oblivion. Some fools believed it and wrote it. Ali enjoyed this hugely and declared Big Red would roll out of town, whatever the risks. 'The King cannot sneak around, I am not afraid,' he said in answer to a suggestion that he might travel by ordinary saloon car. 'We invite you to dare to make the trip on Big Red and be at ringside Tuesday,' he declared to those at breakfast. However, it was true that New York police, who had been investigating Malcolm X's murder, were keeping an eye on him. Detectives William Confrey and John Keeley of the Manhattan Homicide North Department were sent off to Lewiston to 'cooperate with the local police'. Apparently some of those who had been around Malcolm X were 'not in their usual haunts', and so as a precaution, Confrey and Keeley, who knew what these characters looked like, were sent north to 'protect' Big Red's passengers. The officers did not travel on the bus but looked on from the safety of their own convertible.

The only moment of danger came when Otis 5X took a bend too fast and luggage fell out of the overhead racks. One or two sleeping passengers heard the bang and ducked for cover. 'It's all right,' soothed Ali. 'We just being attacked by men on horseback. It's Jesse James . . .' At a Howard Johnson restaurant in Kennebuck, Maine, the champ stopped off for an ice cream and impromptu autograph session.

The anti-tank spin might have been the weirdest exaggeration of the week, but the 'bad-taste award' went to Fred Brooks. Robert Lipsyte, in the *New York Times*, quoted the president of SportsVision as saying: 'If I could assure the people an assassination, I could sell a million tickets.'

Meanwhile, as Ali was on his way, two bear cubs were placed in reception at Poland Springs as props for a publicity stunt. Ali was supposed to pull into Liston's headquarters in Big Red and 'spontaneously' confront Liston in the lobby. Liston had been fed the joke, pointing to the cubs in their cages: 'These are the only bears around here you can handle.' As it happened, Big Red rolled straight on by. Sonny was left rehearsing his lines, then, when it was obvious it was a waste of his time, wandered off.

When the Ali party arrived at the Holiday Inn just off Exit 12 of the Maine Turnpike, five miles out of Lewiston, Bud Collins said fight fans who had followed in Big Red's wake were very uneasy because it was so peaceful and pastoral. They looked around suspiciously. 'Too quiet. Unhealthy,' muttered a gentleman Collins knew only as 'Gaspipe' Vaccola.

Ali escorted Sonji and Lentoy to their rooms on the second floor, then used the moment to make a little noise in a television interview. At first he had seemed sluggish and testy, but when asked if he was afraid, he rose to the job: 'Fear is the Negro's biggest problem. Put into him ever since you brought him here.'

He brandished photographs of Elijah Muhammad and Wallace D. Fard. 'What right has anyone got to come after a righteous, clean-living man like me?' And he deflected the subject into a joke: 'I move too fast to get hit anyway.'

As to the business in hand, he said Liston must be in better shape this time, but it would make no difference: 'He don't have the timing, rhythm, grace or ability to out-think me. It won't go fifteen rounds, or even ten. But if I predicted the round and it happened, they'd say it was a fix.'

After a meal of prime ribs, salad, coffee and tea, Ali also stood on a balcony and addressed the crowd like a politician or, more accurately, a preacher. 'I am the saviour and the resurrection of boxing,' he said. 'I can beat any man on two feet. I like Maine. I've never been here before. It's a beautiful State.'

By this time, Ali's mother and father had arrived. His mother smiled broadly as she climbed the stairs.

'There's the woman who made the greatest boxer in the world,' he declared. Then as he saw his father, he said: 'The royal family is here.'

He wrote out his autograph on slips of paper and let them go from the balcony into the fans' hands. As more people clamoured around, taking photos and asking for his signature, he was heard to say: 'They act like The Beatles are in town.'

Ali, perhaps reflecting on the journey north, declared: 'People don't know other fighters like they know me. Old women, little children, all sorts of men – the whole world knows me.'

He castigated his critics, with a twinkle in his eye:

> When you fellows write all those things about me, all you do is make it hard on Sonny. When I get booed, I get double strong. Boxing is the most important thing in life for making me a living. But to me it's becoming a sideshow. The freedom struggle for 22 million Negroes. That's more important.

Bundini Brown said: 'The boy is gone. What you see now is the man. And what I got to worry about now is that the man don't go trying too hard to prove that he is a man.' Bundini also subscribed to the view that Liston could never again be what he used to be: 'The wait from last November has got to hurt Liston more than the champ,' he said. 'Anyone that old has to get mouldy. We just get fresher.'

Ali enjoyed the subject of Liston's age: 'The Bear got to be more than 35 years of age. Nobody could get that ugly in 35 years . . .'

Jersey Joe Walcott was one of four nominees for the job of referee, along with two other old champs, Jack Dempsey and Jack Sharkey, plus Barney Felix, who had controlled the first fight in Miami. The identity of the referee was kept a secret by the Maine Commission until shortly before fight time. So were the names of the judges, although it was known that they would be local.

Angelo Dundee had no problem with that. 'They might be a little awed by a big title fight, but that doesn't worry me. They'll be the most experienced officials they have. And even if it goes to a decision, there'll probably be a pronounced winner.'

Dundee's own pick was Ali in 11 or 12 rounds. He also said they had looked at films of Liston in training, both before 'the hernia fight' and this time. 'We check how he's moving. We have still pictures, too. We check where his hands are. Those little things tell us a lot. Nobody has to tell us that Liston's going to be tough. He's a man that's desperate.'

32

OF SCIENTIFIC TRIUMPH
AND LOFTY PURPOSE

Closed-circuit business was brisk. Ticket sales for the 258 contracted theatres were around the 630,000 mark. Deals had been done to broadcast the fight live on radio in South America, Britain, Australia, New Zealand, Germany and Austria. The Early Bird satellite would also carry live pictures to Britain and Europe. The worldwide audience was estimated at 80 million, plus 50 million listeners on the radio. The expected financial return from that was at least $1.5 million.

Shirley Povich, in the *Boston Globe*, took a cynical view of the technical accomplishment:

> At the same moment Clay and Liston are bouncing punches off each other's noggins, Early Bird will be bouncing the picture story of the brawl into TV-equipped homes abroad. This, perhaps, is not quite the scientific triumph and the lofty purpose the United States had in mind when it embarked on its billion-dollar satellite program. But now there are communications satellites that are privately owned, and there are nice fees . . . The earlier heavyweight fights in the US were shown in England the next morning, with the kinetoscope films rushed into development and jetted across the Atlantic. But no more of this buggy-wagon stuff. BBC wants the fight live, and is getting it, courtesy of Early Bird.

Both boxers were to be paid 30 per cent of the net gate receipts, and more importantly 30 per cent of the net closed-circuit TV, movie, radio and other ancillary rights.

Astonishingly, the general line from bookmakers was that Liston was a slight favourite. A poll of writers ended 71–48–1 in Ali's favour. The cynic who voted for a draw was not named. Only six others said the fight would go the full fifteen rounds. One of them, again unnamed, somehow envisaged Liston outboxing Ali to win on points.

One of the pro-Liston contingent was Murray Robinson of the *New York Journal-American*. In what now seems a mystifyingly wrong-headed piece, the well-regarded Robinson dismissed Ali with a degree of contempt:

> The champion is a harried, hysterical young man, babbling endlessly of his prowess, but, it seems to me, hiding a nameless fear behind his bragging facade.
>
> He fights scared, which may be a good thing from his point of view, but scarcely a high recommendation. I don't think that Clay has the 'bottom' to be a first-class fighter.

Robinson dismissed the first fight as too bad to be true and went as far as he could within the law to say untoward forces were behind Liston's abject performance. He also believed the fall-out from the Malcolm X assassination, plus the potential effects of the hernia operation, were relevant. Liston would hunt Ali down and knock him out.

Robinson's colleague Dave Anderson felt the opposite – that the bigger, younger, faster champion would be too good. He expected the finish, with Liston cut up, around the ninth. Robinson also wrote an interesting piece about the corkscrew punch, first used extensively by the middleweight champion, Kid McCoy, at the turn of the century. Ali had mentioned using a similar thing to Dave Anderson, and Robinson was intrigued by this. McCoy, he said, would often prolong fights in order to play around with the corkscrew punch, deliberately cutting and bruising his opponent's face:

> Maybe there's a streak of gloating cruelty in Clay's make-up which makes him fond of bloodletting. The corkscrew has been rather rare in boxing because the vast majority of fighters are pros with a job to do and who have no stomach for cruelty per se.

Robinson, who might have been on to something, also compared Ali's defensive skills to those of 'pioneer' champions 'Gentleman Jim' Corbett and Jack Johnson, whom he had seen on film:

> . . . the way he leans back and away from his opponent's leads, guard down, is reminiscent of the way the old-timers boxed on the defence. And, strangely, this gambit has got the current champion a lot of derisive criticism. It was considered classy and masterful when the old boys did it; amateurish, when Cassius does.

Ali was told the Maine police department was still on alert because of the possibility of assassins in the crowd. We can raise eyebrows now, but it must not be forgotten that this was a country that had seen its President gunned down, followed by his alleged killer, and one of his most outspoken critics in Malcolm X. As we know now, it was a spate of high-profile killings that would go on to include among its victims Robert Kennedy and Martin Luther King in the next three years. This was a nation on high alert.

'All those police in the hall just for me,' said Ali, in mock awe. 'I'm a great, great person!'

When he did a spot of roadwork at the side of the Maine Turnpike – the only four-lane highway in the State – a state trooper pulled alongside and chaperoned him, then said it must not happen again.

Someone wrote that the promoters had taken out a $1 million insurance cover on Ali's life. Bob Nilon, seeing a line worth spinning, declared security was of the utmost seriousness. 'Anybody entering the arena or attempting to approach the ring will be scrutinised closely,' he said. 'Those who have the right to be in or near the ring will be given special badges to wear. Others, except the press, will not be allowed near the ring.' This kind of thing is taken as read in the twenty-first century, but 40-odd years ago in Lewiston, Maine, it was considered to be an unusual level of precaution.

John Gillooly wrote a think-piece in the *Boston Record* where he considered the possibility that Ali would have been fretting over a threat to his life. His thread of logic continued that, because he might feel vulnerable in the ring, he might try to take Liston out quickly instead of drawing his sting by boxing on the move – and therefore, might go the way of Floyd Patterson: 'This fight becomes more palpitating, intriguing as post-time nears with new angles, appraisals every ten minutes.'

Gillooly was in danger of baffling himself with his own logic, perhaps a result of being stuck in Maine with not much else to do. However, he eventually backed away from picking Liston on the grounds that Ali knew victory here would take him into paydays that would guarantee his future: '. . . the next heavyweight championship fight could gross $10 million, which would put him on Easy Street at the corner of Secure Avenue.'

Red Smith produced a calm piece of analysis, if one just short of racial stereotyping, for the *New York Herald Tribune*:

> Clay is 23 years old, swift, agile and superbly fit. He is not a deep thinker. He fights, as he talks, by animal instinct, and his reflexes are uninhibited.

He is not an enormously stable character; in adversity, he might come unstrung like a frustrated child.

Smith cited the Henry Cooper fight as the one that proved Ali's heart. He also acknowledged that he had come through the fifth-round difficulties against Liston in Miami. In that fight, he felt Liston's fighting ability might have been permanently damaged:

> Sooner or later every athlete reaches the point of no return physically. With a fighter, it can happen suddenly, in one night. Joe Louis was the best fighter in the world for a dozen years. Then one night he went in against Jersey Joe Walcott and the reflexes were gone . . . It may be that we saw Liston grow old like that on 25 February 1964.
>
> Clay moves with swift grace, hits from all angles with beautiful accuracy. He can put punches together in dazzling combinations, and although they don't look like heavy blows in the gym a swarm of bees can sting a man to death.

Smith's guess was that Ali would stay away early on, cut Liston up and stop him in nine. His colleague, Jesse Abramson, however, picked Liston by knockout by the eighth. It was a strange choice, because the tenor of his preview seemed to suggest he didn't even believe his own pick, as if the newspaper wanted an alternative to Smith's choice just for the sake of readership interest.

Still with the *Herald Tribune*, Jimmy Breslin reminded us that Blinky Palermo was in a federal prison in Lewisburg, Pennsylvania, and Frankie Carbo was in a similar institution on McNeil Island, Washington. Breslin referred to Liston as the Mob's last heavyweight fighter and suggested that in associating himself with the Black Muslims Ali simply belonged to a new breed of gangster:

> They come out of Chicago and they murder and extort, and it is anybody's guess what their leader Elijah Muhammad . . . will do to get at money this simple kid will collect for defending the championship.

Breslin was not reassured by the presence of the Louisville Syndicate: 'The history of fighters protected by businessmen is not good,' he said. 'The businessmen wind up taking care of their business, and the fighter winds up taking care of somebody's shoes.'

Breslin quoted the old fight figure 'Honest' Bill Daly, who declared, with his nether eye on the Nation of Islam: 'We're all in the wrong business. We ought to go out and open a religion.'

On the day before the fight, Ali held a press conference at the Holiday Inn. As he greeted the newspapermen, he sat in a poolside chair, closed his eyes and threw back his head. 'So nice to be alive!' he said, before offering some much-needed copy. He would talk to Liston in the clinches and scare him, he said. He would land his chopping right hand and cut him, he said.

Two disciples of the Nation of Islam stood behind Ali in his chair, nodding when he used a phrase 'community of prayer' for no apparent reason when talking about the substance that got into his eyes in the first fight. The immaculate black suits and black ties had gone, replaced by polo-shirts.

Jimmy Cannon quoted one unnamed insider as saying: 'They must have been told to cool it. They're around all the time. They drop by at night, mostly. But they're around.'

Jimmy Breslin did not, shall we say, find their presence to be a positive element in his working life. He suggested that if Liston won, at least the heavyweight championship would belong to the Mob again: 'They're no good, of course, but at least you can sit down and have a drink with the old gangsters before a heavyweight championship fight.'

Ali understood the effect of bringing the Nation of Islam into the boxing set-up. He said: 'If I lose, I may as well retire, because I'd never get another shot at the title.'

Freelance columnist Al Hirschberg wrote:

> Clay is really an attractive guy. He's young, handsome, bright and bubbly. His outlook is so refreshing, his mimicry so sharp, his doggerel so dreadful, his sense of humour so genuine, that you can accept his outrageous egotism. But you can't accept his devotion to a sect as violently anti-white as the Ku Klux Klan is anti-Negro. And you can't accept Liston, if for no other reason than he can't accept you. He has a grudge against the world.

In another conference Ali offered an illustration of what he believed was the difference between them:

> Liston is tough. He just doesn't think good.
>
> Now if a man were smart, he wouldn't go around rasslin' a dozen cops all the way to the police station when they catch him speedin'. A smart man doesn't do that.
>
> Take me. Couple of months ago I got stopped for speedin' and didn't even have my licence. But I 'Sirred' that man to death. Everything he said, I said, 'Yes, Sir, No, Sir.'

By the time that cop got me to the station, he said, 'Cassius, you've been so obedient I'm gonna let you go.' Now the Bear would have been fightin' the man all the way.

Some who had bought tickets for the Boston fight would not travel to Lewiston because they couldn't find the kind of accommodation they wanted. Or just couldn't get there. The $25 seats at each end of the arena did sell out, but there was not much interest in the others. On-site sales successes rely on the business generated by the mid-price tickets.

The day before the fight, Jesse Abramson reported that hardly anybody turned up at the box office. An unnamed woman, leaving a shop next door, called out: 'Give me a ring when they cut the prices.' Somebody else labelled them 'tourist prices'.

At the weigh-in a little after 12.30 on the day of the fight, the Maine Commission naively put the scales in the ring. As the scales needed a hard even surface in order to be read accurately, this was a waste of time.

Liston arrived first in a white satin robe trimmed with gold, a white towel around his neck. Ali followed a matter of seconds behind him, according to some, looking edgy and nervous in spite of his smiles. He had a white robe with Muhammad Ali inscribed in red. He shadow-boxed. The 500 or so fans in the arena cheered Liston and booed Ali.

Liston stepped on, he was announced as 219½ lb, and Willie Reddish said it was obvious the scales were way out. Then they placed a piece of plywood under them and tried again.

Second time around Liston came up as 215¼ lb. Ali was 206 lb – surprisingly light.

In itself, the weigh-in muddle didn't matter, but it was just one more piece of ammunition for those who believed the heavyweight championship of the world was in the hands of people who didn't know what they were doing.

This time at least, Ali behaved himself, aside from peering closely at the scales to check Liston's weight. Liston did the same to him. In fact, Ali was so well behaved that he didn't react when Liston, feeling he was getting too close, shoved his left shoulder.

They mumbled a couple of things to each other that appeared to have no effect, Ali said something to Willie Reddish, and then the fighters faced each other and exchanged public insults.

'You'll be lucky to stay six rounds this time,' said Ali. 'I'm fast. I'm gonna whup you.'

Liston said: 'I'll bury you. You shut your big mouth. I'll take care of you tonight.'

'You won't be as lucky as you were in Miami,' said Clay.

After the pulse rates of the fighters were announced – 72 for Ali, 60 for Liston – they set off at each other again. It seemed wooden, staged.

'I'm gonna beat you and all your Black Muslim friends tonight,' said Liston.

'I'll beat you so bad I'll make you join the Muslims yourself,' said Ali.

Al Bolan, Floyd Patterson's promoter, said he felt Liston couldn't win unless Ali made a huge defensive mistake. He doubted that would happen. He was expecting to be conducting post-fight negotiations on Patterson's behalf with Ali's team.

Liston had agreed to wear black trunks. Normally he liked white, but Ali wanted white. He didn't care. The black ones were fine. Al Braverman brought him four pairs to try on.

Willie Reddish, according to Jimmy Breslin, was beginning to get nervous. Reddish asked Braverman how Liston had looked in training, especially in cutting down distance, which they had worked on every day. Braverman told him to quit worrying but nothing would stop Reddish doing that. He wasn't dumb.

33

GET UP, YOU BUM!
GET UP, YOU BUM!

Sports fans knew to be prepared for anything from the moment Muhammad Ali and Sonny Liston stepped into the ring in Lewiston, Maine. Bomb-detection experts swept the building before the doors were opened. Police officers checked bags, briefcases, typewriter cases, even purses. State police were on hand, as well as 14 of the 15 men stationed in nearby Mechanics Falls. There were two hundred cops on duty at the arena, near enough one for every ten paying customers. Lewiston police lieutenant Gerald Gilbert said as well as the bomb checks and appearance of plain-clothed New York detectives, his own 'non-uniform' staff would be mingling with fans inside the arena all night.

Newspaper colour writers talked to anyone who was hanging around outside. One lady, Mrs Doretta Pokross, who lived in Maple Street, Lewiston, said: 'I just came to look at the people.'

Just then, somebody called out: 'Here comes Clay!'

At which Mrs Pokross said: 'Clay? Who's he?'

One or two writers felt uneasy at the police pressure. All the talk of assassinations had got people nervous. 'We're on the front row,' said one, quoted in the *Boston Herald*. 'We're sitting ducks for some guy with ideas.'

Lieutenant Gilbert said: 'What disturbs us is the fact that this thing has been given so much publicity. We're afraid some screwball will read all of this stuff and decide to make a name for himself.'

The preliminary bouts went without incident. Jimmy Ellis, Ali's sparring partner, won in a round against 44-year-old Joe 'Bolo' Blackwood. So did Amos Lincoln, Liston's sparring partner, against Abe Davis, a Connecticut loser who hadn't won a fight since 1959. Rahaman Ali took a little longer, two rounds, to knock out Buster Reed, a dreamer who had never had an amateur or professional fight. Reed collapsed in the dressing-room and was taken to hospital. Cody Jones managed to box like a sparring partner even when it came to the real thing and lost a six-round decision to a novice, Mel Turnbow. As entertainment, the undercard was some way less than captivating, but the fans hadn't come to see the bit-part players anyway.

First Liston, accompanied by four police officers, and then Ali, with two policemen and half a dozen Black Muslim security men, entered the ring at around 10.30 p.m. As at the weigh-in, Liston was cheered, Ali booed.

(In Britain, the BBC screened the show live at 3.30 a.m. Normally they closed down before midnight, but for this fight they filled the gap with a string of special programmes. It was said several members of Parliament slipped out of an all-night debate in the House of Commons to watch on television. Harry Carpenter provided the commentary. Former world middleweight champion Terry Downes was, as it turned out, a typically forthright studio guest.)

In the Lewiston ring, 'The Star Spangled Banner' was mangled by a nervous singer, Robert Goulet, whose rendition provoked a mix of amusement and outrage. Goulet, who had played Lancelot opposite Richard Burton and Julie Andrews in the Broadway version of *Camelot*, was born of French-Canadian parents in Massachusetts and raised mostly in Canada. He had not sung the American anthem in public before and had become increasingly worried that he would forget the words.

When the big moment arrived, somehow he managed to turn 'dawn's early light' into 'Dawn's early night', then amended 'gave proof through the night' to 'gave proof through the fight'. His grasp of the tune was a tad experimental.

Watching on the screens in Boston Garden, Pat Horne reported Goulet's performance was greeted by hooting and howling. Someone nearby said: 'Are you sure that was the national anthem?' (It is also said that years later when Goulet was performing on a televised show in Las Vegas, Elvis Presley, watching at home, picked up a handgun and blew his TV set to pieces . . .)

Some of the 2,000-plus customers in St Dominic's Arena not only missed Goulet's big moment but weren't even in their seats when the first bell rang – they were still in long lines at concession stands.

At ringside, the women in Ali's life, his mother Odessa and wife Sonji, sat next to each other. In the corner before the first bell, he bowed his head and prayed, then turned towards Liston.

Ali walked straight out and landed a right lead and moved away, then fired a left hook. Liston ducked low to block or nullify it. Ali set off circling the ring to his left. Liston, in spite of what he said he would not do, chased him, trying to get his jab off. Sometimes he tried to cut Ali off with single rights to the body. Ali blocked them or they fell short.

Ali looked in no hurry, made no attempt to get his jab working, fired off no combinations. There was an authority in his body language that had replaced the nervous energy of the first fight. Liston looked as if he was feeling nothing. Ali just went on circling – then it happened.

Ali checked his advance, feinted to the right, then back to the left, and Liston plodded into range and tried a slow jab just as Ali stopped moving. This time Ali fired a right hand over the jab into Liston's temple. Sonny, who didn't seem to have seen the punch coming, stumbled to his right with the momentum of it, his body bending and his gloves reaching to the canvas. As he touched down, with one minute forty-four seconds gone, his legs gave way and he fell, rolling onto his back.

Referee Jersey Joe Walcott did not react. Ali did not go to the neutral corner, but after ten seconds Liston was on his hands and knees, attempting to get up. His legs gave way again, and he folded over as Ali continued to dance around the ring, at one point leaping into the air. Walcott, who still had not begun a count, looked across at the timekeeper. Liston eventually hauled himself to his feet after being down for 17 seconds.

Walcott spent five seconds more wiping Liston's gloves and checking him, then walked away from the fighters towards where Nat Fleischer, the editor of *Ring*, was sitting next to the knockdown timekeeper, Francis McDonough. Fleischer yelled at Walcott: 'He's out, he's out.' Next to McDonough was the official round timekeeper, a 54-year-old schoolteacher from Auburn named Russell Carroll, who later corroborated McDonough's account of having counted out Liston twice.

Meanwhile, Ali walked to Liston and threw a left hook. Liston tried to crouch but backed away to his left, and Ali threw four more shots before Walcott rushed back and intervened, stopping the fight two minutes and fifteen seconds after the opening bell. Liston said when Walcott stepped in he thought it must be the end of the round. 'I thought maybe I didn't hear the bell.'

When Liston went down, Sonji, in a pink silk dress, leapt to her feet and screamed out. At some point, someone asked how she felt. She shouted: 'I feel beautiful. My man is the king of the world.'

Harold Kaese, in the *Boston Globe*, said when Liston was down, Ali was screaming at him: 'Get up, you bum! Get up, you yellow bum!'

At ringside, Canadian contender George Chuvalo suggested Liston knew exactly what he was doing:

> He got hit on the hairline, looked to his left, looked to his right and went down . . . his eyes were the eyes of a man faking. When a guy is really stunned his eyes roll. His were darting side to side.

Chuvalo's trainer, Ted McWhorter, seemed almost panic-stricken: 'This was no fight. Anybody with any sense knows it [the punch] wasn't anything. This is gonna kill boxing. We'll all be out of work.'

Rocky Marciano once again pronounced boxing dead.

Kaese summed up the brief action: 'Clay was more aggressive and confident, like a fellow who knew the score. All Liston hit him with was three frowns and two scowls.'

Joe Louis had climbed into the ring afterwards. Quite what for, nobody really knew. He probably didn't, either. Leonard Shecter, in the *New York Post*, said the great old champion wore an expression like a man who had just been slapped with a wet sardine. Louis was still trying to come to terms with what happened when he said:

> He got hit by a right hand. But it wasn't no good right hand. He got his jaw broke with a right hand one time and he didn't go down. Clay was on his toes. You don't get that much power on your toes.

BBC commentator Harry Carpenter felt the effect would be far-reaching. 'Boxing,' he said, 'has been set back a good many years by what we have seen here tonight.' Studio guest Terry Downes, the former world middleweight champion from Paddington, declared he had hit his daughter harder than Clay hit Liston – 'and she didn't go down'.

Red Smith wrote that most of the disgruntled customers screaming 'Fix!' and 'Fake!' were very young. Too young, he suspected, to have been able to afford the ticket prices of $25, $50 and $100: 'Possibly they had found a way to get in for less (pronounced nothing) when it began to appear that only about half of the 5,400 seats would be sold.'

Outside Liston's dressing-room, light-heavyweight champion Jose Torres said he felt sorry for Sonny:

> He's my friend. And he's a loser . . . It was a perfect shot. It happens once in a million years. Liston was fighting with his head up, and he moved into it. I don't think he even saw it. It wasn't a fake. You'd have to be a fighter to know it.

Inside the dressing-room, Liston sat on a rubbing table, letting his legs swing, letting his thoughts collect. Geraldine Liston gave him a piece of her mind, telling him he could have got up. He protested his innocence. 'Tell her, Teddy,' he said, to his aide Teddy King. 'Tell her.' Then he changed into blue jeans, a sweatshirt and a white golf cap with the logo 'White Cliffs of Plymouth', a souvenir from one of his training gaffs in Boston.

He stayed in the dressing-room for 40 minutes, accepting visits from Father Edward Murphy, Al Braverman and a few of the Inter-Continental Promotions people, before he emerged, looking and sounding subdued, answering questions as best he could in a near-empty arena. Sam Margolis sat alone in one corner on an empty soft-drinks case, disconsolately shaking his head.

Liston appeared to have had the anger and aggression knocked out of him by that one blow. Perhaps by Geraldine's doubts, too: 'I tried to pick up the count but I couldn't hear any. I was groggy.'

When somebody asked him if he could have got up, he said, 'Yes,' at which Willie Reddish yelled out: 'He didn't know the count.'

Liston tried to explain. 'I didn't quit. I got hit and hurt good . . . I felt all screwed up.'

He said he would fight again against anybody: 'What choice do I have?'

Walcott, who had also made a hash of the Floyd Patterson–Tom McNeeley world title fight when he forgot the mandatory eight rule was in place, said:

> I was trying to keep Clay back, get him to a neutral corner. But I never did get him back. I got him away, but not all the way. Liston was out, though. He got hit a left hook and a right hand. The left on the button, the right on the jaw . . .

He was just letting words go, apparently trying to explain something that he didn't quite remember or understand himself.

Clay, with his Black Muslim friends at his side, said he had tried to tell Liston to get up. 'I wanted him to,' he said. 'I wanted to do a little boxing.'

Having belittled Liston in the ring, he refused to do it afterwards. 'He's a good loser,' said Ali. 'I'm going to have to go and see him and comfort him. When the world turns him down, I'll still be at his side. I wouldn't advise him to retire. Any man looks bad when he fights me.'

Ali said he didn't feel bad about not going to a neutral corner after putting Liston down: 'So I broke a rule about going to a neutral corner . . . Call me an amateur. I'm king of the ring.'

He set off on one of his flights of fancy, declaring the knockdown shot an anchor punch that was first used by Jack Johnson, the first black man to hold the title more than half a century before.

Floyd Patterson's business adviser Al Bolan swung into action, attempting to make a deal with Ali's Louisville syndicate of backers for September 1965. Ali, who had given Patterson a kiss in the ring after the fight, was already doing his bit: 'I want the Rabbit next! He said some bad things about me and maybe he won't last as long as Liston.'

The victory ended Ali's promotional agreement with Inter-Continental Promotions Inc., Liston's backers, and he was now on the open market. 'We are looking for the best deal,' said Angelo Dundee. 'Nobody is going to lick Cassius, not for a long, long time.'

The morning after the fight, Liston took breakfast outside at Poland Springs. Bob Waters of *Newsday* reported that he didn't seem unhappy. In fact, he waved to people who gathered to get a glimpse of him, even smiled.

Jersey Joe Walcott emerged a few minutes after Liston had left. Walcott was a nice man. He had been a popular heavyweight champion almost a decade and a half earlier. At 51, still fit and trim, he moved quickly enough around the ring, but when it had mattered he had not reacted as he should have. In hindsight, a referee more at ease with the pressures and tensions of top-level boxing should have been employed.

Jersey Joe, however, pleaded his case. 'I did all I was supposed to do,' he said.

I tried awful hard. I wanted this to be a good one. You look forward to these things, and then when they're over you wish to God they never happened.

I'm getting most of the blame. I don't think they should blame me, but that's what's happening. It's just that I was the guy in the middle.

The job of a referee is to make sure that when a man is knocked down, he is protected. Then the ref is supposed to pick up the count. That's what I tried to do. I figured Clay was far enough away from Liston, so I ran over to the timekeeper. He told me already he had 12 seconds and that the fight was over.

The way you hear things, you'd think I caused everything.

Frank Butler, for the *News of the World*, said in the ring Walcott had seemed as dazed as the night Rocky Marciano knocked him out in the first round.

The knockdown timekeeper, a 63-year-old retired typesetter for a Portland newspaper, Francis McDonough, was also unhappy. In the Holiday Inn a few miles down the road and across the river in Auburn, he said:

I'll tell you whose fault the whole lousy thing was. It was that lousy bum Clay. If Clay had gone to a neutral corner like he was supposed to, this whole thing wouldn't have happened. The bum shouldn't be allowed to fight any more. He shouldn't be called 'champion'.

McDonough was accompanied by one-third of the three-man Maine Boxing Commission, Duncan MacDonald. The official time, announced in the arena, of one minute of the first round, made the knockout the fastest in heavyweight title history. Some were already querying the accuracy of that, but MacDonald seemed set on grabbing some kind of compensation for the state of Maine in the shape of a chunk of boxing history.

The tape was played out for MacDonald in the Holiday Inn. He watched along with reporters and other interested parties, including Ali, who kept shouting at the screen, celebrating his greatness. 'Watch now,' he said. 'Watch! Wow!' And: 'Look how fast I am in slow motion!'

As Liston was knocked down, a reporter counted on his watch aloud: 'One minute and forty-four seconds.' MacDonald nodded.

As Liston tried to clamber to his feet the first time, the reporter tolled out: 'One minute and fifty-six seconds.' MacDonald nodded again.

When Walcott officially ended the fight, the reporter called: 'Two minutes twelve seconds.' (By my reckoning of the tape I have, he was three seconds out.)

MacDonald walked away, but when questioned about the official time he did what boxing administrators have usually done since somebody first invented the badge and blazer. He stuck to the official line. 'That's the time officially – one minute,' he said, adding as an explanation: 'Cameras sometimes lie. They can speed up the film. I'm going to confer with the other commissioners, but as of now one minute is my time.' However, Fred Brooks, whose company SportsVision provided the tape, said it had not been tampered with, that it was in real time.

Ali was irritated that the facts might get in the way of just about the only accolade that might be attached to this sorry episode. 'What do you want to change my record for?' he said. 'Can't I have a record? This is my day. Don't take it away from me.'

Ali said there should be a public vote on whom he would box next. The title, he said, was the people's, and he was the people's champion. He also said he yelled at Liston to get up because he wanted the world to know he wasn't satisfied: 'I just hollered, "Come on, get up" . . . They cheered him and booed me, and I heard somebody yell, "Hey, Muhammad, your camel is double-parked."'

Ali sympathised with Liston: 'They've taken all his money away and he got nothing . . . I feel really sorry for the man. He's not a bad man.'

He also said: 'I ain't making fun of Sonny. He was used as a tool to stop me. He ain't got no one. He's alone now, all by himself.'

Ali also messed around a little, having fun. He told the media his comedian friend Stepin Fetchit had taught him the punch, which had been passed on to him by the late Jack Johnson. 'I practised it in secret for months and gave it a special twist of my own.'

The condemnation was inevitable.

Frank Butler claimed the disgrace was perpetrated by the Liston camp, not because he took a dive but because he was just so old he couldn't fight any more:

> The Liston–Clay affair was a fraud on the American nation. I emphasise fraud, but it was not a fake-accompli . . . If the fight had been fixed, Liston would have won. The fight mob were on his side. But this still doesn't alter my opinion that this business was the best organised hold-up since the Great Train Robbery.
>
> I exclude Clay from the charge but accuse Liston and his unsavoury backers for cheating about his age and his declining condition. I say he couldn't get up because his legs had gone. Dry rot has set in on a man well over 40, who only admits to 32 . . .

Butler felt Liston's licence should be revoked:

> If he'd gone down fighting, he would have earned respect – perhaps for the first time in his life. Now he's proved an unworthy champion. He will go down in boxing history as a bully and a coward. And I wonder how much cash he will get his hands on when the mathematicians behind him carve up the percentages.

Leonard Shecter wrote in the *New York Post*:

> At this moment of history, not all the perfumes of Araby, not all the Poland Water drunk here by generations of genteel ladies with weak kidneys could wash away the foul odours left by last night's heavyweight championship fight.
>
> It goes down as a one-minute knockout by Cassius Marcellus Clay, who says his name is Muhammad Ali, over Sonny Liston, whose name is mud.

Harold Kaese in the *Boston Globe* suggested:

> The Anasagunticook Indians who sold this town – and a nice little town it is – for a peck of peas were richly rewarded compared to the people who paid to see this travesty of a championship bout.

The Birch St laundry selected to wash the fight canvas before the fight should take it back, wash it again, fumigate it, burn it, and toss the ashes overboard beyond the 12-mile limit.

Red Smith wrote: 'Lewiston's finest stood at the doors of the hockey rink and frisked every lady's handbag for firearms . . . They should have searched Liston for concealed sleeping powders.'

In a case of 'well he would, wouldn't he', Bob Summitt, legal counsel for the World Boxing Association, who no longer recognised Ali as champion, labelled the fight a farce and a fraud. WBA president Merv McKenzie called it 'unfitting, unkempt, illegal and a disgrace to boxing'. Arthur Daley of the *New York Times* seemed so baffled he couldn't write straight. The fight, he said, 'had to be seen to be believed and even then it is hard to believe'.

Reg Gutteridge, for the *London Evening News*, was another who seemed unsure what he had witnessed. The boxing man in him refused to join in with the 'fix' argument, but he could not present an alternative either. The knockout punch, he said, was dubious, a sneaky, half-hearted right hand.

Old Tommy Farr, who once went 15 rounds with Joe Louis for this same heavyweight crown, watched on the Early Bird broadcast in Britain. 'I was always taught that the Early Bird catches the worm,' he said. 'This time it caught two of the greatest slugs it has been my misfortune to see in a boxing ring.'

George Whiting's *London Evening Standard* front-page report recorded 'a dramatic, one-punch conquest over sullen, perspiring Sonny Liston in a high school hockey temple in the middle of nowhere'. He said: 'It was a shambling apology for a world heavyweight championship.'

In North Dakota, *The Rapid City Daily Journal* reported the fight with black borders around its stories. In Virginia, *The Richmond News Leader* removed the report from its sports section and placed it on a business page.

One of the few who was convinced about the nature of Ali's right-hand punch was Alan Hoby. 'Others do not agree with me,' he wrote, when he returned home and filed a reflective piece on the whole mess:

> Well, I thought it was a sweet punch. A swift, perfectly timed chop whipped up and over with a twist of the wrist from the waist. After watching the fight at the ringside, I saw it played back five times on the videotape after the spouting, prancing Clay had completed his degrading rout of the pathetic middle-aged fumbler the Americans have now labelled 'the Deadbeat From Denver'.

Liston understood the grim reality of his situation: 'I'm not in a position to squawk. I have to fight anybody . . .'

When the figures were counted, the official paid attendance came to 2,434. No heavyweight championship since anybody bothered to count had drawn fewer customers to the arena.

The old federal supervision argument resurfaced. Jack Dempsey, Gene Tunney and the former New York State commissioner James Farley all argued for it. Tunney felt it was a fake fight. 'It was a badly arranged knockout,' he said. 'I wish Jack Dempsey and I could go back and take on those two.' Unlike Marciano, however, he didn't feel it was the end of boxing: 'It just shakes the confidence of many people in the sport.'

Dempsey hadn't bothered to watch but felt the criticism was very damaging. Federal supervision could not come soon enough, he said. 'It's the only thing that can save boxing. It's going from bad to worse. It's gotten to be a joke.'

Farley said: 'Boxing, in my opinion, can and should remain alive but only under the supervision of the attorney general. Such a body would prevent local, city or state boxing commissions from having a repetition of what happened in Lewiston.'

A New York senator, Joseph Zaretski, who had paid $5 to watch the fight in an Albany theatre and lost a $1 bet on Liston, was so angry that he attempted to pass a bill to abolish boxing in his state. Several other senators stood in the house to voice their disapproval of the contest and to voice support, in varying degrees, for a federal overseer or a statewide ban.

Having had its taste of world championship boxing, Lewiston wanted to wash its hands of the business as quickly as possible. Quashing the idea of a prolonged, potentially embarrassing and in the end pointless investigation, during which its ringside officials might have to be brought to book, the chairman of the Maine Boxing Commission, George Russo, said: 'There was nothing suspicious about the fight.'

Liston returned to Denver to concentrate on a court case relating to charges of failing to comply with a police order and failing to show his driver's licence. He had come across a minor traffic accident while driving near his training headquarters and stopped to see what was going on. A police officer said he ordered Liston to move his car. He didn't move it and didn't have his licence either, according to the officer. The trial for this heinous offence was set for 6 August 1965.

34

HE'S GONNA MESS HIMSELF UP
SO NOBODY WON'T GO TO SEE HIM

Muhammad Ali agreed to defend next against Floyd Patterson, whose business adviser Al Bolan had begun preliminary negotiations straight after the Lewiston charade.

Eldridge Cleaver, leader of the group which called itself the Black Panthers, saw Ali's fight with Patterson as a part of the ideological struggle that the black man was forced to face. Patterson was the subservient Uncle Tom, while Ali was rebellious, autonomous, forward-thinking.

After an exhibition tour that took in Puerto Rico, Sweden and Britain, on 22 November 1965 Ali toyed with a stubborn Patterson at the Las Vegas Convention Centre. The one-sided fight was finally ended by referee Harry Krause in the 12th round. Patterson, who had gone on after a heavy knockdown, said his movement was restricted by a back injury. He had at least regained his pride after the Liston debacles.

Out of the ring, Ali's marriage to Sonji had ended in a divorce court on 10 January 1966. She would neither convert to Islam nor act as Ali believed a Muslim wife should. Sonji returned home to Chicago, eventually married an attorney, Reynaldo Glover, and made attempts to launch a singing career. Ali remarried, to 17-year-old Belinda Boyd, who became Khalilah Ali, on 17 August 1967.

Attempts were made to produce a unification fight between Ali and the man the WBA recognised as champion, Ernie Terrell of Chicago. This floundered when the New York Commission refused to approve the fight. One of Terrell's associates, Bernard Glickman, was a long-time friend of Frankie Carbo, which was enough to get the fight booted out of New York. In November 1963, Glickman had been interviewed by the FBI following the killing of Lee Harvey Oswald by Jack Ruby. The ensuing report read: 'Bernard Glickman is known to be a close associate of many of Chicago's top echelon criminals and has, in recent years, been active in the management of several ranking prize fighters.'

The California Athletic Commission also issued a statement from its chairman, Dan P. Kilroy, which called on all licensing authorities to refuse to permit Terrell to box under their jurisdiction until he had proved he was free from undesirable influences. Kilroy's statement, circulated by wire service Associated Press, read: 'The California Commission is appalled at the suggestion that Ernest Terrell would be permitted to box for any title so long as Bernard Glickman remains his manager.' The statement reminded authorities of the role California played in the conviction of Carbo and Palermo and went on:

> Glickman was closely associated with Frank Carbo, loaned Carbo money as one friend to another, consulted with Carbo on hundreds of occasions in regard to fights, and called Carbo the Good Will Ambassador of Boxing before the Kefauver committee investigating boxing.

After that, Ben Bentley and Irving Schoenwald tried to put it on in Chicago, only for the plan to become bogged down in a morass of moralistic fervour over Ali's declaration, made early in 1966, in which he demonstrated his doubts about the Vietnam War and his possible role, as a Muslim, in it, to writer Robert Lipsyte: 'I don't have no personal quarrel with those Viet Congs . . .'

The Illinois State Athletic Commission, under political and media pressure, said it had received a telephoned apology from Ali but eventually had to call him to a public hearing to apologise in person. He arrived in the crowded meeting room in Chicago wearing a black suit with gold bow tie and said he did apologise, but only for embarrassing the commission by putting it in a difficult position. He refused to withdraw his words or apologise for them. The Terrell fight was shelved.

His stance sparked outrage in some quarters, applause in others. His family worried for him. His aunt, Mary Turner, who taught maths at a Louisville school, said: 'He's gonna mess himself up so nobody won't go to see him. Most folks feel like I do. When their sons get ready to go to the Army, they'll just pack the suitcases and go.'

Ferdie Pacheco, the physician who observed him closely from before he won the title, said Ali was a whole mix of paradoxes. 'To me, he's just a thoroughly confused person.' Pacheco also felt he had a deliberate tactic of being contrary, citing an occasion when he was to make a speech of acceptance at the 1965 Boxing Writers of America dinner and called people together in a hotel room to work out what they would expect him to say, so that he could say the opposite. Pacheco said Angelo and Chris Dundee were there, so was Herbert Muhammad. The meeting, at the New York Americana Hotel, lasted two hours.

The Vietnam controversy meant Ali was effectively forced to box out of the country. In 1966, he beat George Chuvalo in Toronto, Henry Cooper and Brian London in London, and Karl Mildenberger in Frankfurt.

Ali's contract with the Louisville syndicate who had backed him since the beginning of his professional career ran until October 1966. Bill Faversham said they did not have a renewal option but did have right of first refusal. 'We wouldn't want to hold him,' he said, 'but he's been pretty happy with us.'

Ali agreed he had no general complaints but said while he might sign with the group again, he would want better terms. As it was, the inevitable happened: by the time of the Cleveland Williams fight in November, he was already showing off Herbert Muhammad, the son of Elijah, as his new manager.

When asked about the new deal, Ali seemed a little vague. 'The lawyers are drawing up the agreement,' he said. 'The terms do say if I do not remain true to the Muslim faith as taught by Elijah, the contract is broken. If Herbert goes back on what his father believes, then the contract is broken.'

He said Angelo Dundee would remain but would get a rise in pay. Dundee felt his role would not be changed by a management switch but had been caught by surprise. His brother, Chris, had been negotiating with the syndicate for a defence against Doug Jones in Miami Beach the following February. In fact, as time went on, Dundee's role did lessen. Ali called more of his own shots. But Dundee's influence was still there, and he remained a huge asset during fights themselves because he was, as far as boxing itself was concerned, the man whose judgement Ali could trust above all others.

In order to avoid breaching the anti-trust laws, Herbert Muhammad resigned as president of Main Bouts Inc., which owned the closed-circuit and ancillary rights to the Williams match. Mike Malitz, a top-class television man, was brought in as president. Malitz was steeped in both boxing and television, and his presence was evidence that the Nation of Islam's representatives knew when it was politic to hire a non-believer. Malitz's grandfather, Lew Raymond, matched fighters back in the 1920s, and his father, Lester Malitz, had produced the Wednesday Night Fights in the '50s. Malitz sold the Ali–Williams fight to 125 theatres and arenas in the United States, although Miami Beach city council declined. Malitz worked with lawyer and later promoter Bob Arum.

Reg Gutteridge said Herbert Muhammad had:

> a high voice, an easy smile, a constant giggle and appears to enjoy his role as the remote man of the Ali camp. He seldom shouts, except when Ali is not fighting at his best. Yet he possesses a strength of word that Ali sometimes blindly follows.

Gutteridge was in a New York gym with Herbert when another man, whom the writer described as a 'black wheeler-dealer, not a member of Herbert's clan', had a row with a doorman. Herbert told him quietly: 'Smile at the man, forget it. Then have your friends take care of it later.' It was a rare moment when the mask came down.

Ali treated Elijah Muhammad like a surrogate father. When he got into trouble with the law for some sloppy driving, Ali had his licence taken away not by a law court but by Elijah. 'He makes you live clean and righteous. When he catch you, boy, you caught! I can't drive no more. I have to have a driver.'

In November 1966, Ali produced his classic three-round demolition of the over-the-hill Cleveland Williams in Houston. Ali's performance in that fight was of such a high level, even allowing for Williams' decline, that he was temporarily marketable again.

Texas had no problems licensing the match between Ali and Terrell. The Houston Astrodome was hired again in February 1967. It was the ugliest, nastiest performance of Ali's career. He taunted Terrell through the 15 rounds, yelling at him: 'What's my name?' before smacking another jab or combination into his face. At one point, Ali even rubbed the bewildered, 6 ft 6 in. Terrell's face and eyes against the ropes.

After a more sympathetic seventh-round knockout of the aged father-of-eight Zora Folley in Madison Square Garden in March 1967, Ali was forced into retirement by the escalation of his confrontation with the government. Straight after the Folley fight, he said: 'If I thought going to war would be beneficial in freeing 22 million Negroes to get their freedom, justice and equality, you wouldn't have to draft me. I'd join tomorrow.'

On 28 April 1967, a month after he knocked out Folley, Ali was reclassified as A-1, or eligible, for the armed forces. Because of the escalation of the Vietnam War, the rules of admittance had been altered. Ali was astonished. He had firmly believed that Elijah Muhammad's influence was so great that he would not be called up. Accordingly, he refused the symbolic step forward for induction into the US Armed Forces on the third floor of the US Custom House at 701 Jacinto Street in Houston, Texas. It was pre-arranged. He knew by making that gesture he was enabling his case to go before a civil court. He had already requested exemption on the grounds that he was a Muslim minister and that had been refused by the Service Board of Kentucky and the Appeal Board. The law said that an American citizen wanting a case heard by a court must first explore and exhaust the administrative possibilities. Therefore, he had to attend the induction ceremony.

His argument for his status of minister was that he spent time visiting institutions and talking to crowds and by his example was persuading them to join the Muslim faith. He preached non-violence. According to *Sports Illustrated*, he told his lawyers, while riding in a car from the airport after arriving in Houston: 'Nearly every Negro is a Muslim at heart. The trouble is, first thing you got to do to be a Muslim is live a righteous life. Most people, white or black, don't want to do that.'

On the way, he stopped to talk to people at a bowling alley and to black students crowded on the sidewalk near the university, where there had been disturbances earlier in the week. They were angry and did not appreciate Ali's message of non-violence. He was upset by their negative response.

Three days before he had told writers over lunch in a Houston hotel:

> I've left the sports pages. I've gone on to the front pages.
>
> I want to know what is right, what'll look good in history. I'm being tested by Allah. I'm giving up my title, my wealth, maybe my future.

He said he felt the estimated 600 million Muslims across the world were giving him strength. 'Do you think I'm serious?' he said. 'If I am, then why can't I worship as I want to in America? All I want is justice. Will I have to get that from history?' He estimated that his stand might cost him $10 million, but in the eyes of the people he would still be champion.

For the whole of the week he had been staying in an apartment in what was known as a Negro district of Houston, about six miles from the induction centre downtown. He would have liked to have made the gesture of walking to the Custom House in Jacinto Street but eventually decided against it. Ali, his lawyers and the closest members of his entourage crammed into two cabs.

The night before, he had stayed up until 2 a.m. mulling things over, not with Muslim teachers or ordinary members of the Nation of Islam but with the defiantly Christian Bundini Brown. He slept about four hours and was still in the shower when his lawyers, Hayden Covington and Quinnan Hodges, called to fetch him. Bizarrely, Covington was a Jehovah's Witness, Hodges by his own description 'a southern white Episcopalian'. Offering support was a minister from a local Nation of Islam mosque on Polk Street, Raymond X, formerly Watlington.

When asked if white people could attend his mosque, Raymond was quoted in *Sports Illustrated* as saying: 'Oh my, I don't have that authority. Permission would have to come from Chicago. I'd hate to go back to the ranks, you understand.'

At the Federal District Court hearing before Judge Allen Hannay on the day before the induction was to take place, Hodges and Covington argued

Ali's case, anxious to prevent him from being ruled a delinquent, which was possible once a man had refused to take the step forward. In court, Ali told Judge Hannay he had spoken at 18 mosques, as well as colleges, and his ministry took up an average of 180 hours a month. He also discussed how he had paid expensive divorce costs when he realised his wife Sonji was not a devout Muslim. He also believed the war in Vietnam was directly against the teachings of the Koran because it had not been ordered by Allah or by his messenger: 'We don't take part in Christian wars or wars of any unbelievers. We aren't Christian or Communist.'

By 8 a.m., Ali was at the Custom House. There was no mass protest outside, just 14 or 15 people. (Later in the day, a few more would arrive with a Black Power flag, a few people burned draft cards, songs were sung, slogans shouted, and a passage from the writing of Malcolm X was read out.)

Ali was just one of twenty-six young Americans to be asked the question that day, and the media interest in him and ensuing chaos meant that the proceedings were delayed fifteen minutes. The lunch provided by the Government for Muhammad included a ham sandwich. He threw it away.

Three times he was asked to step forward by Navy Lieutenant C.P. Hartman, three times he refused. Hartman invited him into his office and informed him he had committed a felony punishable by five years in jail and a $10,000 fine. Ali returned to the induction room, refused again and then wrote as instructed: 'I refuse to be inducted into the armed forces of the United States' and signed his name. He was not arrested as a delinquent. This was not unusual, but the possibility that he would be made an example of had been on the minds of those around him. In the end, his lawyers had done their job. Back at the Hotel America, he telephoned his mother to tell her he was all right. Meanwhile, across the street in a plush establishment known as the Brown Derby Lounge, Bundini Brown was refused a soft drink.

Seven weeks later, on 20 June 1967, Ali was convicted of draft evasion by the US Federal Court and sentenced to five years in jail with a $10,000 fine but remained free pending his appeal, which he took all the way to the US Supreme Court. They booted it back to a court in Houston, Texas, where the case was re-examined and ruled to be a correct judgment. Ali was re-sentenced to five years and appealed again. The US Government argued that the Nation of Islam movement did not constitute a religious faith.

On the day he refused to take the step forward, so before he was actually convicted of anything, the New York State Athletic Commission withdrew recognition of him as champion, declaring his action to be 'detrimental to the best interests of boxing'. In other words, they offered their approval of the US involvement in the Vietnam War and felt that any boxer who did not agree to serve in that war should not have the honour of being a world boxing champion. Other states and other organisations followed their lead.

New York Post columnist Al Buck lamented the downfall of a young man he said was once fun. Buck, in his mid-60s and dying, wrote:

> I first met Cassius Marcellus Clay in a small Negro hotel in Miami where he was celebrating his 20th birthday. He was fun then . . . He was fun too when he came to New York to swap poems with the long hairs in Greenwich Village coffee houses . . .
>
> Clay could have been the most popular heavyweight champion since Joe Louis . . .
>
> Clay threw it all away yesterday when he refused to step forward to be inducted in the US Army. He has refused to fight for his native land in which he has earned millions of dollars. Who needs him?

Back home in Louisville, his Aunt Coretta said:

> People don't understand him, but we do, because we lived with him. His image to us is different from the public's. If they knew him, they'd let up on him. They think he's arrogant and insubordinate. But he's a very nice boy.

The World Boxing Association held an elimination tournament to decide his successor, and this was won by Ali's old friend and sparring partner Jimmy Ellis. The New York State Athletic Commission went its own way and recognised Joe Frazier, who had refused to take part in the WBA tournament.

The appeals process meant Ali did not go to prison but he could not box because his licence had been withdrawn. He could command around $2,000 a week in public speaking, but there is no doubt that his anti-Vietnam stand cost him much, much more. He was out of the ring from March 1967, when he knocked out Zora Folley in the seventh round at Madison Square Garden, New York, until October 1970, when he beat Jerry Quarry in three rounds in Atlanta, Georgia.

During his layoff, he said he wanted to resume his career, even though he was disciplined for expressing that desire by Elijah Muhammad, who placed him on a one-year probation and declared that he should no longer use the name Muhammad Ali.

'Clay,' he said, 'has stepped down from the spiritual platform of Islam to see if he can make money in the sports world.' Elijah, in his book *Message To The Black Man*, considered organised 'white man's' sport to be a primary cause of delinquency, murder and theft but had laid that conveniently to one side when the chance had come to embrace Ali, or Clay as he had been then.

Suddenly, Ali faced being expelled from the movement – and, therefore, would have lost his right to claim to be a Nation of Islam minister. Elijah, however, acknowledged that he had to get boxing out of his system.

At various times during his period of exile, Ali was supposed to have fights lined up: in Ohio, Nevada and then Mississippi. Each time, political pressure was brought to bear to stop the project from materialising. He was also subjected to a bitter, eloquent attack by US talk show host and television interviewer David Susskind via a satellite link when Ali was appearing on Eamonn Andrews' UK TV programme in January 1968.

Andrews had shown sympathy for Ali's point of view, but Susskind, who had been in the US forces at Iwo Jima and Okinawa in the Second World War, dismissed Ali as a disgrace to his country and his race, and declared him a convicted felon, a simplistic fool and a pawn.

Ali tried to defend himself by pointing out the financial cost of his action and the possible loss of his liberty. 'I'm not burning draft cards; I still have my draft card. I'm not talking bad about the President, I'm not attacking the country,' he said.

Susskind pressed him about his Islamic references, until an increasingly bewildered Ali tried an old joke. 'You keep talking jive, you'll fall in five,' he said. 'I wish I could get you in a boxing ring.'

Susskind had won, as his intellect and 'safe argument platform' had ensured that he would. He cut Ali down. 'Isn't physical violence the last resort of the exhausted mind?' he asked, then added, 'I believe you're sincere. Grotesquely sincere. I think you're being used, with your modest intelligence quotient, as a pawn by some vicious men.'

Ali had tried to do without boxing. In April 1968, the *Daily Mirror* carried a piece under the byline 'from John Smith in Chicago' in which Ali said:

> What is boxing anyway? It's cheap, child's play. Just beating up an individual with all them gamblers and men with big cigars sitting at the ringside. Everybody patting you on the head and saying, 'Good boy, good brute, good animal . . .'

He was talking in mosques, in colleges, preaching the gospel of segregation, black resistance, black supremacy, the strange interpretation of Islam propounded by Elijah Muhammad.

'Whatever I do, it is all for Allah,' he said. 'I fought in the ring for Allah. I preach for Allah. If my appeal fails I will go to jail for Allah. I am representing my religion. This is beautiful.' He said if he was sent to jail then people would at least understand that he had given up everything for his beliefs. 'Just like Job in the Bible . . . He was tested. I am being tested.'

When a deal was finally done for the Quarry fight to take place in, of all places, Atlanta, Georgia, in October 1970, Ali had been out of the competitive ring for more than three and a half years. He was 28 years old. He tested the public mood in Atlanta with an exhibition there and admitted he felt tired during it, but the crowd accepted him. While he was in Atlanta waiting for the Quarry fight, someone sent a package to his hotel room. In it was a dead puppy with a note attached to it that read: 'We know how to handle black draft-dodging dogs in Georgia.'

Ali was eventually cleared by an 8–0 verdict in the US Supreme Court on 28 June 1971. He was just coming out of a store after buying an orange when the store keeper ran after him to tell him the news that had just been broadcast on the radio. 'I'm not going to celebrate,' he told reporters outside the Lake Travelodge near Chicago:

> I've already said a long prayer to Allah. That's my celebration.
>
> All praises are due to Allah, who came in the person of Master Faroud Muhammad, and I thank Allah for giving to me the Honourable Elijah Muhammad, and I thank the Supreme Court for recognising the sincerity of my religious faith.

By this time, Ali had beaten Quarry, stopped Oscar Bonavena in the 15th round and then lost a mighty struggle with Joe Frazier when challenging for his old crown in Madison Square Garden, New York, on 8 March 1971. Frazier hit the peak of his career that night, outworking and then flooring Ali with a big left hook in the final round. Ali got up, his jaw swollen, and made it to the final bell. The judges voted unanimously for Frazier.

When he was cleared by the Supreme Court, Ali said he had no interest in legal action against those who had cost him the peak years of his career and untold millions of dollars: 'No, they only did what they thought was right at the time. I did what I thought was right. That was all. I can't condemn them for doing what they think was right.' He wasn't even 30.
'Life is full of pressures,' he said:

> I still got a lot of work to do. If I could just wind this whole thing up, taking my title back from Joe Frazier, go on home and say, 'Whew' and quit. Close the doors on all the press, take my little daughters and raise

them, put a fence around my house and get out of all this mess . . .

I just want to sit one day and be an ordinary citizen, go to the hardware store, cut the grass. Don't be in no more papers, don't talk to nobody, no more lectures. Just rest.

He said he wanted to retire in four more fights, including a rematch with Frazier. When someone pointed out there would be pressure for a third fight with Smokin' Joe, he said: 'No, not a third fight. I'd be too tired. You must realise that training is harder. I got up to run this morning, I ran two miles and I quit.'

He recalled his effervescent youth when he could run five fast miles in the morning, mess around afterwards in the town and then go to the gym. Now, after a run he needed to lie down and recover:

I'm not an old man, I'm 29. But you feel it. I get hit in the chin with punches I never got hit with before. I don't dance around every minute . . .

I got another year and that's it. I could fight for eight more years, but I'd be flat-footed. I'd start getting bruised up. I'd start getting knocked down more.

With hindsight, it was one of the most important press conferences he ever gave.

While most people in boxing welcomed the overturning of his conviction, there were those whom it disappointed, even outraged. Herbert R. Rainwater, commander-in-chief of the Veterans of Foreign Wars of the United States, issued a statement from Washington DC:

Naturally, I, like millions of Americans, am very disappointed and embarrassed by the Supreme Court decision to reverse Cassius Clay's draft evasion conviction. This is certain to have a demoralising effect on our American men in uniform as well as those who are about to fulfil that obligation of citizenship and enter the Armed Services.

By the time Ali was cleared by the US Supreme Court, Sonny Liston had been dead six months.

35

SONNY'S LAST YEARS

Unpromotable in the United States after the fiasco in Lewiston, Liston toyed with a strange idea of having Cus D'Amato manage him. Cus talked about it too, but it came to nothing. Sonny and Geraldine left Denver for Las Vegas. In March 1966, Sonny bought a house that belonged to casino and airline owner Kirk Kerkorian at 2058 Ottawa, for $65,000. It was said he paid cash. Or someone did. When he moved in, as an ex-con he had to register his presence with the police. He was told he would not be allowed to carry a gun, but those who knew him said he usually had a .38 handgun on him somewhere. There were no fights on offer in the US, but at the time, in the wake of the popularity of Ingemar Johansson, Sweden was interested in heavyweight boxing. Floyd Patterson and Jimmy Ellis boxed there. So Liston went too. He and Geraldine liked it there. They adopted a Swedish boy, Daniel.

His first fight back, in June 1966, 13 months after Lewiston, he cut up and knocked out the German champion, a 6 ft 5 in. southpaw named Gerhard Zech, before 12,000 fans in Stockholm. Liston was wild, over-eager to please and hurled his punches from too far out, but in round seven a left hook put Zech over. Zech got up but was counted out on his feet.

A three-round win over the still capable 27-year-old Amos Johnson followed in Gothenburg in August. Johnson had been on a good run in Europe: an 'away' draw with Karl Mildenberger in Berlin, a points win over Henry Cooper at the Empire Pool, Wembley, and a disqualification defeat when he out-butted Brian London at Liverpool Stadium. After Liston knocked him out, Johnson was never the same again.

On paper, that should have been enough to earn Sonny a world rating again. After all, only the world heavyweight champion had beaten him in the past decade. However, the fall-out from Lewiston was still such that in the United States nobody wanted to know, especially as his wins had been in a country that some Americans might have struggled to pinpoint on a map of the world. There was also the question of his age. Officially, and quite possibly in reality, he was still only 34. The public perception was that he might have been 44, perhaps even older.

When *Ring* editor Nat Fleischer drew up the rankings at the end of 1966, Liston was excluded. Selected in preference in the top ten contenders for Ali's title were Zora Folley and Floyd Patterson, whom Liston had outclassed in their primes. Then there was Karl Mildenberger – who had only drawn with Amos Johnson, whom Liston had knocked out – Ernie Terrell, Thad Spencer, Doug Jones, Amos Lincoln, George Chuvalo, Henry Cooper and Oscar Bonavena.

In the March 1967 issue, as usual Fleischer looked at each division, categorising world class boxers as Groups 1, 2 and 3, and beneath those listing boxers in alphabetical order in Classes A, B, C and D. The list totalled more than 200 heavyweights. Liston wasn't one of them.

Fleischer hid behind the decision by the New York Commission to deny Liston a licence, a decision which had been taken on 27 April 1962 in view of his alleged connection with the criminal underworld and which had not been revoked. The British Boxing Board of Control also had Liston under suspension as he had not fulfilled his contractual obligations in his 1963 tour.

In fact, as editor of the trade Bible, Fleischer should have risen above, not hidden behind, commission licensing issues. After all, he had rated Liston when he was challenging Ali in 1965, and the New York suspension had stood then. Given Fleischer's influence, his deliberate exclusion of Liston was a scandalously wrong-headed piece of journalism.

According to a *Ring* story in September 1967, Liston confronted Fleischer in Europe. 'Isn't it time to give me a break?' he asked. 'What did I do wrong to begin with? Why was I denied a licence in New York and other states?'

Fleischer told him he could not be rated because he was ineligible virtually everywhere in the United States. 'You have a licence in Nevada and nowhere else in the US,' said Fleischer. 'Thus there is no basis for rating you.' The aged writer added: 'Were you to get reinstated in the United States and fought there, we would have no option but to rate you. As things stand, you present no basis for ranking. Frankly, you are the Forgotten Man.' (Nevada had licensed Liston on 1 October 1966 after he had appeared before the commission in person.)

Dan Daniel reported that several dozen letters a month were arriving at *Ring*'s offices supporting Liston, and in Ali's absence some fans still believed the old champ had the power to clear out the division. 'This must be disputed strongly,' he wrote – and then, once again without the slightest shred of evidence, he fell in with the theory that Liston had persistently lied about his age and was not born in 1932. 'Liston has attained an age at which competent action from him no longer may be expected. He doubtless is more than 45 years of age and very rusty.'

Daniel talked to the 1967 version of the New York Commission and asked if they saw Liston's case differently five years on.

'Not a chance,' said commissioner Eddie Dooley. 'We would turn him down now, as he was turned down five years ago. His situation has not changed.' Dooley also implied that he suspected external influence on Liston's performance in Lewiston.

The truth appeared to be that whatever Liston might have said in his defence, those in authority would not have listened.

Daniel pointed out the inconsistency of the treatment handed down to Liston and Patterson, both of whom had flopped all too pathetically in world title fights, but in the end he complied with his editor's stance: 'From his days in St Louis, where he served as a labour goon, Sonny had a penchant for hooking up with the wrong guys,' he wrote.

(When Liston was eventually allowed into the *Ring* round-up at the end of 1967, Fleischer placed him in Group 3. He did not return to the top ten until August 1968 when he came in at number 7 following a seventh-round stoppage of Henry Clark in San Francisco.)

In Sweden in the spring of 1967, Liston knocked out Dave Bailey in one round of a horrible mismatch – ironically, in view of the events of the Ali rematch, local critics said they didn't see the knockout punch – and stopped Elmer Rush, who was at least better than Bailey, in six. Joe Polino, who had managed the Swedish adventure, went home to the United States, and soon after the Listons returned as well, taking up permanent residence at their house in Las Vegas.

Hank Greenspun, editor of the *Las Vegas Sun*, told Bruce Jay Friedman of *Esquire* after Sonny's death: 'He loved Vegas. There were many of, shall we say, his element here.' Greenspun, by the way, believed Liston did die of an overdose.

Although the police in Las Vegas were infinitely more low key than their counterparts in St Louis, Philadelphia or Denver, he continued to complain that they harassed him, especially on the road. He loved his two Cadillacs. One was pink, the other blue. His driving, though, was always wayward. In spite of the sporadic police attention, he seemed to settle in and feel relaxed. He already had acquaintances from his Thunderbird Hotel days and soon found plenty of others who could help him out. For a price, of course.

Lenny Banker had met Liston in the Thunderbird Hotel in 1963, when he was preparing for the Patterson fight. He owned health clubs at the Sahara and the Riviera, where Sonny would take steam baths, and he liked to call himself Liston's closest friend. 'He was a nice guy,' he said. 'That stare was just hype.

He had a nice sense of humour, and he wasn't stupid.' Banker said Sonny was a good father, too, and enjoyed going off on fishing trips with Daniel to Lake Mead.

Sonny and Geraldine lived in their split-level luxury house two miles east of the Strip, overlooking the golf course that belonged to the Stardust Hotel and Casino. When he was training, Sonny would go out on to the golf course at dawn to do his run. The rest of the Paradise Valley neighbourhood was 'white'. Sonny didn't care. 'Anybody who burns a cross on my lawn, he won't burn anything ever again if I catch him.' It was said he and Geraldine had a bigger swimming pool than anybody else there. It was 30 feet long. 'We're going to stay here,' said Geraldine. 'Because everything is just right and the place is growing.'

Sonny settled down. Geraldine persuaded him to take her to see Liberace. He said:

> Liberace, who wants to hear Liberace? Well, I told my friends, 'This is gonna be a dull evening.' I kept thinking, Liberace oh no, not Liberace . . . I got to tell you this, nobody, but nobody, had a better time than me.

One of his contacts even got him a bit-part in the knockabout teen-movie *Head*, which starred The Monkees, and in another one called *Moonfire*. Even if many considered him beyond redemption, he was enjoying life again.

His first fight back in the USA was in Reno, Nevada, in March 1968: a fourth-round victory over a fair-class Sacramento journeyman Bill McMurray. Two months later, Liston stopped Billy Joiner in seven in Los Angeles. Joiner was poor. Then came the win that even *Ring* magazine could not ignore: the seventh-round stoppage of 23-year-old Henry Clark at the old Cow Palace arena in San Francisco in July 1968. Clark had won his previous seven fights, including decisions over veteran Eddie Machen and the improving Leotis Martin. The result was what mattered most, but the ringside report was less than complimentary. Clark, wrote Don Fraser, opted for the wrong tactics, staying inside with Liston instead of using his speed and boxing him on the move the way Ali had. Maybe Fraser was right, maybe not. In the old days, Bert Whitehurst, who fought Liston twice, said the safest place was on the inside. Liston weighed 219 lb, only 4 lb heavier than when he destroyed Floyd Patterson in his prime.

Through the rest of 1968, Liston was active, winning quickly against S.D. 'Sonny' Moore in Phoenix; Willis Earls in Juarez, Mexico; Roger Rischer in Pittsburgh; and Amos Lincoln in Baltimore. None of that quartet lasted more than three rounds. By the end of the year, he was up to number 3.

Altogether there were 14 wins from the rematch with Ali in May 1965 until his ninth-round knockout defeat by Leotis Martin, who had been his sparring partner years before, in December 1969. In that fight, Liston controlled things early on with his jab and floored Martin in round four. By the seventh, however, Liston's nose was leaking blood and he was fading. In the ninth, a right cross over Liston's sloppy, tired jab set him up for a left hook that put him down, out cold. He fell face first.

Liston's last fight was when he stopped Chuck Wepner in the tenth round in Jersey City in June 1970. Wepner needed more than 50 stitches in cuts on his face and head. Johnny Tocco, who ran Liston's corner, said: 'It was like blood was coming out of a hydrant.'

Afterwards, Liston was paid $13,000 in cash. Usually he was close with his money, but on the plane home, he counted out $10,000 and handed it to one of his friends, Lenny Banker, who had placed a bet for that amount for him weeks before on the outcome of the Jerry Quarry–Mac Foster fight. Liston had bet on Foster. Quarry had won.

The remaining $3,000 he shared between his corner team, which left him with nothing. No money put aside either for the tax man. That was his only fight in the whole of 1970. He was getting his money from somewhere.

Although he was never in serious trouble with the law courts in Las Vegas, in 1969 he was fined $200 for reckless driving and on 2 December 1970 he was taken to hospital after a car smash. He was lucky. The steering wheel was crushed against him, but he escaped with a gashed forehead that needed 20 stitches and some chest injuries, apparently minor. Johnny Tocco said the accident wasn't Liston's fault. 'This broad rear-ended him and put him in the hospital,' said Tocco, who went to visit him and said even then Liston was worried about the possibility of needing an injection.

Banker said Liston was by then in the habit of seeing other women in Vegas, sometimes wives of executives at the casinos, sometimes hookers, whom he mostly didn't pay. *Esquire* quoted Red Greb, who had been involved in the second Patterson fight and by then was working the craps tables in Caesars Palace, as saying the last two years of Sonny's life were ruined by a 'tall junkie girl'. The same piece suggested the girl was a hooker who had led him into the hard drug world. Greb said Liston was also funding a drug dealer's runs across the border to Mexico and back. A hustler named Hank Bloomfield told *Esquire*: 'The thing to remember about Liston is that he was a convict at heart. He always carried a pistol. He was very rough with people and it was nothing for him to pistol-whip people.'

Tocco said the Las Vegas police had been staking a house on the notorious west side of Las Vegas. The west side was so lawless only one cab company in the city would go there. The police believed the house in question to be the centre of a drug operation. Liston was seen several times going in and out. Whether he was using illegal substances and going there for his supply, or working for whoever was inside, or just friends with them, is a matter for conjecture.

His old friends at this time said they were not aware of a significant drug habit, and although he drank alcohol it was to nowhere near the extent he had several years earlier when he was drowning his sorrows in Philadelphia, Chicago and Denver. In December 1970, just before Christmas, Sonny and Geraldine had dinner at the house of Davey Pearl, a top-class referee who ran a bar named Davey's Locker behind the Sands Hotel. Sonny didn't even have a drink. Pearl also insisted he would have had nothing to do with injecting himself.

36

NOBODY NEVER GETS
KILLED IN VEGAS

When Geraldine Liston returned to Ottawa Drive in a cab from McCarran Airport with their adopted son Daniel following a New Year stay with her mother, Eva, in St Louis, it was between 8.30 and 9 p.m. on Wednesday, 6 January 1971. During her break, she had tried to talk to Sonny, but he had not answered the phone. She had presumed he was out with friends. Now lights were on all over the house, windows were open and doors unlocked. In their bedroom, Sonny lay dead.

The body was decomposing, swollen and foul-smelling, but he had apparently fallen onto the bed, with its gold-coloured bedspread, and then across an upholstered bench, a rail of which had broken under his weight. There was dried blood on his white vest, a fingernail file beneath him. He was wearing shorts and a T-shirt that might have been underwear. Other clothes were nearby. A gun was in a holster on the dresser. It had not been fired. The television was on. Outside in the carport, where the delivery boy deposited the daily paper, there were copies of the *Las Vegas Sun* dating back to 29 December. Sonny's black Fleetwood car was there. So was her own pink Cadillac convertible.

The Clark County coroner's office issued a preliminary statement saying there were no wounds or any evidence of foul play. Geraldine Liston had, said police, fallen apart and left Daniel to stay with friends. She said she recalled a bad dream she had in St Louis on the night of the 28th. In it, Sonny was falling over in the shower and calling out her name. It had left her edgy, but her mother had eased her mind.

At first she had thought the smell in the house was due to food having been left out and gone rotten. The moment she walked into the bedroom, however, she knew what she was looking at. Daniel asked what was wrong, and she remembered saying, 'Sonny's dead' and whisking him out of the house.

No one will ever know what killed him. It is possible the Mob-execution theory is correct, that someone attacked him in his home, or got him drunk to the point of stupor and then injected him with a lethal dose of something and planted drugs the police say they found: heroin and marijuana. It is also possible the persistent chest pains he suffered following the car accident at the beginning of December were indicative of a problem with his heart, though after the car accident the hospital had not identified a medical condition that might cause his life to be in danger.

'I was shocked, I was very shocked,' said Harold Conrad. 'Especially the way it happened. They said he might have OD'd. I know that was a lot of crap. I was really pissed off about that.'

Conrad said Liston had been working collecting outstanding debts for loan sharks and had been arguing for a rise. 'He was working for some tough guys . . . black part of Las Vegas. Really tough guys. He didn't give a shit.'

Bill Cayton, who co-managed Mike Tyson, heard Sonny had upset the 'wiseguys' of Las Vegas. Floyd Patterson said he heard something similar.

Conrad was not surprised by what he felt was a high-level cover-up: 'Vegas sits on that stuff. Nobody never gets killed in Vegas. There's no murders. None.' It was Conrad who first came out with the line: 'Sonny died the day he was born.'

In his obituary, Harry Carpenter suggested Liston's mysterious life and death would keep him in the public eye long after his passing. He seemed to feel that Liston's failure to communicate actually increased his allure. It is possible. It is also possible that a general refusal to listen to what he was trying to say made him believe it was pointless attempting to explain himself and therefore aggravated his deep-rooted suspicion and obstinacy.

'I detested interviewing him,' said Carpenter:

> You couldn't get anywhere. The black bullet head would droop as if he were falling asleep during the question. There would be a long silence. Finally the head would come up slowly, those baleful eyes would look right through you and the heavy lips would mumble 'Yeah' or 'No'.

Peter Moss, in the *Daily Mail*, recalled how Liston was hostile even when he answered his phone. 'Your dime, my time – make it quick,' he would say. Moss ceded that while Liston was the least loved of champions he might also have been the least understood. 'But that was his own fault,' he wrote. 'He regarded would-be friends in the same way as opponents. He stared at well-wishers as he did across the ring – frozen-faced, forbidding, dead-eyed.'

Peter Wilson, as judgemental in his generalisations as he ever was, declared: 'It is idle to pretend that Liston was anything but a thug outside the ring and a bully, turned coward, inside it.' As if to balance the argument, he offered another sweeping statement that meant little: 'But if ever there was a boy who never had a chance it was Liston.'

Lionel Crane of the *Sunday Mirror*, who got to know Liston a little when he was ghosting his story for the newspaper, said: 'He always seemed to me one of the loneliest men I ever met. Even in a crowd he still lived in solitary confinement.'

The corpse was in an advanced state of decomposition because the heating was on in the closed house, but the autopsy was able to reveal traces of morphine and codeine in the body, which happens when heroin breaks down. The coroner suggested the amount did not appear to have been enough to be lethal. Rather than do the logical thing and rule an 'open verdict', the coroner decided death was from natural causes, possibly from a heart attack or as a result of lung congestion.

One of the investigating officers, Sergeant Gary Beckwith, said he found marijuana and heroin with a syringe in the house. The police report also said there were fresh needle track marks on his arm. When he spoke to *Esquire*, Captain Gene Clark said he and his men had nothing to be embarrassed about.

That didn't wash with Johnny Tocco. Tocco said in a *Flash* magazine interview in 1988:

> They never found no dope, no needle, no nothing. They never found a needle mark other than the ones the hospital put there.
>
> I'll go to my grave knowing Sonny Liston didn't shoot dope. They found a glass that might have had some booze in it. All Liston did was drink. I know . . . I ran the bar here. Vodka on the rocks was all.

Geraldine Liston said: 'He never took any drugs as far as I knew, and I knew a dopehead when I saw one.' She believed he died of a heart attack. He had high blood pressure, she said.

Harold Conrad would have none of it either:

> I was once with him when he refused to let a doctor give him a shot. He wanted to throw the doctor out the window. And when I told him about Joe Louis and heroin, he was shocked, absolutely shocked.
>
> He got mad at me and wouldn't talk to me the whole night. Two days later, he found out I wasn't lying. He called me and for the first time I heard Sonny apologise.
>
> Sonny smoked a little pot once in a while and he was a heavy boozer. But the guy wasn't on hard drugs.

Years on, the word was that the Las Vegas police department stuck to their belief that Liston had injected himself with heroin on a regular basis. Another theory, said to have originated with the police, was that he was executed on the orders of Ash Resnick, his old friend from the Thunderbird Hotel.

Father Edward Murphy flew in from Detroit to give the eulogy at the funeral service. Back home, the Jesuit priest broke down. He wept for an hour before he could talk of the events of the day to his friend, Father Kelly. He said:

> They had the funeral procession down the Strip. Can you imagine that? People came out of the hotels to watch him pass. They stopped everything.
>
> They used him all his life. They were still using him on the way to the cemetery. There he was, another Las Vegas show. God help us.

Ella Fitzgerald and Doris Day were among the mourners, and Joe Louis was a pall-bearer as Liston was laid to rest in the Paradise Memorial Gardens, near the area where they bury children and babies. In a moment of bizarre irony, as the cortège entered the gates of the cemetery, a policeman saluted.

Geraldine Liston worked as a casino hostess at the Riviera for nine years after Sonny's passing, then she returned to St Louis, where she took a job as a medical technician. She had nothing bad to say about him: 'He was a great guy, great with me, great with kids, a gentle man.'

37

I'M NOT SCARED TO DIE.
I'VE MADE MY PEACE

Muhammad Ali was still in his 20s when Sonny Liston died. He was still unbeaten, had just floored the previously unstoppable Oscar Bonavena three times for a fifteenth-round victory. He was still nine weeks away from the first fight, and first defeat of his professional career, against Joe Frazier at Madison Square Garden.

After Frazier floored and outpointed him, Ali was humility itself:

> Just lost a fight, that's all. There are more important things to worry about in life. Probably be a better man for it.
>
> News don't last long. Plane crash, 90 people die, it's not news a day after. My losing's not so important as 90 people dying.
>
> Presidents get assassinated, civil rights leaders get assassinated. The world goes on. You'll all be writing about something else soon.

Ali's intense rivalry with Frazier would go on to the second fight in New York in January 1974 and then culminate in the epic struggle in the Philippines in 1975. His career would take him, at the age of 32, to the incredible 'Rumble in the Jungle' victory over George Foreman and, in his dotage, his 15-round revenge win over Leon Spinks. It would take him all the way to the inexpressibly sad performances against Larry Holmes and, last of all, Trevor Berbick, in the Bahamas in 1981. Even as he struggled through those last two fights, there were signs of the illness that clouded his middle and later years, but his faith brought him a serenity far removed from the noise of his exciting, brash, uncertain, unpredictable youth. He married four times, eventually found contentment at home and fulfilled his mission of becoming a spokesman for Islam, and saw, of all things, his daughter Laila make good money for a while as a professional boxer.

Ali distanced himself from the Nation of Islam gradually, and the organisation changed its direction following the death of Elijah Muhammad in 1975, when Elijah's son guided it towards a more liberal approach. Herbert admitted white members and renamed it the Muslim American Society. Offshoots still catered for those wanting a harder line, but life had changed.

Ali's view altered as he aged. He said he saw the positives that Elijah provided in terms of helping to increase the self-esteem of African Americans, to help them find a focus in faith and become more disciplined. 'One of the things he did was to make people feel it was good to be black,' said Ali. However, he came to reject Elijah's insistence that the white man was a devil. Souls and hearts, said Ali, had no colour. Black people and white people were made of the same human flesh, and therefore one was not superior to another.

In the 1980s, as his illness tightened its grip, Ali said:

> I'm not scared to die. I've made my peace. I know that people have taken advantage of me. There have been people I should never have been associated with. I know who they are . . . and I know who the good people are . . . that's just the price you pay. The price for doing what I did.
>
> God gave me this gift for a reason. And he gave me Parkinson's Disease for a reason. To show me I'm just a man, just like everybody else. To show me I've got human frailties like everybody else has. That's all I am – a man.

AFTERWORD

It's nearly 30 years since Muhammad Ali stopped boxing and 40 since Sonny Liston met his premature end. The world they grew up in, were young, strong men in, has gone. We are all another generation further away from the time when men and women were owned as slaves, when their family and heritage was denied them, along with the most basic of human rights. The plight of those people, and of their sons and daughters, grandsons and granddaughters, should be a constant reminder of what was done in the name of culture and civilisation. In their different ways, with their contrasting personalities and personal histories, Liston and Ali can teach us much about the way the world was in the 1940s, '50s and '60s, and maybe we can learn something about the nature of human existence, too. From Liston perhaps we learn that sometimes a person cannot shake free from what others perceive them to be, and that the rejected reject. From Ali, perhaps we learn that sometimes we might not quite know what it is that we follow or seek out, but that it's sometimes worth the journey, the effort to be dedicated and disciplined, that peace and serenity are worthwhile objectives and are sometimes achievable in the most unexpected circumstances.

As to boxing, what is it that we know? That in his youth Ali told everyone he was 'the Greatest' and nobody believed him, but to many critics now he was just that: the best heavyweight of all time. That in his youth Liston told nobody anything very much and there were those who said he was unbeatable, but to many now he's just another boxing bully who couldn't take it when things got rough.

In my opinion, it's a fair assessment to say Ali was the most successful heavyweight in history, though I find it hard to judge one generation against the next. All a man can do is beat his contemporaries. Ali did that. As for Liston, I think he's harshly treated because nobody can ever forgive those two inept performances against Ali in 1964 and 1965. And perhaps they cannot forgive them because of the reputation he had of being a heavyweight monster, an unstoppable force. In the end, he disappointed, and because he was not perceived as an attractive personality, because he represented the nihilistic, self-serving world of the career criminal, he could not be forgiven his failures or recognised for the flawed, vulnerable soul that he was.

For generations, people have tried to decide who is the best heavyweight of all time. In 1958, before Liston and Ali came into the argument, Nat Fleischer, editor of *Ring* magazine, said the best was Jack Johnson, the first black champion, who held the title and played to his own life-rules from 1908 until 1915. Fleischer put Joe Louis down as low as six, behind Bob Fitzsimmons, which today would seem a bizarre piece of judgement. But in 40 or 50 years from now, who knows how boxing historians will see it. Modern technology has led to all kinds of computerised attempts to provide some kind of logical order. The excellent website www.boxrec.com uses its own computer system for ranking active and all-time boxers, and the data it has analysed has produced some results that, were they advocated by a human being, might be considered eccentric. Ali is the number one heavyweight in history, followed by Louis, and, then, at three comes Floyd Patterson. Sonny Liston, who demolished Patterson twice in a total time that is less than it takes to boil an egg, is down in 16th place. Poor Sonny. Even the computer refuses to recognise him.

POSTSCRIPT

On 20 January 2009, with the winter sun casting its shadows early, Barack Obama was inaugurated as the 44th president of the United States before a crowd of more than one million Americans in Washington DC.

Long before the ceremony began, a middle-aged woman and an elderly man moved quietly into their seats. The man was dressed in an immaculate black overcoat with a brown scarf and a wide-brimmed black trilby hat. The coat was buttoned high against the cold. As he sat down, the woman bent to lay a blue rug over his lap and legs and then, satisfied he was comfortable, sat down next to him. This was the 67-year-old Muhammad Ali and his wife Lonnie, who had travelled from their home in Michigan to be a part of a day that was so special for African Americans in particular and the world as a whole, a day that when they were young must have seemed an impossibility.

'My fellow citizens,' said President Obama, 'I stand here today humbled by the task before us, grateful for the trust you have bestowed, mindful of the sacrifices borne by our ancestors . . . The time has come to reaffirm our enduring spirit; to choose our better history; to carry forward that precious gift, that noble idea, passed on from generation to generation: the God-given promise that all are equal, all are free, and all deserve a chance to pursue their full measure of happiness . . . because we have tasted the bitter swill of civil war and segregation, and emerged from that dark chapter stronger and more united, we cannot help but believe that the old hatreds shall someday pass; that the lines of tribe shall soon dissolve; that as the world grows smaller, our common humanity shall reveal itself; and that America must play its role in ushering in a new era of peace . . .

'What is required of us now is a new era of responsibility – a recognition, on the part of every American, that we have duties to ourselves, our nation and the world, duties that we do not grudgingly accept but rather seize gladly, firm in the knowledge that there is nothing so satisfying to the spirit, so defining of our character than giving our all to a difficult task.

'This is the price and the promise of citizenship. This is the source of our confidence: the knowledge that God calls on us to shape an uncertain destiny. This is the meaning of our liberty and our creed, why men and women and children of every race and every faith can join in celebration across this magnificent mall, and why a man whose father less than 60 years ago might not have been served at a local restaurant can now stand before you to take a most sacred oath.

'So let us mark this day in remembrance of who we are and how far we have travelled . . .'

Amen, amen.

APPENDIX

THE PROFESSIONAL RECORD OF SONNY LISTON (WEIGHTS WHERE KNOWN)

rsf – referee stopped fight	(s) – spilt
rtd – retired	(m) – majority
pts – points	ko – knockout

1953

2 Sep	w rsf 1 Don Smith, St Louis 200½
17 Sep	w pts 4 Ponce DeLeon, St Louis 200
21 Nov	w pts 6 Ben Thomas, St Louis 198

1954

25 Jan	w rsf 6 Martin Lee, St Louis 201
31 Mar	w pts 6 Stan Howlett, St Louis 203
29 Jun	w pts 8 John Summerlin, Detroit 206
10 Aug	w pts 8 (s) John Summerlin, Detroit 201
7 Sep	l pts 8 (s) Marty Marshall, Detroit 204

1955

1 Mar	w pts 8 Neil Welch, St Louis 202
21 Apr	w rsf 6 Marty Marshall, St Louis 202
5 May	w rsf 5 Emil Brtko, Pittsburgh 202
25 May	w rsf 2 Calvin Butler, St Louis 206½
13 Sep	w rsf 6 Johnny Gray, Indianapolis 212
13 Dec	w rsf 4 Larry Watson, St Louis 209

1956

6 Mar	w pts 10 Marty Marshall, Pittsburgh 203

1957

inactive

1958

20 Jan	w ko 2 Bill Hunter, Chicago 210
11 Mar	w ko 4 Ben Wise, Chicago 210
3 Apr	w pts 10 Bert Whitehurst, St Louis 205
14 May	w rsf 3 Julio Mederos, Chicago 204
6 Aug	w rsf 1 Wayne Bethea, Chicago 204
7 Oct	w ko 1 Frankie Daniels, Miami Beach 212
24 Oct	w pts 10 Bert Whitehurst, St Louis 212½
18 Nov	w rsf 8 Ernie Cab, Miami Beach 211

1959

18 Feb	w rsf 8 Mike DeJohn, Miami Beach 209½
15 Apr	w rsf 3 Cleveland Williams, Miami Beach 212½
5 Aug	w ko 3 Nino Valdes, Chicago 211
9 Dec	w rsf 7 Willi Besmanoff, Cleveland 210

1960

23 Feb	w rsf 8 Howard King, Miami Beach 212¼
21 Mar	w rsf 2 Cleveland Williams, Houston 212½
25 Apr	w rsf 1 Roy Harris, Houston 212½
18 Jul	w ko 3 Zora Folley, Denver 212½
7 Sep	w pts 12 Eddie Machen, Seattle 211

1961

8 Mar	w ko 3 Howard King, Miami Beach 219½
4 Dec	w ko 1 Albert Westphal, Philadelphia 212¼

1962

25 Sep	w ko 1 Floyd Patterson, Chicago 213 (World heavyweight title)

1963

22 Jul	w ko 1 Floyd Patterson, Las Vegas 215 (World heavyweight title)

1964

25 Feb	l rtd 6 Cassius Clay, Miami Beach 218 (World heavyweight title)

1965

| 25 May | l ko l Muhammad Ali, Lewiston 215¼ |
| | (World heavyweight title) |

1966

| 29 Jun | w ko 7 Gerhard Zech, Stockholm 221 |
| 19 Aug | w ko 3 Amos Johnson, Gothenburg 218¼ |

1967

| 30 Mar | w ko 1 Dave Bailey, Gothenburg 221½ |
| 28 Apr | w rsf 6 Elmer Rush, Stockholm 220 |

1968

16 Mar	w ko 4 Bill McMurray, Reno 223
23 May	w rsf 7 Billy Joiner, Los Angeles 222
6 Jul	w rsf 7 Henry Clark, San Francisco 219
14 Oct	w rsf 3 Sonny Moore, Phoenix 221
3 Nov	w ko 2 Willis Earls, Juarez 223
12 Nov	w ko 3 Roger Rischer, Pittsburgh 219
10 Dec	w ko 2 Amos Lincoln, Baltimore 215¾

1969

28 Mar	w pts 10 Billy Joiner, St Louis 219½
19 May	w rsf 7 George Johnson, Las Vegas 217
23 Sep	w ko 3 Sonny Moore, Houston 226
6 Dec	l ko 9 Leotis Martin, Las Vegas 219½

1970

| 29 Jun | w rsf 10 Chuck Wepner, Jersey City 219 |

Fights 54 Won 50 Lost 4

THE PROFESSIONAL RECORD OF CASSIUS CLAY AKA MUHAMMAD ALI

1960

| 29 Oct | w pts 6 Tommy Hunsaker, Louisville 186 |
| 27 Dec | w rsf 4 Herb Siler, Miami Beach 193 |

1961

17 Jan	w rsf 3 Tony Esperti, Miami Beach 195
7 Feb	w rsf 1 Jim Robinson, Miami Beach 193½
21 Feb	w rsf 7 Donnie Fleeman, Miami Beach 190½
19 Apr	w ko 2 Lamar Clark, Louisville 192
26 Jun	w pts 10 Duke Sabedong, Las Vegas 194
22 Jul	w pts 10 Alonzo Johnson, Louisville 192
7 Oct	w rsf 6 Alex Miteff, Louisville 188
29 Nov	w rsf 7 Willi Besmanoff, Louisville 193

1962

10 Feb	w rsf 4 Sonny Banks, New York 194½
28 Feb	w rsf 4 Don Warner, Miami Beach 189½
23 Apr	w rsf 4 George Logan, Los Angeles 196½
19 May	w rsf 7 Billy Daniels, New York 196
20 Jul	w ko 5 Alejandro Lavorante, Los Angeles 199
15 Nov	w rsf 4 Archie Moore, Los Angeles 202

1963

24 Jan	w ko 3 Charley Powell, Pittsburgh 205
13 Mar	w pts 10 Doug Jones, New York 202½
18 Jun	w rsf 5 Henry Cooper, London 207

1964

| 25 Feb | w rtd 6 Sonny Liston, Miami Beach 210½ |
| | (World heavyweight title) |

1965

25 May	w ko 1 Sonny Liston, Lewiston 206
	(World heavyweight title)
22 Nov	w rsf 12 Floyd Patterson, Las Vegas 210
	(World heavyweight title)

1966

29 Mar	w pts 15 George Chuvalo, Toronto 214½
	(World heavyweight title)
21 May	w rsf 6 Henry Cooper, London 201½
	(World heavyweight title)

6 Aug	w ko 3 Brian London, London 209½
	(World heavyweight title)
10 Sep	w rsf 12 Karl Mildenberger, Frankfurt 203½
	(World heavyweight title)
14 Nov	w rsf 3 Cleveland Williams, Houston 212¾
	(World heavyweight title)

1967

6 Feb	w pts 15 Ernie Terrell, Houston 212¼
	(World heavyweight title)
22 Mar	w ko 7 Zora Folley, New York 211½
	(World heavyweight title)

1968–69

inactive

1970

| 26 Oct | w rsf 3 Jerry Quarry, Atlanta 213½ |
| 7 Dec | w rsf 15 Oscar Bonavena, New York 212 |

1971

8 Mar	l pts 15 Joe Frazier, New York 215
	(World heavyweight title)
26 Jul	w rsf 12 Jimmy Ellis, Houston 220½
17 Nov	w pts 12 Buster Mathis, Houston 227
26 Dec	w ko 7 Jurgen Blin, Zurich 220

1972

1 Apr	w pts 15 Mac Foster, Tokyo 226
1 May	w pts 12 George Chuvalo, Vancouver 217½
27 Jun	w rsf 7 Jerry Quarry, Las Vegas 216½
19 Jul	w rsf 11 Alvin Lewis, Dublin 217½
20 Sep	w rsf 7 Floyd Patterson, New York 218
21 Nov	w ko 8 Bob Foster, Stateline 221¼

1973

14 Feb	w pts 12 Joe Bugner, Las Vegas 217¼
31 Mar	l pts 12 (s) Ken Norton, San Diego 221
10 Sep	w pts 12 (s) Ken Norton, Los Angeles 222

20 Oct   w pts 12 Rudi Lubbers, Jakarta 217½

1974

28 Jan   w pts 12 Joe Frazier, New York 212

30 Oct   w ko 8 George Foreman, Kinshasa 216½
                (World heavyweight title)

1975

24 Mar   w rsf 15 Chuck Wepner, Cleveland 223½
                (World heavyweight title)

16 May   w rsf 11 Ron Lyle, Las Vegas 224½
                (World heavyweight title)

1 Jul   w pts 15 Joe Bugner, Kuala Lumpur 224½
                (World heavyweight title)

1 Oct   w rtd 14 Joe Frazier, Manila 224½
                (World heavyweight title)

1976

20 Feb   w ko 5 Jean-Pierre Coopman, San Juan 226
                (World heavyweight title)

30 Apr   w pts 15 Jimmy Young, Landover 230
                (World heavyweight title)

24 May   w rsf 5 Richard Dunn, Munich 220
                (World heavyweight title)

28 Sep   w pts 15 Ken Norton, New York 221
                (World heavyweight title)

1977

16 May   w pts 15 Alfredo Evangelista, Landover 221¼
                (World heavyweight title)

29 Sep   w pts 15 Earnie Shavers, New York 225
                (World heavyweight title)

1978

15 Feb   l pts 15 Leon Spinks (s), Las Vegas 224¼
                (World heavyweight title)

15 Sep   w pts 15 Leon Spinks, New Orleans 221
                (World heavyweight title)

1979

inactive

1980

2 Oct   l rtd 10 Larry Holmes, Las Vegas 217½
              (World heavyweight title)

1981

11 Dec   l pts 10 Trevor Berbick, Nassau 236¼
              Fights 61 Won 56 Lost 5

ENDNOTES

1 / MAYBE THEY THINK I'M SO OLD BECAUSE I NEVER WAS REALLY YOUNG

A Quaker from Virginia . . .: *Unchained Memories: Readings from the Slave Narratives* (New York: Bulfinch, 2002), p. 23.

'poisoned by a lady': Nick Tosches, *Night Train: The Sonny Liston Story* (London: Hamish-Hamilton, 2000), p. 15.

'My mother had either 12 or 13 children . . .': Gilbert Rogin and Morton Sharnik, 'Can't a fellow make a mistake?', *Sports Illustrated*, 17 July 1961, p. 24.

'All my children grew fast . . .': A.S. Young, *Sonny Liston: The Champ Nobody Wanted* (Chicago: Johnson, 1963), p. 33.

Not many believed his mother, Helen: ibid., p. 32.

'We tried to get his birth certificate . . .': Bob Waters, *Newsday* (undated).

'When guys would write that he was 32 . . .': as cited by William Nack, 'O unlucky man', *Sports Illustrated*, 4 February 1991, reprinted 1994.

'Maybe they think I'm so old . . .': ibid.

'He didn't whip them as much . . .': Young, *The Champ Nobody Wanted*, p. 33.

2 / THIS IS THE ATOMIC AGE, PEACHES

'Yes, indeed, the original Cassius . . .': Jack Olsen, *Cassius Clay* (London: Pelham, 1967), p. 46.

'There's some people say colored folks are lazy . . .': Jack Olsen, 'Growing up scared in Louisville', *Sports Illustrated*, 18 April 1966, p. 96.

'The car was cold . . .': Olsen, *Cassius Clay*, p. 89.

'You gotta cut 'em off . . .': ibid., p. 90.

'And then I ran into his father': Olsen, 'Growing up scared in Louisville', p. 98.

3 / I FIGURED I HAD TO PAY FOR WHAT I DID

'I figured the city would be like the country . . .': Young, *The Champ Nobody Wanted*, p. 51.

'Those guys treated me like a man . . .': Wendell Smith, *Chicago's American*, 1962; also Associated Press, quoted by Young, *The Champ Nobody Wanted*, p. 40.

'We broke into this restaurant . . .': Smith, *Chicago's American*, 1962.

'Nobody don't want a bum . . .': Lionel Crane, 'The man who never came out of solitary', *Sunday Mirror*, 10 January 1971, p. 25.

'No, it hurts me when I think about . . .': ibid.

'I figured I had to pay for what I did . . .': Gilbert Rogin, 'Heavyweight in waiting', *Sports Illustrated*, 17 July 1961, p. 27.

'We had no trouble with him at all . . .': Young, *The Champ Nobody Wanted*, p. 59.

'He was very shy . . .': Bob Waters, *Newsday* (undated).

'I tried to teach him the alphabet . . .': Rogin, 'Heavyweight in waiting', p. 27.

Another inmate, Joe Gonzalez: Young, *The Champ Nobody Wanted*, p. 59.

'He's no fool . . .': ibid., p. 61.

'I have a fighter down at the penitentiary . . .': Robert L. Burnes, 'Heavyweight with a past', *St Louis Globe Democrat*, repeated *Saturday Evening Post*, 13 August 1960.

'I made Frank publisher . . .': Rogin, 'Heavyweight in waiting', p. 28.

'He's going to kill me . . .': ibid.

'He's on the roly-poly side . . .': Burnes, 'Heavyweight with a past'.

'I don't know how . . .': Rogin, 'Heavyweight in waiting', p. 27.

'He was a loner . . .': William Nack, 'O lucky man', p. 159.

'And I've seen them for more than 30 years . . .': Maurice Shevlin, 'Potential of Liston obvious back in 1953', *Chicago Daily Tribune*, 26 September 1962, p. 4.

'He likes to train . . .': ibid.

'he's an ideal boy to handle . . .': ibid.

'Whatever you tell me to do . . .': Burnes, 'Heavyweight with a past'.

4 / THAT'S WHY YOU CAN'T BE RICH

'When I was a boy . . .': Jack Olsen, 'Learning Elijah's advanced lesson in hate', *Sports Illustrated*, 2 May 1966, p. 44.

'It's according to how you look at things . . .': Olsen, *Cassius Clay*, p. 123.

'Look there. That's why you can't be rich . . .': 'The dream', *Time*, 22 March 1963, p. 40.

'If we were in the wrong place . . .': Thomas Hauser, *Muhammad Ali: His Life and Times* (London: Robson, 2004), p. 170.

'I'm sure every last Anglo-Saxon one of you . . .': 'The murder of Emmett Till', http://www.watson.org/~lisa/blackhistory/early-civilrights/emmett.html (Also various others, including: http://www.pbs.org/wgbh/amex/till/).

'I'm no bully . . .': William Bradford Huie, 'The shocking story of approved killing in Mississippi' http://www.nathanielturner.com/emmetttill2.htm (Also http://www.trutv.com/library/crime/notorious_murders/famous/emmett_till/index.html).

'It really did, because what happened . . .': Devery S. Anderson, 'Interview with Mamie Till-Mobley', 3 December 1996, http://www.emmetttillmurder.com/Mamie%20Interview.htm

'I mean, to hear they hung people on a tree . . .': ibid.

'I had plenty to do without going to jail . . .': Cheryl Corley, 'Civil rights icon Rosa Parks dies', http://www.npr.org/templates/story/story.php?storyId=4973548

'We are . . . asking every Negro . . .': Rita Dove, 'Heroes and icons: Rosa Parks', *Time*, 14 June 1999.

'In the past 20 years . . .': Huston Horn, 'Who made me is me', *Sports Illustrated*, 25 September 1961, p. 40.

'Oh, he's a real Joe Louis!': Dale Shaw, 'Cassius Clay: the man and the challenge', *Sport* (undated), p. 59.

'He'd box three or four rounds . . .': William Nack, 'Young Cassius Clay', *Sports Illustrated*, 13 January 1992, p. 78.

'He was always a loudmouth . . .': Jack Olsen, 'Hysteria is a sometime thing', *Sports Illustrated*, 25 April 1966, p. 54.

'Our greatest claim to fame': Nack, 'Young Cassius Clay', p. 81.

'... look like a lady': ibid., p. 75.

'Pretty soon, we're gonna get married . . .': ibid., p. 75.

'Get him off me . . .': ibid., p. 79.

'I never did bother nobody': Olsen, 'Hysteria is a sometime thing', p. 61.

'I've changed my religion . . .': Hauser, *Muhammad Ali*.

'I had to drink water . . .': Izyaslav Koza and Gennadi Komarnitsky, 'Soviet legends: Gennadi Ivanovich Shatkov – city, legend, hero', http://www.eastsideboxing.com/news.php?p=3885&more=1, 17 June 2005.

'I saw him at the very beginning . . .': Nack, 'Young Cassius Clay'.

'Last Sunday, some cats I know . . .': Horn, 'Who made me is me', p. 39.

'Let's just say he fell off the Christmas tree . . .': ibid., p. 42.

'Daddy had enough on his mind . . .': Huston Horn, 'The eleven men behind Cassius Clay', *Sports Illustrated*, 11 March 1963, pp. 63–70.

After becoming involved in Clay's career: ibid.

'Either One knows Cassius . . .': ibid.

'Dundee is the best trainer . . .': ibid.

'In Cassius we saw a good local boy . . .': Horn, 'Who made me is me', p. 42.

'The hardest part of the training . . .': ibid., p. 53.

'All this temptation . . .': ibid., p. 53.

5 / I AM NOT A SOCIAL FRIEND OF MR CARBO'S, MR CHAIRMAN

'moved by the mob': Pedro Fernandez, 'Tocco talks Liston', *Flash*, September 1988, p. 3.

'king fight-fixer': Jim Brady, *Boxing Confidential* (Preston: Milo Books, 2002).

'He was surrounded at all times . . .': Barney Nagler, *James Norris and the Decline of Boxing* (Indianapolis: Bobbs-Merrill, 1964), p. 20.

'When the empire tumbled . . .': ibid., p. 80.

'About 15 years ago . . .': Brady, *Boxing Confidential*, pp. 54–5.

They contacted Genovese: Nagler, *James Norris*, pp. 122–3.

'In 1961, it was revealed that Carbo, unknown to Basilio . . .': Brady, *Boxing Confidential*, p. 83.

'I had to do it': ibid., p. 67.

Mordini, aka Brown, had a piece of Nathan Mann: Nagler, *James Norris*, p. 100.

'Carbo had his fingers on the throat': Teddy Brenner, *Only The Ring Was Square* (New Jersey: Prentice-Hall, 1981).

'Two fights I had . . .': Peter Heller, *In This Corner: Forty-Two World Champions Tell Their Stories* (London: Robson, 1985), p. 272.

'He started crying': ibid.

Jimmy Breslin recalled a story: Jimmy Breslin, *New York Herald Tribune*, 25 May 1965, p. 27.

'it looked . . . better on our record': Gilbert Rogin, 'Norris' last stand', *Sports Illustrated*, 19 December 1960.

6 / WHERE YOU GOING? I DON'T KNOW

'You fight good': *The Detroit Free Press*, September 1954.

'When Harrison died . . .': Robert L. Burnes, *Saturday Evening Post*.

'They've raked me over the coals . . .': Rogin and Sharnik, 'Can't a fellow make a mistake?', p. 28.

'Sonny has the mind of a 12 year old . . .': ibid.

'Every time we could jump Liston . . .': Rogin and Sharnik, 'Can't a fellow make a mistake?'.

'If they don't belong in St Louis . . .': ibid.

'He's dumb . . .': ibid.

'You better unroll . . .': ibid.

'All I tried to do is work . . .': ibid.

Years later, though: Rob Steen, *Sonny Boy: The Life and Strife of Sonny Liston* (London: Methuen, 1993), p. 220.

'He hangs out with a bunch of dogs . . .': Rogin: 'Heavyweight in waiting'.

. . . Vitale lent him $200: Martin Kane, 'Big punch, small chance', *Sports Illustrated*, 9 May 1960.

'Sonny saw no action in 1957 . . .': Lew Eskin, 'Heavyweight hopefuls', *Ring Magazine*, August 1958, p. 49.

'Liston might be the shot in the arm the division needed': *Boxing Illustrated*.

'When he hits you with the left . . .': Tom Phillips, *Daily Herald*, as quoted by Edward Prell, 'London Writer Scoffs at Liston's Right Hand', *Chicago Daily Tribune* (undated).

'I took a good beating . . .': Morton Sharnik, 'The four who baffled Liston', *Sports Illustrated*, 10 February 1964, p. 65.

'His jab is the best I've seen since Joe Louis . . .': Al Buck, 'Sonny Liston big 13', *Ring Magazine*, June 1959, p. 17.

'He can't fight': ibid., p. 47.

'The Ring Record Book makes me 27 . . .': ibid.

'Take a look at those hands . . .': ibid.

'I really found out about myself': Jack McKinney, 'He's mad and getting madder', *Sports Illustrated*, 24 September 1962.

'I got a contender . . .': Joseph Page, 'Everybody is talking about Sonny Liston', *Boxing Illustrated*, December 1959, p. 29.

'Because he's big and strong . . .': Burnes, 'Heavyweight with a past', p. 58.

'Liston is the president of the Don't Wanna Know club . . .': George Whiting, 'The face that doesn't fit' (date and publication unknown).

'I wouldn't bet on a grizzly bear . . .': Whiting, ibid.

'I had his ticket number . . .': McKinney, 'He's mad and getting madder', p. 120.

'What happened? . . .': Rogin, 'Heavyweight in waiting', p. 50.

'Come on, Big Punch . . .': Sharnik, 'The four who baffled Liston', p. 67.

'I needed the money': ibid.

7 / JUST ADDRESS THE ENVELOPE 'CASSIUS CLAY, USA'

'I tried everything I knew . . .': Hauser, *Muhammad Ali*, p. 31.

'What does this kid do? . . .': *Time*, 22 March 1963, p. 42.

'He don't have it': Huston Horn, 'Fast talk and a slow fight', *Sports Illustrated*, 31 July 1961, p. 44.

'I feel like a millionaire . . .': Gilbert Rogin, 'Cautious comes of age', *Sports Illustrated*, 16 October 1961, p. 23.

'I'm not talking this fight . . .': ibid., p. 22.

'I was embarrassed to get in the ring . . .': Shaw, 'Cassius Clay: the man and the challenge' p. 60.

'Nobody has the right to call another fighter a bum': ibid.

'I don't care if this kid can't fight a lick . . .': *Time*, 22 March 1963, p. 42.

'The boy with the big mouth': Shaw, 'Cassius Clay: the man and the challenge', p. 58.

'I can't take no more . . .': ibid., p. 60.

'When he first hit me . . .': Tex Maule, 'Liston's edge, lethal left', *Sports Illustrated*, 24 February 1964, p. 20.

'Clay has such good movement . . .': *Time*, 22 March 1963, p. 42.

Former middleweight champion Paul Pender: ibid.

'Eating, that's my only weakness . . .': Alan Hoby, *Sunday Express*, 13 January 1963.

'I'm gonna drive down Walnut Street . . .': *Time*, 22 March 1963, p. 40.

8 / IT'S NICE TO BE NICE

'I wouldn't pass judgement on no one . . .': Nack, 'O unlucky man'; also Steen, *Sonny Boy*, p. 82.

'I got to get me a manager that's not hot . . .': ibid.

'No ifs, no buts, no nothings': Rogin, 'Heavyweight in waiting', p. 49.

'As matters stand . . .': Lester Bromberg, *New York World Telegram*.

He wasn't training: Lester Bromberg, 'Liston the kidder may laugh away a fortune', *New York World Telegram* (undated).

'I haven't been able to find him since . . .': John Gold, 'Four terrifying hours with Sonny Liston', *London Evening News and Star*, 21 March 1962, p. 15.

'If I get time . . .': Nack, 'O unlucky Man'.

'Sonny's the type of person that needs understanding . . .': Rogin, 'Heavyweight in waiting'.

'You now stand at the crossroads . . .': Red Smith, 'Prodigal Sonny', *New York Herald Tribune* (undated, but 1961).

. . . 5–1 anti-Liston: Hal Hennesey, 'Forget about Liston's police record', *Boxing Illustrated* (undated).

'Like some guys buy racehorses . . .': George Whiting, *London Evening Standard*, 20 July 1963, p. 14.

'Let me make this clear . . .': Alan Hubbard, 'This big overgrown kid', *World Sports*, June 1962, p. 11.

9 / DON'T DUMP YOUR TRASH ON US

'He is pictured as a fearsome . . .': John Hanlon, 'Liston – an ogre built up on ballyhoo', *The Observer*, 10 December 1961.

'Liston is not stupid . . .': Jack McKinney, *Philadelphia Daily News* (undated).

The dwindling army of boxing fans: Steve Snider, 'Liston talks good fight', *The Jersey Journal*, 20 April 1962, p. 9.

'Little Lord Fauntleroys . . .': Hennesey, 'Forget about Liston's police record'.

'What do I have to do to get it? . . .': Pete Evans, 'Floyd is afraid of the dynamite in my mitts', *The Police Gazette*, March 1962, p. 8.

'All that publicity didn't do me any good . . .': ibid.

'I still don't know what he asked me . . .': David Condon, 'In the wake of the news', *Chicago Tribune*, September 1962.

'I'm disappointed in the way he has been treated . . .': Gay Talese, 'Sonny's plight Shocks Patterson', *New York Times*, 28 April 1962, p. 18.

'One night in bed I made up my mind . . .': ibid.

'The spectacle of boxing commissioners . . .': Joe Williams, *New York World Telegram and Sun*, 28 April 1962.

'I don't feel Liston has sufficiently rehabilitated himself . . .': Deane McGowen, 'State Commission denies licence to Liston', *New York Times*, 28 April 1962, p. 18.

'If they want to bring the fight to Chicago . . .': ibid.; also Lester Bromberg, *New York World Telegram and Sun*, 28 April 1962.

'unfair, unjust and un-American': McGowen, 'State Commission denies licence to Liston', p. 18.

'I'm totally ignorant of the fight business . . .': Jimmy Cannon, 'Shadow of Carbo over Liston camp', *New York Journal-American* (undated).

'He thinks he's Sonny Liston . . .': Budd Schulberg, *Playboy*, October 1964, p. 138.

10 / A BLUES SONG JUST FOR FIGHTERS

'They made him a monster': Johnny Tocco interview with Pedro Fernandez, *Flash*, September 1988, p. 3.

'that scowling slab of boxing zombie': Sam Leitch, 'Saint versus sinner', *Sunday Pictorial*, 23 September 1962, p. 31.

'He looks like a fugitive from a horror film': Peter Wilson, 'Nobody wants Liston to win', *Daily Mirror*, 25 September 1962, pp. 16–17.

'The man is like something . . .': Peter Wilson, 'The human hammer', *Daily Mirror*, 21 February 1964.

'A boxing match is like a cowboy movie . . .': Rogin, 'Can't a fellow make a mistake?'; also George Whiting, 'No. 63723 gets a chance to make good', *London Evening Standard*, 19 July 1963, p. 7.

'To Geraldine Liston . . .': *New York Times Magazine*.

'In the beginning I want to emphasise . . .': Wendell Smith, 'Sonny's story of childhood squalor', *Chicago's American*, 19 September 1962.

'I'm the poorest and I need the moorest . . .': Jack R. Griffin, 'Liston to press: things I read, it's ridiculous', *Chicago Sun-Times*, 21 September 1962.

'I don't like this business . . .': Jack McKinney, 'Sonny Liston – a smell of rain and victory', *Sports Illustrated*, 27 August 1962.

'Sonny likes to talk about training . . .': ibid.

'If someone had a question . . .': Sharnik, 'The four who baffled Liston', p. 66.

'I guess I annoyed him . . .': ibid.

'See, the different parts of the brain . . .': McKinney, 'Sonny Liston – a smell of rain and victory'.

'No workout. I smell rain': ibid.

'That's the way it has to be from here on in . . .': ibid.

'Some day they'll write a blues song just for fighters . . .': ibid.

'If I win this fight . . .': ibid.

'I don't have to talk to you': Milton Gross, 'Mind over (ring) matter', *New York Post*, 22 September 1962; also Jimmy Cannon, 'Gloves', *New York Journal-American*, 18 September 1962, p. 21.

'That kid didn't come hear for no handout . . .': McKinney, 'He's mad and getting madder', p. 25.

'The poor guy could go nuts . . .': ibid.

'One dollar seventy five-cents an hour . . .': George Whiting, 'Old Stone Face warns champion', *London Evening Standard*, 19 September 1962, p. 30.

'Favours aren't special . . .': David Condon, 'In the wake of the news' column, *Chicago Tribune* (undated); also quoted in Young, *The Champ Nobody Wanted*, p. 200.

'You fellers look at the sun . . .': Budd Schulberg, *Playboy*, October 1964, p. 138.

'And when Liston did talk . . .': ibid.

'He has a list of them . . .': Leonard Shecter, *New York Post*.

'There's nothing to see . . .': Gerald Kersh, *Playboy* (undated), p. 148.

'All time I read how fast this Patterson is . . .': Griffin, 'Liston to press: things I read, it's ridiculous', p. 82.

'What did he do this guy? . . .': ibid.

'I didn't box with him': ibid.

'If it's a cold night, not very long': McKinney, 'He's mad and getting madder', p. 25; also Al Buck, *New York Post*, 20 September 1962, p. 68, and Jack R. Griffin, *Chicago Sun-Times*, 21 September 1962, p. 82.

'I can't see Patterson beating him . . .': Lester Bromberg, 'Man who broke Sonny's jaw picks him to beat champ', *New York World Telegram and Sun*, 21 September 1962.

11 / HE MUST HAVE DIED LAST NIGHT

'When this gets printed . . .': Gross, 'Mind over (ring) matter'.

'For the first time in my life . . .': Floyd Patterson with Milton Gross, *Victory Over Myself* (London: Pelham, 1962), p. 25.

'Patterson appeared in a boilermaker blue shirt . . .': Reg Gutteridge, *London Evening News and Star*, 20 September 1962, p. 19.

'I gotta make him mad': ibid.

'It's a word I hate . . .': ibid.

'Even if I beat Liston . . .': Arthur Daley, 'At the crossroads', *New York Times* (undated).

'If you dig deeply beneath Sonny's hate . . .': Gross, 'Mind over (ring) matter'.

'I've attended only two Patterson press conferences . . .': Joe Williams, 'Preacher Patterson's sermons lack a punch', *New York World Telegram and Sun*, 21 September 1962.

'You must keep writing . . .': Gross, 'Mind over (ring) matter'.

'For a guy who said he'd fight me for nothing . . .': George Whiting, *London Evening Standard*, 20 September 1962.

'Liston is the unknown quantity . . .': Joe Williams, 'Chicago's battle of the bums', *New York World Telegram and Sun*, 19 September 1962.

'This is the column that called . . .': Red Smith, 'Which one?', *New York Herald Tribune* (undated).

'They're going to psychoanalyse . . .': ibid.

'We will then have a heavyweight champion . . .': ibid.

'I don't see how he can lose . . .': Al Buck, *New York Post*.

'unless he's fooled me . . .': Joe Louis, 'Liston's confidence big asset in bid', *New York Journal-American*, 21 September 1962, p. 29.

'He responds when he is going . . .': ibid.

'Welcome home! . . .': Leo Fischer, 'Leo gets into the act, with an assist from Ben Bentley', *Chicago's American* (undated).

'Certainly, but has there been any worthy . . .': ibid.

'Those were friends of mine . . .': ibid.

'A live gate may soon be . . .': ibid.

'I don't think Floyd is scared . . .': Wendell Smith, 'Experts see fast fight finish', *Chicago's American*, 23 September 1962.

Gerald Kersh . . .went for Liston by the sixth': ibid.

'I am pulling for Floyd . . .': ibid.

'You keep quiet . . .': Jack R. Griffin, 'Tempers flare at boxing meeting', *Chicago Sun-Times*, 18 September 1962, p. 76.

'You tell England . . .': George Whiting, 'Big fight fury', *London Evening Standard* (undated).

'We'll be here all day . . .': Edward Prell, 'Liston jabs at aid: who's doin' fightin'?', *Chicago Daily Tribune*, 25 September 1962, p. 2.

'I believe Floyd's assets . . .': John P. Carmichael, 'Cus: Sonny "predictable"', *Chicago Daily News* (undated).

'Absolutely. I look at boxing coldly . . .': ibid.

'How do I know? . . .': Prell, 'Liston jabs at aid: who's doin' fightin'?', p. 2.

'Patterson is a pretty good fighter . . .': Reg Gutteridge, *London Evening News and Star*, 25 September 1962, p. 1.

'I am champion and I mean to stay . . .': ibid.

'See you tonight': Red Smith, 'Day of the fight', *New York Herald Tribune*, 25 September 1962.

'Just act very calm . . .': ibid.

'If he wins . . .': Georgie Anne Geyer, 'Meet "better half" of Liston family', *Chicago Daily News*, 26 September 1962, p. 69.

'I just saw a dead man walking . . .': Frank Graham, *New York Journal-American*, 15 July 1963.

'I never look at any of my opponents . . .': Gilbert Rogin, 'The facts about the big fight', *Sports Illustrated*, 8 October 1962.

'Hell, let's stop kidding . . .': *New York Post*.

'The other bum can't fight': Red Smith, 'Day of the fight', *New York Herald Tribune*, 25 September 1962.

'against the weight of evidence . . .': George Whiting, *London Evening Standard*, 25 September 1962, p. 7.

'The big problem . . .': Wendell Smith, 'Marciano here, analyzes bout', *Chicago's American* (undated).

12 / THAT BLANKNESS OF NOT KNOWING

'He was a hollow shell': Hugh Bradley, 'Sonny aims to be good champion', *New York Journal-American*, 26 September 1962, p. 39.

'Eyes open, Floyd. Keep 'em open': ibid.; also Reg Gutteridge, *London Evening News and Star*, 26 September 1962.

'He didn't say anything . . .': Pete Hamill, 'Cus doesn't think Floyd should quit', *New York Post*, 26 September 1962, p. 99.

'I must have still been groggy . . .': Rogin, 'The facts about the big fight'.

'I'm not afraid of Floyd getting beat . . .': *New York Journal-American*.

'He didn't get hurt . . .': Al Coxon, 'Gates no bar to our Al', *Chicago Daily News*, 26 September 1962, p. 72.

'I'm upset . . .': Frank Mastro, 'Patterson to go thru with return match', *Chicago Daily Tribune*, 26 September 1962, p. 2.

'Were you impressed by Floyd's speed?': Murray Robinson, *New York Journal-American*, 26 September 1962, p. 39.

'bewildered, disgusted, resentful': Red Smith, *New York Journal-American*.

'Peanuts, ten cents!': Red Smith, 'The big fight', *New York Journal-American*, 27 September 1962, p. 28; also Budd Schulberg, *Playboy*, October 1962, p 9.

'Maybe this is corny . . .': Bradley, 'Sonny aims to be good champion', p. 39.

'Three left hooks to the head did it . . .': Reg Gutteridge, *London Evening News and Star*, 26 September 1962.

'If the public let bygones be bygones . . .': ibid.; also Peter Wilson, 'Just a cold and brutal execution!', *Daily Mirror*, 27 September 1962, p. 30, and Edgar Munzel, 'Give me a chance, I'll be worthy champ', *Chicago Sun-Times*, 26 September 1962, p. 73.

'Only once . . .': ibid.

'We had hard times . . .': Geyer, 'Meet "better half" of Liston family', p. 69.

'As he came into the room . . .': Milton Gross, 'For Floyd – a sad story', *New York Post*, 26 September 1962, p. 99.

'My feelings were hurt . . .': Reg Gutteridge, *London Evening News and Star*, 26 September 1962 and Gross, 'For Floyd – a sad story'; also Wilson, 'Just a cold and brutal execution!', and others.

'Sonny can be a nice fellow . . .': Bradley, 'Sonny aims to be good champion', p. 39.

'Our plan was to make Liston miss . . .': ibid.

'It wasn't as if he took a brutal beating . . .': Hamill, 'Cus doesn't think Floyd should quit', *New York Post*, 26 September 1962, p. 99.

'He took a punch in the gym . . .': ibid.

'He never did the things he trained . . .': Rogin, The facts about the big fight'.

'I never realised . . .': unidentified contemporary newspaper; also quoted by Mike Puma, 'Liston KO'd popular Patterson for title', http://espn.go.com/classic/s/add_liston_sonny. html espn.com, 19 November 2003.

'It was a disgrace . . .': Leonard Shecter, *New York Post*, 26 September 1962.

'I'm glad for Sonny . . .': Al Buck, *New York Post*, 26 September 1962.

'I told him I was very proud . . .': Associated Press wire (no byline), 'Be good boy, ma to Sonny', Forrest City, Arkansas, 26 September 1962.

'Paid attendance: 18,894 . . .': Associated Press (no byline), Chicago, 26 September 1962, and *New York Times*, 27 September 1962, p. 45; also *Chicago Sun-Times*, 26 September 1962, p. 79.

'The picture was a Picasso . . .': Murray Robinson, 'Pay-TV lays a golden egg', *New York Journal-American*, 26 September 1962, p. 39.

'Harlem had an early curfew . . .': Ted Poston, 'Ringside in Harlem', *New York Post*, 26 September 1962.

'There will be a disposition on the part of . . .': Dan Parker, *New York Mirror*.

'A rogue elephant . . .': Wilson, 'Just a cold and brutal execution!', p. 30.

'A scowling mass of a man . . .': Hugh Bradley, *New York Journal-American*, 26 September 1962.

'He was gone . . .': Frank Graham, *New York Journal-American*, 26 September 1962.

'plain, old-fashioned murder . . .': John P. Carmichael, 'It was plain old-fashioned M-U-R-D-E-R', *Chicago Daily News*, 26 September 1962, p. 69.

'a muscular mass of menace . . .': Reg Gutteridge, *London Evening News and Star*, 26 September 1962, p. 1 (p. 9 later editions).

'The heavyweight champion of the world . . .': Arthur Daley, 'A final look', *New York Times*, September 1962.

'That final right was the one . . .': ibid.

'Liston and Sikora were closest to the operation . . .': ibid.

'What did he get hit with?': Milton Gross, 'For Floyd, a sad journey', *New York Post*, 26 September 1962, p. 99.

'the most wretched show . . .': Frank Butler, *News of the World,* 30 September 1962.

'Nobody got their money's worth . . .': Robert L. Teague, *New York Times,* 27 September 1962, p. 45.

'It will be a long time . . .': Budd Schulberg, 'The anatomy and mystique of championship boxing', *Playboy,* October 1962, p. 136.

'it was here old J.J. Walcott . . .': Smith, 'The big fight', *New York Herald Tribune,* 27 September 1962, p. 28.

Eventually a hacksaw did the job: Bob Smith, *Chicago Daily News.*

'Floyd's a man that has a lot of pride . . .': Gay Talese, 'Patterson, a former champion, seeking obscurity of solitude', *New York Times,* 27 September 1962, p. 45.

'If I had lost to McNeeley . . .': Gilbert Rogin, *Sports Illustrated.*

'No bank robber . . .': Jimmy Cannon, *New York Journal-American.*

'I thought he would win . . .': Robert Samuels and Paul Meskil, *New York World Telegram and Sun,* 26 September 1962.

'From what I hear on TV this morning . . .': Red Smith, 'The big fight', *New York Herald Tribune,* 27 September 1962, p. 28.

'Soon as I get paid': ibid.

'Leave the bum talk': ibid.

'I call you a bum . . .': ibid., repeated in Young, *The Champ Nobody Wanted,* p. 18.

'Maybe a better man can knock me off . . .': Hugh Bradley, 'Liston sees six-year reign', *New York Journal-American,* 27 September 1962, p. 29.

'No comment': ibid.

'Geraldine would like the travelling . . .': ibid.

'Boy, that was a terrible performance . . .': Rogin, 'The facts about the big fight'.

'He was so frightened . . .': Associated Press (no byline), Seattle, Washington, 27 September 1962.

'You can't say Patterson was scared . . .': Jimmy Powers, 'The powerhouse' column, *New York Daily News,* 27 September 1962.

'There is no reason for a return . . .': Jimmy Cannon, *New York Journal-American,* 27 September 1962, p. 29.

'[He] used the dirty statesmanship . . .': ibid.

13 / STILL THE BAD GUY

'I want to reach my people . . .': quoted in William Nack, 'O unlucky man'.

'There's a big difference between having fear: Rogin, 'The facts about the big fight'.

'I watched Sonny . . .': ibid.; also McKinney, quoted in Nack, 'O unlucky man', and in Nigel Collins, *Boxing Babylon* (New York: Citadel, 1990), p. 128.

'First thought was . . .': Rogin, 'The facts about the big fight', p. 27.

'I'm not tough . . .': Joan Younger Dickinson, *Ladies Home Journal & Philadelphia Bulletin,* 27 October 1962.

'I'd rather be a lamp post in Denver . . .': Peter Wilson, *Daily Mirror,* 22 February 1964, p. 22.

'You could smell him in the mornings . . .': Nack, 'O unlucky man'.

'Liston has had the championship for almost a year . . .': Robert H. Boyle, *Sports Illustrated,* 29 July 1963.

'Now one must speculate . . .': Frank Butler, 'Sonny's on top to stay', *World Sports,* January 1963.

'Clay is too young . . .': ibid.

14 / EVEN CLEOPATRA WAS RINGSIDE

'You've missed my best line . . .': John Gold, *London Evening News and Star*, 13 March 1963.

'That ugly little man . . .': *Time*, 22 March 1963, p. 42.

'The Garden is too small for me . . .': ibid.

'See, I'm pretty as a girl . . .': *Time*, 22 March 1963, p. 43; also quoted by John Cottrell, *Man of Destiny* (London: Frederick Muller, 1967), p. 101.

'Clay is nothing . . .': Shaw, 'Cassius Clay: the man and the challenge'.

'I'll get locked up for murder . . .': (no byline), 'Clay outpoints Jones', *Boxing News*, 22 March 1963, p. 11.

fought like an amateur: Huston Horn, 'A comeuppance for the cocksure Cassius', *Sports Illustrated*, 25 March 1963.

'The strutting 21-year-old pretender . . .': Desmond Hackett, 'Great? No, Clay is just lucky', *Daily Express*, 15 March 1963.

'When I get that championship . . .': *Time*, 22 March 1963, p. 43.

15 / I PITY A MAN WHO HATES

'They don't need to bury survivors': Robert H. Boyle, 'Sonny slams ahead', *Sports Illustrated*, 29 July 1963, p. 15.

'Liston has no feelings . . .': ibid., p. 13.

'That's all you people write about . . .': ibid.

'He's frustrated . . .': ibid.

'It's just like marriage and divorce . . .': Hugh Bradley, *New York Journal-American*, 16 July 1963.

'Clay's demanding great big money . . .': ibid.

'They're just trying to stir me up . . .': ibid.

'How should I know? . . .': ibid.

'Thought people with mental problems . . .': ibid.

'I got the punk's heart now': Nack, 'O unlucky man'; also Collins, *Boxing Babylon*, p. 128.

'You just stand there . . .': Shaw, 'Cassius Clay: the man and the challenge', p. 46.

'Hey, Liston, you're an animal . . .': George Whiting, *London Evening Standard*, 19 July 1963, p. 22.

'This is something you'll never get': Arthur Daley, *New York Times* (undated).

'You burn me up . . .': George Whiting, *London Evening Standard*, 19 July 1963, p. 22.

'He's a man who hates and hates hard . . .': John Gold, *London Evening News and Star*, 22 July 1963, p. 12.

'My husband got letters . . .': Helen Sutton, *New York Journal-American*.

'The only question is . . .': Hugh Bradley, *New York Journal-American*, 15 July 1963, p. 23.

'That's about all the prediction I will make . . .': ibid.

'I think I'm going to win . . .': (no byline), *New York Journal-American*, 14 July 1963.

'I feel like I'm going to a dance': (no byline), 'Just like going to a dance', *New York World Telegram and Sun*, 23 July 1963.

'Clay's a good fighter . . .': George Whiting, *London Evening Standard*, 20 July 1963, p. 1.

16 / GOD SAVE THE KING, GOD SAVE BOXING

'a mouse of a man': Lester Bromberg, 'Shouldn't have fought . . . insult to people', *New York World Telegram and Sun*, 23 July 1963, p. 16.

'If he couldn't make a better fight . . .': ibid.

'From some hole in the ring . . .': John Gold, 'Two-minute terror', *London Evening News and Star*, 23 July 1963, p. 1.

'If the bum whips me . . .': Associated Press, 23 July 1963, used in *New York World Telegram and Sun*, p. 16.

'I'm gonna make my entrance . . .': Shaw, 'Cassius Clay: the man and the challenge', p. 46.

'Liston's biggest worry . . .': Donald Saunders, 'Liston retains title of lonely champion', *Daily Telegraph*, 23 July 1963.

'Sonny Liston is still the heavyweight king: Robert H. Boyle, *Sports Illustrated*, 29 July 1963, p. 12.

'At the post-fight press conference': whole question and answer session with the media quoted in the *New York World Telegram and Sun*, 23 July 1963 (no byline).

'Yes, I think he is . . .': George Whiting, *London Evening Standard*, 23 July 1963; also John Gold, *London Evening News and Star*, 23 July 1963, p. 1.

'It could be a combination of both . . .': Oscar Fraley, 'Patterson says wasn't afraid', *United Press International*, used in *New York World Telegram and Sun*, 23 July 1963, p. 16; also John Gold, *London Evening News and Star*, 23 July 1963.

'I do feel disgraced terrible . . .': George Whiting, *London Evening Standard*, 23 July 1963.

'Who is Clay? . . .': ibid.; also Lester Bromberg, *New York World Telegram and Sun*, 23 July 1963, p. 16.

'Come on over here . . .': Associated Press wire, published *New York World Telegram and Sun*, 23 July 1963, p. 16.

'Servile before mobsters . . .': Barry Gottehrer, *New York Herald Tribune*, July 1963.

'The public is not with me . . .': John Gold, *London Evening News and Star*, 23 July 1963, p. 1.

'. . . the world of sport now realises . . .': Jim Murray, *Los Angeles Times*, July 1963.

'I was thrilled . . .': Robert H. Boyle, *Sports Illustrated*, 29 July 1963, p. 15.

'It's really nice . . .': ibid.

'No smoke, no smog': ibid.

17 / I'LL BE AS GOOD AS PEOPLE WILL LET ME BE

'Those engagements went well . . .': Mickey Duff with Bob Mee, *Twenty and Out* (London: Collins Willow, 1999), pp. 71–2.

'a fundamental honesty . . .': John Rafferty, 'The scorched but human champion', *The Scotsman*, September 1963.

'I don't think I get treated right back home . . .': Alex Cameron, *Scottish Daily Mail*, 12 September 1963.

'Why take one payday . . .': ibid.

'I reckon this boy has something . . .': ibid.

'I've never lost a street fight in my life': Duff with Mee, *Twenty and Out*, p. 75.

'Man, he couldn't wash that colour off quick enough . . .': (no byline), 'No one pushes me around', *World Sports*, November 1963, p. 6.

'Take a bow': Reg Gutteridge, *Uppercuts and Dazes* (London: Blake, 1998), pp. 148–9.

'I had to go to Roehampton Limb Fitting Centre': ibid., p. 150.

'. . . a bully with a soft centre': ibid., p. 147.

'It was never easy': Lionel Crane, 'The man who never came out of solitary', *Sunday Mirror*, 10 January 1971, p. 25.

'Ever since I been fighting, I been a loner': Lionel Crane, *Sunday Mirror*, 1 September 1963.

'Nobody never gave me nothing': ibid.

'Sure, he's a good boy . . .': ibid.

'I've done some rough things, man . . .': ibid.

'From one broad to another . . .': Duff with Mee, *Twenty and Out*, p. 74.

'You mustn't ask him anything like that': Danny Blanchflower, 'It's no noble art when Liston is around', *Sunday Express*, 15 September 1963.

'Why should there be more indignation . . .': J.L. Manning, 'Liston and I have to skip it together', *Daily Mail*, 11 September 1963, p. 6.

'I'm ashamed to be an American': (no byline), 'No one pushes me around', *World Sports*, November 1963, p. 6.

'It's the bombing in Birmingham': ibid.

'I ain't got no dog-proof ass': Nack, 'O unlucky man'.

'They don't fight fair': Boyle, 'Sonny Slams Ahead', p. 13.

'He was a great world champion while he was up there . . .': Peter Moss, 'Stone-Face', *Daily Mail*, 7 January 1971.

'He had a chip on his shoulder . . .': ibid.

'The tour wasn't set up right': Barbara La Fontaine, 'He's just got that look', *Sports Illustrated* (undated), pp. 32–8.

18 / I WANT TO MAKE A BEAUTIFUL LIFE

'He's a real easy, nice person . . .': Joan Younger Dickinson, *Ladies Home Journal & Philadelphia Bulletin*, 27 October 1962.

'Don't ask me a lot of questions about them . . .': Lionel Crane, *Sunday Mirror*, September 1963.

'. . . broke up the interview and howled with glee': FBI file, 24 February 1964.

'I been married to my present wife . . .': Lionel Crane, *Sunday Mirror*, September 1963.

'She was there when the going was rough': ibid.

'Often he won't talk to me': Harry Carpenter, 'The secret Liston has taken to his grave', *The Sun*, 7 January 1971.

'He isn't moody': Boyle, 'Sonny slams ahead', p. 15.

'I get tired of all that killing': ibid.

'She manages his money': Robert L. Burnes, *Saturday Evening Post*, 13 August 1960, p. 58.

'I don't have to read': Rogin, 'Heavyweight in waiting', p. 50.

'Every day I got to read what a big bum I am': Joan Younger Dickinson, *Ladies Home Journal & Philadelphia Bulletin*, 27 October 1962.

'All right Charles, come out . . .': Boyle, 'Sonny slams ahead', p. 15.

'Charles tries to play jokes . . .': Pete Hamill, 'Sonny Liston – Heavyweight Champ', *New York Post*, 26 September 1962, p. 98.

'If it were up to me . . .': Young, *The Champ Nobody Wanted*, p. 17.

'Now you run along': La Fontaine, 'He's just got that look'.

'Somebody pinch me': Huston Horn, 'A rueful dream come true', *Sports Illustrated*, 18 November 1963, pp. 26–7.

'You eat like you headed to the electric chair': ibid.

19 / HE'S JUST A LITTLE BOY IN THE DARK AND HE'S SCARED

'You can't sell to everybody': Gilbert Rogin, 'The many faces of Mr Mac', *Sports Illustrated*, 17 February 1964, pp. 55–62.

'. . . it's an ugly business . . .': ibid.

'I figure if this man Jack Nilon don't take it, he can't count': ibid.

'It's going to be a breath of fresh air': ibid.

'I figure Clay wins it': ibid.

'Well, I think there was some kind of a handout . . .': J.L. Manning, *Daily Mail*, 21 February 1964.

'Chris Dundee had begun boxing in 1926 . . .': Angelo Dundee with Mike Winters, *I Only Talk Winning* (Chicago: Contemporary Books Inc., 1985), p. 24.

'I got to be known as a dependable kid . . .': Graham Houston and Angelo Dundee, 'The man the champs rely on', *Boxing News*, 15 November 1974, pp. 8–9.

'We had Luis Rodriguez and Sugar Ramos . . .': ibid.

'He scared the shit out of Patterson . . .': Dan Hirschberg, 'Sonny Liston: the mystery remains', *Boxing Today* (undated).

'He made that colossal misjudgement': Nack, 'O unlucky man'.

'You ever hear that saying "whistlin' in the dark"?': Carpenter, 'The secret Liston has taken to his grave'.

'This is an angry man . . .': Reg Gutteridge, 'Moral: don't talk to a bear when he's eating', *London Evening News* (undated).

'Is he fast?': Wilson, 'The human hammer'.

'So help me, I'm not making him up': Peter Wilson, 'The barefoot boy and the buffalo', *Daily Mirror*, 19 February 1964, p. 22.

'He's my baby, my million-dollar baby . . .': Frank Butler, *News of the World*, 23 February 1964; also by other writers at the press conference, including Alan Hoby, George Whiting and others.

'Jeez, how good do I have to be?': George Whiting, 'Clay is my baby', *London Evening Standard*, 17 February 1964.

'But for the 16 oz gloves . . .': ibid.

'The only way Cassius can hurt me . . .': Associated Press, 29 January 1964.

'Security has made a different man of him': *Miami News*, 24 February 1964, Section B, p. 2.

'But what the hell': George Whiting, 'Cassius Clay in awaits dividends – or 22 ulcers', *London Evening Standard*, 21 February 1964.

'. . . remarkably amateurish': ibid.

'I can't be beat. No one can beat me': Al Buck, *New York Post*, 22 February 1964; also George Whiting, *London Evening Standard*, 21 February 1964.

'I don't think I could make a score doing that': Hugh Bradley, *New York Journal-American* (undated).

'After I finish with Liston': Wilson, 'The barefoot boy and the buffalo'.

'If Liston beats me . . .': ibid.

'I'll go to my dressing-room . . .': ibid.

'Cassius has trouble getting off stage': Reg Gutteridge, *London Evening News and Star* (undated).

'Cassius might be scared and tense . . .': ibid.

'I ain't gonna wait around': television interview reported by Robert Lipsyte, 'Clay and Liston slug it out in TV battle of barbs', *New York Times*, 14 February 1964.

'We have many assets': Maule, 'Liston's edge: lethal left', p. 19.

'He's young and restless and foolish sometimes': ibid.

'I'm going to be the greatest of all time': film footage.

20 / RUMBLE, YOUNG MAN, RUMBLE

'Float like a butterfly, sting like a bee': Various pieces of TV footage; also Tex Maule, 'The sting of the Louisville Lip', *Sports Illustrated*, 17 February 1964.

'Man that's arson': Tommy Fitzgerald, *Miami News* (undated).

'You trying to shame me?': Reg Gutteridge, *London Evening News and Star* (undated, but February 1964).

'Sonny demonstrated what a man can do': Bob Waters, *Newsday* (undated).

'No but you are': Robert Lipsyte, *New York World Telegram and Sun*, 21 February 1964, repeated in *The Times*, 21 February 2004.

'My dog plays drums better than that kid with the big nose': Sonny Liston talking off-set on the *Ed Sullivan Show*, Deauville Hotel, Miami, 1964.

'That's what I mean by naive': Edwin Pope, 'Cassius makes a pretty picture but Liston brushes off artist', *Miami Herald*, 22 February 1964.

'They think I talk too much': Jim Jacobs television interview.

'You are forty if you are a day': ibid.

'a total eclipse of the Sonny' ibid.

'as popular as a barracuda': Jim Murray, *Los Angeles Times* (undated).

'I was frazzled and crushed': Al Taylor, 'The jinx that chilled the Clay–Liston bout', *Boxing Illustrated*, 1964, p. 46.

21 / THIS KID IS OUT OF HIS MIND

'Liston is angry and might knock out the kid . . .': Wilson, 'The barefoot boy and the buffalo', p. 22.

'Yes, they can, and he can pay': Olsen, 'Hysteria is a sometime thing', p. 49.

'it was worse than handling Caruso': ibid., p. 50.

'I'll take you on right now': ibid., p. 50, and Bob Waters, *Newsday*, 25 February 1964.

'My God, he's scared to death': Olsen, 'Hysteria is a sometime thing', p. 50.

'. . . Drew, shut up, will you?': ibid.

'He [Liston] lost the fight right there': Hirschberg, 'Sonny Liston: the mystery remains'.

'You ain't nothing. You ain't nothing': film footage.

'Clay is fined . . .': film footage; also quoted by Peter Wilson, *Daily Mirror*, 26 February 1964, p. 31.

'in an extreme state of excitement . . .': wire service report quoted by Olsen, 'Hysteria is a sometime thing', p. 50; also Peter Wilson, different version of the quote, *Daily Mirror*, 26 February 1964, back page.

'He is emotionally unbalanced . . .': Bob Waters, *Newsday*, 25 February 1964.

'Maybe you think he's nuts . . .': ibid.

'He just didn't know what to make of the kid': *New York Times*, 26 February 1964, p. 26.

'Oh, don't worry about that': Olsen, 'Hysteria is a sometime thing', p. 50.

'Cassius, I'm here as a doctor': ibid., p. 53.

'He's just overcoming that cowardice . . .': ibid., p. 54.

22 / A DANCING BEAR AND A FREAK WHO NEVER STOPS TALKING

'He's a murderous puncher': Reg Gutteridge, *London Evening News and Star*, February 1964.

'No man can get away with that forever': Sharnik, 'The four who baffled Liston', p. 67.

'You've got to confuse him . . .': Associated Press, used in *New York Herald Tribune*, 25 February 1964, p. 22.

'If Clay moves, he has a chance': (no byline), *New York Journal-American*, 24 February 1964, p. 22.

'Clay can't take that kind of a punch': Maule, 'Liston's edge: lethal left', p. 21.

'I think Sonny Liston will put him away . . .': Rocky Marciano, 'That Clay image vanishes', *Daily Sketch*, 24 February 1964, p. 15.

'Liston has the killer instinct . . .': Al Buck, *New York Post*, 22 February 1964.

'Liston has got to kill Clay as soon as he touches him': Dan Parker, *New York Journal-American*, 25 February 1964, p. 27.

'They each have two legs . . .': ibid.

'Who's my choice?': ibid.

'I boxed with Clay more rounds than anybody . . .': ibid.

'. . . past the edge of discretion into disaster': Maule, 'Liston's edge: lethal left'.

'comparative greenhorn': Peter Wilson, *Daily Mirror*, 25 February 1964, p. 1.

'Sonny does it in three' and other quotes in this section: *New York World Telegram and Sun*, 25 February 1964, p. 21.

'Not only is that illegal, but it's downright impossible': Bob Waters, *Newsday*, 25 February 1964.

'Boxing, owned by hoods until the fuzz chased . . .': Murray Robinson, 'TV takes over', *New York Journal-American*, 25 February 1964, p. 26.

23 / WHAT THE HELL IS THIS? WHAT DID THEY DO?

'We fought so often I got diabetes': a version of this line is in Harry Mullan, *The Book of Boxing Quotations* (London: Stanley Paul, 1988), p. 117. La Motta repeatedly used this line in fun from the 1950s onwards, amended and altered from time to time, sometimes using 'almost got diabetes' instead. He used it in his stand-up act.

'Clay's supporters stormed the press section . . .': Dan Parker, *New York Journal-American*, 26 February 1964.

'What the hell is this?': Reg Gutteridge, *London Evening News and Star*, 19 May 1965, p. 21; also Jimmy Cannon, 'What the hell is this?' *New York Journal-American*, 26 February 1964; also Cannon in a subsequent *KO Magazine*, 'What the hell is this?'

'I borrowed the line from Caesar': Hugh Bradley, 'I came, I saw, I conquered', *New York Journal-American*, 26 February 1964, p. 34. Other editions headlined 'Cass credits Sugar Ray's help'.

'He's a big guy . . .': *New York Journal-American*, 27 February 1964, p. 22.

'My arm was killing me': William Tucker, 'Eight doctors X-ray Sonny at hospital', *Miami News*, 26 February 1964, p. 1; also Rick Pezdirtz, 'I threw a hook, something snapped', *Miami News*, 26 February 1964, p. 5B.

'We came to the conclusion . . .': *New York World Telegram and Sun*, 26 February 1964, p. 1.

'Please make this positively accurate': Tucker, 'Eight doctors X-ray sonny at hospital', p. 1.

'Put a Bible before me . . .': ibid.; also Pezdirtz, 'I threw a hook, something snapped', p. 5B.

After six rounds, Peter Wilson said he had Liston ahead: Peter Wilson, 'The big quit', *Daily Mirror*, 27 February 1964, p. 31.

'We had over 400 sportswriters . . .': Joe Williams, 'MacDonald has a brainstorm', *New York World Telegram and Sun*, 27 February 1964, p. 19.

'. . . don't forget he was no kid any more': Hirschberg, 'Sonny Liston: the mystery remains'.

'Hypocrites, hypocrites, hypocrites . . .': *New York World Telegram and Sun*, 26 February 1964, p. 34.

'I don't know what happened to Liston': Hugh Bradley, *New York Journal-American*, 26 February 1964.

'It was just an unfortunate accident': Milton Gross, *North American Newspaper Alliance*, 26 February 1964.

'What are they saying out there?': Hirschberg, 'Sonny Liston: the mystery remains'; also Nack, 'O unlucky man'.

'Sonny was tired, so he quit': Fernandez, 'Tocco talks Liston', p. 3.

'peculiar even by the standards of this mean racket': Jimmy Cannon, 'Real champs don't quit', *New York Journal-American*, 26 February 1964, p. 1.

'Real champions don't quit . . .': ibid.

'I think it was an honest fight . . .': Hugh Bradley, *New York Journal-American*, 27 February 1964, p. 22.

'The horizon is his, and all its rainbows': George Whiting, *London Evening Standard*, 26 February 1964, p. 1.

'We had a choice of two national product endorsements . . .': Joe Williams, 'Ali still Clay to tax people', *New York World Telegram and Sun*, 30 April 1964.

'I go to a Muslim meeting and what do I see?': Jack Mahon, *New York Journal-American*, 27 February 1964, p. 22; also Alan Hoby, 'Was it a fix? No – Liston ran out of steam', *Sunday Express*, 1 March 1964.

'I started to teach Cassius the tricks of the white man': *New Muslims*, available at http://www.isesco.org.ma/.

'They've ruined my two boys': Pat Putnam, 'Dad says Cassius Muslim prisoner', *Miami Herald* (undated).

'My white blood came from the slave-masters . . .': quoted by Jack Olsen, from a speech at an undated public rally, 'Growing up scared in Louisville', p. 95.

'I am with myself and my own kind': Olsen, 'Learning Elijah's advanced lesson in hate', p. 53.

'He's an old man.': Bob Waters, *Newsday*, 27 February 1964, p. 48.

'There was something hot in my eyes . . .': ibid.

'I told him this was for the big apple . . .': ibid.

'by a wise, wise person': John Crittenden, *Miami News*, 26 February 1964.

'He's not as good as Machen or Folley or Williams': Bob Waters, *Newsday*, 27 February 1964, p. 48.

'Sure, I want to fight him again': Hugh Bradley, 'Liston hurt, won't quit', *New York Journal-American*, 26 February 1964, p. 1.

'Like I did when the President got shot': Wilson, 'The big quit', p. 1; also Bob Waters, *Newsday*, 27 February 1964, p. 48.

'. . . his hand was completely numb': *New York Journal-American*, 26 February 1964.

'We thought we could get away with it': Associated Press, used in *New York Times*, 26 February 1964; also John Cashman, 'Liston: hurt before fight, Clay: Sonny has to wait', *New York Post*, 26 February 1964, back page.

'I was the one who made the decision': Hugh Bradley, *New York Journal-American*, 26 February 1964, p. 32; also *United Press International* report, *New York Times* (no byline), 'We're out of business, says Nilon', 26 February 1964, p. 27.

'a paralysing sensation': Milton Gross, *North American Newspaper Alliance*.

'clean, well run and well ordered': Hugh Bradley, *New York Journal-American*, 27 February 1964, p. 22; also Bob Waters, *Newsday*, 27 February 1964, p. 48.

'left me wondering': Hugh Bradley, *New York Journal-American*, 27 February 1964, p. 22; also William Tucker, 'Gerstein orders report on Liston's fight injury', *Miami News*, 26 February 1964.

'We have the right to name the opponent . . .': Hugh Bradley, 'An injured Liston has piece of Clay', *New York Journal-American*, 27 February 1964, p. 32.

'I don't think he'll want it': Wilson, 'The big quit', p. 31; also Al Buck, *New York Post*, 26 February 1964, back page.

'We're out of business': Bradley, 'An injured Liston has piece of Clay', p. 32; also *United Press International* wire report, in *New York Times*, 26 February 1964.

The financial breakdown shows just how badly MacDonald was burned: Huston Horn, 'The first days in the new life of the Champion of the World', *Sports Illustrated*, 9 March 1964, p. 24.

'I thought Clay fought a real good fight': *United Press International* report (no byline), in *New York Journal-American*, 26 February 1964; also Associated Press (no byline), *New York Times*, 26 February 1964.

'Liston heaved punches as if they were cobblestones': Jimmy Cannon, *New York Journal-American*.

'. . . a fumbling automaton': Reg Gutteridge, *London Evening News and Star*, 26 February 1964, p. 16.

'A smell has gone round the world . . .': Sam Leitch, 'Nobody dare rig that world title', *Sunday Mirror*, 1 March 1964, p. 39.

'I don't think the shoulder made him quit': Jimmy Cannon, *New York Journal-American*, 4 November 1964.

'I was the first one in Liston's corner . . .': ibid.

'I was shocked because I saw things that Liston could have done . . .': Dave Anderson, 'Jones claims he's now no. 1', *New York Times*, 26 February 1964, p. 33.

'I don't regard Cassius Clay as a worthy champion': *London Evening News*, 26 February 1964, p. 16.

'We'll win it back': Horn, 'The first days in the new life of the Champion of the World', p. 24.

24 / I AM HIS BEST FRIEND, AT LEAST IN PHILADELPHIA

'a pudgy and pious Philadelphian . . .': (no byline), 'Prizefighting', *Time*, 10 April 1964.

'I am his best friend, at least in Philadelphia': ibid.

'there's a lot of bread in that life': ibid.

. . . Jimmy Cannon interviewed Sam Margolis: *New York Journal-American*, 20 May 1965, p. 24.

'Look, I'm not scholarly': ibid.

'The lawyers made a mistake': ibid.

25 / TO BOSTON AND SUITCASE SAM

'I said I was the greatest, not the smartest': Jose Torres with Bert Sugar, *Sting Like A Bee: The Muhammad Ali Story* (London: Coronet, 1972), p. 149.

'I am probably dead already': news conference televised interview, 8 June 1964, widely available, including youtube.com.

'Nobody listens to that Malcolm any more': Olsen, 'Learning Elijah's advanced lesson in hate', p. 51.

'He was so controversial, so bold, so courageous': *Lifestyle*, 1998.

'I froze on the spot': Gilbert Rogin, 'Still hurt and lost', *Sports Illustrated*, 16 November 1964, p. 25.

'Man, you don't marry that girl': Robert H. Boyle, *Sports Illustrated*, April 1964, p. 26.

'I can be a good wife to this man': ibid.

'This is everything he wants': Rogin, 'Still hurt and lost', p. 24.

'One word from them, and the fight mob does as it pleases': Jimmy Cannon, *New York Journal-American* (undated).

'My Board have very strong views . . .': J.L. Manning, *Daily Mail*, 25 August 1964.

'The promoters claim Boston outbid . . .': Jimmy Cannon, *New York Journal-American* (undated).

'sneaking into the back of the pictures': Leonard Shecter, *New York Post*, 15 September 1964.

'Ain't no use of my trying to answer questions . . .': ibid.

'When you go out and your feet start hurting . . .': ibid.

'There ain't but one way to catch a 'coon': ibid.

'You ask [Barry] Goldwater about his faith?': ibid.

'Please, call me Muhammad Ali': ibid.

26 / EVERY GANGSTER WANTS TO BE AL CAPONE

'Do Clay's insults bother you?': Doug Ibbotson, *London Evening News and Star*, 11 November 1964, p. 2.

'One day you're the champ . . .': Rogin, 'Still hurt and lost', p. 24.

'Willa!': Robert Lipsyte, 'Liston drills with usual charm', *New York Times*, 5 November 1964.

'I'm kinda special': Mark Kram, 'The prefight moods of Sonny Liston', *Sports Illustrated*, 2 November 1964, p. 38.

'I fought a stupid fight': Lipsyte, 'Liston drills with usual charm'.

'I thought it was Cassius Clay . . .': ibid.

'The polices [sic] are just like gangsters': La Fontaine, 'He's just got that look', p. 38.

'Time to go': Lipsyte, 'Liston drills with usual charm'.

'I don't know': Jimmy Cannon, *New York Journal-American*.

'Cook on him, Brother Muhammad': Rogin, 'Still hurt and lost', p. 23.

'In Miami, I was Columbus': ibid.

'The event is hardly a job for a sportswriter': J.L. Manning, 'New creed for the apostles of pugilism', *Daily Mail*, 13 November 1964.

'I know his moods, I know his moods': Kram, 'The prefight moods of Sonny Liston', p. 40.

'I'll tell ya, the man is vicious': ibid.

'Oh, man, someday I'm gonna write a book . . .': ibid., p. 42.

'Lightest in three years': Jimmy Cannon, *New York Journal-American*, 9 November 1964.

'. . . healthy, well-fed and sound in wind and limb . . .': George Whiting, 'Cassius gets up steam', *London Evening Standard*, 10 November 1964, p. 30.

'One thing is sure': Peter Wilson, *Daily Mirror*, November 1964.

'. . . I don't smoke and I don't drink and I'm happily married': Doug Ibbotson, *London Evening News and Star*, 12 November 1964, p. 9.

'I ain't making any exact predictions': ibid.

'Liston will be harder to lick this time': George Whiting, *London Evening Standard*, 21 May 1965, p. 5.

'Clay may be nuts': ibid.

'Liston's going to try to grab my jab': Rogin, 'Still hurt and lost', p. 26.

'you only seen one quarter of the things this kid can do': ibid.

27 / HE COULD HAVE DIED

'He asked us to send for an ambulance': Frank Butler, 'The sleeping prince', *News of the World*, 15 November 1964.

'What fun and games is Cassius up to now?': ibid.; also Doug Ibbotson, *London Evening News and Star*, 14 November 1964.

He smiled and said: 'Not tonight': ibid.

'He could have died': Peter Wilson, 'The day boxing almost died', *Daily Mirror*, 16 November 1964, p. 29.

'Thank God it did not happen in the ring . . .': J.L. Manning, 'Postponed – the lame duck championship', *Daily Mail*, 16 November 1964, p. 20.

lost by a technical knockout: ibid.

'slipped a Mickey Finn': Wilson, 'The day boxing almost died', p. 29.

'Holy shit, I'd better start washing dishes . . .': Hirschberg, 'Sonny Liston: the mystery remains'.

Clay may have thought he was dying . . .': Milton Gross, 'Sonny Liston: What Next?', *New York Post*, November 1964.

'I was getting ready to pick Sonny': Joe Louis, 'Time runs out for old Sonny', *Daily Sketch*, 16 November 1964, p. 8.

'Could have been worse. Could have been me': George Whiting, 'Doctors count Clay out', *London Evening Standard*, 14 November 1964, and Doug Ibbotson, *London Evening News and Star*, 14 November 1964.

'I can do with all the nickels going . . .': Butler, 'The sleeping prince'.

28 / SONNY? YOU OUT THERE?

'There was an explosion in the dining alcove . . .': La Fontaine, 'He's just got that look'.

'The money means more to the Government': ibid.; also Reg Gutteridge, *London Evening News and Star*, May 1965.

'Following a dinner party thrown by his wife . . .': *Los Angeles Herald Examiner*, quoted by La Fontaine, 'He's just got that look'.

'I picked up a little boy . . .': quoted in People section (no byline), *Sports Illustrated*, 1996, p. 104.

'I never had a problem with the son of a bitch . . .': Steen, *Sonny Boy*, p. 191.

'Win, lose or draw, you will always be our champ': Tex Maule, *Sports Illustrated*, 24 May 1965, p. 25.

29 / YES, IT'S ME IN YOUR TOWN

'Not with that boy with you': Bud Collins, *Boston Globe*, 29 May 2005.

'Out the back. Food's just the same': George Plimpton, 'The world champion is refused a meal, *Sports Illustrated*, 17 May 1965.

'My head don't belong between my knees': ibid., p. 26.

'Malcolm X got just what he preached': Elijah Muhammad speech, February 1965; also a version of this in Karl Evanzz, *The Messenger – The Rise and Fall of Elijah Muhammad* (New York: Pantheon Books, 1999).

'I don't see how any DA could stand by . . .': Robert Lipsyte, *New York Times*, 10 May 1965.

'In the same time, Liston has grown old': Bud Collins, *Boston Globe*, 21 May 1965.

'Sonny has a very old face . . . like somebody's wife': ibid.

30 / OF MOOSE AND MEN

'Lewiston has been the capital of schoolboy hockey . . .': Red Smith, *New York Herald Tribune*, May 1965.

'The smaller the ring the more it favours Liston': Dave Anderson, 'They're not going to fence Clay in', *New York Times*, May 1965.

'Is that so? Well, we'll just have to put in a new one': ibid.

But where the heck are we going to put all the people?': Associated Press.

'Moose Area Next Eighteen Miles': Red Smith, *New York Herald Tribune* (undated).

'We took Billy Graham down and put Sonny Liston up': Milton Gross, *New York Post*, 20 May 1965, p. 53.

'. . . banned in Boston': Arthur Daley, 'The unwanted', *New York Times* (undated, but May 1965).

'We were the last I knew . . .': Roland Wirths, *Portland Press Herald*, 24 May 1965, p. 13.

'Liston will win because it's his turn . . .': Sam Leitch, *Sunday Mirror*, 23 May 1965.

'sleazy stripper going to flesh': Milton Gross, *New York Post*, 20 May 1965, p. 53.

'Miss Misty Knight': George Whiting, 'Was it a fiddle?', *London Evening Standard*, 23 May 1965.

'. . . our town will be filled with thieves and thugs . . .': Milton Gross, *New York Post*, 20 May 1965, p. 53.

'stuck out in the wilds of Maine': Peter Wilson, 'Liston in the priest country', *Daily Mirror*, May 1965.

'. . . the Grossingers of the north': Red Smith, *New York Herald Tribune*.

'. . . if you stop for a moment you can hear it still': Leonard Shecter, *New York Post*, 21 May 1965.

'sit down while drinking intoxicants': George Whiting, *London Evening Standard*, 19 May 1965.

'Sonny is more sinned against than sinner': Herb Ralby, 'Prison chaplain roots for Liston', *Boston Globe*, 24 May 1965.

'Any man who likes children as much as he does . . .': ibid.

'Liston does not look quite as old as the Mansion House': Bud Collins, *Boston Globe*, 21 May 1965.

'Boxing is dead': Bucky Yardume, 'Marciano: boxing's dead everywhere', *Boston Traveler*, repeated in *New York Herald Tribune*, 8 May 1965.

'Marciano still makes a pretty good living . . .': Joe O'Day, *New York Daily News*.

'It is light, airy and immaculate . . .': Red Smith, *New York Herald Tribune* (undated).

'Liston looked at times like an old bull moose . . .': Alan Hoby, *Sunday Express*, 23 May 1965.

'Sparring in the 200-year-old ballroom . . .': ibid.

'. . . the cleanest and most beautiful arena in the whole country': Gene Ward, *New York Daily News* (undated).

'Sonny Liston is a man of few words . . .': ibid.

'the stony face has a wizened scowl': Sam Leitch, *Sunday Mirror*, 23 May 1965.

'His tree-trunk left jab . . .': Frank Butler, *News of the World*, 23 May 1965.

'The hernia operation has not troubled him . . .': ibid.

'Well, I couldn't say': Arthur Daley, *New York Times*, 24 May 1965, p. 40.

'Only cowards run': Reg Gutteridge, *London Evening News and Star*, 21 May 1965.

'Don't tell me I'm afraid . . .': George Whiting, *London Evening Standard*.

'. . . we got a couple of police dogs waiting for him': ibid.

'Lewiston is surrounded by breathtakingly beautiful countryside . . .': Leonard Shecter, *New York Post*, 21 May 1965.

'You've got to get off the horse . . .': Peter Wilson, *Daily Mirror*, 19 May 1965.

'The fittest man I ever examined': Bud Collins, *Boston Globe*, 21 May 1965.

'the most perfect physical specimen . . .': ibid.

'"This bum belongs in an oxygen tent"': ibid.

'Maine is the land of the bear': Al Buck, *New York Post*, 20 May 1965, p. 52.

'. . . a likeable actor . . .': Alan Hoby, *Sunday Express*, 23 May 1965.

'The money, I want the money, honey . . .': Reg Gutteridge, *London Evening News and Star*, 24 May 1965.

Reg Gutteridge felt Ali had grown up . . .: ibid.

'All you can see is if they're in shape': Red Smith, 'Liston to prove whether Clay bonafide champ', unusually in the *Boston Globe*, 23 May 1965.

'The forces of evil are still at work': Deane McGowen, *New York Times* (undated).

'Ain't I the fastest you ever saw, Joe?': Red Smith, 'Situation normal', *New York Herald Tribune* (undated).

'If you even dream it, you should apologise': ibid.

'He's as ready as he'll ever be': Anderson, 'They're not going to fence Clay in'.

Sonji agreed to an interview with Tim Moriarty . . .: Tim Moriarty, *United Press International*, 21 May 1965.

31 / THE BOY IS GONE

'Fall, Bear, fall!': Bud Collins, *Boston Globe*, 24 May 1965.

E.J. Cogut of Springfield . . .: Steve Cady, *New York Times*, 24 May 1965.

'What a guy the champ is!': (no byline), 'Clay fulfils promise to Brighton schoolboy', *Boston Traveler*, 24 May 1965.

'. . . dare to make the trip on Big Red . . .': Bud Collins, *Boston Globe*, 24 May 1965.

'It's Jesse James . . .': ibid.

'If I could assure the people an assassination . . .': Robert Lipsyte, *New York Times*, 24 May 1965, p. 40.

'Too quiet. Unhealthy': Bud Collins, *Boston Globe*, 29 May 2005.

'Fear is the Negro's biggest problem': Reg Gutteridge, *London Evening News and Star*, 24 May 1965.

'I move too fast to get hit anyway': Associated Press (no byline), in *Portland Press Herald*, 24 May 1965.

'He don't have the timing . . .': Reg Gutteridge, *London Evening News and Star*, 24 May 1965.

'I can beat any man on two feet': Bob Gardner, newspaper unknown.

'The royal family is here': ibid.; also Reg Gutteridge, *London Evening News and Star*, 24 May 1965.

'They act like The Beatles are in town': Reg Gutteridge, *London Evening News and Star*, 24 May 1965.

'The freedom struggle for 22 million Negroes': ibid.

'The boy is gone': Arthur Daley, *New York Times*, 23 May 1965; also Tex Maule, *Sports Illustrated*, 24 May 1965, p. 24.

'Nobody could get that ugly in 35 years . . .': Arthur Daley, *New York Times*, 23 May 1965.

'They might be a little awed . . .': Anderson, 'They're not going to fence Clay in'.

'He's a man that's desperate': ibid.

32 / OF SCIENTIFIC TRIUMPH AND LOFTY PURPOSE

'At the same moment Clay and Liston are bouncing punches off . . .': Shirley Povich, 'World will watch fight on early bird satellite', *Boston Globe*, 21 May 1965.

'I don't think that Clay has the "bottom" to be a first-class fighter': Murray Robinson, *New York Journal-American*, 21 May 1965.

'. . . a streak of gloating cruelty in Clay's make-up . . .': ibid.

'All those police in the hall just for me': Alan Hoby, *Sunday Express*, 23 May 1965.

'others, except the press, will not be allowed near the ring': Milton Gross, *New York Post*, 20 May 1965, p. 54.

'. . . more palpitating, more intriguing. . .': John Gillooly, *Boston Record* (undated).

'. . . a swarm of bees can sting a man to death': Red Smith, *New York Herald Tribune*, 25 May 1965.

'We're all in the wrong business': Jimmy Breslin, *New York Herald Tribune*, 25 May 1965.

'So nice to be alive!': ibid.

'They must have been told to cool it': Jimmy Cannon, *New York Journal-American*, 23 May 1965.

'. . . at least you can sit down and have a drink with the old gangsters . . .': Jimmy Breslin, *New York Herald Tribune*, 25 May 1965.

'If I lose, I may as well retire . . .': (no byline), *Boston Traveler* (undated).

'Clay is really an attractive guy': Al Hirschberg, *Boston Traveler*, 25 May 1965.

'Liston is tough. He just doesn't think good': Will McDonough, *Boston Globe*, 24 May 1965, p. 23.

'tourist prices': Jesse Abramson, *New York Herald Tribune*, 24 May 1965.

'I'll make you join the Muslims yourself': (no byline), *Boston Traveler*, 25 May 1965.

33 / GET UP, YOU BUM! GET UP, YOU BUM!

'Clay? Who's he?': D. Leo Monahan and Bill McSweeny, *Boston Record American*, 26 May 1965.

'We're on the front row': *Boston Herald*; also Will Grimsley, *Boston Globe*, 26 May 1965, p. 37.

'We're afraid some screwball . . .': Will Grimsley, *Boston Globe*, 26 May 1965, p. 37.

'Are you sure that was the national anthem?' Pat Horne, *Boston Record American*, 26 May 1965.

'. . . Elvis Presley, watching at home . . .': Associated Press, Woody Baird.

'He's out, he's out': almost all of the reports included this; see Reg Gutteridge, *London Evening News*; George Whiting, *London Evening Standard*; Peter Wilson, The *Daily Mirror*, and so on.

'I thought maybe I didn't hear the bell': (no byline), 'Liston says he got fast shuffle', *New York Journal-American*, 27 May 1965.

'My man is king of the world': Bud Collins, *Boston Globe*, 26 May 1965.

'Get up, you bum!': Harold Kaese, *Boston Globe*, 26 May 1965.

'His were darting side to side': ibid.

'We'll all be out of work': ibid.

'. . . three frowns and two scowls': ibid.

slapped by a wet sardine: Leonard Shecter, *New York Post*, 26 May 1965.

Harry Carpenter felt the effect would be far-reaching: quoted by Reuters, 26 May 1965.

'Possibly they had found a way to get in for less . . .': Red Smith, *Boston Globe*, 26 May 1965.

'You'd have to be a fighter to know it': Leonard Shecter, *New York Post*, 26 May 1965, p. 80.

'Tell her, Teddy': Nack, 'O unlucky man'; also Collins, *Boxing Babylon*, p. 134.

'He didn't know the count': Milton Gross, *New York Post*, 26 May 1965; also *United Press International* report, *Boston Record American*, 26 May 1965.

'I felt all screwed up': George Whiting, 'I didn't quit, I was hurt good', *London Evening Standard*, 26 May 1965, p. 16.

'The left on the button, the right on the jaw . . .': Milton Gross, *New York Post*, 26 May 1965.

'Call me an amateur': (no byline), *New York Post*, 26 May 1965.

'I want the Rabbit next!': ibid.

'Nobody is going to lick Cassius, not for a long, long time': ibid.

Liston took breakfast outside: Bob Waters, *Newsday*, 27 May 1965.

'I tried awful hard': ibid.

'It was that lousy bum Clay': ibid.

'Two minutes twelve seconds': ibid.

'Cameras sometimes lie': ibid.

'Can't I have a record?': ibid.

'I ain't making fun of Sonny': Jimmy Cannon, *New York Journal-American*, 27 May 1965, p. 26.

'I practised it in secret . . .': George Whiting, *London Evening Standard*, 26 May 1965, p. 16.

'. . . a fraud on the American nation': Frank Butler, *News of the World*, 30 May 1965.

'. . . not all the perfumes of Araby . . .': Leonard Shecter, *New York Post*, 26 May 1965.

'The Anasagunticook Indians who sold this town . . .': Harold Kaese, *Boston Globe*, 26 May 1965.

'They should have searched Liston for concealed sleeping powders': Red Smith, *New York Herald Tribune*, 27 May 1965, p. 24.

a farce and a fraud: George Whiting, *London Evening Standard*, 26 May 1965.

'unfitting, unkempt, illegal and a disgrace to boxing': Reg Gutteridge, 'Fiasco, but a fix? I say no', *London Evening News and Star*, 26 May 1965, p. 1.

'even then it is hard to believe': Arthur Daley, *New York Times*, 27 May 1965, repeated *London Evening News and Star*, 26 May 1965, p. 1.

a sneaky, half-hearted right hand: Reg Gutteridge, *London Evening News and Star*, 26 May 1965, p. 1.

'I was always taught that the Early Bird catches the worm': ibid.

'a dramatic, one punch conquest . . .': George Whiting, 'A fix! A fix! A fix!', *London Evening Standard*, 26 May 1965, p. 1.

'Others do not agree with me': Alan Hoby, *Sunday Express*, 30 May 1965.

'It was a badly arranged knockout': (no byline), *New York Herald Tribune*, 27 May 1965.

'It's gotten to be a joke': ibid.

'Boxing, in my opinion, can and should remain alive . . .': ibid.

'There was nothing suspicious about the fight': Al Buck, *New York Post*, 27 May 1965, p. 84.

34 / HE'S GONNA MESS HIMSELF UP SO NOBODY WON'T GO TO SEE HIM

'Glickman was closely associated with Frank Carbo . . .': Associated Press (undated, *c*.1965).

'I don't have no personal quarrel with those Viet Congs . . .': Robert Lipsyte, *New York Times*, repeated in various sources, including William Barry Furlong, 'The wind that blew in Chicago', *Sports Illustrated*, 7 March 1966.

'He's gonna mess himself up so nobody won't go see him': Jack Olsen, 'A case of conscience', *Sports Illustrated*, 11 April 1966, p. 90.

'To me, he's just a thoroughly confused person': Olsen, 'Hysteria is a sometime thing', p. 67.

'The lawyers are drawing up the agreement': Al Buck, 'The champion senses danger', *New York Post*, November 1966.

'Smile at the man, forget it': Reg Gutteridge, 'The faceless force behind Ali's success', *London Evening News*, 2 October 1976, p. 21.

'When he catch you, boy you caught!': Olsen, 'Learning Elijah's advanced lesson in hate', p. 51.

'If I thought going to war would be beneficial . . .': Robert Lipsyte, 'Clay gets a cut but not in fight', *New York Times* (undated).

'Nearly every Negro is a Muslim at heart': Edwin Shrake, 'Taps for the champ', *Sports Illustrated*, 8 May 1967, p. 19.

'I've left the sports pages': ibid.

'I'd hate to go back to the ranks . . .': ibid., p. 22.

'We don't take part in Christian wars . . .': ibid., p. 23.

'He has refused to fight for his native land . . .': Al Buck, 'Poor Cassius', *New York Post* (undated).

'People don't understand him, but we do . . .': Olsen, 'Growing up scared in Louisville', p. 98.

'. . . stepped down from the spiritual platform . . .': Elijah Muhammad statement in *Muhammad Speaks*, 11 April 1969.

'I believe you're sincere. Grotesquely sincere': Sam Leitch, *Sunday Mirror*, 14 January 1968, p. 39.

'"Good boy, good brute, good animal . . ."': John Smith, 'The next martyr', *Daily Mirror*, 23 April 1968, p. 9.

'Whatever I do, it is all for Allah': ibid.

'I've already said a long prayer to Allah': Dave Anderson, 'A day for victory outside the ring', *New York Times*, 29 June 1971.

'I got another year and that's it': ibid.

'Naturally I, like millions of Americans, am very disappointed . . .': ibid.

35 / SONNY'S LAST YEARS

'Sonny had a penchant for hooking up with the wrong guys': Dan Daniel, 'The Liston mystery', *Ring*, September 1967, pp. 10–13, and p. 37.

'He loved Vegas': Bruce Jay Friedman, 'Requiem for a heavy', *Esquire*, August 1971.

'Anyone burns a cross on my lawn . . .': Cal McCrystal, 'Why the big bear came back for more', *TV Times*, 1969, p. 51.

'Because everything is just right and the place is growing': ibid.

'Liberace, who wants to hear Liberace?': ibid.

opted for the wrong tactics: Don Fraser, 'Liston back in ratings after stopping Clark', *Ring*, October 1968, pp. 12–13.

'It was like blood was coming out of a hydrant': Nack, 'O unlucky man'.

'This broad rear-ended him . . .': Fernandez, 'Tocco talks Liston', p. 3.

sometimes hookers, whom he mostly didn't pay: Friedman, 'Requiem for a heavy'.

'He always carried a pistol': ibid.

Liston was seen several times going in and out: ibid.

36 / NOBODY NEVER GETS KILLED IN VEGAS

'Sonny's dead': Nack, 'O unlucky man'.

'He didn't give a shit': Hirschberg, 'Sonny Liston: the mystery remains'.

Sonny had upset the 'wiseguys' of Las Vegas: Rob Steen, 'The champion nobody wanted', *Total Sport* (undated).

Floyd Patterson said he heard something similar: ibid.

'Sonny died the day he was born': Nack, 'O unlucky man'.

'I detested interviewing him': Harry Carpenter, 'The secret Liston has taken to his grave'.

'Your dime, my time . . .': Moss, 'Stone-Face'.

'But if ever there was a boy who never had a chance . . .': Peter Wilson, 'The rise and fall of the big ugly bear', *Daily Mirror*, 7 January 1971, p. 7.

'Even in a crowd he still lived in solitary confinement': Lionel Crane, 'The man who never came out of solitary', *Sunday Mirror*, 10 January 1971, p. 25.

'They never found no dope, no needle, nothing': Fernandez, 'Tocco talks Liston', p. 3.

'. . . I knew a dopehead when I saw one': HBO documentary, Unsolved Mysteries: *Sonny Liston: The Mysterious Life and Death of a Champion*.

'But the guy wasn't on hard drugs': Hirschberg, 'Sonny Liston: the mystery remains'.

'There he was, another Las Vegas show. God help us': Nack, 'O unlucky man'.

'He was a great guy . . .': ibid.

37 / I'M NOT SCARED TO DIE. I'VE MADE MY PEACE

'Just lost a fight, that's all': quoted in Bob Mee, *Boxing News*, 17 January 1992.

'That's all I am, a man': ibid.

BIBLIOGRAPHY

Bingham, Howard and Wallace, Max. *Muhammad Ali's Greatest Fight: Cassius Clay vs the United States of America*. London: Robson Books, 2004.

Brady, Jim. *Boxing Confidential: Power, Corruption and the Richest Prize in Sport*. Preston: Milo Books, 2002.

Brenner, Teddy as told to Barney Nagler. *Only The Ring Was Square*. New Jersey: Prentice Hall, 1981.

Bromberg, Lester. *Boxing's Unforgettable Fights*. New York: Ronald Press Co., 1962.

Butler, Frank. *The Good, The Bad and The Ugly: Illustrated History of Boxing*. London: Stanley Paul, 1986.

Cannon, Jimmy and Cannon, T. *Nobody Asked Me But . . . : The World of Jimmy Cannon*. New York: Holt, Rinehart and Winston, 1978.

Collins, Nigel. *Boxing Babylon: Behind the Shadowy World of the Prize Ring*. New York: Citadel, 1990.

Cottrell, John. *Man of Destiny: The Story of Muhammad Ali, formerly Cassius Clay*. London: Frederick Muller, 1967.

Duff, Mickey with Mee, Bob. *Twenty and Out: A Life in Boxing*. London: Collins Willow, 1999.

Dundee, Angelo with Winters, Mike. *I Only Talk Winning*. Chicago: Contemporary Books Inc., 1985.

Gutteridge, Reg with Batt, Peter. *Uppercuts and Dazes: My Autobiography*. London: Blake, 1998.

Hauser, Thomas. *Muhammad Ali, His Life And Times*. London: Robson Books, 2004.

Heller, Peter. *In This Corner: Forty-Two World Champions Tell Their Stories*. London: Robson Books, 1985.

Nagler, Barney. *James Norris and the Decline of Boxing*. Indianapolis: Bobbs-Merrill, 1964.

Olsen, Jack. *Cassius Clay*. London: Pelham, 1967.

Pacheco, Ferdie. *Muhammad Ali: A View From The Corner*. New York: Birch Lane, 1992.

Patterson, Floyd with Gross, Milton. *Victory Over Myself*. London: Pelham, 1962.

Plimpton, George. *Shadow Box: An Amateur in the Ring*. London: Andre Deutsch, 1978.

Remnick, David. *King of the World*. Random House, 1998.

Robinson, Sugar Ray with Anderson, Dave. *Sugar Ray*. London: Robson Books, 1970.

Schulberg, Budd. *Loser And Still Champion, Muhammad Ali*. New York: Doubleday, 1972.

Sheed, Wilfred. *Muhammad Ali: A Portrait in Words and Photographs*. Signet, 1975.

Steen, Rob. *Sonny Boy, The Life and Strife of Sonny Liston*. London: Methuen, 1993.

Tanner, Michael. *Ali In Britain*. Edinburgh: Mainstream, 1995.

Torres, Jose with Sugar, Bert. *Sting Like A Bee: The Muhammad Ali Story*. London: Coronet, 1972.

Tosches, Nick. *Night Train: The Sonny Liston Story*. London: Hamish-Hamilton, 2000.

Various. *Unchained Memories: Readings from the Slave Narratives*. New York: Bulfinch, 2002.

Walker, Robert. *Muhammad Ali: His Fights in the Ring*. Midas, 1978.

Whiting, George. *Great Fights of the Sixties*. London: Leslie Frewin, 1967.

Wilson, Peter. *The Man They Couldn't Gag: An Autobiography*. London: Stanley Paul, 1977.

Wilson, Peter. *Boxing's Greatest Prize*. London: Stanley Paul, 1980.

Young, A.S. *The Champ Nobody Wanted*. Chicago: Johnson, 1963.

INDEX